Please note

We believe accurate, plain-English legal information should help you solve many of your own legal problems. But this text is not a substitute for personalized advice from a knowledgeable lawyer. If you want the help of a trained professional—and we'll always point out situations in which we think that's a good idea— consult an attorney licensed to practice in your state.

9th edition

IRAs, 401(k)s & Other Retirement Plans

Taking Your Money Out

by Twila Slesnick, Ph.D., Enrolled Agent
& Attorney John C. Suttle, CPA

NINTH EDITION	JUNE 2009
Editor	CATHERINE CAPUTO
Cover Design	SUSAN PUTNEY
Production	MARGARET LIVINGSTON
Proofreading	ANI DIMUSHEVA
Index	SONGBIRD INDEXING
Printing	DELTA PRINTING SOLUTIONS, INC.

Slesnick, Twila.
  IRAs, 401(k)s & other retirement plans : taking your money out / by Twila Slesnick &
John C. Suttle. -- 9th ed.
     p. cm.
  ISBN-13: 978-1-4133-1031-3 (pbk.)
  ISBN-10: 1-4133-1031-1 (pbk.)
  1. Individual retirement accounts--Law and legislation--United States--Popular works. 2.
401(k) plans--Law and legislation--Popular works. 3. Deferred compensation--Law and
legislation--United States--Popular works. I. Suttle, John C. II. Title. III. Title: IRAs,
401(k)s, and other retirement plans.
  KF3510.Z9S55 2009
  343.7305'233--dc22
                    2009011288

Acknowledgments

Thanks to Nolo editor Robin Leonard for her intelligent and skillful editing of the first edition—and for adding a dose of levity to the entire process. For multitudes of subsequent editions, thanks to Nolo editor Amy DelPo for her keen eye and clear thinking. She smoothed the way for editors to come, and permanently endeared herself to the authors. For the most recent edition, thanks to Nolo editor Cathy Caputo for taking on the project and speeding things along.

Table of Contents

Your Retirement Companion

1 Types of Retirement Plans

Qualified Plans...6

Individual Retirement Accounts...12

Almost-Qualified Plans...15

Nonqualified Plans..16

2 An Overview of Tax Rules

Taxation Fundamentals...21

General Income Tax Rules for Retirement Plans.....................................26

Income Tax on Qualified Plans and Qualified Annuities.......................30

Special Income Tax Rules for Tax-Deferred Annuities...........................52

Special Income Tax Rules for IRAs...53

How Penalties Can Guide Planning...57

3 Early Distributions: Taking Your Money Out Before the Law Allows

Exceptions to the Early Distribution Tax..62

Calculating the Tax...68

Reporting the Tax..69

Special Rules for IRAs...75

4 Substantially Equal Periodic Payments

Computing Periodic Payments..84

Implementing and Reporting Your Decision...92

Modifying the Payments..94

5 Required Distributions: Taking Money Out When You Have To

Required Distributions During Your Lifetime 101

Death Before Required Beginning Date 102

Death After Required Beginning Date 103

Special Rules for Tax-Deferred Annuities 104

Special Rules for Roth IRAs 105

Penalty 106

Reporting the Penalty 110

Waiver 111

6 Required Distributions During Your Lifetime

Required Beginning Date 117

Computing the Required Amount 120

Designating a Beneficiary 125

Special Rules for Annuities 128

Divorce or Separation 131

7 Distributions to Your Beneficiary If You Die Before Age 70½

Determining the Designated Beneficiary 139

Distribution Methods 141

Spouse Beneficiary 144

Nonspouse Beneficiary 150

No Designated Beneficiary 154

Multiple Beneficiaries, Separate Accounts 155

Multiple Beneficiaries, One Account 155

Trust Beneficiary 161

Estate as Beneficiary 164

Annuities 165

Divorce or Separation 166

Reporting Distributions From IRAs 167

8 Distributions to Your Beneficiary If You Die After Age 70 ½

Administrative Details 171

Spouse Beneficiary 173

Nonspouse Beneficiary 180

No Designated Beneficiary 183

Multiple Beneficiaries, Separate Accounts 183

Multiple Beneficiaries, One Account 183

Trust Beneficiary 187

Estate as Beneficiary 189

Annuities 190

Divorce or Separation 190

9 Roth IRAs

Taxation of Distributions 196

Early Distribution Tax 205

Ordering of Distributions 207

Required Distributions 209

10 Roth 401(k) Plans

Taxation of Distributions 212

Early Distribution Tax 216

Ordering of Distributions 217

Required Distributions 217

Appendixes

A IRS Forms, Notices, and Schedules

Form 4972, *Tax on Lump-Sum Distributions* 220

Tax Rate Schedule for 1986 224

Form 5329, *Additional Taxes on Qualified Plans (Including IRAs) and Other Tax-Favored Accounts* 225

Form 5330, *Return of Excise Taxes Related to Employee Benefit Plans* 233

Form 5498, *IRA Contribution Information* 252

Form 8606, *Nondeductible IRAs* 253

Revenue Ruling 2002-62 264

B Life Expectancy Tables

Table I: Single Life Expectancy 272

Table II: Joint Life and Last Survivor Expectancy 273

Table III: Uniform Lifetime Table 291

Table IV: Survivor Benefit Limits 292

Index

Your Retirement Companion

Let's start with the basics. There are many kinds of retirement plans and many possible sources for owning one. This book is about how to take money out of your retirement plans.

You might have a retirement plan at work, an IRA that you set up yourself, or a plan or IRA you've inherited. Or you might have all three. You might still be contributing to a plan, or you may be retired. No matter what your situation, you will find information in this book to help you through the minefield of rules.

There are many reasons to take money out of a retirement plan. You might want to borrow the money for an emergency and pay it back—or not pay it back. Maybe you quit your job and you want to take your share of the company's plan. Perhaps you're required by law to withdraw some of your retirement funds because you've reached a certain age.

Whatever your situation, you probably have a lot of questions about your plan—and how to take money out of it. This book can answer:

- How do I know what kind of retirement plan I have? (See Chapter 1.)
- Do I have to wait until I retire to get money out of my plan or my IRA? (See Chapter 3.)
- Can I borrow money from my 401(k) plan to buy a house? (See Chapters 3, 4, and 5.)
- What should I do with my retirement plan when I leave my company or retire? (See Chapter 2.)
- When do I have to start taking money out of my IRA? (See Chapter 5.)
- How do I calculate how much I have to take? (See Chapter 6.)
- Can I take more than the required amount? (See Chapter 6.)
- What happens to my retirement plan when I die? (See Chapters 7 and 8.)
- Can my spouse roll over my IRA when I die? (See Chapters 7 and 8.)
- What about my children? Can they put my IRA in their names after I die? Do they have to take all the money out of the account right away? (See Chapters 7 and 8.)

- If I inherit a retirement plan, can I add my own money to it? Can I save it for my own children, if I don't need the money? (See Chapters 7 and 8.)
- Am I allowed to set up a Roth IRA? Should I? (See Chapter 9.)
- Can I convert my regular IRA to a Roth IRA? Should I? (See Chapter 9.)
- How is a Roth 401(k) plan different from a Roth IRA? (See Chapter 10.)

To help you answer these and other questions, we include many examples to guide you through the decision-making process and take you through calculations. You will also find sample tax forms that the IRS requires, along with instructions for how to complete them.

This book contains tables to help you calculate distributions. It also contains sample letters and worksheets you can use to communicate with the IRS or with the custodian of your IRA or retirement plan. We've even included some important IRS notices so you can read firsthand how IRS personnel thinks about certain critical issues.

The tax rules for pensions, IRAs, 401(k)s, and other types of retirement plans are notoriously complex, which can be all the more frustrating because they are important to so many people. The good news is that help is here: This book makes the rules clear and accessible.

Types of Retirement Plans

Qualified Plans...6

    Profit-Sharing Plans...7

    Stock Bonus Plans 9

    Money Purchase Pension Plans...9

    Employee Stock Ownership Plans (ESOPs) 10

    Defined Benefit Plans..10

    Target Benefit Plans..10

    Plans for Self-Employed People (Keoghs) 11

Individual Retirement Accounts..12

    Traditional Contributory IRAs 12

    Rollover IRAs...13

    Simplified Employee Pensions...13

    SIMPLE IRAs 14

    Roth IRAs..15

Almost-Qualified Plans...15

    Qualified Annuity Plans...16

    Tax-Deferred Annuities 16

Nonqualified Plans 16

Who Should Read Chapter 1

SKIP AHEAD
Read this chapter if you aren't certain which types of retirement plans you have—either through your employer or as a self-employed person. Also read this chapter if you have an IRA but aren't sure which type.

How many people have warned you that you'll never see a penny of the hard-earned money you've poured into the Social Security system and that you'd better have your own retirement nest egg tucked away somewhere? Perhaps those doomsayers are overstating the case, but even if you eventually do collect Social Security, it is likely to provide only a fraction of the income you will need during retirement.

Congress responded to this problem several decades ago by creating a variety of tax-favored plans to help working people save for retirement. One such plan is set up by you, the individual taxpayer, and is appropriately called an individual retirement account or IRA. Another, which can be established by your employer or by you if you are self-employed, is referred to by the nondescript phrase "a qualified plan." A qualified plan is one that qualifies to receive certain tax benefits as described in Section 401 of the U.S. Tax Code.

There are other types of retirement plans, too, which enjoy some of the same tax benefits as qualified plans but are not technically qualified because they are defined in a different section of the Tax Code. Many of these other plans closely follow the qualified plan rules, however. The most common of these almost-qualified plans are tax-deferred annuities (TDAs) and qualified annuity plans. (Don't be thrown by the name. Even though it may be called a qualified annuity plan, it is not defined in Section 401 and therefore is not a qualified plan in the purest sense.) Both of these plans are defined in Section 403 of the Tax Code. Because many of the rules in Section 403 are similar to those in Section 401, TDAs and qualified annuity plans are often mentioned in the same breath with qualified plans.

All qualified plans, TDAs, and qualified annuity plans have been sweetened with breaks for taxpayers to encourage them to save for retirement. And working people have saved, often stretching as far as they can to put money into their retirement plans. But saving is only half the equation. The government also wants you to take money out of the plan and spend it chiefly on your retirement. For that reason, the government has enacted a series of rules on how and when you can—or, sometimes, must—take money out of your retirement plan. (Taking money out is called a distribution.)

What does this mean for you? If you or your employer have ever put money into a

Helpful Terms

Adjusted gross income (AGI). Total taxable income reduced by certain expenses such as qualified plan contributions, IRA contributions, and alimony payments.

Beneficiary. The person or entity entitled to receive the benefits from an insurance policy or from trust property, such as a retirement plan or IRA.

Deductible contribution. A contribution to a retirement plan that an employer may claim as a business expense to offset income on the employer's tax return. You may know it as simply the employer's contribution. In the case of an IRA, a deductible contribution is one that an individual taxpayer may use to offset income on the individual's tax return.

Distribution. A payout of property (such as shares of stock) or cash from a retirement plan or IRA to the participant or a beneficiary.

Earned income. Income received for providing goods or services. Earned income might be wages or salary or net profit from a business.

Eligible employee. An employee who qualifies to participate in the employer's plan because he or she has met the eligibility requirements (such as having worked for the employer for a specified number of years).

Nondeductible contribution. A contribution to a retirement plan or IRA that may not be claimed as a business expense or used as an adjustment to offset taxable income on an income tax return.

Nondiscrimination rules. The provisions in the U.S. Tax Code that prohibit certain retirement plans from providing greater benefits to highly compensated employees than to other employees.

Participant, or active participant. An employee for whom the employer makes a contribution to the employer's retirement plan.

Tax-deductible expense. An item of expense that may be used to offset income on a tax return.

Tax deferral. The postponement of tax payments until a future year.

Vested benefit. The portion of a participant's retirement plan accumulation that a participant may keep after leaving the employer who sponsors the plan; or the portion that goes to a participant's beneficiary if the participant dies.

retirement plan and received tax benefits as a result, then you cannot simply take the money out whenever you want, nor can you leave it in the plan indefinitely, hoping, for example, to pass all of the funds on to your children.

Instead, you must follow a complex set of rules for withdrawing money from the plan during your lifetime, and your beneficiaries must follow these rules after your death. These rules are called distribution rules, and if you or your beneficiaries don't follow them, the government will impose penalties— sometimes substantial ones.

This chapter identifies and briefly describes the types of retirement plans to which these distribution rules apply. If you have a retirement plan at work or if you have established one through your own business, you should find your plan listed below. Also, if you have an IRA, you will find your particular type among those described below.

There is also an entire category of plans known as nonqualified plans to which distribution rules do not apply. Such plans are used by employers primarily to provide incentives or rewards for particular— usually upper management—employees. These plans do not enjoy the tax benefits that IRAs and qualified plans (including TDAs and qualified annuities) do, and they consequently are not subject to the same distribution restrictions. Although this chapter helps you identify nonqualified plans, such plans have their own

distribution rules, which fall outside the scope of this book.

Identifying your particular retirement plan probably won't be as difficult as you think. This is because every plan fits into one of four broad categories:

- qualified plan
- IRA
- plan that is neither an IRA nor a qualified plan, but that has many of the characteristics of a qualified plan, or
- plan that is neither an IRA nor a qualified plan, and that does not have the characteristics of a qualified plan.

Qualified Plans

A qualified plan is a type of retirement savings plan that an employer establishes for its employees and that conforms to the requirements of Section 401 of the U.S. Tax Code. Why is it called "qualified"? Because if the plan meets all of the requirements of Section 401, then it qualifies for special tax rules, the most significant of which is that contributions the employer makes to the plan on behalf of employees are tax deductible. Probably the best-known qualified plan is the 401(k) plan, discussed below.

The advantages to you, the employee, working for an employer with a qualified plan, are not only the opportunity to accumulate a retirement nest egg, but also to postpone paying income taxes on money contributed to the plan. Neither the contributions you make nor any of the investment returns are taxable to you until you take money out of the plan. In tax jargon, the income tax is deferred until the money is distributed and available for spending—usually during retirement. Congress built in some safeguards to help ensure that your plan assets are around when you finally do retire. For example, the assets are required to be held in trust and are generally protected from the claims of creditors.

In return for these tax benefits, the plan must comply with a number of procedural rules. First, the plan must not discriminate in favor of the company's highly compensated employees. For example, the employer may not contribute disproportionately large amounts to the accounts of the company honchos. Also, the employer may not arbitrarily prevent employees from participating in the plan or from taking their retirement money with them when they leave the company. Finally, the plan must comply with an extremely complex set of distribution rules, which is the focus of this book.

Seven of the most common types of qualified plans are described below. Those plans are:

- profit-sharing plans, which include 401(k) plans and Roth 401(k) plans
- stock bonus plans
- money purchase pension plans
- employee stock ownership plans
- defined benefit plans

- target benefit plans, and
- plans for self-employed people, called Keogh plans.

Profit-Sharing Plans

A profit-sharing plan is a type of qualified plan that allows employees to share in the profits of the company and to use those profits to help fund their retirement. Despite the plan's title and description, an employer doesn't have to make a profit in order to contribute to a profit-sharing plan. Similarly, even if the employer makes a profit, it does not have to contribute to the plan. Each year, the employer has discretion over whether or not to make a contribution, regardless of profitability.

When the employer contributes money to the plan on behalf of its employees, the contributions are generally computed as a percentage of all participants' compensation. The annual contribution to all accounts can be as little as zero or as much as 25% of the total combined compensation of all participants. For the purposes of making this calculation, the maximum compensation for any individual participant is capped at $245,000. (The $245,000 increases from time to time for inflation.) No individual participant's account can receive more than $49,000 in a single year. (The $49,000 cap also increases from time to time for inflation.) There is an exception to the $49,000 limit for individuals who are older than 50 and who contribute to a 401(k) plan.

EXAMPLE: Joe and Martha participate in their company's profit-sharing plan. Last year, the company contributed 25% of their respective salaries to the plan. Joe's salary was $120,000 and Martha's was $230,000. The company contributed $30,000 for Joe (25% x $120,000). The company's contribution for Martha was limited to the $49,000 ceiling, however, because 25% of Martha's salary was actually $57,500, which is above the limit.

This year, however, the company's profits tumbled, so the company decided not to make any contributions to the profit-sharing plan. Thus, the company will not contribute any money to the plan on Joe or Martha's behalf.

401(k) Plans

A special type of profit-sharing plan, called a 401(k) plan, is named imaginatively after the subsection of the Tax Code that describes it. A traditional 401(k) plan allows you to direct some of your compensation into the plan, and you do not have to pay income taxes on the portion of your salary you direct into the plan until you withdraw it.

The plan may or may not provide for employer contributions. Some employers make matching contributions, depositing a certain amount for each dollar the participant contributes.

EXAMPLE: Fred participates in his company's 401(k) plan. His company has promised to contribute 25¢ for each dollar of Fred's salary that he directs into the plan. Fred's salary is $40,000. He directs 5% of his salary, which is $2,000, into the plan. The company matches with a $500 contribution (which is 25¢ x $2,000).

Other employers contribute a fixed percentage of compensation for each eligible employee, whether or not the employee chooses to contribute to the plan.

EXAMPLE: Marilyn's salary for the current year is $60,000. Her company has a 401(k) plan that does not match employee contributions. Instead, the company contributes a flat 3% of each eligible employee's salary to the plan. Marilyn is saving to buy a house, so she is not currently directing any of her salary into the 401(k) plan. Nonetheless, the company will contribute $1,800 (which is 3% x $60,000) to the plan for Marilyn.

Roth 401(k) Plans

Employers can also establish a special type of 401(k) plan called a Roth 401(k). This plan is similar to a traditional 401(k) plan in that it allows employees to defer salary into the plan. The difference comes in the tax treatment. Whereas contributions to traditional 401(k) plans are tax deductible, contributions to Roth 401(k) plans are not. Rather, the tax benefits for Roth 401(k)s come when you take distributions, which will be tax free so long as you meet certain requirements. (See Chapter 10 for a complete discussion of Roth 401(k) plans.)

Stock Bonus Plans

A stock bonus plan is like a profit-sharing plan, except that the employer must pay the plan benefits to employees in the form of shares of company stock.

> **EXAMPLE:** Frankie worked for the Warp Corp. all her working life. During her employment, she participated in the company's stock bonus plan, accumulating $90,000 by retirement. When she retired, Warp Corp. stock was worth $100 per share. When the company distributed her retirement benefits to her, it gave her 900 shares of Warp Corp. stock.

Money Purchase Pension Plans

A money purchase pension plan is similar to a profit-sharing plan in the sense that employer contributions are allocated to each participant's individual account. The difference is that the employer's contributions are mandatory, not discretionary. Under such a plan,

the employer promises to pay a definite amount (such as 10% of compensation) into each participant's account every year. In that sense, money purchase pension plans are less flexible for employers than are profit-sharing plans.

As with a profit-sharing plan, the maximum amount that an employer can contribute to the plan for all participants combined is 25% of the total combined compensation of all participants (although each participant's compensation is limited to $245,000 for purposes of making this calculation).

The maximum that the employer can contribute to any given participant's account in a year is either $49,000 or the agreed-to amount of the participant's compensation—whichever is less.

(The $245,000 and $49,000 caps increase from time to time for inflation.)

> **EXAMPLE:** Sand Corp. has a money purchase plan that promises to contribute 25% of compensation to each eligible employee's account. Jenna made $45,000 last year and was eligible to participate in the plan, so the company contributed $11,250 (25% x $45,000) to her account for that year. This year, the company is losing money. Nonetheless, the company is still obligated to contribute 25% of Jenna's salary to her money purchase plan account for the current year.

Employee Stock Ownership Plans (ESOPs)

An employee stock ownership plan, or ESOP, is a type of stock bonus plan that may have some features of a money purchase pension plan. ESOPs are designed to be funded primarily or even exclusively with employer stock. An ESOP can allow cash distributions, however, as long as the employee has the right to demand that benefits be paid in employer stock.

Because an ESOP is a stock bonus plan, the employer cannot contribute more than 25% of the total compensation of all participants and no more than $49,000 into any one participant's account.

Defined Benefit Plans

A defined benefit plan promises to pay each participant a set amount of money as an annuity beginning at retirement. The promised payment is usually based on a combination of factors, such as the employee's final compensation and the length of time the employee worked for the company. If the employee retires early, the benefit is reduced.

> **EXAMPLE:** Damien is a participant in his company's defined benefit plan. The plan guarantees that if Damien works until the company's retirement age, he will receive a retirement benefit equal to 1% of his final pay times the number of years he worked for the company. Damien will reach the company's retirement age in 20 years. If Damien is making $50,000 when he retires in 20 years, his retirement benefit will be $10,000 per year (which is 1% x $50,000 x 20 years). If he retires early, he will receive less.

Once the retirement benefit is determined, the company must compute how much to contribute each year in order to meet that goal. The computation is not simple—in fact, it requires the services of an actuary, who uses projections of salary increases and investment returns to determine the annual contribution amount. The computation must be repeated every year to take into account variations in investment returns and other factors and then to adjust the amount of the contribution to ensure the goal will be reached.

Even though, under certain circumstances, defined benefit plans permit much higher contributions than other qualified plans, they are used infrequently (especially by small companies) because they are so complex and expensive to administer.

Target Benefit Plans

A target benefit plan is a special type of money purchase pension plan that incorporates some of the attributes of a defined benefit plan. As with a money purchase plan, each participant in a target benefit plan has a separate account. But instead of contributing a fixed percentage of pay to every account, the employer projects a retirement benefit for each employee, as with a defined benefit plan. In fact, the contribution for the first year is computed in the same way a defined benefit plan contribution would be computed—with the help of an actuary. The difference, though, is that after the first year, the contribution formula is fixed. While a defined benefit plan guarantees a certain retirement annuity, a target benefit plan just shoots for it by estimating the required annual contribution in the employee's first participation year and then freezing the formula. The formula might be a specific dollar amount every year or perhaps a percentage of pay.

If any of the original assumptions turn out to be wrong—for example, the investment return is less than expected—the retirement target won't be reached. The employer is under no obligation to adjust the level of the contribution to reach the original target if there is a shortfall. Conversely, if investments do better than expected, the employee's retirement benefit will exceed the target, and the increased amount must be paid to the employee.

EXAMPLE: Jack is 35 when he becomes eligible to participate in his company's target benefit plan. Jack's target retirement benefit is 60% of his final pay. Assuming Jack will receive wage increases of 5% each year and will retire at 65 after 30 years of service, Jack's final pay is projected to be $80,000. His target retirement benefit, then, is $48,000 (60% of $80,000). In order to pay Jack $48,000 a year for the rest of his life beginning at age 65, the actuaries estimate that the company must contribute $4,523 to Jack's account every year. The company will contribute that amount, even if Jack doesn't receive 5% raises some years, or if other assumptions turn out to be wrong. Thus, Jack may or may not receive his targeted $48,000 during his retirement years. It might be more or it might be less.

Plans for Self-Employed People (Keoghs)

Qualified plans for self-employed individuals are often called Keogh plans, named after the author of a 1962 bill that established a separate set of rules for such plans. In the ensuing years, Keoghs have come to look very much like corporate plans. In fact, the rules governing self-employed plans are no longer segregated, but have been placed under the umbrella of the qualified plan rules for corporations. Nonetheless, the Keogh moniker lingers—a burr in the side of phonetic spellers.

If you work for yourself, you may have a Keogh plan that is a profit-sharing plan, money purchase pension plan, or defined benefit plan. If so, it will generally have to follow the same rules as its corporate counterpart, with some exceptions.

Individual Retirement Accounts

Most people are surprised to learn that individual retirement accounts, or IRAs, exist in many forms. Most common is the individual retirement account or individual retirement annuity to which any person with earnings from employment may contribute. These are called contributory IRAs. Some types of IRAs are used to receive assets distributed from other retirement plans. These are called rollover IRAs. Still others, such as SEPs and SIMPLE IRAs, are technically IRAs even though their rules are quite similar to those of qualified plans. Finally, Roth IRAs combine the features of a regular IRA and a savings plan to produce a hybrid that adheres to its own set of rules. You can learn more about each type of IRA in the following sections.

Traditional Contributory IRAs

If you have income from working for yourself or someone else, you may set up and contribute to an IRA. The IRA can be a special depository account that you set up with a bank, brokerage firm, or other institutional custodian. Or it can be an individual retirement annuity that you purchase from an insurance company.

You may contribute a maximum of $5,000 each year, or $6,000 if you will reach age 50 by the end of the year. If you are not covered by an employer's retirement plan, you may take a deduction on your tax return for your contribution.

If you are covered by an employer's plan, your IRA might be fully deductible, partly deductible, or not deductible at all depending on how much gross income you have.

For example, in 2009, if you are single and covered by an employer's plan, your contribution is fully deductible if your adjusted gross income, or AGI, is less than $55,500, and not deductible at all when your AGI reaches $65,500. Between $55,500 and $65,500 the deduction is gradually phased out. For married individuals, the phaseout range is from $89,000 to $109,000, if the IRA participant is covered by an employer plan. For an IRA participant who is not covered by a plan but whose spouse is covered, the phaseout range is $166,000 to $176,000.

> **EXAMPLE ONE:** Jamie, who is single and age 32, works for Sage Corp. and participates in the company's 401(k) plan. This year he will make $30,000. Eager to save for retirement, Jamie decides to contribute $5,000 to an IRA. Since his income is less than $55,500, Jamie will be able to take a $5,000 deduction on his tax return for the IRA contribution, even though he also participated in his employer's retirement plan.

> **EXAMPLE TWO:** Assume the same facts as in Example One except that Jamie's salary is $70,000. Although Jamie is permitted to make an IRA contribution,

he may not claim a deduction for it on his tax return because his income is more than $65,500.

EXAMPLE THREE: Assume Jamie made $75,000, but Sage Corp. does not have a retirement plan for its employees. Because Jamie is not covered by an employer's retirement plan, his $5,000 IRA contribution will be fully deductible even though he made more than $65,500.

Rollover IRAs

If you receive a distribution from a qualified plan, you might decide to put some or all of it into an IRA. (See Chapter 2 for information about how and why you might do this.) The IRA that receives the qualified plan distribution is called a rollover IRA.

Although rollover IRAs used to have some special features, the 2001 pension law eradicated most of the differences between contributory and rollover IRAs.

Simplified Employee Pensions

A simplified employee pension, or SEP, is a special type of IRA that can be established by your employer or by you, if you are self-employed. Designed for small businesses, SEPs have many of the characteristics of qualified plans but are much simpler to set up and administer.

Under a SEP, each participant has his or her own individual retirement account to which the employer contributes. The contributions are excluded from the participant's pay and are not taxable until they are distributed from the plan. If you are self-employed, you may set up a SEP for yourself, even if you have no employees.

The advantage of a SEP over a regular IRA is that the contribution limits are higher. The contribution can be as much as 25% of your annual compensation, up to a maximum contribution of $49,000.

The disadvantage of a SEP, from an employer's perspective, is that the participation and vesting rules for SEPs are less favorable than those for qualified plans. Participation rules determine which employees must be covered by the plan and must receive contributions to their plan accounts. Vesting rules determine how much an employee is entitled to if the employee leaves the job or dies. An employer who establishes a SEP is required to make contributions on behalf of virtually all employees. Furthermore, the employees must be 100% vested at all times, which means that they must be allowed to take 100% of their plan account with them when they leave the company, no matter how long they have been employed there. Those can be costly requirements for small employers whose staff often includes many short-term, part-time employees. By contrast, 401(k) plans (and other qualified plans) can stretch the period before an employee is fully vested to as long as six years.

SIMPLE IRAs

A Simplified Incentive Match Plan for Employees, or SIMPLE IRA, is yet another type of IRA designed specifically to make it easier for small employers (those with 100 or fewer employees) to establish a retirement plan. A SIMPLE IRA is a salary reduction plan that, like a 401(k) profit-sharing plan, allows employees to divert some compensation into retirement savings.

As with a SEP, contributions to a SIMPLE IRA are deposited into a separate IRA for each participating employee. The participant may select any percentage of compensation to defer into the plan—even zero—but the total dollar amount cannot exceed $11,500 per year ($14,000 if you are at least age 50 by the end of the year).

 TIP

Dollar amounts change. From time to time, the dollar amounts are increased for inflation. Each year, usually in October, the IRS publishes the contribution levels for the following year. You can find the new numbers on the IRS website at www.irs.gov. Search for "Pension Plan Limitations" to find out what the numbers will be for the upcoming year.

Unlike the employee, the employer is absolutely required to make a contribution. The employer has two options:

- It can match the employee's contribution up to 3% of the employee's compensation. (Under certain circumstances, the employer may match less than 3%, but never more.)
- As an alternative to matching, the employer may contribute a flat 2% of compensation (up to a maximum compensation of $245,000) to the accounts of all eligible employees, whether or not the employee directs any salary into the plan.

EXAMPLE ONE: Tabor Corp. has four employees, who earned the following salaries:

Jane	$25,000
Jake	$20,000
Bree	$35,000
Holly	$50,000

Tabor's SIMPLE IRA offers to match employees' contributions up to 3% of compensation. All four employees are eligible to participate. Jane and Jake each direct $9,000 of their salaries into the plan, while Bree and Holly direct none of their salaries into the plan. Tabor Corp. contributes $750 (which is 3% x $25,000) for Jane and $600 (3% x $20,000) for Jake. It contributes nothing for Bree or Holly.

EXAMPLE TWO: Assume the same facts as in Example One except that instead of matching contributions, Tabor's plan requires a contribution of 2% of compensation to the accounts of all eligible employees. So, Tabor contributes $500 for Jane (which is 2% of $25,000) and $400 (2% of $20,000) for Jake. It also contributes $700 (2% of $35,000) for Bree and $1,000 (2% of $50,000) for Holly, even though Bree and Holly did not direct any of their salaries into the plan.

Roth IRAs

At first glance, a Roth IRA looks a lot like a traditional contributory IRA because annual contribution limits are the same. Beyond that, though, the similarities are more difficult to see. For one thing, none of your contributions to a Roth IRA are ever deductible on your tax return. Furthermore, your ability to make a Roth IRA contribution begins to phase out when your AGI exceeds $166,000 (for joint filers) or $105,000 (for single filers). And you are not permitted a contribution at all when your AGI exceeds $176,000 (for joint filers) or $120,000 (for single filers). (Recall that with a traditional IRA, you may make a contribution even if your income is high and you are covered by an employer's plan. You might not be able to deduct the contribution on your tax return, however.)

The big advantage of a Roth IRA is that if you qualify to make contributions, all distributions from the IRA are tax free—even the investment returns—as long as the distribution satisfies certain requirements. Furthermore, unlike traditional IRAs, you may contribute to a Roth IRA for as long as you continue to have earned income. (In the case of traditional IRAs, you can't make any contributions after you reach age 70½.)

Although Roth IRAs belong to the IRA family and are subject to many of the IRA rules, the abundant exceptions and variations in treatment make it difficult to rely on what you know about traditional IRAs when trying to figure out what to do with a Roth IRA. Consequently, we devote all of Chapter 9 to Roth IRAs. In that chapter, we point out the distinguishing characteristics of the Roth IRA and identify which of the distribution rules in this book apply to it and which do not. Before you take any action on a Roth IRA based on what you know about the traditional IRA rules, be sure to read Chapter 9.

Almost-Qualified Plans

Tucked into the voluminous Tax Code are a number of hybrid plans that are not strictly qualified plans, but that share many of the benefits and restrictions of qualified plans. The two most common, and the two that most closely mirror the qualified plan rules, are qualified annuity plans and tax-deferred annuities.

Qualified Annuity Plans

The rules for qualified plans require that the assets of the plan be held by an administrator in a trust. Congress carved out an exception to this rule by adding Section 403(a) to the Tax Code. Section 403(a) allows employers to use contributions to purchase annuities for employees directly from an insurance company. This alternative to holding the contributions in a trust can simplify administration. In almost every other respect, the rules and regulations that apply to qualified plans also apply to qualified annuity plans.

Tax-Deferred Annuities

If you are a university professor or an employee of a public school, odds are that you are covered by an annuity plan of a public charity or public school, more commonly referred to as a tax-deferred annuity, or TDA. TDAs, defined in Section 403(b) of the Tax Code, are typically funded with individual annuity contracts purchased from an insurance company. When you retire, your benefits are usually paid to you as a monthly annuity for the rest of your life, although some TDAs offer other distribution options, such as a lump sum payment.

TDAs are not qualified plans and do not track the qualified plan rules as closely as qualified annuity plans do. For example, distributions from TDAs are not eligible for special tax options, such as averaging and capital gains treatment. (See Chapter 2 for more information about tax options.) However, the vast majority of the distribution rules that apply to qualified plans also apply to TDAs. The exceptions are noted where relevant.

Nonqualified Plans

Big business being what it is—subject to the sometimes wise and sometimes questionable judgment of the boss—many companies offer special incentives and compensation packages to key employees. The incentives might come in the form of deferred cash bonuses, stock certificates, or stock options. Very often, the boss doesn't offer the same deal to everyone.

Because the incentives are not available to everyone, such plans generally do not satisfy the nondiscrimination requirements of qualified plans and are therefore called nonqualified plans. Because they are nonqualified, they are not subject to the same rigorous vesting, participation, and distribution requirements.

Nonqualified plans have some additional distinctive features: An employer may not deduct contributions to the plan, assets of the plan are not required to be held in trust, and the assets of the individual participants are not protected from the claims of creditors. Because nonqualified plans are not subject to the same distribution rules as IRAs, qualified plans, qualified annuities, and TDAs, they are not covered in this book.

Creditor and Bankruptcy Protection

Corporate retirement plans have long been safe from creditors, thanks to the Employee Retirement Income Security Act of 1974, commonly known as ERISA. Unfortunately, that law does not protect retirement plans for self-employed individuals, nor does it protect IRAs of any kind.

Protection for those plans came in 2005 through a new law titled The Bankruptcy Abuse Prevention and Consumer Protection Act. That law provides debtors in bankruptcy with an exemption for retirement assets in qualified plans, qualified annuities, tax-sheltered annuities, and self-employed plans.

In addition, the law exempts all assets in an IRA that are attributable to rollovers from a retirement plan described above. If you happen to have a traditional IRA or Roth IRA containing assets that are not attributable to a rollover from some other type of retirement plan (for example, the assets are from amounts you contributed directly to the IRA), then you will also be allowed an exemption of up to $1 million total for the assets in those contributory IRAs.

Key Tax Code Sections

§ 401(a)
Qualified Plans in General (including Keoghs): profit sharing, stock bonus, money purchase pension, defined benefit plans.

§ 401(k)
Cash or Salary Deferral Plan: A special type of qualified plan. Can be profit-sharing or stock bonus plan.

§ 403(a)
Qualified Annuity Plan: Plan established by employer that is not a public charity or public school. Funded by the employer with purchased annuities.

§ 403(b)
Annuity Plan of Public Charity or Public School: Commonly called tax-deferred annuity or TDA. Usually funded with purchased annuities owned by the employee.

§ 408
IRAs: Contributory, rollover, SEP, SIMPLE.

§ 408A
Roth IRAs.

An Overview of Tax Rules

Taxation Fundamentals...21

    Defer the Payment of Tax...21

    Pay Tax at the Lowest Rate..25

    Avoid Tax Penalties...25

General Income Tax Rules for Retirement Plans...26

    Distributions Are Taxable Immediately 26

    Your Basis Is Not Taxable 26

    You Don't Have to Withdraw Cash 28

    You May Not Claim Losses...29

    Divorce or Inheritance Doesn't Change the Basic Tax Rules 30

Income Tax on Qualified Plans and Qualified Annuities 30

    Options for Paying Taxes at Retirement 30

    Options for Paying Taxes Before Retirement 40

    Options for Paying Taxes on Inherited Plans..41

    Options for Paying Taxes on Qualified Plans Received at Divorce..................43

    Withholding Money to Pay Taxes 46

    Loans From Qualified Plans 49

    Hardship Distributions From Qualified Plans..51

Special Income Tax Rules for Tax-Deferred Annuities..52

Special Income Tax Rules for IRAs..53

    Ordinary Income Tax Applies..53

    Rollover Allowed...54

    Averaging and Capital Gain Treatment Not Allowed 55

Special Rules at Divorce or Separation 55

Mandatory Withholding Doesn't Apply..56

Loans Not Allowed 56

Hardship Distributions Not Allowed..56

How Penalties Can Guide Planning..57

Who Should Read Chapter 2

 SKIP AHEAD
Everyone should read this chapter. It describes the basic tax rules that apply to your retirement plan when you leave your job. (Chapters 3–6 contain more specific rules.) If the only retirement plan you have is an IRA, you can skip the following sections below: "Income Tax on Qualified Plans and Qualified Annuities" and "Special Income Tax Rules for Tax-Deferred Annuities."

O ur tax laws provide both incentive and opportunity to sock away significant sums for retirement. The combination of an up-front tax deduction for contributions to retirement plans, years of tax-deferred growth, and eventual taxation at relatively low rates (such as during retirement) can produce dramatic returns on retirement savings.

Taxation Fundamentals

To reap maximum benefit from your retirement plan, you must contribute as much as you can through the years, and you must adhere to certain guidelines when you draw money out. Keep in mind that your financial goal should be to maximize your after-tax wealth. It won't do you much good to accumulate a comfortable nest egg if you lose the bulk of it to taxes. As you pursue this goal, the following fundamentals will serve you well when you are not sure how to proceed:

- defer the payment of tax
- pay tax at the lowest rate, and
- avoid tax penalties.

Read the following sections to learn more about each of these strategies.

Defer the Payment of Tax

When you have a choice, it is usually best to delay or defer the payment of income tax for as long as possible. During the deferral period, you will have the use of money that would otherwise have gone to taxes; if you invest it, that money will help generate more tax-deferred income. The easiest way to defer the payment of tax is by deferring the receipt of income. For example, if you have the option of taking a distribution from your retirement plan this year or next, it is often better to wait. As the tables below show, even a one-year delay can be beneficial. Your money grows while the tax man waits.

Many people vastly underestimate the benefits of tax-deferred compounding of investment returns inside a retirement plan account. Take a look at Tables I and II below. Both cases assume a simple 8% return on your investment and a flat 28% tax rate. Table I shows what happens if you take $10,000 out of your IRA, pay tax on it, and invest the remainder for 15 years. Because the investment is outside your IRA, each year you will pay tax on your interest, dividends, and capital gains.

Helpful Terms

After-tax dollars. The amount of income left after all income taxes have been withheld or paid.

Amortization. The reduction of a debt through periodic payments of principal and interest.

Basis. An amount treated as the purchase price or cost of an asset for purposes of determining the taxable gain or loss when the asset is sold.

Custodian. A person or entity who is in possession of property belonging to another. For example, the custodian of an IRA is the institution that holds the stocks, bonds, cash, or other property of the IRA, even though the assets actually belong to the individual who established and funded the IRA.

Distribution. A payout of property (such as shares of stock) or cash from a retirement plan or IRA to the participant or a beneficiary.

Fair market value (FMV). The price at which an item could be sold at retail by a willing seller to a willing buyer.

Net unrealized appreciation. The amount by which an asset has increased in value before it is sold.

Nondeductible contribution. A contribution to a retirement plan or IRA that may not be used as a business expense or an adjustment to offset taxable income on an income tax return.

Pre-tax dollars. Total taxable income before income taxes have been paid.

Pro rata. Proportionately. For example, an amount distributed *pro rata* over four years is distributed evenly over those four years. Property that is distributed *pro rata* to its owners is distributed according to the percentage of each owner's interest.

Tax bracket or marginal tax bracket. The rate at which each additional dollar of income will be taxed. Under the Internal Revenue Code, a certain amount of income is taxed at one rate, and additional income is taxed at another. Therefore, it is possible that if you have one more dollar of income it will be taxed at a different rate than the previous dollar. Your marginal rate is the rate at which your next dollar of income will be taxed.

Trustee. A person or entity who holds legal title to the property in a trust. For example, a qualified retirement plan is a trust that is administered by a trustee who manages the trust property for the plan participant.

Table I

Withdraw from IRA:	$10,000
Pay income tax:	$2,800
Invest remainder:	$7,200
Investment return:	8%
Tax Rate:	28%

Year	Initial Investment Beginning of Year	Interest Earned	Current Year Tax on Interest	Total Investment Year End
1	$ 7,200	$ 576	$ 161	$ 7,615
2	7,615	609	171	8,053
3	8,053	644	180	8,517
4	8,517	681	191	9,007
5	9,007	721	202	9,526
6	9,526	762	213	10,075
7	10,075	806	226	10,655
8	10,655	852	239	11,268
9	11,268	902	252	11,918
10	11,918	953	267	12,604
11	12,604	1,008	282	13,330
12	13,330	1,066	299	14,097
13	14,097	1,128	316	14,909
14	14,909	1,193	334	15,768
15	15,768	1,262	353	16,677

Table II

Leave inside IRA: $10,000
Investment return: 8%
Tax Rate: 28%

Year	Initial Investment Beginning of Year	Interest Earned	Current Year Tax on Interest	Total Investment Year End	Tax If Distributed	Net If Distributed*
1	$ 10,000	$ 800	$ 0	$ 10,800	$ 3,024	$ 7,776
2	10,800	864	0	11,664	3,266	8,398
3	11,664	933	0	12,597	3,527	9,070
4	12,597	1,008	0	13,605	3,809	9,796
5	13,605	1,088	0	14,693	4,114	10,579
6	14,693	1,175	0	15,868	4,443	11,425
7	15,869	1,269	0	17,138	4,799	12,340
8	17,138	1,371	0	18,509	5,183	13,327
9	18,509	1,481	0	19,990	5,597	14,393
10	19,990	1,599	0	21,589	6,045	15,544
11	21,589	1,727	0	23,316	6,529	16,788
12	23,316	1,865	0	25,182	7,051	18,131
13	25,182	2,015	0	27,196	7,615	19,581
14	27,196	2,176	0	29,372	8,224	21,148
15	29,372	2,350	0	31,722	8,882	22,840

*Compare last column with last column of Table I.

Now look at Table II, which shows what happens if you leave the $10,000 inside the IRA. The table projects the value of your investment after one year, two years, or more. After 15 years, the total value of your IRA will be $31,722, almost twice as much as the balance shown in Table I after 15 years. If you take the money out and pay the tax on the distribution, your balance will be $22,840, which is still $6,162 more than you would have if you had paid the tax in year one and invested the money outside the IRA. This is true even though you start with the same amount of money, earn the same investment return, and are subject to the same tax rate in both situations.

Occasionally, it may be better not to defer distributions—if you expect to be in a permanently higher tax bracket in the future, for example. Or perhaps the income you earn outside the IRA will be taxed at a capital gains rate that is lower than your ordinary income tax rate. Bear in mind, however, that a slightly higher tax bracket or a temporary spike in your tax rate is not usually enough justification to accelerate distributions. Your tax rate would have to increase significantly to offset the enormous benefits of compounded growth.

Pay Tax at the Lowest Rate

Generally, your goal should be to pay tax on all of your retirement income at the lowest possible rate. But how will you know when the time is right to take the money out? Most people will be in a lower tax bracket after retirement, which provides yet another reason to defer distributions as long as possible.

Avoid Tax Penalties

A raft of penalty taxes awaits you if you fail to comply with the myriad distribution laws. Some penalties are designed to discourage you from withdrawing money before you retire. Others target individuals who want to leave their retirement funds to their heirs. Penalties are discussed at length in subsequent chapters, but be advised: It is rarely wise to take a distribution and pay a tax penalty, even if it seems like a small amount to you. Not only will you have to pay the penalty when you file your next tax return, but you will also have to report the distribution as income and pay regular income tax on it. When you factor in the loss of tax-deferred compounded growth, you might even be better off borrowing the money you need, rather than dipping into your retirement plan.

At some point, though, you certainly will take money out of your retirement plan, whether it is because your employer distributes it to you when you leave your job, because you need the money, or because the law requires you to withdraw it. When that time comes, you must understand how retirement plans are taxed and know your options. You will also need to be aware of potential penalties in order to stay out of harm's way.

General Income Tax Rules for Retirement Plans

When you take money out of a retirement plan, whether it is an IRA, qualified plan, qualified annuity, or TDA, some basic income tax rules apply. They are:

- distributions are taxable immediately
- your basis is not taxable
- you don't have to withdraw cash
- you may not claim losses, and
- divorce or inheritance does not change the basic tax rules.

Although each rule has exceptions, expect the rule to apply in most situations. Read more about each rule in the sections below.

Distributions Are Taxable Immediately

First and most basic: All distributions will be taxed in the year they come out of the plan. Exceptions to this rule occur when you roll over your distribution into another retirement plan or a traditional IRA within 60 days, or when your employer transfers the distribution directly into another plan or traditional IRA. In these cases, you do not pay income tax until the money is eventually distributed from the new plan or IRA. (See "Income Tax on Qualified Plans and Qualified Annuities," below, for more about rollovers.)

If you ask your employer to transfer your retirement plan into a Roth IRA (as opposed to a traditional IRA), the transaction will be treated as a conversion to a Roth IRA. Assuming you are eligible to make the conversion, you will be required to pay income tax in the year of the conversion on any pre-tax amounts that are transferred from your employer's plan to your Roth IRA. For more information about conversions, see Chapter 9.

CAUTION

Some money might be withheld! Beware of rules that require your plan administrator to withhold money to cover income taxes you may owe when you take money out of your retirement plan—even if you plan to roll it over. You can avoid the withholding by having your employer transfer the retirement funds directly into another retirement plan or IRA. (See "Income Tax on Qualified Plans and Qualified Annuities," below, for more about these withholding rules.)

Your Basis Is Not Taxable

If you made contributions to a retirement plan or IRA for which you were not permitted to take a tax deduction on your tax return, then you have what is called "basis" in the plan. In other words, you have contributed money to a plan or IRA that you have already reported as income on your tax return. You will not have to pay taxes on those amounts a second time when you take the money out of your plan, but unfortunately, you usually don't have the luxury of deciding when to withdraw the portion of the money attributable to the basis.

If you have a regular IRA or a Keogh (see Chapter 1 for a description of these plans), your basis generally comes out *pro rata*, which means that every time you take a distribution, part of it is taxable and part is not. You compute the taxable and nontaxable portions of each distribution on IRS Form 8606 and submit it with the rest of your tax return at tax time. (A copy of Form 8606 is in Appendix A.) Roth IRAs and Roth 401(k) plans are different—they have special basis rules. (See Chapters 9 and 10, respectively, for more information.) In the case of an employer plan, the contributions you made with dollars on which you already paid taxes are usually distributed as a lump sum when you retire—unless you elect to take your retirement benefits as an annuity. If so, you may have to take your basis out *pro rata*—a little bit with each annuity payment.

EXAMPLE: Over the years, you contributed a total of $10,000 to your IRA. You were not permitted to claim a tax deduction on your tax return for any of those contributions. Thus the $10,000 is all after-tax money, or basis. On December 31, the fair market value of the IRA was $45,000. During the year, you withdrew $5,000 to help cover living expenses. Part of the $5,000 is taxable, and part is not. To determine the tax-free portion, use the following method:

Step One: Add the distributions you took during the year to the fair market value of the IRA on December 31.

$5,000 + $45,000 = $50,000

Step Two: Divide your total basis in the IRA by the amount from Step One.

$10,000 ÷ $50,000 = 0.2 or 20%

Step Three: Multiply the result in Step Two by the amount of the year's distribution.

20% x $5,000 = $1,000

You will not have to pay taxes on $1,000 of the $5,000 distribution, but the remaining $4,000 will be subject to income tax.

CAUTION

Multiple IRAs. If you have more than one IRA, all of your IRAs (including traditional IRAs, SEPs, and SIMPLE IRAs but not Roth IRAs) are combined and treated as one for purposes of computing the tax-free portion of each distribution.

EXAMPLE: You have two IRAs. Over the years, you made nondeductible contributions of $8,000 to IRA #1. All of your contributions to IRA #2 were deductible. Consequently, your total basis for both IRAs is $8,000. On July 19 of this year, you withdrew $5,000 from IRA #1. On December 31, the fair market value of IRA #1 was $45,000 and IRA #2 was $30,000. To determine the tax-free portion of the distribution, you must follow these steps:

Step One: Determine the total fair market value of all of your IRAs as of December 31.

$45,000 + $30,000 = $75,000

Step Two: Add the distributions you took during the year to the total from Step One.

$5,000 + $75,000 = $80,000

Step Three: Determine the total basis (nondeductible contributions) for all IRAs.

$8,000 + $0 = $8,000

Step Four: Divide the total basis from Step Three by the amount from Step Two.

$8,000 ÷ $80,000 = 0.1 or 10%

Step Five: Multiply the result in Step Four by the amount of your distribution.

10% x $5,000 = $500

You will not have to pay tax on $500 of the $5,000 distribution, but you will on the remaining $4,500.

You Don't Have to Withdraw Cash

Generally, when you take a distribution from an IRA, you may choose the assets you want to withdraw; you are not required to take cash. For example, suppose you want to withdraw $20,000. Your portfolio consists of $10,000 in cash and the remainder in stocks and bonds. You may take your $20,000 in any combination of cash and property you choose. You may take part of your distribution in cash and part in stocks and bonds, or even all of it in stock. If you take the distribution in property other than cash, the amount of the distribution is the fair market value of the property (such as the stock) on the day it comes out of the IRA.

EXAMPLE: You decide to take a distribution from your retirement account on June 1. On that day, the total value of your account is $50,000, of which $10,000 is in cash and the remainder in 1,000 shares of MacBlue stock valued at $40 per share. The stock was purchased in the IRA for $10 per share. You decide to withdraw all of the cash and 250 shares of MacBlue stock. The total value of your distribution for tax purposes is $20,000 ($10,000 of cash plus 250 shares of MacBlue stock x $40 per share). After the distribution, you will have no cash inside the IRA, but you will have 750 shares of MacBlue stock. The tax basis of the MacBlue stock in your hands will be $40 per share, not its original cost of $10 per share. Therefore, if you sell the stock at some time in the future, the taxable amount will be the sale price less your basis of $40.

When you receive a distribution from your employer's retirement plan, the plan itself usually dictates which assets must be distributed; you frequently have little control.

You May Not Claim Losses

You may not claim on your tax return losses you incur inside your IRA or retirement plan. Instead, you simply pay tax on each distribution based on the cash value or the fair market value of the property on the date it is distributed from the plan. For example, if you purchased 100 shares of LM Corp. at $12,000 and the fair market value of the stock is $5,000 when you withdraw all 100 shares from your IRA, you are not permitted to take a loss of $7,000. But before you cry foul, remember that you didn't pay tax on the money you used to purchase the stock, either. It was purchased inside your retirement plan with tax-deferred money. The value of the stock at distribution is $5,000, and that is the entire taxable amount. In fact, you will have obtained a tax benefit from the loss through the reduction of the taxable distribution.

One extremely rare exception to this rule might occur if you have made contributions with after-tax dollars and never managed to withdraw all of your basis. For example, if your basis in your IRA exceeds the fair market value of the entire IRA (or all of your IRAs combined, if you have more than one) when you take a final distribution, you may claim the loss as a miscellaneous itemized deduction on your tax return. But the loss will be deductible only to the extent that it, along with other miscellaneous itemized deductions, exceeds 2% of your AGI.

EXAMPLE: In 1990 you made a non-deductible $2,000 contribution to an IRA. You invested all of the money in junk bonds. Because the investment started to go bad immediately, you never made any additional contributions. Now the account is worth $1,500. If you take a distribution of the entire $1,500 and close the account, you may claim a loss of $500 on Schedule A of your tax return. When you combine this amount with your other miscellaneous itemized deductions (in the amount of $450), the total of your miscellaneous deductions is $950 ($500 + 450). You are permitted to deduct your miscellaneous deductions only to the extent that they exceed 2% of your AGI. If your AGI is $42,000, 2% of that is $840 ($42,000 x 2%). Therefore, you may deduct only $110 ($950 − $840).

 TIP

Roth IRAs and Roth 401(k) plans are different. If you have a Roth IRA or a Roth 401(k) plan, all of your contributions (but not your investment returns) are after tax, so your basis in your Roth IRA or Roth 401(k) is likely to be higher than in your regular IRA or 401(k) plan.

Divorce or Inheritance Doesn't Change the Basic Tax Rules

If you inherit a retirement plan or IRA, or if you receive one from your spouse in a divorce settlement, the four rules just discussed apply to you as though you were the original owner. For example, when you take money or property out of an IRA you inherited from your mother, you pay tax on the fair market value of the assets on the date of distribution. And if your mother had some basis left in the account, that remaining basis is passed on to you.

 CAUTION

Step-up rules don't apply to retirement plans. Many assets receive what is called a step-up in basis when the owner of those assets dies. In other words, the basis of the asset is deemed to be its value when the owner dies rather than what the owner originally paid for it. Because investment assets usually increase in value over time, this benefit is referred to as a step-up.

Assets in IRAs and other retirement plans are not permitted a step-up in basis. The assets in the IRA will be subject to tax at their fair market value whenever they are distributed. Death only determines who will pay the tax. The original owner pays during his lifetime; after that, the beneficiary of the plan pays the tax.

Income Tax on Qualified Plans and Qualified Annuities

A variety of circumstances could lead to a distribution from your retirement plan during your working years. Or you might not take money out until you actually retire. If you wait until retirement, you have many options for paying the tax on the money you receive. If you take a distribution before retirement, you will encounter a minefield of restrictions, and you might even have to pay tax penalties.

Options for Paying Taxes at Retirement

In general, when you receive a distribution from a qualified plan or qualified annuity, you should consider four tax options:

- You can report the distribution on your return as ordinary income.
- You can roll over the distribution into a traditional IRA or another retirement plan, which means you can continue to delay paying taxes.
- If you qualify, you can use ten-year averaging, which is a method of computing the tax as though the distribution were spread over a ten-year period.
- If you qualify, you can roll over or transfer the distribution into a Roth IRA. This is called a conversion and you must pay tax on all of the pre-tax amounts that you transfer from the plan to the Roth IRA.

CAUTION

After-tax contributions aren't taxable. If part of your distribution includes after-tax contributions you made to your plan, those amounts will not be taxable and should not be included when computing your income tax using any of the above methods.

Pay Ordinary Income Tax

Some people are tempted to choose the path of least resistance. This is true in life generally, but especially true in that part of life that requires dealing with the IRS. When taking distributions from a retirement plan, the easiest option is simply to take the money, deposit it in your regular bank account, and report the amount of the distribution as ordinary income on your tax return at tax time.

But if your retirement plan distribution is large, you ordinarily would not choose to pay tax on the entire amount unless you need the money immediately and don't qualify for any special tax options.

Another reason you might have to use the ordinary income tax option is if you made a procedural error when attempting to use one of the other tax options, which left you no choice but to use the ordinary income tax option.

Who Is Eligible?

Anyone who receives a distribution from a retirement plan can choose to have the distribution taxed in this way.

Which Distributions Are Eligible?

All distributions you receive from a retirement plan that are attributable to pretax contributions or to investment returns may be taxed at ordinary income tax rates. This is true whether the distribution represents only part of your account or the entire balance.

CAUTION

Roth 401(k)s are different. Note that in the case of a distribution from a Roth 401(k) plan, investment returns, as well as your original after-tax contributions, will not be subject to tax, provided you have met the age and holding period requirements. (See Chapter 10 for a complete discussion of Roth 401(k) plans.)

Advantages and Disadvantages

The advantage of this tax option is that once the money comes out of the retirement plan and you pay the taxes owed, you have unrestricted use of the funds. The money that you withdraw is no longer subject to the terms of the plan.

But that peace of mind is expensive. Paying tax at ordinary rates on the money in the same year you receive it is usually the least advantageous option—at least from a financial perspective. If your distribution is large, it could easily push you into a higher tax bracket. It's hardly cheery to think of starting your retirement by handing the government 40% or more of your nest egg.

Roll Over Your Distribution

Rather than paying ordinary income tax on your entire retirement plan distribution, you might consider a more versatile and attractive strategy: Rolling some or all of the distribution into a traditional IRA or another employer's plan.

A rollover is usually accomplished by having your employer transfer your funds directly to another employer's plan or an IRA through a transaction called a direct rollover. If the funds are distributed directly to you, however, you have 60 days to deposit them into another plan or an IRA. The portion that is rolled over will continue to be tax deferred and will be subject to all the rules of the new plan or IRA. Any portion that is not rolled over within 60 days will be subject to ordinary income tax.

 TIP

Rollovers into another qualified plan after retirement are unusual. This is because once a person retires, he or she probably doesn't have another plan. Distributions at retirement are usually rolled into an IRA, unless you are taking your benefits as an annuity, in which case no rollover of any kind is permitted.

Who Is Eligible?

Anyone who receives a distribution from a qualified plan or qualified annuity is permitted to roll it over. It doesn't matter how old you are or how long you have been a participant in the plan.

Which Distributions Are Eligible?

Generally, all distributions and partial distributions from qualified plans and qualified annuities are eligible to be rolled over. The most significant exceptions are:

- distributions that are required to be distributed to you because you have passed age 70½ (see Chapters 5–8 for information about required distributions), and
- distributions in the form of a life annuity or periodic payments that last for ten years or more.

Advantages and Disadvantages

If you don't need to use your retirement money right away, rolling it over is a big advantage. It allows you to defer paying income tax until you are ready to spend the money (or until you are required to take it out by the new plan). If you take money out only when you need it, you may be able to withdraw it in small enough chunks to keep yourself in a low tax bracket. Meanwhile, whatever you don't need can be left to grow inside the new plan or IRA.

The disadvantage of rolling over the distribution is that you don't have unrestricted use of the money. As long as it's in an IRA or qualified plan, it is subject to all the rules and restrictions of the plan.

Pitfalls

If you are about to receive a distribution from a qualified plan or qualified annuity and you want to roll it over into another plan or an IRA, arrange for a direct rollover. In other words, have the funds transferred directly from your old employer's plan into the new plan or IRA. If you don't and instead receive the funds yourself before delivering them to the new plan, the distribution will be subject to income tax withholding, which could cause you some serious problems. (See "Withholding Money to Pay Taxes," below, for more information about withholding.) Your employer is required to offer you the option of a direct rollover (except to a defined benefit plan) if the amount of the distribution is at least $200. In addition to the withholding problem, you could encounter other traps.

Trap One: 60-Day Rule. You have 60 days from the time you receive a distribution to roll it over into another plan or IRA, and the clock starts ticking when you have the distribution in hand. The IRS is devilishly unforgiving when it comes to enforcing this rule, so if you're on your way to the bank on the 60th day, don't stop to tie your shoes. Also, not all types of plans can be mixed. For example, if you want to roll over your Roth 401(k) plan to a new employer's plan, the new employer must have a Roth 401(k) plan. Or if you want to roll over your Roth 401(k) plan to an IRA, it must be a Roth IRA.

Trap Two: Changing Your Mind. Once you actually complete the rollover of your retirement plan into another plan or IRA, there is no going back.

For example, suppose you instruct the plan administrator of your employer's plan to transfer your retirement money directly into an IRA. A week after the money is deposited to your IRA, you decide that you really should have taken the distribution and elected ten-year averaging. (Read on to learn more about this issue.) Unfortunately, you cannot undo a rollover. Once the rollover is complete, you may not pull the money out of the account and elect averaging, even if the 60 days has not yet expired.

If you do pull the money out, it will be treated as another retirement plan distribution, and you will have to pay income tax—and you might even have to pay an early distribution tax. (See Chapter 3 for information about the early distribution tax.)

Trap Three: Rolling Over Ineligible Funds. Some of the money you receive from a retirement plan might not be eligible to be rolled over. You cannot roll over annuity payments or money that must be distributed to you when you are age 70½ or older.

If you accidentally roll over ineligible funds, you have a certain amount of time to correct the problem—usually until the due date of your tax return. (That's April 15 of the following year, unless you request an extension of time for filing your return. In that case, you will have until the extended deadline.) If you do not remove the funds in time, you will have to pay a penalty for each calendar year or part of a year those funds remain in the plan or IRA.

Trap Four: Plan Rules Govern. Sometimes you might find that the law permits you to take certain steps with your retirement plan, but the terms of your plan are more restrictive. In that case, the plan's rules will govern. For example, the law generally allows you to roll over qualified plans and qualified annuities into almost any other type of retirement plan. Some plans, however, do not permit mixing and matching. Qualified annuity plan administrators often will not accept rollovers from other qualified annuities. However, you can always roll over a qualified plan or qualified annuity distribution into a traditional IRA.

Convert to a Roth IRA

Not only are you permitted to roll over a qualified plan distribution to another plan or to a traditional IRA, but you may also roll over the distribution to a Roth IRA. If you choose this option, however, you are technically converting the assets to a Roth IRA and all of the usual rules for Roth IRA conversions will apply. Specifically, you must be eligible to make the conversion in the first place. If you are, then you must pay income tax on all the pre-tax money that is transferred out of your employer's plan into your Roth IRA. And you must pay it in the year of the conversion. There is one exception to this rule for conversions that take place in the year 2010. You are permitted to spread the income from the conversion over two years, beginning in 2011 (half

in 2011 and half in 2012). For conversions after 2010, however, all of the income from the conversion must be included on the tax return for the year of conversion. (See Chapter 9 for more information about converting to a Roth IRA.)

Who is Eligible?

For the year 2009, you are eligible to convert to a Roth IRA if your modified AGI is $100,000 or less. (See Chapter 9 for more information about computing your modified AGI.) And if you are married, you must file a joint return with your spouse. (In other words, those who are married filing separately do not qualify to convert plan assets to a Roth IRA.) Beginning in 2010, everyone qualifies to convert to a Roth IRA.

Which Distributions Are Eligible?

As is the case with rollovers to other plans or to traditional IRAs, all distributions and partial distributions from qualified plans and qualified annuities are eligible to be rolled over to a Roth IRA, with the exception of required distributions and annuities or periodic payments that last for ten years or more.

Advantages and Disadvantages

Once you make the decision to roll over your employer's plan into an IRA, the next question you must ask yourself is: traditional IRA or Roth IRA? The decision involves a variety of factors. The disadvantage of converting to a Roth IRA is that you must pay tax on the entire amount of the distribution right away. The tax is not deferred. The advantage, however, is that all future distributions, including investment earnings, are potentially tax free no matter how large the account grows. Another advantage is that you are not required to take distributions from a Roth IRA during your lifetime, so the account can be left to grow tax free for as long as you live.

If you will not need to draw on the Roth IRA for living expenses during your retirement years, it is almost certainly right to convert to a Roth IRA. It can then be left alone to grow tax-free for years until your beneficiaries must draw on the funds.

If you do need the Roth IRA to live on, then it makes sense to do some calculations, taking into account tax rates at the time of conversion compared with expected retirement tax rates, living expenses, and other factors to determine the optimum amount (if any) you should convert to a Roth IRA. You might want to consult with a tax professional to help with those calculations.

Pitfalls

As with any rollover, you will want to arrange a direct rollover from the plan to the Roth IRA to avoid mandatory income tax withholding (see "Withholding Money to Pay Taxes," below).

If you choose to receive the distribution and roll it over yourself, not only will you have mandatory withholding to deal with, but you have a 60-day window during which the transaction must be completed. If you fail to complete the rollover

(actually, conversion) you won't owe any additional tax, but once the 60 days have passed, your opportunity to put that distribution into the Roth IRA will have expired.

See Chapter 9 for detailed information about conversions to Roth IRAs.

Use Ten-Year Averaging to Compute Tax

It may be that you cannot afford to roll over all of your retirement distribution because you need the money. And if you do need the money, you don't want to give up a large chunk of the distribution to income taxes. Although there is no way to avoid paying taxes if you elect not to roll over the distribution, you may be able to compute the tax using a method called ten-year averaging, which can reduce your total bill.

Who Is Eligible?

You are eligible to use ten-year averaging if you satisfy all of the following conditions:

- you were born before 1936
- you have not used ten-year averaging on any distribution since 1986, and
- you participated in the plan for at least five years, which means you or your employer made a contribution to your plan account in at least five separate years before the year of the distribution.

TIP

Figuring the length of participation.
If your account is transferred from one plan to another, you don't have to start the participation clock ticking all over again. The years you participated in the old plan count toward the five-year requirement.

Which Distributions Are Eligible?

Even if you are eligible, you may use ten-year averaging only if your distribution also qualifies. Your distribution will qualify only if both of the following are true:

- The distribution to be averaged must be the entire amount of your qualified plan or qualified annuity. You cannot roll over part of the distribution and you cannot have rolled over part of it in the past.
- You must receive the distribution all within one tax year, even if you receive more than one payment.

CAUTION

You might have two plans that the IRS treats as one for ten-year averaging.
For example, money purchase pension plans and defined benefit plans must be combined and considered one plan for purposes of the ten-year averaging rules. Let's say you receive a distribution of your defined benefit plan one year and roll it over. The next year you receive a distribution of your money purchase pension plan and want to use ten-year averaging. You cannot, however, because the distributions were received in different years.

How Is It Computed?

If you receive a distribution and elect to use ten-year averaging, the tax on the distribution itself is computed on IRS Form 4972 (see Appendix A) and recorded on a separate line of your tax return. You must pay that amount to the IRS even if you owe no other income taxes.

The tax is calculated as though you were a single individual (even if you are married) and as though you received the distribution in ten installments over ten years. Despite this calculation, you pay the total tax due in the year of the distribution, not over ten years. These are the steps:

Step One: Determine the taxable amount of the distribution.

This is usually the entire amount of the distribution reduced by any after-tax contributions you made. Your employer or the administrator of the plan should provide this information.

Step Two: Determine the Minimum Distribution Allowance.

If your distribution is less than $70,000, you may exclude some of it from your income when computing the tax. The excludable portion is called your minimum distribution allowance, or MDA. To determine the MDA:

1. Reduce the taxable amount of the distribution by $20,000, but not below zero.
2. Multiply the result by .2 or 20%.
3. Subtract the result from $10,000 or from one-half of the taxable

amount (the number from Step One), whichever is less. The result is your MDA.

Step Three: **Subtract your MDA from the taxable amount (Step One minus Step Two).**

Step Four: **Divide the result by 10.**

Step Five: **Compute the income tax on the amount from Step Four.**

You must use the 1986 tax rates for a single person. (A schedule of 1986 tax rates is in Appendix A.)

Step Six: **Multiply the result by 10.**

EXAMPLE: You receive a lump sum distribution of $50,000 that qualifies for ten-year averaging. You want to use the money to build your retirement dream house, so you decide to pay the tax. Here's how it is computed:

Step One: Taxable amount = $50,000

Step Two: Since the distribution is under $70,000, you will be entitled to an MDA as follows:

$50,000 − $20,000 = $30,000
$30,000 x 0.2 = $6,000
$10,000 − $6,000 = $4,000 (your MDA)

Step Three: $50,000 − $4,000 = $46,000

Step Four: $46,000 ÷ 10 = $4,600

Step Five: Tax on $4,600 at 1986 single rates = $597

Step Six: $597 x 10 = $5,970

Thus, you will owe $5,970 of federal income tax on your $50,000 distribution in the year you receive it. By contrast, if you simply reported the $50,000 as additional income without using the special averaging, you could owe as much as $19,800 of federal income tax on that $50,000, if you are in the top tax bracket.

Advantages and Disadvantages

When should you use averaging? Although it is usually better to roll over a distribution and continue your tax deferral rather than pay a ten-year averaging tax, those guidelines go right out the window if you need the money. In such a situation, ten-year averaging could mean big tax savings.

You might also choose ten-year averaging if your distribution is small enough to be taxed at a rate lower than you are likely to see in the future. But if your distribution is large, ten-year averaging is rarely a good choice. For one thing, you give up substantial compounded growth on the money that would otherwise remain in the retirement account. But also, the tax advantages of averaging decline as the distribution increases in amount. In addition, the top tax rates in 1986 were quite a bit higher than top rates today.

EXAMPLE: You receive a retirement plan distribution of $100,000. If you use ten-year averaging, the entire tax would be $14,470—all of it taxed at less than 15%. In contrast, if your distribution is $500,000 and you choose ten-year averaging, more than $150,000 would be taxed at rates higher than any current tax rate. In this case, you may be better off rolling over the $500,000 and spreading distributions out over your retirement years.

Bottom line: it's easy to be seduced by the lure of lower tax rates and ready money. But if your goal is to accumulate substantial sums for your retirement, you are usually better off rolling over your distribution and deferring the payment of tax.

Pitfalls

If you still think ten-year averaging is your best option, consider these traps.

Trap One: One-Time Election. Ten-year averaging is a once-in-a-lifetime election. If you choose to use it on a distribution, you may never again use ten-year averaging on a future distribution from any plan.

Trap Two: Multiple Distributions. If you receive distributions from more than one retirement plan in a single year and want to use ten-year averaging, you must use it on all the distributions you receive that year. If you want to use ten-year averaging on only one distribution, you must arrange to receive the distribution you want to average in a separate year, if possible. This rule is different from the aggregation rule covered above. Under the aggregation rule, if two plans are of the same type, for example both are profit-sharing plans, they are

considered one plan for ten-year averaging purposes. In that case, the distributions from both plans must be received in the same year or you may not use ten-year averaging on either distribution.

Use Capital Gain Rates to Compute Tax

If you were born before 1936 and you began participating in your employer's plan before 1974, you have another option available to you in addition to ten-year averaging: You may treat part of your distribution as capital gain subject to a flat 20% tax rate. The amount of your distribution that is eligible for this rate is computed by the plan administrator and is based on the number of years you participated in the plan before 1974. The administrator will report the eligible amount to you so that you can decide if you want to elect the 20% tax option. You may elect to use this special rate whether you choose to use ten-year averaging or ordinary income tax rates on the remaining portion of your distribution.

Special Rules for Employer Stock

Your retirement account distribution may include some shares of your employer's stock. If the total current value of the shares of stock purchased in your plan account is greater than the total basis, the difference is called the net unrealized appreciation.

Net unrealized appreciation is the difference between the fair market value of the stock and the stock's basis. Basis for this purpose means the cost of the stock when the plan purchased it. For example, suppose your employer contributed $1,000 to your retirement account on your behalf. The plan then used that $1,000 to purchase 100 shares of company stock at $10 per share. The stock's basis is $10 per share or $1,000 total. Many years later, when you retire, those 100 shares are worth $20,000. The net unrealized appreciation is $19,000, which is the fair market value less the plan's basis in those shares ($20,000 – $1,000).

You have several options for paying income taxes on employer stock that is part of a retirement plan distribution:

- If you elect ten-year averaging, you can exclude the net unrealized appreciation when computing the tax. In that case, you would include only the plan's basis in the ten-year averaging calculation (assuming, of course, that the stock was purchased with pretax dollars). If you use this tax strategy, you will pay tax on the net unrealized appreciation using long-term capital gains rates when you later sell the company stock.

- You can include the net unrealized appreciation when calculating your tax using ten-year averaging. You might do this if your tax rate using averaging is lower than the long-term capital gains rate.

- You can pay ordinary income tax (as opposed to using ten-year averaging) on all but the net

unrealized appreciation (paying tax on the plan's basis, for example, if the stock was purchased with pretax dollars). You would use this strategy if you did not qualify for ten-year averaging but did not want to roll over all of your employer stock into an IRA. Using this strategy you would pay capital gains tax on the net unrealized appreciation only when you sell the stock.

- You can roll over your entire distribution, including employer stock, into a traditional IRA. If you do so, the net unrealized appreciation in the stock becomes irrelevant because all future distributions from the IRA will be taxed as ordinary income, not as capital gains.

 TIP

Paying taxes to preserve capital gains rates. It might well be to your advantage not to roll over all of your employer stock into an IRA. This might be true if your net unrealized appreciation is large relative to the plan's basis in the stock, because the bulk of the distribution (the net unrealized appreciation) could be taxed at low capital gains rates when you eventually sell the stock. Remember, once the stock is rolled over into an IRA, all future distributions from the IRA will be taxed at ordinary rates—not capital gains rates. Note, too, that this strategy might work for you even if you are younger than age 59½. Although the portion of the distribution that you must pay tax on at the time of distribution (typically the basis) will be subject both to ordinary income tax and an early distribution penalty, the tradeoff—taxing the bulk of the distribution at capital gains rates instead of ordinary rates—could easily offset any disadvantage. But just how large the net unrealized appreciation must be relative to the plan's basis for this strategy to work might require a calculation by you or your accountant.

> **CAUTION**
>
> **No step-up for net unrealized appreciation.** Your inclination may be to exclude the net unrealized appreciation from your income tax and keep the stock, passing it on to your heirs when you die. You might do this if you think your heirs will obtain a step-up in the basis of the stock when you die. The step-up would allow them to avoid all tax on the net unrealized appreciation. But this strategy won't work. The Tax Code specifically denies any step-up in basis for net unrealized appreciation in employer stock.

Options for Paying Taxes Before Retirement

It is quite possible that you will receive a distribution from your retirement plan before you retire. Here are some common situations in which that might occur:

- you change jobs
- your company terminates its retirement plan, or
- you are self-employed and terminate your own plan.

The retirement plan rules were written to discourage distributions before retirement. For this reason, you'll find your options for paying taxes somewhat limited if you receive a retirement plan distribution while the government thinks you are too young to be retired.

Pay Ordinary Income Tax

If you do not need the distribution you receive from your retirement plan for living expenses, you will almost certainly want to do something with it other than spend it or put it in a regular bank account. If you don't, you will have to report the distribution on your tax return and pay ordinary income tax on it. Furthermore, you might have to pay penalties for withdrawing the money early.

Roll Over Your Distribution

If you have not yet reached age 59½ and you receive a distribution from a qualified plan or qualified annuity, you can roll over the distribution into a traditional IRA or another retirement plan to continue deferring the tax and to avoid paying an early distribution penalty. Alternatively, you can roll over the distribution into a Roth IRA, which constitutes a conversion of the assets to a Roth IRA. If you choose this option, you must pay income tax on the converted amounts. See Chapter 9 for more information about converting to a Roth IRA.

○! CAUTION

Arrange a direct rollover. If you receive a distribution from a qualified plan, intending to roll it over into another plan or into an IRA, arrange to have the administrator of your old employer's plan transfer the funds directly into the new plan or IRA instead of sending the money to you. Otherwise, the administrator of the old plan may be required to withhold money to cover taxes you might owe. (See below for more information about withholding.)

Use Ten-Year Averaging to Compute Tax

As long as you satisfy the requirements described above, averaging is an option for you.

Options for Paying Taxes on Inherited Plans

If you are the beneficiary, rather than the owner, of a qualified plan and you receive a distribution as a result of the owner's death, the rules for paying income taxes are a little different from the general rules described in "Options for Paying Taxes at Retirement," above. You can:

- pay ordinary income tax
- roll over your distribution
- convert to a Roth IRA, or
- use ten-year averaging.

Pay Ordinary Income Tax

If the plan assets are distributed outright to you and you simply take the money and put it into your regular bank account, then you will have to report the distribution as income on your tax return and pay tax on it, as you might expect. You may be able to reduce the total amount of the tax or gain some breathing room in paying the tax, however, by taking the distribution in installments over a number of years.

There is a bit of good news, too. If you receive a distribution from a plan you inherited, you will not have to pay an early distribution tax, even if you are younger than 59½. The penalty is waived for inherited plans. (See Chapter 3 for information about the early distribution tax.)

Roll Over Your Distribution

If you inherit a qualified plan or qualified annuity and you were the spouse of the original owner, you can roll over the distribution into a traditional or Roth IRA in your name or into your employer's plan.

If you inherit a retirement plan, such as a 401(k) plan, and you were not the spouse of the original owner, then you may roll over the plan assets into a traditinal IRA only if you follow these rules:

- You may not roll over the assets into a plan or IRA that is in your own name. Instead, you must establish a new IRA that is titled in the name of the deceased with you as the designated beneficiary: "Father Doe, deceased, for benefit of Daughter Doe." When an IRA is titled this way, it is called an inherited IRA, even though it was just established.

- The transfer of assets from the qualified plan to the newly established inherited IRA must occur as a trustee-to-trustee transfer. In other words, the assets must go directly from the retirement plan into the new IRA without going through you first. You cannot take possession of the funds.
- You must not mix assets from any other qualified plan or IRA with the inherited funds.

 CAUTION

Transfer to IRA might not be permitted. Although the law permits nonspouse beneficiaries to transfer assets from an inherited retirement plan to a new inherited IRA, the plan itself is not required to offer the option to a nonspouse beneficiary. If the plan doesn't allow it, the strategy will not be available to the beneficiary.

See Chapters 7 and 8 for more information about inherited plans and IRAs, including how to title accounts.

Convert to a Roth IRA

When a spouse inherits a retirement plan or IRA, the spouse is accorded virtually all of the distribution options offered to the deceased plan participant. For that reason, it has always been an easy matter for a spouse beneficiary to convert retirement assets to a Roth IRA if he or she wants to do so. In the past, nonspouse beneficiaries did not enjoy the same privileges. But in

2008, the IRS issued a notice indicating that not only are nonspouse beneficiaries now permitted to transfer qualified plan assets into a traditional IRA (in the decedent's name), but they also have the option to transfer (or convert) the assets to a Roth IRA. Again, there are some conditions:

- The beneficiary must first qualify to convert assets to a Roth IRA. That means, through the year 2009, the beneficiary's modified AGI cannot exceed $100,000 and the beneficiary may not use the filing status married filing separately. After 2009, there are no income or filing status restrictions on converting to a Roth IRA. (See Chapter 9 for more information about modified AGI.)
- As is the case when transferring assets to a traditional IRA, the beneficiary must establish a new Roth IRA in the decedent's name. The new Roth IRA will be treated as an inherited Roth IRA.
- The transfer from a qualified plan to a new Roth IRA must occur as a trustee-to-trustee transfer.
- The new Roth IRA should not contain any other assets except those that were converted from the qualified plan.
- The beneficiary must pay income tax on the converted amounts for the year of conversion. One exception: If the beneficiary converts assets to a Roth IRA in the year 2010, the

taxes for the conversion may be paid over two years, beginning in 2011. The taxes due on conversions in any year except 2010 must be paid in full with the tax return for the year of conversion.

See Chapter 9 for more information about converting assets to a Roth IRA and about how to take distributions from an inherited Roth IRA.

CAUTION

Transfer to Roth IRA might not be permitted. As is the case with transfers to traditional IRAs, even though the law permits nonspouse beneficiaries to transfer assets from an inherited retirement plan to a new inherited Roth IRA, the plan itself might disallow it and the plan's rules will govern.

Use Ten-Year Averaging to Compute Tax

If you inherit a qualified plan or qualified annuity, you can use ten-year averaging provided that the distribution is a qualified distribution and that the original owner satisfied all the eligibility requirements (except the five-year participation require-ment) at the time of death.

CAUTION

Meeting the eligibility requirements. It is not you, the person who inherited the plan, who must meet the eligibility requirements for ten-year averaging, it is the original owner. It

doesn't matter how old you are, nor would it matter if you had used averaging on one of your own distributions. As long as the original owner would have qualified for averaging, you qualify.

Options for Paying Taxes on Qualified Plans Received at Divorce

Congress has gone to great lengths to protect your qualified plan assets. The cornerstone of that protection is a provision known as the anti-alienation rule, which attempts to ensure that you cannot be forced to give away your qualified plan assets.

Divorce presents a unique problem, however. What if you want to use your retirement plan as part of a property settlement? Can you give away some or all of your plan assets in that situation? And if you can, who should be responsible for the taxes and penalties (if any) on the part you give away?

Congress addressed these concerns by giving divorcing couples a vehicle for protecting plan assets and minimizing tax penalties. It's called a Qualified Domestic Relations Order or QDRO (pronounced "Quadro"). The QDRO rules spell out the circumstances under which your qualified plan benefits can go to someone else—an alternate payee—such as your soon-to-be former spouse.

A QDRO is a judgment, decree, or order (including a court-approved property settlement agreement) that satisfies all of the following:

- It relates to child support, alimony, or the marital property rights of a spouse, a former spouse, a dependent child, or some other dependent of the qualified plan participant.
- It gives an alternate payee, such as a spouse, former spouse, dependent child, or other dependent, the right to receive all or a portion of the participant's plan benefits.
- It does not alter the form or the amount of the benefit originally intended for the participant even though the benefit might now go to an alternate payee. For example, the QDRO cannot require the plan to pay a larger annuity to the alternate payee than it would have paid to the participant.
- It contains certain language. Specifically:
  - The alternate payee must be referred to as "the alternate payee" in the QDRO.
  - The QDRO must identify the plan, as well as the amount of each payment and the number of payments to be made.
  - The QDRO must contain the name and address of both the participant and the alternate payee.

If you are in the process of divorcing and you and your spouse agree that you will receive an interest in your spouse's qualified plan, you may be able to preserve some of the tax benefits of the plan for yourself. But this is possible only if there is a QDRO in place. If you and your spouse write up your agreement but it does not meet the above four requirements and is not court-approved, then your agreement is not a QDRO. In such a situation, distributions to a spouse, former spouse, or child could be subject to penalties.

In most cases, QDRO payments are made to a spouse or former spouse as alimony or as part of a property settlement. Payments might also be used for child support. If you receive a qualified plan distribution under a QDRO, the rules for how it is taxed and what you can do with it will depend upon your relationship to the original owner or plan participant.

Options for a Nonspouse Alternate Payee

If the recipient of a QDRO payment is not the spouse or former spouse of the plan participant, then the plan participant must report all distributions from the qualified plan as income on the participant's own tax return and pay taxes on them. If the distribution qualifies for special tax treatment, however, the plan participant can opt for the special rules. For example, the plan participant may use ten-year averaging on a distribution to figure the tax liability, provided the participant is eligible. If you are the recipient, you would pay no taxes when you receive the distribution.

Although the tax burden falls heavily on the plan participant, a couple of special rules provide a little tax relief:

- The participant will not have to pay an early distribution tax on any QDRO distribution paid to a nonspouse recipient, no matter how old the participant is or how old the recipient is. (See Chapter 3 for more information about the early distribution tax.)

- If the participant separates the recipient's share of the plan, perhaps by rolling it over into a new IRA, the participant can use ten-year averaging on the remaining portion—provided the remaining portion would have qualified for averaging if it had been the participant's entire plan balance. The participant may not treat the recipient's portion alone as a distribution eligible for averaging, however, unless that portion constitutes the participant's entire plan balance.

Options for a Spouse or Former Spouse Alternate Payee

If you are a spouse or former spouse receiving a distribution under a QDRO, you are treated in almost every respect as though you are the plan participant. Specifically:

- You may roll over some or all of the distribution to your own IRA or employer plan.

- You must pay tax on the distribution if you do not roll it over.

- The distribution is subject to mandatory withholding rules as though you were the plan participant. (See "Withholding Money to Pay Taxes," below.)

As you might expect, there are exceptions to the general rule that you are to be treated as though you were the plan participant:

- Although you may elect ten-year averaging on the distribution you receive, your eligibility for averaging depends on the participant's eligibility. In other words, if the participant was born before 1936, has not made an averaging election since 1986, and has participated in the plan for at least five years, then you may elect ten-year averaging. If the plan participant does not qualify, neither do you.

- Although you may elect averaging, you are not permitted to use the special capital gain rules for pre-1974 accumulations, nor may you exclude from income the net unrealized appreciation in employer stock.

- Any distribution you keep in a regular account instead of rolling it over will not be subject to an early distribution tax, regardless of your age or the participant's age. (See Chapter 3 for information about early distributions.)

Once you do roll over the distribution into an IRA or another retirement plan in your name, the assets become yours in every respect, as though they never belonged to the original participant.

Withholding Money to Pay Taxes

Congress, in its increasingly creative efforts to improve the Treasury's cash flow, passed a mandatory withholding law in 1993 for qualified plans. The law requires your plan administrator to keep 20% of all qualified plan distributions to pay federal income tax before distributing the remainder to you.

> **EXAMPLE:** You leave your job and plan to travel around the world for six months. Your employer distributes your retirement plan to you. The total value of your account is $10,000. The plan administrator gives you $8,000 and sends the rest to the government to pay the taxes you will owe on the distribution.

Exceptions to Mandatory Withholding

There are some exceptions to the mandatory withholding law.

- Amounts that are transferred directly from the trustee of your retirement plan to the trustee of another plan or to the custodian of your IRA are not subject to the withholding. This is called a direct rollover and is the most appropriate action to take if your intention is to roll over your distribution.

> CAUTION
>
> **Standard rollovers are not exempt from the mandatory withholding rule.** If you take a distribution of your retirement plan—for example, you receive a check payable to you—intending to roll it over into an IRA, your employer must withhold 20% for taxes. The direct rollover exception works only if the money is delivered directly from your retirement plan trustee to the trustee of another plan or to the custodian of your IRA. (Read on for more information about direct rollovers.)

- Any after-tax contributions you made to the plan are not subject to withholding when they are distributed to you.
- If you elect to receive your distribution in roughly equal periodic payments over ten or more years, those payments will not be subject to mandatory withholding.
- Small distributions of $200 or less are not subject to mandatory withholding.

Pitfalls of Mandatory Withholding

Unless you use a direct rollover, the withholding law can pose some serious problems for you and maybe even take a permanent bite out of your retirement nest egg by doing the following:

- reducing your retirement accumulation
- imposing penalties and taxes, and
- forcing you to sell assets to pay taxes.

Let's look at each of these in more detail.

Reducing Your Retirement Accumulation

If it is your intention to roll over your entire retirement plan distribution into an IRA or another retirement plan and continue the tax deferral, and you don't use a direct rollover, mandatory withholding could put a crimp in those plans. Because the withholding is usually paid out of the distribution, you will have a smaller amount to roll over.

> **EXAMPLE:** You have just retired. You accumulated $200,000 in your employer's retirement plan. You plan to roll over your distribution into an IRA. However, when you receive the check from your employer, it is only $160,000. Because of the mandatory withholding rules, your employer was required to send 20% or $40,000 to the IRS to cover any income taxes you might owe on the distribution, even if it was always your intention to roll over the entire amount. So now you only have $160,000 in your retirement nest egg. (You may be able to replace the amount withheld, however. See below.)

Imposing Penalties and Taxes

If your distribution was subject to withholding, you may claim a refund of the tax withheld for the portion that was rolled over. However, the portion of the distribution that was sent to the government for taxes was part of your distribution, too, and it wasn't rolled over, so it will be subject to income tax. Worse, if you are not yet 59½, you might have to pay an early distribution tax on the portion withheld for taxes, even though the withholding was mandatory. (See Chapter 3 for more information about the early distribution tax.)

> **EXAMPLE:** You decide to retire in November of the year you turn 61. You have accumulated $300,000 in your employer's retirement plan. When you receive your distribution, the amount is only $240,000 because your employer was required to send 20% or $60,000 to the IRS for taxes. When you file your next tax return, you will report the $60,000 of withholding as tax you have already paid along with any other amounts withheld from your regular paychecks during the year.
>
> In addition, you must report $60,000 of the retirement plan distribution as income. The $240,000 that was rolled over is not subject to tax, but the $60,000 that was sent to the IRS to pay taxes is. Even though the withholding was mandatory, it is still treated as a taxable distribution. In essence you took money out of your retirement account to pay your taxes.
>
> On the plus side, you should be entitled to a big tax refund when you file your tax return, since you paid $60,000 (through withholding) for taxes due on your distribution, but

the taxable portion itself was only $60,000. The remaining $240,000 was rolled over.

Similarly, if you borrow money from your plan and don't pay it all back by the time you are to receive your distribution, the unpaid loan amount counts as part of your distribution and is subject to both income tax and mandatory withholding. You might need to liquidate assets (except employer securities) in order to cover the withholding.

> **EXAMPLE:** When you retire, you will have $10,000 of cash in your retirement plan and 5,000 mutual fund shares valued at $20 per share. The total value of your account is $110,000. However, you also borrowed money from the plan last year and still owe $20,000 on that loan. The plan will report a distribution of $130,000 to the IRS ($10,000 in cash plus $100,000 in mutual fund shares plus the outstanding loan balance of $20,000). The mandatory 20% withholding is based on the full $130,000, and therefore is $26,000. Because you have only $10,000 in cash, the plan must sell 800 of your mutual fund shares to come up with enough cash to cover the withholding. Thus, although a distribution of $130,000 is reported to the IRS, the amount you actually receive will be only $84,000, which is $130,000 reduced by the loan amount and reduced further by the 20%

withholding ($130,000 − $20,000 − $26,000 = $84,000).

Forcing You to Sell Assets to Pay Taxes

What happens if there's not enough cash in your account to cover the required withholding? The news is not good. The plan administrator must withhold taxes even if it means selling property in the account to generate enough cash. If you hold stock you don't want to sell, you might be out of luck—unless one of these exceptions applies:

- The plan permits you to come up with the money for withholding from sources outside the plan. This requires that you have a stash of cash.
- If your retirement assets consist solely of cash and employer securities (as opposed to other securities or property) and you don't have enough cash to cover the 20% mandatory withholding, the administrator will withhold only the cash. In other words, you are not required to liquidate employer securities in order to pay the withholding.

> **EXAMPLE:** On the day you retire from Flush Corp., your retirement plan assets consist of $5,000 in cash and 3,000 shares of Flush Corp. stock valued at $50 per share or $150,000. The total value of your retirement plan is $155,000, which means that the mandatory withholding is $31,000 (20% x $155,000). Because you do not have $31,000 in cash and you are

not required to liquidate employer stock, your mandatory withholding is limited to the amount of cash in your retirement account, which is $5,000.

Avoiding or Correcting Mandatory Withholding

Happily, you can avoid the withholding pitfalls altogether through direct rollover. Simply request that the plan administrator transfer your entire distribution directly into another qualified plan or an IRA. If you never have access to the funds during the transfer, the administrator is not required to withhold any money. The rule applies even if your distribution check is sent to you personally, as long as it is payable to the trustee or custodian of the new plan, and not to you.

It is possible to elect a direct rollover for part of your distribution, saving you at least some of the mandatory withholding. Only the portion paid directly to you will be subject to mandatory withholding.

If you fail to request a direct rollover and instead receive a distribution check reduced by the 20% withholding amount, you may still be able to make yourself whole. If you can come up with the cash to cover the amount withheld, you can deposit it into the new plan or IRA as though you received it as part of your distribution. Then at tax time, you can claim a refund of the entire withholding amount. You avoid income taxes and penalties and manage to roll over every dollar of the distribution.

Although this approach works, you must have adequate cash on hand to take advantage of it. And of course, the government has free use of your money until you file your next tax return.

You can use a similar strategy if you have an outstanding loan from your plan. In other words, you can use cash you have outside the plan to roll over the amount of the loan into the new plan.

Notification of Mandatory Withholding

Are you worried that if you miss the direct rollover option you'll feel foolish? Take heart: It's not as easy to miss as you might think. Not only must the plan administrator give you the option to elect a direct rollover, but the administrator must notify you of the option at least 30 days (and no more than 90 days, lest you forget) before the distribution is to take place. Failure to give notice will cost the administrator $100 per incidence, up to $50,000 per year. However, once the administrator provides notice, he has satisfied his obligation. The administrator is not required to make sure you read the notice.

Loans From Qualified Plans

The law generally permits employees to borrow money from their qualified plans, although some plans do not allow it. Most do, however, because employees consider the ability to borrow from their retirement plan an important benefit. But the borrowing rules are stringent.

A loan from a qualified plan is considered a taxable distribution unless it satisfies certain requirements:

- The loan must be repaid at a reasonable rate of interest with well-defined repayment terms.
- The loan amount cannot exceed $50,000.
- The loan amount cannot exceed the greater of $10,000 or 50% of your vested account balance. (The vested amount is the portion you may take with you when you leave the company.) In other words, the loan is limited to 50% of your vested balance unless your account is under $20,000. Then you may borrow up to $10,000 as long as you have that much in your account and the plan allows it.

EXAMPLE: You have a vested account balance of $70,000 in your employer's retirement plan. You would like to borrow as much as you can from the plan. The loan may not exceed $50,000. But it also may not exceed 50% of your vested account balance, which is $35,000 (50% x $70,000). Thus the maximum you may borrow from the plan is $35,000.

- If you have more than one outstanding loan, the total of all loans from the plan cannot exceed $50,000 reduced by the difference between the highest loan balance for the previous 12 months and the current balance.

EXAMPLE: On January 15, your vested benefit in your employer's retirement plan is $150,000. You borrow $25,000 from the plan. On December of the same year, you realize that you need to borrow some additional money to get through the holiday season. Although you had begun to pay back the first loan, you still owe $20,000. To compute the amount you may borrow now, you begin with the $50,000 limit and reduce it by the amount of money you still owe to the plan. That reduces your limit to $30,000 ($50,000 – $20,000). The $30,000 must be reduced further by the difference between the highest outstanding balance in the last 12 months (which was $25,000) and the current outstanding balance (which is $20,000). That difference is $5,000. Thus the $30,000 is further reduced to $25,000, which is the maximum you may now borrow from the plan.

- The loan must be repaid within five years, using a level amortization schedule (like a home mortgage) with payments to be made at least quarterly. There is an exception to the five-year repayment rule if the loan is used to purchase (but not improve) a principal residence. In that case, you may simply repay the loan in a reasonable amount of time. (The Tax Code does not define "reasonable"—however, the IRS has been known to approve loans outstanding for as long as 30 years when they are used to make mortgage payments.)

As long as the above five requirements are met, the amount of the loan will not be considered a taxable distribution to you, either at the time it is made or during the repayment period.

> **CAUTION**
>
> **You may owe taxes on an out-standing loan.** If you haven't repaid your loan by the time your share of the plan assets is distributed to you, the loan amount will be subject to income tax. (See "Pitfalls of Mandatory Withholding," above.)

Hardship Distributions From Qualified Plans

A special relief provision in the Tax Code allows participants in 401(k) plans and other profit sharing plans—but no other type of qualified plan—to withdraw money in the event of hardship. It is not sufficient that the law permits such withdrawals; the plan itself must specifically allow them as well.

The Tax Code defines hardship withdrawal to be a distribution because of "immediate and heavy financial need." The plan must establish objective and nondiscriminatory ways of determining whether such a need exists and measuring the amount of money necessary to satisfy that need.

The IRS provides a list of expenses that qualify as hardship withdrawals. That means that if your expenses fall into one of the listed categories and your plan allows hardship withdrawals, your distribution will generally qualify as a hardship withdrawal. The IRS expenditures are as follows:

- medical expenses for you, your spouse, or your dependents
- expenses to purchase a principal residence (but not money to make mortgage payments)
- expenses to pay postsecondary education for a 12-month period, including tuition, room, and board, and
- expenses to stave off eviction from your principal residence or to forestall a foreclosure.

Expenses can qualify for hardship withdrawals even if they don't fall into one of the above categories. In that case, the plan document must provide some method of determining whether an expense constitutes immediate and heavy financial need. You must also provide a statement to the IRS declaring that you have exhausted other available resources. For example, if you have a vacation home, you would be required to sell it and use the proceeds before you would qualify to take money out of your plan.

Now the coup de grace. Suppose you jump through all the hoops and are eligible for a hardship withdrawal. What you gain is access to your funds without disqualifying the plan. But a hardship withdrawal is still subject to income tax. And you will also owe a 10% early distribution penalty if you are younger than 59½, unless the withdrawal qualifies for one of the exceptions described in Chapter 3.

CAUTION

Hardship distributions are not eligible to be rolled over into an IRA or another qualified plan. So if you take a distribution from your 401(k) plan under its hardship provisions, and then you decide you don't need the money after all, you are stuck. You cannot roll it into an IRA, nor can you put it back into the plan.

Special Income Tax Rules for Tax-Deferred Annuities

Although tax-deferred annuities, or TDAs, closely track the taxation rules for qualified plans, there are some important differences. (See Chapter 1 for more information about TDAs.)

Ordinary income tax applies. In general, distributions from TDAs will be taxed along with the rest of your income at normal tax rates unless you roll over the distribution. But you may not exclude from your income the net unrealized appreciation in employer stock, as you can with a qualified plan.

Rollover. As with qualified plan distributions, you may roll over any portion of a TDA distribution into an IRA or another retirement plan. However, if you roll over the TDA distribution into a qualified plan, you forfeit the right to use ten-year averaging on any future distribution from that qualified plan.

Averaging and capital gain treatment not allowed. Ten-year averaging is not permitted for distributions from TDAs, and neither is capital gain treatment for pre-1974 accumulations. Distributions from TDAs must be rolled over or they will be subject to ordinary income tax at the tax rates in effect in the year of distribution.

QDRO rules apply. The QDRO rules apply to TDAs just as they do to qualified plans, except that the alternate payee is not permitted to use ten-year averaging or the special capital gain treatment.

Hardship distributions permitted. Hardship distributions from TDAs are permitted and are subject to the same rules as hardship distributions from 401(k) plans.

Special Income Tax Rules for IRAs

Unlike TDAs, which mimic qualified plans in most respects, IRAs are quite different, and in many ways more restrictive.

CAUTION

Roth IRAs are not standard IRAs. If you have a Roth IRA, the following rules may not apply. See Chapter 9 for a detailed description of Roth IRAs and the taxes, penalties, and distribution rules that apply to them.

Ordinary Income Tax Applies

All distributions from traditional IRAs are subject to ordinary income tax unless you have made nondeductible contributions to the IRA over the years. In that case, a portion of each distribution will be tax free. The fair market value of the taxable portion is simply included with your income and taxed at your normal rates. You may not use capital gain rates, nor may you claim losses.

Tax Free Distribution From IRA for Charity

For years 2006 through 2009 only, you may make a charitable donation directly from your IRA (or an IRA you inherited) and not pay tax on the amount you withdraw. Here's the fine print:

- You must be at least age 70½ on the day the money is distributed from the IRA.
- Only traditional IRAs and Roth IRAs qualify—not active SEPs or SIMPLE IRAs.
- The money must be sent directly from the custodian of the IRA to the charity. In other words, you cannot take the money out and deposit it in one of your bank accounts and then give it to charity.
- The amount you may give to charity without paying tax on the IRA distribution is limited to $100,000.
- You may give the charity pretax money only. So, for example, your after-tax contributions in your Roth IRA are not eligible for donation under this provision.

If you follow the above rules, then you may exclude your IRA distribution from your income at tax time. Furthermore, you may use the distribution to satisfy part or all of your required minimum distribution from your IRA for the year. (See Chapter 6 for information about required minimum distributions.)

Rollover Allowed

You can roll IRA distributions into another IRA or even into your employer's plan—with certain restrictions.

Roll to Another IRA

You may roll over an IRA or part of an IRA into a different IRA or even back into the same IRA, but you must follow two important rules:

Rule Number One: 60-Day Time Limit. If you take a distribution with the intention of rolling it into a different IRA, you have 60 days from the time you receive the distribution to deposit it into the new IRA. If you miss the deadline, you will owe income tax and perhaps penalties, such as an early distribution tax. (See Chapter 3.)

TIP

If you need a short-term loan. It is quite acceptable to take money from your IRA as long as you deposit it into another IRA, or back into the same IRA, within 60 days. Just be careful to redeposit the precise amount of cash you distributed in the first place. Don't buy stock with the distributed funds and then try to deposit the stock into the IRA in lieu of the cash. If cash came out, cash must go back in.

Rule Number Two: Only One Per Year. You are permitted only one rollover per year from each IRA that you own. For example, if your IRA #1 has $50,000 in it and you decide to roll over $20,000 to your IRA

#2, you may not roll over any other funds from IRA #1 for 12 months. (Note that the restriction is for a full 12 months, not just a calendar year.)

CAUTION

The same funds can be rolled over only once in a 12-month period. For example, if you roll over $10,000 from one of your IRAs into a new IRA, you may not later roll over that same $10,000 into yet another IRA until 12 months have passed.

TIP

The one-rollover-per-year rule applies only to rollovers. This rule does not apply to transfers that go directly from one IRA custodian to another. For example, if you want to roll funds from IRA #1 to IRA #2, you could simply ask the custodian of IRA #1 to send you a check. When you receive it, you deliver it to the custodian of IRA #2. That is considered a rollover. But if you instruct the custodian of IRA #1 to transfer funds directly to the custodian of IRA #2, so that you never personally receive the funds, that is considered a transfer. The IRS is more lenient with transfers, because you don't have access to the funds and presumably can't do anything improper. The IRS allows you to make as many transfers as you like during the year.

Roll to an Employer Plan

You may also roll over some or all of your IRA distribution into your employer's plan—provided the plan permits such rollovers. Be careful, though; you are not permitted to roll over any after-tax amounts from the IRA to the employer plan. Thus, if you have made nondeductible contributions to the IRA, you cannot roll these into an employer plan.

60-Day Rule

For many years, the IRS adamantly refused to entertain even the most heartbreaking excuse for why a taxpayer was unable to complete a rollover from one plan or IRA to another within 60 days. But eventually, the IRS issued a compassionate revenue procedure (Rev. Proc. 2003-16) promising to grant waivers "where failure to waive … would be against equity or good conscience." The revenue procedure lists the following circumstances under which a waiver is likely to be granted:

- financial institution error (the waiver will generally be automatic if the error is corrected within a year)
- death
- disability
- hospitalization, or
- incarceration.

To obtain a waiver, the taxpayer must formally apply for one and pay a fee that ranges from $500 to $3,000 depending on the size of the rollover.

Averaging and Capital Gain Treatment Not Allowed

Neither ten-year averaging nor capital gain treatment is permitted on distributions from an IRA.

Special Rules at Divorce or Separation

The QDRO rules for qualified plans do not apply to IRAs. It is still possible to give a spouse or former spouse an IRA or a portion of an IRA, however, as part of a marital property settlement without subjecting the distribution to current income tax or penalties. To do so, you must have a valid divorce decree, a written instrument incident to divorce, a written agreement incident to a legal separation, or a maintenance or alimony decree.

With one of those documents in place, the IRA may be transferred in whole or in part to a spouse or former spouse through one of the following methods:

- The custodian of the participant's IRA may transfer the IRA directly to the trustee of the spouse or former spouse's IRA.
- The participant may direct the custodian to change the title of the IRA to an IRA in the spouse's or former spouse's name.
- The original participant or owner may roll over the IRA into an IRA in the name of the spouse or former spouse.

Under no circumstances, however, should the spouse or former spouse initiate the transfer of the participant's IRA or take possession of the funds before they are deposited into an IRA in the spouse's name. Only the participant may direct the transfer or rollover. Once the funds are in an IRA in the name of the spouse or former spouse, the IRA is treated in every respect as though the spouse or former spouse were the original owner. When assets are later distributed, they will be subject to ordinary income tax and perhaps penalties, for which the spouse or former spouse will be liable.

CAUTION

You'll still owe the early distribution tax. Although there is an exception to the early distribution tax for distributions to an alternate payee under a QDRO, that exception does not apply to IRAs. (See Chapter 3 for more information about the early distribution tax.)

Mandatory Withholding Doesn't Apply

Distributions from IRAs are not subject to the mandatory withholding rules discussed earlier in this chapter that apply to distributions from qualified plans.

Loans Not Allowed

You are not permitted to borrow from an IRA. There are no exceptions. If you do, the consequences are disastrous. If you borrow any amount at all, the entire IRA is disqualified and all assets deemed distributed. The distribution will be subject to income taxes and perhaps other penalties as well, such as the early distribution tax.

Hardship Distributions Not Allowed

There is no such thing as a hardship distribution from an IRA—any type of IRA. That's because hardship distributions are not necessary. Unlike a qualified plan, which restricts your access to funds, you can take money out of your IRA any time you want. Of course, you will have to pay income tax and, if you are younger than 59½, you'll also have to pay an early distribution tax. But you always have access to the money.

How Penalties Can Guide Planning

In this chapter and the previous one, we have defined the most common types of retirement plans, highlighted their differences, and discussed the income tax consequences of distributions. In the remaining chapters, we discuss distribution rules that apply across the board—to qualified plans, qualified annuities, TDAs, and IRAs. Those rules come with punishing penalties for violations. The penalties are in the form of an additional tax, but are usually avoidable if you understand the rules.

The following two penalty taxes will drive many of the decisions you make about your retirement plan or IRA:

Early distribution penalty. You will be hit with an early distribution tax if you take a retirement plan distribution too early—usually before age 59½. This penalty is discussed in depth in Chapters 3 and 4.

Required distribution penalty. Once you reach a certain age, usually 70½, you will be required to take a minimum amount from your retirement plan each year. If you don't, you will be subject to a huge penalty—50% of the shortfall. Similar rules apply after you inherit a retirement plan. These required distributions are discussed in Chapters 5 through 8.

Permissible Rollovers	
Original plan	New plan
Qualified plan—401(a)	Traditional IRA Roth IRA SEP Qualified plan—401(a) Qualified annuity plan—403(a) Tax deferred annuity—403(b)
Qualified annuity plan—403(a)*	Traditional IRA SEP Qualified plan—401(a) Qualified annuity plan—403(a) Tax deferred annuity—403(b)
Tax deferred annuity—403(b)	Traditional IRA Roth IRA SEP Qualified plan—401(a) Qualified annuity plan—403(a) Tax deferred annuity—403(b)
SEP	Traditional IRA Roth IRA SEP Qualified plan—401(a)** Qualified annuity plan—403(a)** Tax deferred annuity plan—403(b)**
SIMPLE IRA	SIMPLE IRA Traditional IRA (after two years) Roth IRA (after two years)
Traditional IRA	Traditional IRA Roth IRA SEP Qualified plan—401(a)** Qualified annuity plan—403(a)** Tax deferred annuity plan—403(b)**
Roth IRA	Roth IRA
Roth 401(k) plan	Roth 401(k) plan Roth IRA

* 403(a) plans often don't permit rollovers to or from any other plan even though the law itself permits it.

** Can receive pretax portion only.

Key Tax Code Sections

§ 401(a)(31)

Direct Rollover

§ 402

Rollovers; Ten-Year Averaging

§ 414(p)

Qualified Domestic Relations Orders (QDROs)

§ 3405

Qualified Plan Withholding Rules

§ 4975

Prohibited Transactions

Early Distributions: Taking Your Money Out Before the Law Allows

Exceptions to the Early Distribution Tax 62

    Age 59½ 63

    Death 64

    Disability 64

    Substantially Equal Periodic Payments 65

    Leaving Your Job After Age 55 66

    Dividends From ESOPs 66

    Medical Expenses 66

    QDRO Payments 68

    Federal Tax Levy 68

    Refunds 68

Calculating the Tax 68

Reporting the Tax 69

Special Rules for IRAs 75

    Rules Applicable to All IRAs Except Roth IRAs 75

    One Rule Applicable Only to SIMPLE IRAs 79

Who Should Read Chapter 3

 SKIP AHEAD
Read this chapter if you are younger than 59½ and want to withdraw money from your retirement plan or IRA. If you are older than 59½, this chapter does not apply to you.

If you take money out of a qualified plan, qualified annuity, tax-deferred annuity, or IRA before you reach age 59½, your withdrawal is called an early distribution, and you will have to pay a 10% early distribution tax on the money unless you can meet one of the exceptions.

This chapter describes those exceptions, and it also tells you how to calculate and report the tax just in case your distribution doesn't fit within one of those exceptions. In addition, it describes special rules for IRAs.

CAUTION

Don't forget regular income taxes. The exceptions we describe in this chapter help you escape the early distribution tax, not income taxes.

Exceptions to the Early Distribution Tax

The 10% early distribution tax feels more like a penalty than a tax, and no wonder: It is the cornerstone of the government's efforts to discourage us from plundering our savings before our golden years. Fortunately, there are many exceptions to the rule:

- if you are age 59½
- if you die
- if you become disabled
- if you choose to take substantially equal periodic payments
- if you are at least 55 years old when you leave your job
- if the distributions are dividends from an ESOP
- if you withdraw the money to pay medical expenses
- if you withdraw the money to pay child support or alimony or as part of a QDRO
- if you use the money to pay a federal tax levy, or
- if the money is actually a refund.

You can read more about each of these exceptions in the sections below.

Helpful Terms

Adjusted gross income (AGI). Total taxable income reduced by certain expenses such as qualified plan or IRA contributions or alimony payments. Note: Adjusted gross income does not take into account any itemized deductions (see definition below).

After-tax contribution. A contribution to a retirement plan or IRA for which no deduction was taken on an income tax return.

Ancestor. A person from whom an individual is descended. For example, an individual's parents, grandparents, and great grandparents are among his or her ancestors.

Distribution. A payout of property (such as shares of stock) or cash from a retirement plan or IRA to the participant or a beneficiary.

Itemized deductions. Expenses, such as medical payments, mortgage interest, and charitable contributions, that may be used to reduce AGI to arrive at the total amount of income subject to tax.

Principal residence. The home in which an individual lives most of the time. ("Most" is not defined in the Tax Code. It is established by your actions.)

Separation from service. Termination of employment.

Standard deduction. A fixed dollar amount that may be used instead of itemized deductions to reduce AGI before computing tax liability.

Age 59½

Although it's a little nonsensical to call being 59½ an exception to the tax on early distributions (after all, if you are 59½, your distribution isn't early in the first place), the Tax Code views it as an exception, so that is the way we discuss it here.

Before taking money out, make sure you will be at least 59½ on the day of the withdrawal. Otherwise, you'll pay the tax. In other words, it's not good enough that you turn 59½ during the year of the withdrawal. You must be at least 59½ on the day that you get the funds.

CAUTION

Escaping the early distribution tax doesn't mean you get free access to your money. Just because you have passed age 59½ doesn't guarantee that you can take money out of your retirement plan. Many qualified plans do not permit distributions before you terminate your employment. Attaining age 59½ simply ensures that if you are able to take money out, it will not be subject to the early distribution tax.

Death

Another straightforward exception to the tax, albeit a less attractive one, is death. None of the funds distributed from your retirement plan after your death will be subject to the early distribution tax, as long as the account is still in your name when the distribution occurs.

If you are the beneficiary of your spouse's retirement plan or IRA, then upon your spouse's death you may roll over a distribution from your spouse's retirement plan or IRA to a retirement plan or IRA of your own. (See Chapters 7 and 8 for more information about post-death distributions.) This benefit is available only to you as a spouse-beneficiary. But once the funds have been rolled over into an IRA in your name, the post-death exception to the early distribution tax no longer applies, because the account is no longer in the deceased owner's name.

If you want to roll over a post-death distribution from your deceased spouse's retirement plan into an IRA or plan of your own, but need to hold back some of the money for living expenses, this could pose a problem. If you take a distribution from a retirement plan while the plan is still in your deceased spouse's name, the distribution will indeed avoid the 10% tax. But the IRS has ruled that when a surviving spouse invokes this exception, the spouse forfeits the option to roll over the remainder into an IRA in his or her own name. Although this conclusion arises from a private letter ruling (which

means that other taxpayers may not rely on the result when planning their own tax strategies), it serves as a warning.

The logical solution to this problem is for the spouse to roll over only the amount that is not needed for living expenses, leaving the remainder in the deceased spouse's name. The remaining portion could then be tapped to pay expenses without incurring the 10% tax. The IRS has not yet ruled on such a strategy, however.

About Private Letter Rulings

Many taxpayers who are unclear about how to proceed in a murky area of the tax law and who feel they have too much at stake to take a wait-and-see posture with the IRS will request private letter rulings. These rulings are just what their title implies—private—meaning the ruling applies only to the taxpayer who requested it and only to the situation in question. The result of the ruling will not serve as precedent and cannot be relied upon by anyone else with similar or even identical circumstances. But the rulings can provide valuable insights into which way the IRS leans on a particular issue.

Disability

If you become disabled, you can take money out of your retirement plan without worrying about the early distribution tax.

But what does it mean to be disabled? And who decides? The law defines disabled as the inability to "engage in any substantial gainful activity by reason of any medically determinable physical or mental impairment which can be expected to result in death or to be of long-continued and indefinite duration." Is this helpful?

The key to the disability exception seems to lie in the permanence of the condition, not the severity. Disability exceptions have been denied for chemical dependence and chronic depression, even when the taxpayers were hospitalized for those conditions. It also appears that the disability must be deemed permanent at the time of the distribution, whether or not it is later found to be permanent. For example, the IRS denied the disability exception for a taxpayer, even knowing that the taxpayer later qualified for Social Security disability benefits.

Successful disability claims have included a dentist who suffered nerve damage to his thumb and who produced documents from four insurance companies declaring his disability permanent. Another successful claim involved a taxpayer who had been granted a disability retirement by his company. The IRS relied on the company's determination of the individual's disability. These cases reveal that the IRS is most concerned about the timing and the nature of the disability. Using the cases as a guide, if your disability prevents you from working and is deemed permanent at the time you take your retirement plan

distribution, then you should qualify for the disability exception. But there are no guarantees in this arena.

The IRS regulations do clarify one point, however. Gainful activity refers specifically to the type of work you were doing before becoming disabled. Thus it would seem that you need not be unfit for all work—just the work you customarily do.

Substantially Equal Periodic Payments

The substantially equal periodic payment exception is available to anyone with an IRA or a retirement plan, regardless of age, which makes it an attractive escape hatch. Theoretically, if you begin taking distributions from your retirement plan in equal annual installments, and those payments are designed to be spread out over your entire life or the joint life of you and your beneficiary, then the payments will not be subject to an early distribution tax.

The fly in the ointment is that you are not permitted to compute payments any way you please. The payment method must conform to IRS guidelines, which sanction three computation methods. Nonetheless, the guidelines are somewhat flexible, making the exception at once versatile and complex. For these reasons, Chapter 4 is devoted exclusively to interpreting the IRS's computational guidelines and related rulings.

If you think you might need to tap your retirement plan early, this is the option that is most likely to work for you. One caveat: If you want to begin taking substantially equal periodic payments from your employer's plan, you must have terminated your employment before payments begin. If the payments are from an IRA, however, the status of your employment is irrelevant.

Leaving Your Job After Age 55

If you are at least 55 years old when you leave your job, you will not have to pay the early distribution tax on money that you take out of your retirement plan. This exception applies per employer, meaning that you can go to work for another employer and still meet this exception to your previous employer's plan.

This exception is relevant only if you are between ages 55 and 59½. After age 59½, the early distribution tax does not apply to any retirement plan distribution.

As with other exceptions, you must pay attention to certain details. For example, you need not be age 55 on the day you leave your job, as long as you turn 55 by December 31 of the same year. The strategy falls apart if you retire in a year that precedes the year you turn 55, even if you postpone receiving the retirement benefits until you reach age 55.

EXAMPLE: You retire at age 53 and convince your employer to keep your retirement plan benefits in the plan

until you reach age 55. The day after your 55th birthday, you receive $100,000 from your former employer's plan. You buy a Jaguar and spend the rest of the money on a trip around the world. At tax time, you will owe regular income tax on the $100,000 plus a 10% early distribution tax.

If instead you had retired in the same year you turned 55, the $100,000 would be subject to regular income tax, but you would not have to pay an early distribution tax.

CAUTION

The age 55 exception is not available for IRAs. See "Special Rules for IRAs," below, for other rules that apply only to IRAs.

Dividends From ESOPs

You do not have to pay the early distribution tax on distributions of dividends from employer stock held inside an ESOP, no matter when you receive the dividend. (See Chapter 1 for more information about ESOPs.)

Medical Expenses

If you withdraw money from a retirement plan to pay medical expenses, a portion of that distribution might escape the early distribution tax. But once again, the exception is not as simple or as generous as it sounds. The tax exemption applies only to the portion of your medical expenses that would be deductible if you itemized deductions on your tax return. Medical expenses are deductible if they are yours, your spouse's, or your dependent's. But they are deductible only to the extent they exceed 7.5% of your adjusted gross income. Consequently, your retirement plan distribution will avoid the early distribution tax only to the extent it also exceeds the 7.5% threshold.

EXAMPLE: You are single and your adjusted gross income is $50,000. You had medical bills of $6,000 during the year, which you paid with funds you withdrew from your retirement plan. For income tax purposes, you are permitted to deduct medical expenses that exceed 7.5% of your adjusted gross income. Thus,

Adjusted gross income (AGI) = $50,000

Nondeductible expenses
  7.5% of AGI (.075 x 50,000) = $ 3,750
Deductible expenses
  Excess (6,000 – 3,750)   = $ 2,250

Although you took $6,000 from your retirement plan to pay medical expenses, only $2,250 will escape the early distribution tax. The remaining $3,750 will be subject to the 10% additional tax (unless you qualify for another exception). And don't forget that the entire $6,000 is subject to regular income tax, as well.

On the plus side, the medical expense exception is available even if you don't itemize deductions. It applies to those amounts that would be deductible if you did itemize.

EXAMPLE: As in the preceding example, your adjusted gross income is $50,000. You have $6,000 of medical expenses, which you paid with funds from your retirement plan. Only $2,250 of those expenses are deductible (as calculated above). Your deductible items for the year are as follows:

Deductible medical:	$2,250
Deductible taxes:	$1,000
Charitable contributions:	$ 500
Total	$3,750

The standard deduction for a single individual is greater than $3,750. When computing your tax liability, you are permitted to reduce your adjusted gross income by the larger of your itemized deductions or the standard deduction. In this case, because the standard deduction is larger, you will not itemize deductions on your tax return. You may still exclude $2,250 of your retirement plan distribution from the early distribution tax computation, however.

QDRO Payments

If you are paying child support or alimony from your retirement plan, or if you intend to distribute some or all of the plan to your former spouse as part of a property settlement, you will not have to pay an early distribution tax on any of those payments as long as there is a QDRO in place that orders the payments. (See Chapter 2 for more information about QDROs.) A QDRO usually arises from a separation or divorce agreement and involves court-ordered payments to an alternate payee, such as a former spouse or minor child. Although the QDRO exception applies to all distributions from a qualified plan to any named alternate payee, it is critical that the payments arise from a valid QDRO, not just a private agreement between you and your former spouse.

> ! **CAUTION**
>
> **The exception to the early distribution tax for QDRO payments does not apply to IRAs.** See "Special Rules for IRAs," below, for more information.

Federal Tax Levy

If you owe back taxes, you can be reasonably certain the government will try to collect them. If you have assets in a retirement plan, the government can take those assets (in other words, the IRS can put a levy on the assets of the plan) to pay your debt. If it does, then those amounts taken for taxes will not be subject to the early distribution penalty. This shouldn't be too much of a worry for you because IRS policy frowns on the government grabbing retirement plans to satisfy back tax debts unless the debtor is uncooperative and has no other assets.

Refunds

If you receive a refund of a contribution to your retirement plan because you contributed more than the law permits, you will not have to pay the early distribution tax on those corrective distributions.

Calculating the Tax

If you take money out a retirement plan before you reach age 59½ and cannot meet one of the exceptions described above, you will have to pay a 10% early distribution tax on the money. This tax applies to the taxable portion of your distribution only. So if you receive a distribution that includes after-tax contributions that you made to your retirement plan, the 10% tax will not apply to that portion. Similarly, if you receive a distribution of employer stock and elect to exclude the net unrealized appreciation from your taxable income, the excluded portion will not fall under the 10% tax. (See Chapter 2 for more information about employer stock and net unrealized appreciation.)

EXAMPLE: You retire at age 51 and take $80,000 out of your retirement plan. The distribution includes $15,000 of after-tax contributions that you make to the plan over the years. The remaining $65,000 consists of employer contribution and investment returns. You plan to use the money to buy a vacation home, so you don't meet any of the exceptions to the early distribution tax. At tax time, you will owe regular income tax and the 10% early distribution tax on the $65,000 portion; you will owe not taxes on the $15,000 portion.

Reporting the Tax

If you take a distribution from a retirement plan during the year, the trustee or custodian of your retirement plan will send you a copy of IRS Form 1099-R, which reports the amount distributed to you. (See the following page for a sample Form 1099-R.) The trustee or custodian will also send a copy to the IRS. You don't need to attach a copy of Form 1099-R to your tax return unless income tax was withheld from your distribution. In that case, you must attach the 1099-R just as you would attach your W-2 to show how much tax was withheld.

If you are younger than 59½ at the time of the distribution, a Code 1 should appear in Box 7 of the form, indicating that the early distribution tax applies. If you are younger than 59½ but you qualify for

another exception (including having left your job after age 55), Box 7 should reflect that information as well. Code 3 indicates a disability exception, Code 4 is a post-death distribution, and Code 2 is for most other exceptions.

EXAMPLE: At age 30, Geoff Sute quit his job with Tech Inc. for a higher paying job with another company. Tech Inc. distributed $1,500 to Geoff, which represented the entire balance of his 401(k) plan account. Geoff decided to spend the $1,500 on a new suit. At tax time, Tech Inc. sent Geoff a Form 1099-R reporting the distribution. (See sample form on following page.) Note that Box 7 correctly shows a Code 1.

If the Form 1099-R is accurate, your only responsibility is to compute and pay the extra 10%. This early distribution tax is reported as an additional tax under "other taxes" on page 2 of Form 1040, your regular income tax form. Even if you do not owe the IRS any regular income tax, you must still report the early distribution tax on your tax return and pay it at tax time.

EXAMPLE: Using the same facts as in the previous example, Geoff should report his $1,500 distribution on Form 1040, as shown below. Then he should report the early distribution tax of $150 on page 2 of Form 1040.

Sample: Form 1099-R From Plan Trustee or Custodian to Report Distribution

9898 ☐ VOID ☐ CORRECTED		

PAYER'S name, street address, city, state, and ZIP code	1 Gross distribution	OMB No. 1545-0119	Distributions From Pensions, Annuities, Retirement or Profit-Sharing Plans, IRAs, Insurance Contracts, etc.
Tech Inc. 401(k) Plan	$ 1,500	**2008**	
786 Chipstone Way	2a Taxable amount		
Sunburn, California	$ 1,500	Form **1099-R**	

		2b Taxable amount not determined ☐	Total distribution ☒	Copy A For Internal Revenue Service Center
PAYER'S federal identification number	RECIPIENT'S identification number	3 Capital gain (included in box 2a)	4 Federal income tax withheld	
99-9999	555-55-5555	$	$ 300	File with Form 1096.

RECIPIENT'S name	5 Employee contributions /Designated Roth contributions or insurance premiums	6 Net unrealized appreciation in employer's securities	For Privacy Act and Paperwork Reduction Act Notice, see the 2008 General Instructions for Forms 1099, 1098, 5498, and W-2G.
Geoff Sute	$	$	

Street address (including apt. no.)	7 Distribution code(s)	IRA/ SEP/ SIMPLE	8 Other	
42 Rising Ave.	1	☐	$	%

City, state, and ZIP code	9a Your percentage of total distribution %	9b Total employee contributions
Sand City, CA		$

	1st year of desig. Roth contrib.	10 State tax withheld	11 State/Payer's state no.	12 State distribution
		$		$
		$		$

Account number (see instructions)	13 Local tax withheld	14 Name of locality	15 Local distribution
	$		$
	$		$

Form **1099-R**   Cat. No. 14436Q   Department of the Treasury - Internal Revenue Service

Do Not Cut or Separate Forms on This Page — Do Not Cut or Separate Forms on This Page

Sample: Form 1040, Page 1, to Report Early Distribution

Form 1040
Department of the Treasury—Internal Revenue Service
U.S. Individual Income Tax Return 2008 (99) IRS Use Only—Do not write or staple in this space.

For the year Jan. 1–Dec. 31, 2008, or other tax year beginning , 2008, ending , 20 | OMB No. 1545-0074

Label
(See instructions on page 14.)
Use the IRS label.
Otherwise, please print or type.

LABEL HERE

Your first name and initial: Geoff | Last name: Sute | Your social security number: 555 55 5555

If a joint return, spouse's first name and initial | Last name | Spouse's social security number

Home address (number and street). If you have a P.O. box, see page 14. | Apt. no. | ▲ You **must** enter your SSN(s) above. ▲
42 Rising Avenue

City, town or post office, state, and ZIP code. If you have a foreign address, see page 14.
Sand City, CA

Checking a box below will not change your tax or refund.

Presidential Election Campaign ▶ Check here if you, or your spouse if filing jointly, want $3 to go to this fund (see page 14) ▶ ☐ You ☐ Spouse

Filing Status
Check only one box.

1 ☐ Single
2 ☐ Married filing jointly (even if only one had income)
3 ☐ Married filing separately. Enter spouse's SSN above and full name here. ▶
4 ☐ Head of household (with qualifying person). (See page 15.) If the qualifying person is a child but not your dependent, enter this child's name here. ▶
5 ☐ Qualifying widow(er) with dependent child (see page 16)

Exemptions

6a ☐ **Yourself.** If someone can claim you as a dependent, **do not** check box 6a
b ☐ **Spouse**
c **Dependents:**

(1) First name	Last name	(2) Dependent's social security number	(3) Dependent's relationship to you	(4) ✔ if qualifying child for child tax credit (see page 17)
				☐
				☐
				☐
				☐

Boxes checked on 6a and 6b ___
No. of children on 6c who:
• lived with you ___
• did not live with you due to divorce or separation (see page 18) ___
Dependents on 6c not entered above ___

If more than four dependents, see page 17.

d Total number of exemptions claimed

Add numbers on lines above ▶ ☐

Income

Attach Form(s) W-2 here. Also attach Forms W-2G and 1099-R if tax was withheld.

If you did not get a W-2, see page 21.

Enclose, but do not attach, any payment. Also, please use Form 1040-V.

7 Wages, salaries, tips, etc. Attach Form(s) W-2 | 7
8a Taxable interest. Attach Schedule B if required | 8a
b Tax-exempt interest. **Do not** include on line 8a | 8b
9a Ordinary dividends. Attach Schedule B if required | 9a
b Qualified dividends (see page 21) | 9b
10 Taxable refunds, credits, or offsets of state and local income taxes (see page 22) | 10
11 Alimony received | 11
12 Business income or (loss). Attach Schedule C or C-EZ | 12
13 Capital gain or (loss). Attach Schedule D if required. If not required, check here ▶ ☐ | 13
14 Other gains or (losses). Attach Form 4797 | 14
15a IRA distributions | 15a | b Taxable amount (see page 23) | 15b
16a Pensions and annuities | 16a 1,500 00 | b Taxable amount (see page 24) | 16b 1,500
17 Rental real estate, royalties, partnerships, S corporations, trusts, etc. Attach Schedule E | 17
18 Farm income or (loss). Attach Schedule F | 18
19 Unemployment compensation | 19
20a Social security benefits | 20a | b Taxable amount (see page 26) | 20b
21 Other income. List type and amount (see page 28) | 21
22 Add the amounts in the far right column for lines 7 through 21. This is your **total income** ▶ | 22

Adjusted Gross Income

23 Educator expenses (see page 28) | 23
24 Certain business expenses of reservists, performing artists, and fee-basis government officials. Attach Form 2106 or 2106-EZ | 24
25 Health savings account deduction. Attach Form 8889 | 25
26 Moving expenses. Attach Form 3903 | 26
27 One-half of self-employment tax. Attach Schedule SE | 27
28 Self-employed SEP, SIMPLE, and qualified plans | 28
29 Self-employed health insurance deduction (see page 29) | 29
30 Penalty on early withdrawal of savings | 30
31a Alimony paid b Recipient's SSN ▶ | 31a
32 IRA deduction (see page 30) | 32
33 Student loan interest deduction (see page 33) | 33
34 Tuition and fees deduction. Attach Form 8917 | 34
35 Domestic production activities deduction. Attach Form 8903 | 35
36 Add lines 23 through 31a and 32 through 35 | 36
37 Subtract line 36 from line 22. This is your **adjusted gross income** ▶ | 37

For Disclosure, Privacy Act, and Paperwork Reduction Act Notice, see page 88. | Cat. No. 11320B | Form **1040** (2008)

Sample: Form 1040, Page 2, to Report Early Distribution

Form 1040 (2008)   Page **2**

Tax and Credits	38	Amount from line 37 (adjusted gross income)	38	
	39a	Check { You were born before January 2, 1944, ☐ Blind. } Total boxes if: { ☐ Spouse was born before January 2, 1944, ☐ Blind. } checked ▶ 39a		
	b	If your spouse itemizes on a separate return or you were a dual-status alien, see page 34 and check here ▶ 39b ☐		
Standard Deduction for—	c	Check if standard deduction includes real estate taxes or disaster loss (see page 34) ▶ 39c ☐		
	40	**Itemized deductions** (from Schedule A) **or** your **standard deduction** (see left margin) .	40	
	41	Subtract line 40 from line 38	41	
• People who checked any box on line 39a, 39b, or 39c **or** who can be claimed as a dependent, see page 34.	42	If line 38 is over $119,975, or you provided housing to a Midwestern displaced individual, see page 36. Otherwise, multiply $3,500 by the total number of exemptions claimed on line 6d .	42	
	43	**Taxable income.** Subtract line 42 from line 41. If line 42 is more than line 41, enter -0-	43	
	44	**Tax** (see page 36). Check if any tax is from: **a** ☐ Form(s) 8814 **b** ☐ Form 4972 .	44	
• All others:	45	**Alternative minimum tax** (see page 39). Attach Form 6251	45	
Single or Married filing separately, $5,450	46	Add lines 44 and 45 . . . . ▶	46	
	47	Foreign tax credit. Attach Form 1116 if required	47		
	48	Credit for child and dependent care expenses. Attach Form 2441	48		
Married filing jointly or Qualifying widow(er), $10,900	49	Credit for the elderly or the disabled. Attach Schedule R . .	49		
	50	Education credits. Attach Form 8863	50		
	51	Retirement savings contributions credit. Attach Form 8880 .	51		
Head of household, $8,000	52	Child tax credit (see page 42). Attach Form 8901 if required .	52		
	53	Credits from Form: **a** ☐ 8396 **b** ☐ 8839 **c** ☐ 5695	53		
	54	Other credits from Form: **a** ☐ 3800 **b** ☐ 8801 **c** ☐	54		
	55	Add lines 47 through 54. These are your **total credits**	55	
	56	Subtract line 55 from line 46. If line 55 is more than line 46, enter -0- . . . . . . ▶	56	
Other Taxes	57	Self-employment tax. Attach Schedule SE	57	
	58	Unreported social security and Medicare tax from Form: **a** ☐ 4137 **b** ☐ 8919	58	*150*
	59	Additional tax on IRAs, other qualified retirement plans, etc. Attach Form 5329 if required .	59	
	60	Additional taxes: **a** ☐ AEIC payments **b** ☐ Household employment taxes. Attach Schedule H	60	
	61	Add lines 56 through 60. This is your **total tax** . . . . ▶	61	
Payments	62	Federal income tax withheld from Forms W-2 and 1099 .	62		
	63	2008 estimated tax payments and amount applied from 2007 return	63		
If you have a qualifying child, attach Schedule EIC.	64a	**Earned income credit (EIC)**	64a		
	b	Nontaxable combat pay election	64b			
	65	Excess social security and tier 1 RRTA tax withheld (see page 61)	65		
	66	Additional child tax credit. Attach Form 8812	66		
	67	Amount paid with request for extension to file (see page 61)	67		
	68	Credits from Form: **a** ☐ 2439 **b** ☐ 4136 **c** ☐ 8801 **d** ☐ 8885	68		
	69	First-time homebuyer credit. Attach Form 5405	69		
	70	Recovery rebate credit (see worksheet on pages 62 and 63) .	70		
	71	Add lines 62 through 70. These are your **total payments** . . . . ▶	71	
Refund Direct deposit? See page 63 and fill in 73b, 73c, and 73d, or Form 8888.	72	If line 71 is more than line 61, subtract line 61 from line 71. This is the amount you **overpaid**	72	
	73a	Amount of line 72 you want **refunded to you.** If Form 8888 is attached, check here ▶ ☐	73a	
	b	Routing number ▶ c Type: ☐ Checking ☐ Savings		
	d	Account number		
	74	Amount of line 72 you want **applied to your 2009 estimated tax** ▶ 74		
Amount You Owe	75	**Amount you owe.** Subtract line 71 from line 61. For details on how to pay, see page 65 ▶	75	
	76	Estimated tax penalty (see page 65) 76		
Third Party Designee		Do you want to allow another person to discuss this return with the IRS (see page 66)? ☐ **Yes.** Complete the following. ☐ **No**		
		Designee's name ▶	Phone no. ▶ ( )	Personal identification number (PIN) ▶	
Sign Here Joint return? See page 15. Keep a copy for your records.		Under penalties of perjury, I declare that I have examined this return and accompanying schedules and statements, and to the best of my knowledge and belief, they are true, correct, and complete. Declaration of preparer (other than taxpayer) is based on all information of which preparer has any knowledge.		
		Your signature	Date	Your occupation	Daytime phone number ( )
		Spouse's signature. If a joint return, **both** must sign.	Date	Spouse's occupation	
Paid Preparer's Use Only		Preparer's signature ▶	Date	Check if self-employed ☐	Preparer's SSN or PTIN
		Firm's name (or yours if self-employed), address, and ZIP code ▶		EIN :	
				Phone no. ( )	

Form **1040** (2008)

Sample 1: Form 5329 to Report Early Distribution, No Code on 1099-R

Form **5329**	**Additional Taxes on Qualified Plans (Including IRAs) and Other Tax-Favored Accounts**	OMB No. 1545-0074
Department of the Treasury Internal Revenue Service (99)	► Attach to Form 1040 or Form 1040NR. ► See separate instructions.	2008 Attachment Sequence No. **29**

Name of individual subject to additional tax. If married filing jointly, see instructions.	Your social security number
Geoff Sute	555	55	5555

Fill in Your Address Only If You Are Filing This Form by Itself and Not With Your Tax Return ►	Home address (number and street), or P.O. box if mail is not delivered to your home	Apt. no.
	City, town or post office, state, and ZIP code	If this is an amended return, check here ► ☐

If you **only** owe the additional 10% tax on early distributions, you may be able to report this tax directly on Form 1040, line 59, or Form 1040NR, line 54, without filing Form 5329. See the instructions for Form 1040, line 59, or for Form 1040NR, line 54.

Part I — Additional Tax on Early Distributions

Complete this part if you took a taxable distribution (other than a qualified disaster recovery assistance or qualified recovery assistance distribution), before you reached age 59½, from a qualified retirement plan (including an IRA) or modified endowment contract (unless you are reporting this tax directly on Form 1040 or Form 1040NR—see above). You may also have to complete this part to indicate that you qualify for an exception to the additional tax on early distributions or for certain Roth IRA distributions (see instructions).

1	Early distributions included in income. For Roth IRA distributions, see instructions	**1**	*1,500*
2	Early distributions included on line 1 that are not subject to the additional tax (see instructions). Enter the appropriate exception number from the instructions: _____	**2**	*0*
3	Amount subject to additional tax. Subtract line 2 from line 1	**3**	*1,500*
4	Additional tax. Enter 10% (.10) of line 3. Include this amount on Form 1040, line 59, or Form 1040NR, line 54	**4**	*150*

Caution: *If any part of the amount on line 3 was a distribution from a SIMPLE IRA, you may have to include 25% of that amount on line 4 instead of 10% (see instructions).*

Part II — Additional Tax on Certain Distributions From Education Accounts

Complete this part if you included an amount in income, on Form 1040 or Form 1040NR, line 21, from a Coverdell education savings account (ESA) or a qualified tuition program (QTP).

5	Distributions included in income from Coverdell ESAs and QTPs	**5**	
6	Distributions included on line 5 that are not subject to the additional tax (see instructions) . .	**6**	
7	Amount subject to additional tax. Subtract line 6 from line 5	**7**	
8	Additional tax. Enter 10% (.10) of line 7. Include this amount on Form 1040, line 59, or Form 1040NR, line 54	**8**	

Part III — Additional Tax on Excess Contributions to Traditional IRAs

Complete this part if you contributed more to your traditional IRAs for 2008 than is allowable or you had an amount on line 17 of your 2007 Form 5329.

9	Enter your excess contributions from line 16 of your 2007 Form 5329 (see instructions). If zero, go to line 15	**9**	
10	If your traditional IRA contributions for 2008 are less than your maximum allowable contribution, see instructions. Otherwise, enter -0-	**10**	
11	2008 traditional IRA distributions included in income (see instructions)	**11**	
12	2008 distributions of prior year excess contributions (see instructions)	**12**	
13	Add lines 10, 11, and 12	**13**	
14	Prior year excess contributions. Subtract line 13 from line 9. If zero or less, enter -0- . . .	**14**	
15	Excess contributions for 2008 (see instructions)	**15**	
16	Total excess contributions. Add lines 14 and 15	**16**	
17	Additional tax. Enter 6% (.06) of the **smaller** of line 16 **or** the value of your traditional IRAs on December 31, 2008 (including 2008 contributions made in 2009). Include this amount on Form 1040, line 59, or Form 1040NR, line 54	**17**	

Part IV — Additional Tax on Excess Contributions to Roth IRAs

Complete this part if you contributed more to your Roth IRAs for 2008 than is allowable or you had an amount on line 25 of your 2007 Form 5329.

18	Enter your excess contributions from line 24 of your 2007 Form 5329 (see instructions). If zero, go to line 23	**18**	
19	If your Roth IRA contributions for 2008 are less than your maximum allowable contribution, see instructions. Otherwise, enter -0-	**19**	
20	2008 distributions from your Roth IRAs (see instructions)	**20**	
21	Add lines 19 and 20	**21**	
22	Prior year excess contributions. Subtract line 21 from line 18. If zero or less, enter -0- . . .	**22**	
23	Excess contributions for 2008 (see instructions)	**23**	
24	Total excess contributions. Add lines 22 and 23	**24**	
25	Additional tax. Enter 6% (.06) of the **smaller** of line 24 **or** the value of your Roth IRAs on December 31, 2008 (including 2008 contributions made in 2009). Include this amount on Form 1040, line 59, or Form 1040NR, line 54	**25**	

For Privacy Act and Paperwork Reduction Act Notice, see page 6 of the instructions.   Cat. No. 13329Q   Form **5329** (2008)

Sample 2: Form 5329 to Report Exception to Early Distribution Tax

Form **5329**	**Additional Taxes on Qualified Plans (Including IRAs) and Other Tax-Favored Accounts** ▶ Attach to Form 1040 or Form 1040NR. ▶ See separate instructions.	OMB No. 1545-0074 **20**08
Department of the Treasury Internal Revenue Service (99)		Attachment Sequence No. **29**

Name of individual subject to additional tax. If married filing jointly, see instructions.		Your social security number
Irwin Hirsh		444 : 44 : 4444

Fill in Your Address Only If You Are Filing This Form by Itself and Not With Your Tax Return ▶	Home address (number and street), or P.O. box if mail is not delivered to your home	Apt. no.
	City, town or post office, state, and ZIP code	If this is an amended return, check here ▶ ☐

If you **only** owe the additional 10% tax on early distributions, you may be able to report this tax directly on Form 1040, line 59, or Form 1040NR, line 54, without filing Form 5329. See the instructions for Form 1040, line 59, or for Form 1040NR, line 54.

Part I   **Additional Tax on Early Distributions**

Complete this part if you took a taxable distribution (other than a qualified disaster recovery assistance or qualified recovery assistance distribution), before you reached age 59½, from a qualified retirement plan (including an IRA) or modified endowment contract (unless you are reporting this tax directly on Form 1040 or Form 1040NR—see above). You may also have to complete this part to indicate that you qualify for an exception to the additional tax on early distributions or for certain Roth IRA distributions (see instructions).

1	Early distributions included in income. For Roth IRA distributions, see instructions	**1**	25,000
2	Early distributions included on line 1 that are not subject to the additional tax (see instructions). Enter the appropriate exception number from the instructions: _01_	**2**	25,000
3	Amount subject to additional tax. Subtract line 2 from line 1	**3**	0
4	**Additional tax.** Enter 10% (.10) of line 3. Include this amount on Form 1040, line 59, or Form 1040NR, line 54	**4**	0
	Caution: If any part of the amount on line 3 was a distribution from a SIMPLE IRA, you may have to include 25% of that amount on line 4 instead of 10% (see instructions).		

Part II   **Additional Tax on Certain Distributions From Education Accounts**

Complete this part if you included an amount in income, on Form 1040 or Form 1040NR, line 21, from a Coverdell education savings account (ESA) or a qualified tuition program (QTP).

5	Distributions included in income from Coverdell ESAs and QTPs	**5**	
6	Distributions included on line 5 that are not subject to the additional tax (see instructions) . .	**6**	
7	Amount subject to additional tax. Subtract line 6 from line 5	**7**	
8	**Additional tax.** Enter 10% (.10) of line 7. Include this amount on Form 1040, line 59, or Form 1040NR, line 54	**8**	

Part III   **Additional Tax on Excess Contributions to Traditional IRAs**

Complete this part if you contributed more to your traditional IRAs for 2008 than is allowable or you had an amount on line 17 of your 2007 Form 5329.

9	Enter your excess contributions from line 16 of your 2007 Form 5329 (see instructions). If zero, go to line 15		**9**	
10	If your traditional IRA contributions for 2008 are less than your maximum allowable contribution, see instructions. Otherwise, enter -0-	**10**		
11	2008 traditional IRA distributions included in income (see instructions)	**11**		
12	2008 distributions of prior year excess contributions (see instructions)	**12**		
13	Add lines 10, 11, and 12		**13**	
14	Prior year excess contributions. Subtract line 13 from line 9. If zero or less, enter -0-		**14**	
15	Excess contributions for 2008 (see instructions)		**15**	
16	Total excess contributions. Add lines 14 and 15		**16**	
17	**Additional tax.** Enter 6% (.06) of the **smaller** of line 16 **or** the value of your traditional IRAs on December 31, 2008 (including 2008 contributions made in 2009). Include this amount on Form 1040, line 59, or Form 1040NR, line 54		**17**	

Part IV   **Additional Tax on Excess Contributions to Roth IRAs**

Complete this part if you contributed more to your Roth IRAs for 2008 than is allowable or you had an amount on line 25 of your 2007 Form 5329.

18	Enter your excess contributions from line 24 of your 2007 Form 5329 (see instructions). If zero, go to line 23		**18**	
19	If your Roth IRA contributions for 2008 are less than your maximum allowable contribution, see instructions. Otherwise, enter -0- . . .	**19**		
20	2008 distributions from your Roth IRAs (see instructions)	**20**		
21	Add lines 19 and 20		**21**	
22	Prior year excess contributions. Subtract line 21 from line 18. If zero or less, enter -0- . . .		**22**	
23	Excess contributions for 2008 (see instructions).		**23**	
24	Total excess contributions. Add lines 22 and 23		**24**	
25	**Additional tax.** Enter 6% (.06) of the **smaller** of line 24 **or** the value of your Roth IRAs on December 31, 2008 (including 2008 contributions made in 2009). Include this amount on Form 1040, line 59, or Form 1040NR, line 54		**25**	

For Privacy Act and Paperwork Reduction Act Notice, see page 6 of the instructions.   Cat. No. 13329Q   Form **5329** (2008)

If the Form 1099-R is not properly coded, you must still compute and pay the additional tax, but you must also complete IRS Form 5329 to show your computation of the tax. Include it with your other forms when you file your tax return. (A sample Form 5329 is in Appendix A.)

EXAMPLE ONE: The facts are the same as in the previous example except that Tech Inc. failed to enter Code 1 in Box 7 of Form 1099-R. As a result, Geoff must complete Part I of Form 5329 and include the form when he files the rest of his tax return. Part I should be completed as shown in Sample 1, above.

EXAMPLE TWO: Irwin retired from Tech Inc. at age 56. The company distributed $25,000 to Irwin, which represented the entire balance in his 401(k) plan. When Irwin received his Form 1099-R from Tech Inc. at tax time, the form showed a Code 1 in Box 7, indicating that Irwin had received an early distribution. Because Irwin left the company after age 55, his distribution is not subject to an early distribution tax. He must complete and attach Form 5329 to his tax return to tell the IRS which exception applies. The instructions for Form 5329 indicate that the age 55 exception is number 01. Irwin must enter 01 on line 2 of Part I. Irwin completes the rest of the form as shown in Sample 2, above.

Special Rules for IRAs

The early distribution tax applies to IRAs in much the same way it applies to qualified plans, with just a few exceptions and variations described in this section. Bear in mind, however, that the Roth IRA is not a typical IRA, so the following rules do not necessarily apply to it. For a complete discussion of the Roth IRA rules, see Chapter 9.

Rules Applicable to All IRAs Except Roth IRAs

Six special rules apply to rollover IRAs, contributory IRAs, SEP IRAs, and SIMPLE IRAs.

Rule One: No Age 55 Exception

As we explained earlier in this chapter, employees who are at least age 55 when they terminate their employment will not have to pay an early distribution tax on distributions from their former employer's qualified plan. This rule does not apply to IRAs, however. If you have an IRA, you must be at least 59½ to use the age exception to the early distribution tax. Of course, you may still qualify for an exception that is unrelated to your age.

Rule Two: No QDRO Exception

The special QDRO rules in the Tax Code do not apply to IRAs. This means the QDRO exception to the early distribution tax is available for qualified plan distributions, but not for IRA distributions. Even if your divorce agreement or court order mandates child support or alimony payments from an IRA, the payments will be subject to an early distribution tax unless one of the other exceptions applies. Sometimes the divorce agreement simply requires the distribution to a spouse of his or her interest in the IRA (for example, a community property interest), but in that case, too, the distribution could be subject to an early distribution tax.

There is one way around this, but it is available only to the former spouse of the IRA participant, and only if the spouse is to receive some or all of the IRA as directed by a divorce or maintenance decree or a written separation agreement. The IRA participant may direct the custodian of the IRA to transfer some or all of the IRA assets directly into an IRA in the former spouse's name. Alternatively, the participant could roll over the spouse's share into a new IRA in the participant's name and then direct the custodian to change title on the new IRA to the spouse's name. The participant might even roll over the spouse's interest into an IRA in the spouse's name (instead of using a direct transfer). The key in each case is for the spouse not to take possession of the funds before they are deposited into an IRA in the spouse's own name.

Once the funds are in an IRA in the spouse's name, however, they belong to the spouse in every way. Thereafter, all IRA rules apply to the assets as though

the spouse had been the original IRA participant. If the spouse takes a distribution, the spouse will have to pay an early distribution tax unless an exception applies.

CAUTION

Get it in writing! The transfer of IRA assets to an account in the name of a spouse or former spouse must be as a result of a written divorce or separation agreement. You may not transfer funds from your IRA into your current spouse's IRA simply because you want to increase the value of his or her account for some reason.

CAUTION

Child support cannot go into an IRA. The above transfer strategy is available only for payments that are made to a separated or former spouse. Child support payments may not be transferred to an IRA in either the child's name or the former spouse's name.

Health Insurance Premiums

An early distribution tax exception unique to IRAs concerns health insurance premiums. If you are unemployed or were recently unemployed and use money from your IRA to pay health insurance premiums, the IRA funds used specifically for that purpose will not be subject to an early distribution tax, as long as you satisfy the following conditions:

- you received unemployment compensation for at least 12 consecutive weeks
- you received the funds from the IRA during a year in which you received unemployment compensation or during the following year, and
- the IRA distribution is received no more than 60 days after you return to work.

EXAMPLE: You are 45. You lost your job in 2008 and began receiving unemployment compensation on September 22, 2008. You want to maintain your health insurance even during your unemployment. You pay $400 per month on the first day of each month beginning October 1. Because you are short of cash, you withdraw the $400 from your IRA each month to cover the cost of the premiums. You land a job and begin working on March 15, 2009. Unfortunately, your new employer does not provide any health benefits, so you continue to pay premiums of $400 per month, withdrawing the money from your IRA each time. Only the premiums you pay after December 15, 2008 (12 weeks after your unemployment compensation payments began), and before May 15, 2009 (60 days after you began work), are eligible for the exception to the early distribution tax. Thus your distributions of $400 on January 1, February 1, March 1, April 1, and May

1 totaling $2,000 all escape the early distribution tax. Distributions after May 15 are subject to the early distribution tax unless another exception applies.

You may also make a penalty-free withdrawal from your IRA to pay for health insurance if you were self-employed before you stopped working, as long as you would have qualified for unemployment compensation except for the fact that you were self-employed.

Higher Education Expenses

Distributions that you use to pay higher education expenses will not be subject to the early distribution tax, as long as those distributions meet the following requirements:

- The distributions are used to pay for tuition, fees, books, supplies, and equipment. They may also be used for room and board if the student is carrying at least half of a normal study load (or is considered at least a halftime student).
- The expenses are paid on behalf of the IRA owner, spouse, child, or grandchild.
- The distributions do not exceed the amount of the higher education expenses. Furthermore, the total expenses (tuition, fees, and so on) must be reduced by any tax-free scholarships or other tax-free assistance the student receives, not including loans, gifts, or inheritances.

First Home Purchase

In 1997, Congress enacted an exception to the early distribution tax to make it easier for people to buy their first homes. When the dust settled, the benefit was not as dramatic as people had hoped—not because it was difficult to qualify for, but because the lifetime distribution limit was only $10,000. Here are the details:

- The IRA distribution must be used for the acquisition, construction, or reconstruction of a home.
- The funds must be used within 120 days of receipt. If it happens that the home purchase is canceled or delayed, the funds may be rolled over into another IRA (or back into the same one) as long as the rollover is complete within 120 days of the initial distribution.
- The funds must be used to purchase a principal residence for a first-time home buyer. A first-time home buyer is someone who has had no interest in a principal residence during the two years ending on the date of purchase of the new home. If the individual happens to be married, then neither the individual nor the spouse may have owned any part of a principal residence during the preceding two-year period.
- The first-time home buyer must be the IRA owner, or the owner's spouse, or an ancestor (such as a parent, grandparent, or great grandparent), child, or grandchild of either the IRA owner or the owner's spouse.
- The lifetime limit of $10,000 applies regardless of whose home is purchased or improved. If the IRA owner withdraws $10,000 and gives it to his or her child, the lifetime limit for the IRA owner is used up. The IRA owner may not invoke the first home exception for any future distribution even if it is to buy a house for a different relative or for himself. The $10,000 does not have to be distributed all at once or even in a single year. For example, the IRA owner could withdraw $5,000 one year, giving it to a qualified person for a home purchase, and then withdraw another $5,000 in a later year.

Refunds

There is a limit to how much you may contribute to an IRA each year. If you contribute too much, then you have made an excess contribution. If you withdraw the excess by the time you file your tax return (including extensions, if you filed a request and were granted an extension), you will not have to pay an early distribution tax on the excess. You must also withdraw the income earned on the excess while it was in the IRA, however, and that portion will be subject to the early distribution tax, unless it qualifies for another exception.

EXAMPLE: You are self-employed. In January you open an IRA and contribute $3,000 for the current tax year. On December 31, when you compute your net income for the year, you discover that you only made $2,500 in self-employment income. Because your IRA contribution is limited to the lesser of $3,000 or your net income, you have made an excess contribution of $500. Also, you earned 10% on the IRA investment during the year. To correct the excess contribution, you must withdraw not only the $500, but the $50 of earnings on that excess (10% of $500) as well. If you withdraw these amounts by April 15 of the year after the excess contribution (or the due date of your tax return, if you received an extension of time for filing the return), there will be no penalty on the $500 distribution. The $50 of earnings will be subject to ordinary income tax and a 10% early distribution tax of $5.

If you fail to correct an excess contribution to an IRA by the time you file your tax return, but make a corrective distribution later, the entire amount of the distribution is subject to the early distribution tax unless it qualifies for another exception.

One Rule Applicable Only to SIMPLE IRAs

SIMPLE IRAs are described in Chapter 1. All the special IRA rules discussed above apply to SIMPLE IRAs, but there is one additional rule. If you are a participant in a SIMPLE IRA and you receive a distribution within two years of the date you began contributing to it, the early distribution tax increases from 10% to 25%. At the end of two years, it falls back to 10%. Of course, if the distribution qualifies for an exception, the early distribution tax will not apply at all.

Key Tax Code Sections and IRS Pronouncements
§ 72(t) Early Distribution Tax
§ 402(g)(2)(C) Distribution of Excess Deferrals
§ 4972 Nondeductible Contributions to Qualified Plans
§ 4973 Excess Contributions to IRAs
§ 4979 Excess Contributions to Qualified Plans (in Violation of Nondiscrimination Rules)
Revenue Procedure 92-93 Treatment of Corrective Distributions

Substantially Equal Periodic Payments

Computing Periodic Payments 84

    Method One: Required Minimum Distribution...85

    Method Two: Fixed Amortization..87

    Method Three: Fixed Annuitization...90

Implementing and Reporting Your Decision..92

Modifying the Payments 94

    The No-Modification Rule...94

    Exceptions to the No-Modification Rule 95

    Penalties for Breaking the No-Modification Rule 96

Who Should Read Chapter 4

SKIP AHEAD
Read this chapter if you are younger than 59½ and want to learn about using substantially equal periodic payments to escape the early distribution tax.

Chapter 3 introduced you to all of the exceptions to the early distribution tax. Here, we take an in-depth look at the most complicated of those exceptions: Substantially equal periodic payments.

As you may recall, the exception essentially means that you do not have to pay the early distribution tax on money that you take out of your plan in regular payments over either your life expectancy or the joint life expectancy of you and your beneficiary, even if you are younger than 59½.

Here are some basic rules about the exception:

- There are no age restrictions. So, for example, you could be 25 and start taking substantially equal periodic payments.
- The payments must be substantially equal, which means you cannot alter the payment each year to suit your needs, perhaps by taking a few dollars one year and a few thousand the next.

- You must compute the payments as though you intend to distribute the retirement plan over your entire life, or over the joint life of you and your beneficiary.
- Payments from your employer's plan must begin after you leave your job. (This restriction does not apply to IRAs.)
- You may not discontinue payments or alter the computation method for at least five years. And if you have not reached age 59½ at the end of the five-year period, you must wait until you do reach that age before making a change. If you modify payments too soon, the early distribution tax (plus interest) will be applied retroactively to all of the payments you have received. There is one exception to the rule that you may not modify the payments: You are permitted a one-time switch to the required minimum distribution method if you started out using another method. ("Computing Periodic Payments," below, discusses the various methods you can use to compute your payments. "Modifying the Payments," below, describes how to discontinue or alter the size of payments.)

RESOURCE
Learn more. If you'd like to read more about these guidelines, refer to IRS Revenue Ruling 2002-62, which you can find in Appendix A to this book.

Helpful Terms

Amortize. To liquidate or reduce (as in the case of a debt) through periodic payments of principal and interest.

Annuity. A contract, sold by an insurance company, that promises to make monthly, quarterly, semiannual, or annual payments for life or for a specified period of time.

Distribution. A payout of property (such as shares of stock) or cash from a retirement plan or IRA to the participant or a beneficiary.

Joint life expectancy. The number of years expected to pass before the second of two individuals dies.

Recalculated life expectancy. Life expectancy that is revised each year according to statistically accurate measures of mortality.

Payments that are part of a series of substantially equal periodic payments are not eligible to be rolled over. Perhaps in your zeal to withdraw from your retirement plan precisely the amount you need and no more, you devise a plan to begin periodic withdrawals and then roll over into an IRA the portion of each payment you don't use. That strategy is creative, logical, reasonable—and prohibited. The Tax Code specifically denies rollover treatment to periodic payments. You should be able to achieve a similar result by splitting the account first before beginning periodic payments. At least that strategy is not specifically forbidden. (You can learn more about this strategy in "If You Don't Want to Withdraw All of Your Money," below.)

Periodic payments are also exempt from the mandatory income tax withholding rules for qualified plan distributions. (See Chapter 2 for more information about withholding.) Mandatory withholding applies only to those plan distributions that are eligible to be rolled over. Because periodic payments are not eligible to be rolled over, they are not subject to mandatory withholding.

If You Don't Want to Withdraw All of Your Money

Because the methods described below require that the whole plan be distributed eventually, some people find that they end up with larger payments from their plan than they need. That's not a good thing, because taking more money out of your plan than is necessary means paying income tax on money when you don't really have to.

If you have two or more retirement plans, you might be able to solve your problem by taking periodic payments from one plan and leaving the other(s) alone.

But if you have only one plan, you're in a bit of a pickle. Some taxpayers split an existing plan or IRA into two accounts so that one of the accounts is the right size to produce the payment they want. They then leave the other account alone. If you choose this method, however, be warned that no one knows for certain if the IRS will routinely condone it.

Computing Periodic Payments

The basic requirement for periodic payments is that they be spread over your lifetime in roughly equal payments. This is trickier than it first appears. For one thing, you probably don't know how long you are going to live, and you also probably don't know how your investments are going to do over the years. If you did (and more important, if the IRS did) the calculation would be simple.

But because most of us have pretty murky crystal balls, the IRS requires us to use some generally accepted life expectancy assumptions and interest rates. Although the IRS does not hand us the numbers we are to use, the agency has put its stamp of approval on three methods for computing required distributions. These are the required minimum distribution, fixed amortization, and fixed annuitization methods. Each has its own set of guidelines for determining life expectancy and selecting an interest rate or an expected investment return. The section that follows discusses each method in detail.

You are permitted to use any of the methods you want, but before you choose, you should be aware of the principles that are common to all three computation methods:

- Using a joint life expectancy instead of your single life expectancy will reduce the size of your payments.
- Reducing the interest rate assumption will reduce the size of your payments.
- The IRS is more likely to object to large periodic payments than small ones.

If You Stray From the Guidelines

The computation methods outlined in Revenue Ruling 2002-62 and described in this chapter serve as safe harbors. As long as you use one of those methods, you can be certain that the IRS will not challenge you. You are free to stray from these guidelines, but if you do—by using an alternative method, for example, or by altering the variables (such as the interest rate) in one of the IRS methods—you will lose the safe harbor protection, and the IRS can challenge your method. You would then have to successfully defend your method or pay penalties. As a result, the IRS recommends that you request a private letter ruling if you will not be following one of the three methods precisely.

Method One: Required Minimum Distribution

In this relatively simple method, you determine your retirement account balance and divide it by a life expectancy factor each year. The result is your periodic payment for that year. The life expectancy factor can be plucked right out of tables provided by the IRS. (See Tables I, II, and III in Appendix B.) You don't have to worry about choosing an interest rate because your year-end account balance reflects the actual investment returns you earned during the year.

As simple as this method is, you must still decide whether to use your single life expectancy, the Uniform Lifetime Table, or the joint life expectancy of you and your beneficiary. A joint life expectancy and the Uniform Table (which assumes a joint life expectancy) will produce a smaller payment than a single life expectancy will. The size of the payment you need should be the only factor in your decision, given that your choice will affect no other aspect of your retirement plan.

After you make your decision about life expectancies, follow the steps below to arrive at a payment.

Step One: Determine your life expectancy factor.

If you use your single life expectancy, you will look up your age each year in Table I in Appendix B, and use the number from the table.

If you use the Uniform Lifetime Table, you will look up your age each year in Table III in Appendix B and use the number you find there.

If you have one or more beneficiaries, you may (but are not required to) use the joint life expectancy table (Table II in Appendix B) to find the appropriate factor. To use a joint life expectancy, the person whose life you use along with your own must be your actual beneficiary. If you have named more than one beneficiary, then you must use the oldest beneficiary's age for determining your joint life expectancy.

If you choose to use either the single life table or the Uniform Lifetime Table, you must use the same table in all subsequent years.

If you choose the joint life table, you must continue to use that table while the beneficiary whose life you are using remains the oldest beneficiary of the account. If during a year a beneficiary dies, is removed as beneficiary, or is no longer the oldest (for example, if you add an older beneficiary), do not change the calculation for the year of change. For the next year, however, you must use the oldest beneficiary's life when determining your joint life factor. If you have no beneficiary in that next year, you must use the single life table.

Step Two: Determine your account balance.
IRS guidelines state that the account balance you use to calculate your payment "must be determined in a reasonable manner." That statement in and of itself is not terribly useful. But fortunately, the statement is followed by an example in which the IRS makes it clear that using the account balance as of December 31 of the year before periodic payments are to begin is reasonable. And, according to the IRS, it is also reasonable to use the account balance for any date "within a reasonable period before the distribution." For example, if you take your first distribution on July 15, the IRS says it would be reasonable to choose an account balance as of any date between December 31 of the previous year and your distribution date.

Step Three: Calculate the payment.
Divide the account balance by the factor you determined in Step One, above. The result is the amount that must be distributed during the first year. For the second year, you follow a similar procedure, using the account balance either as of December 31 of the first payment year or as of a date within a reasonable period of your next distribution.

> **EXAMPLE:** You quit your job last year and rolled over your retirement plan into an IRA. The balance of your IRA at the end of the year you retired was $100,000. This year, you will turn 50. You need to draw on the IRA to help make ends meet, so you plan to begin periodic payments.
>
> **Year One**
>
> **Step One:** From Table I you see that your single life expectancy (for age 50) is 34.2 years.
>
> **Step Two:** Your December 31 balance for the year before payments are to begin was $100,000.
>
> **Step Three:** Your first annual periodic payment is $2,924, or $100,000 divided by 34.2.
>
> **Year Two**
>
> Assume that the balance of your IRA at the end of the first year of periodic payments was $110,000. (You earned more in interest than you withdrew

the first year.) Follow these steps to compute the second year payment.

Step One: Refer again to Table I. You will turn 51 this year. Thus, your life expectancy is 33.3.

Step Two: Your account balance as of December 31 of the first year of periodic payments was $110,000.

Step Three: Your second periodic payment is $3,303, or $110,000 divided by 33.3.

CAUTION

Be exact. Although this method is referred to as the required minimum distribution method, the payment does not represent the minimum you must take, but the exact amount. Once you compute your periodic payment for the year, you must distribute precisely that amount—no more, no less.

Advantages of the Required Minimum Distribution Method

The IRS has declared that payments computed under the required minimum distribution rules will be considered substantially equal periodic payments. Nonetheless, the payments could vary significantly from one year to the next, depending on how well or poorly your portfolio performs. Thus, the advantage of this method is that it reflects your actual investment returns. And if your intention is to spread payments over your lifetime, this method can accomplish your goal. Not to be overlooked is the fact that this calculation method is simple and straightforward. And if you choose it, the IRS is unlikely to challenge your payment size or your methodology.

Disadvantages of the Required Minimum Distribution Method

Although this method might accurately reflect your investment returns, it is the least flexible. Except by choosing to use a joint life expectancy or the Uniform Lifetime Table, there is no way to tweak payments to produce the distribution you want. And because of market fluctuations, you might find your payments too large one year and not quite large enough the next. Even without market fluctuations, this method will tend to skew payments so that they are small in the early years and larger in later years. That's fine if you expect to need more income later, but if you need more now, there's no way to skew payments in the other direction.

Method Two: Fixed Amortization

This method is favored by many taxpayers because it is flexible enough to produce a range of payments, and the computation is straightforward. Once you compute your annual payment, the payment remains fixed for all subsequent years. To compute your payment under this method, you must first decide which table you will use: the single, joint life, or Uniform Lifetime Table. (Remember, a joint life expectancy produces lower payments.) Then you follow these steps.

Step One: Choose an interest rate.

This is where most of the flexibility comes in, although your choice isn't completely open-ended. IRS safe-harbor guidelines (in Revenue Ruling 2002-62) state that you may use any interest rate that does not exceed 120% of the federal midterm rate for either of the two months before the month distributions begin.

You can find federal midterm rates at www.irs.gov/app/picklist/list/federalRates.html. Because the payments must be made at least annually, you may use the "annual" interest rate found at this site.

Remember, the IRS guidelines provide a safe harbor, but nothing in the law prohibits you from using a higher rate. (Higher rates produce higher payments.) However, as mentioned above, the IRS recommends—but does not require—that you obtain a private letter ruling if you stray from the guidelines.

In past private letter rulings, the IRS has approved rates that range from 5% to 10.6%. However, those private letter rulings were issued before the safe harbor guidelines in Revenue Ruling 2002-62.

Step Two: Determine your life expectancy.

You may choose to use the Single Life Table (Table I) or the Uniform Lifetime Table (Table III). If you have one or more designated beneficiaries of your account, you may use a Joint Life Expectancy (Table II) with the oldest beneficiary.

Step Three: Determine your account balance.

As is the case with the required minimum distribution method, your account balance may be determined on one of two dates: as of December 31 of the year before your first distribution or as of a date "within a reasonable period" before the first distribution. Thus, presumably, if the account balance has dropped (or increased) dramatically between the end of the prior year and the date you take your first distribution, your choice of valuation date could make a significant difference in the size of your periodic payment.

Step Four: Calculate the payment.

Amortize your account balance using the life expectancy and interest rate you have chosen. Use the same method you would use to amortize a home mortgage or other loan. You can make the computation with a financial calculator, on a computer spreadsheet, or with an amortization program that might be included with other financial software you have. Fortunately, several financial sites on the Internet have free calculators you can use for this purpose:

- First Source Bank at www.1stsrce .com/calculators.cfm, and
- Financial Visions at www.fincalc.com.

Enter your account balance when asked for the loan amount and your life expectancy when asked for the number of years or months you will take to repay the loan. Then enter the interest rate you have chosen. The calculator then computes the payment amount.

EXAMPLE: You have decided to start taking substantially equal periodic payments annually from your IRA beginning in the year you turn 52. Your IRA account balance as of December 31 of the preceding year was $82,000.

Step One: You decide to use 120% of the federal midterm rate for December of the year before you begin distributions. That rate is 7%.

Step Two: You will take distributions over your own single life expectancy, which is 32.3 (from Table I) for age 52.

Step Three: Your account balance on December 31 of the year before payments are to begin was $82,000.

Step Four: Using a financial calculator, you compute your annual payment to be $6,467

($82,000 amortized over 32.3 years at 7%). Your payment for the second and future years will also be $6,467. If you are using Hewlett Packard's financial calculator (the HP-12C) you will reach a slightly different result: $6,620 instead of $6,467. This is because the HP-12C rounds up to the next integer when you use a fractional period (number of years) in the equation.

Advantages of the Fixed Amortization Method

One significant attraction of this method is its simplicity. Once you determine your payment, you never have to compute it again. No looking up numbers in tables every year or trying to remember computation formulas. You do it once and it's done.

Along with the simplicity comes some flexibility. You can choose from a range of interest rates, and you may use one of three life expectancy tables. That flexibility should get you close to the payment you want unless you need an exceptionally large amount. And if you really want to use a higher interest rate than the guidelines suggest, you can always request a private letter ruling.

Disadvantages of the Fixed Amortization Method

The amortization example in the IRS guidelines, as well as in most of the favorable private letter rulings, computes a fixed payment—one that doesn't vary at all from year to year. Fixed payments, by definition, do not take into account recalculation of life expectancies, actual investment returns on your account, or inflation. The payments are constant. Consequently, if inflation surges, you might find yourself stuck with a payment that is too low for your needs and that doesn't reflect either the real returns on your investments or the changing economic climate.

However, recent private letter rulings give hope to taxpayers who want to modify their payments to keep up with inflation. In one case, for example, the taxpayer amortized his account balance anew each year, using 120% of the current federal midterm rate and his updated life expectancy. The IRS took the position that although the payment changed, the method of computing the payment was exactly the same each year. If you choose to do something like this, keep in mind that it doesn't follow the method precisely and therefore does not enjoy safe harbor protection.

Method Three: Fixed Annuitization

Although the underlying arithmetic in the annuitization method is essentially the same as in the amortization method, the computation is performed simply by dividing your account balance by an annuity factor. The annuity factor is derived from a formula used mostly by actuaries.

As with the amortization method, once you determine your annual payment, it should remain the same every year, if you want to stay within the safe harbor.

The factor is based on certain interest rate and mortality assumptions. Those of us who are inexperienced with these calculations rely on actuaries and other number crunchers to produce tables we can use to look up the appropriate factor.

IRS regulations state that you may use any reasonable mortality table to come up with your annuity factor. The IRS has provided a safe harbor mortality table in Revenue Ruling 2002-62. As you might expect, this mortality table produces a smaller payment than many of the mortality tables used by insurance companies or even in other sections of the Tax Code.

Step One: Choose an interest rate.

Your criterion for choosing an interest rate should be no different for this method than for the amortization method. Higher rates will produce higher payments; but the safe harbor is an interest rate that does not exceed 120% of the federal midterm rate.

Step Two: Find your annuity factor.

Although the IRS provided a safe-harbor mortality table, it didn't go so far as to actually compute the factors for us. Does that mean you need to hire your own actuary? Fortunately, at least one website, www.72t.net, has popped up to fill in this gap. When you go to the website, click "Calculators" and then "SEPP Calculators," and finally "SEPP Calculator, RR." The calculator that comes up will not only calculate your payment under the annuitization method, but it will also allow you to choose another safe harbor method and compare the payment sizes.

Step Three: Determine your account balance.

You use the same guidelines for determining your account balance under the annuitization method as you would under the amortization method. You may use the balance as of December 31 of the year before the first distribution or you may use the balance as of a date within a reasonable period before the date of your first distribution.

Step Four: Compute the payment.

Divide the account balance by the annuity factor to arrive at your payment.

> **EXAMPLE:** You will turn 52 this year. You decide to begin substantially equal periodic payments from your IRA, and you plan to use your own single life expectancy. Your IRA account balance as of December 31 of the preceding year was $82,000.
>
> **Step One:** You choose an interest rate of 7%, which is 120% of the federal midterm rate.
>
> **Step Two:** You use the annuity factor calculator you downloaded to come up with an annuity factor of 13.031.
>
> **Step Three:** Your account balance on December 31 of last year was $82,000.
>
> **Step Four:** Your periodic payment for this year, your first payment year, is $6,239 (Step Three divided by Step Two, or $82,000 divided by 13.031.)

CAUTION

Only fixed payments are officially approved by the IRS. Bear in mind that although some private letter rulings sanction variable payments under the annuity factor method, only fixed payments have been approved officially by the IRS.

Advantages of the Fixed Annuitization Method

The only substantive difference between this method and the amortization method is that this method allows you to use mortality figures other than those provided by the IRS. Thus, theoretically, you have the flexibility to choose a table that accurately reflects your situation or produces a payment that better suits your needs.

If you choose a mortality table other than the IRS's, however, you fall outside the safe harbor.

Disadvantages of the Fixed Annuitization Method

The disadvantages of this are the same as those under the amortization method: Because your payment is fixed (if you use the safe harbor), it will not reflect a changing economy or the actual performance of your investments.

Implementing and Reporting Your Decision

Once you have selected your computation method, prepare a worksheet illustrating the computation. (See sample, below.) Keep it with your other important tax papers in case the IRS should ever ask you to explain the methodology you chose. Next, arrange with your plan administrator or IRA custodian to begin periodic payments. After that, your only remaining task is to report the payments on your tax return.

Sample Worksheet for Your Tax Files

Computation of Substantially Equal Periodic Payments Using Amortization Method
Annual distributions to be made each January 1, beginning in the year 2009.
December 31, 2008, value of IRA Account # 01234: $100,000.
My single life expectancy at age 52 in the year 2009 (from IRS Publication 590, Appendix C, Table 1): 32.3 years.
120% of the federal midterm rate for December 2008: 4.28%.
Annual payment ($100,000 amortized over 32.3 years at 4.28%): $5,770.

After the end of the year, you will receive a Form 1099-R from either the trustee of your plan or the custodian of your IRA. This form will report the total amount of distributions you received during the year. If the form shows a Code 2 in Box 7, you do not need to file any special forms with your tax return. (Code 2 means that the distribution qualifies for an exception to the early distribution tax.) You will simply report your periodic payments as ordinary income on your tax return. (See Chapter 3 for more information about Form 1099-R codes and the reporting

Sample: Form 5329 to Report Incorrectly Coded 1099-R

Form **5329**	**Additional Taxes on Qualified Plans (Including IRAs) and Other Tax-Favored Accounts** ► Attach to Form 1040 or Form 1040NR. ► See separate instructions.	OMB No. 1545-0074 **2008**
Department of the Treasury Internal Revenue Service (99)		Attachment Sequence No. **29**

Name of individual subject to additional tax. If married filing jointly, see instructions. | Your social security number

Fill in Your Address Only If You Are Filing This Form by Itself and Not With Your Tax Return	Home address (number and street), or P.O. box if mail is not delivered to your home	Apt. no.
	City, town or post office, state, and ZIP code	If this is an amended return, check here ► ☐

If you **only** owe the additional 10% tax on early distributions, you may be able to report this tax directly on Form 1040, line 59, or Form 1040NR, line 54, without filing Form 5329. See the instructions for Form 1040, line 59, or for Form 1040NR, line 54.

Part I   **Additional Tax on Early Distributions**

Complete this part if you took a taxable distribution (other than a qualified disaster recovery assistance or qualified recovery assistance distribution), before you reached age 59½ , from a qualified retirement plan (including an IRA) or modified endowment contract (unless you are reporting this tax directly on Form 1040 or Form 1040NR—see above). You may also have to complete this part to indicate that you qualify for an exception to the additional tax on early distributions or for certain Roth IRA distributions (see instructions).

1	Early distributions included in income. For Roth IRA distributions, see instructions	1	*24,000*
2	Early distributions included on line 1 that are not subject to the additional tax (see instructions). Enter the appropriate exception number from the instructions: *02*	2	*24,000*
3	Amount subject to additional tax. Subtract line 2 from line 1	3	*0*
4	**Additional tax.** Enter 10% (.10) of line 3. Include this amount on Form 1040, line 59, or Form 1040NR, line 54	4	*0*

Caution: If any part of the amount on line 3 was a distribution from a SIMPLE IRA, you may have to include 25% of that amount on line 4 instead of 10% (see instructions).

Part II   **Additional Tax on Certain Distributions From Education Accounts**

Complete this part if you included an amount in income, on Form 1040 or Form 1040NR, line 21, from a Coverdell education savings account (ESA) or a qualified tuition program (QTP).

5	Distributions included in income from Coverdell ESAs and QTPs	5	
6	Distributions included on line 5 that are not subject to the additional tax (see instructions) . .	6	
7	Amount subject to additional tax. Subtract line 6 from line 5	7	
8	**Additional tax.** Enter 10% (.10) of line 7. Include this amount on Form 1040, line 59, or Form 1040NR, line 54	8	

Part III   **Additional Tax on Excess Contributions to Traditional IRAs**

Complete this part if you contributed more to your traditional IRAs for 2008 than is allowable or you had an amount on line 17 of your 2007 Form 5329.

9	Enter your excess contributions from line 16 of your 2007 Form 5329 (see instructions). If zero, go to line 15	9	
10	If your traditional IRA contributions for 2008 are less than your maximum allowable contribution, see instructions. Otherwise, enter -0-	10	
11	2008 traditional IRA distributions included in income (see instructions)	11	
12	2008 distributions of prior year excess contributions (see instructions)	12	
13	Add lines 10, 11, and 12	13	
14	Prior year excess contributions. Subtract line 13 from line 9. If zero or less, enter -0- . . .	14	
15	Excess contributions for 2008 (see instructions)	15	
16	Total excess contributions. Add lines 14 and 15	16	
17	**Additional tax.** Enter 6% (.06) of the **smaller** of line 16 **or** the value of your traditional IRAs on December 31, 2008 (including 2008 contributions made in 2009). Include this amount on Form 1040, line 59, or Form 1040NR, line 54	17	

Part IV   **Additional Tax on Excess Contributions to Roth IRAs**

Complete this part if you contributed more to your Roth IRAs for 2008 than is allowable or you had an amount on line 25 of your 2007 Form 5329.

18	Enter your excess contributions from line 24 of your 2007 Form 5329 (see instructions). If zero, go to line 23	18	
19	If your Roth IRA contributions for 2008 are less than your maximum allowable contribution, see instructions. Otherwise, enter -0- . . .	19	
20	2008 distributions from your Roth IRAs (see instructions) . . .	20	
21	Add lines 19 and 20	21	
22	Prior year excess contributions. Subtract line 21 from line 18. If zero or less, enter -0- . . .	22	
23	Excess contributions for 2008 (see instructions).	23	
24	Total excess contributions. Add lines 22 and 23	24	
25	**Additional tax.** Enter 6% (.06) of the **smaller** of line 24 **or** the value of your Roth IRAs on December 31, 2008 (including 2008 contributions made in 2009). Include this amount on Form 1040, line 59, or Form 1040NR, line 54	25	

For Privacy Act and Paperwork Reduction Act Notice, see page 6 of the instructions.   Cat. No. 13329Q   Form **5329** (2008)

requirements for IRA and qualified plan distributions.)

If Box 7 of Form 1099-R does not show Code 2, you must complete Part I of Form 5329 and file it with the rest of your tax return. Part I of Form 5329 asks you to report the total amount of your early distributions (on line 1) and the distributions that are eligible for an exception to the early distribution tax (line 2). Line 2 also provides a space for you to write in the exception number. The exception number for substantially equal periodic payments is 02. You can find exception codes in the instructions for Form 5329, which is in Appendix A.

> **EXAMPLE:** At age 52, you began receiving substantially equal periodic payments of $2,000 per month from your IRA. After the end of the year, you receive your 1099-R from your IRA custodian, reporting distributions of $24,000 from your IRA. Box 7 incorrectly shows a Code 1. Consequently, you must complete Part I of Form 5329 and file it with the rest of your tax return. Lines 1–4 of Form 5329 should look like the sample form on the previous page.

Modifying the Payments

In general, the substantially equal periodic payment exception will save you from the early distribution tax only if you do not discontinue your payments or alter your

computation method (other than in the approved ways, such as recalculation based on annual changes in life expectancy or account balance under the required minimum distribution method) once payments have begun. If you change your computation method, the early distribution tax can be applied retroactively to all distributions.

Fortunately, Congress didn't intend that your payments remain fixed until your death—just for a well-defined period of time. And, of course, there are exceptions to the no-modification rule that allow you to change the payments under certain circumstances, even if you don't satisfy the time-period requirement.

The No-Modification Rule

Once you establish a schedule and begin receiving substantially equal periodic payments, you may not modify them or discontinue them for five years or until you attain age 59½, whichever period is longer. For example, if you are age 49 when you begin receiving payments, you will be only 54 after five years. Therefore, you must continue the payments until you reach 59½. On the other hand, if you begin payments when you are 58, you must continue them for five full years, even though you will have passed the age 59½ milestone in the meantime.

The time-period requirement is quite literal. If you begin monthly payments at 49 and wish to stop at age 59½, you must take your last payment on or after the day you reach age 59½. You may not simply stop payments on January 1 of the year you turn 59½. Similarly, if you begin monthly payments on your 58th birthday, you must continue them at least until your 63rd birthday, when five full years will have passed.

As mentioned above, you may not prematurely discontinue or alter the size of the payments. Furthermore, if you transfer any additional amounts into the account or transfer any amounts to another retirement account, the IRS will consider those actions a modification of your payment. And of course, you may not withdraw additional amounts in excess of the periodic payment because the IRS sees that as a simple (and disallowed) increase in the amount of the annual payment.

Exceptions to the No-Modification Rule

There are four exceptions to the rule that payments cannot be modified.

Death

If you die before the required period has passed, your beneficiary may discontinue the payments.

Disability

If you become disabled, you are no longer tied to your periodic payment schedule, and subsequent distributions will not be subject to the early distribution tax. For this exception to apply, you must satisfy the IRS's definition of disabled. (See Chapter 3 for more information on the disability exception.)

Complete Depletion of Assets

If your account balance goes to zero while you are taking substantially equal periodic payments, the IRS will not penalize you for failing to continue the payments. Even the IRS recognizes that your investment losses should be penalty enough.

One-Time Change to Required Minimum Distribution Method

In the early years of the new millennium, taxpayers watched their retirement funds shrink in lockstep with the tumbling stock market. The IRS sought to offer some relief to those who had started periodic payments at the market peak and now faced a rapidly depleting retirement nest egg because of high periodic payments.

Had taxpayers chosen to use the required minimum distribution method at the outset, their payments would have fluctuated with their retirement plan account balance. If you now think you would be better off with that method, the IRS will allow anyone currently using either the amortization or the annuitization method to make a one-time permanent switch to the required minimum distribution method.

If you choose to switch, you may not switch back to either of the other methods. Furthermore, if you are currently using the required minimum distribution method, you may not switch to the amortization or the annuitization methods. Once you choose the required minimum distribution method, you are stuck with it.

Bear in mind that if you switch to the required minimum distribution method, you will almost certainly be reducing your payments, so make some calculations first to be sure you can get by on the smaller amounts.

Penalties for Breaking the No-Modification Rule

If you modify your payments in any but the approved ways before the required period has expired, then all distributions you have received since you initiated periodic payments will be subject to the early distribution tax. Because a modification invalidates the substantially equal periodic payment exception, all of the payments are treated (retroactively) as though they were normal discretionary distributions. Therefore, funds that were distributed before you turned 59½ are subject to an early distribution tax, but amounts received after age 59½ are not.

The cumulative payments for all years must be reported on your tax return for the year in which you first modify the payments. You must pay the taxes with that return. You must also pay interest on

any early distribution taxes that would have been due from and after the year of the first periodic payment.

EXAMPLE ONE: You began taking substantially equal periodic payments of $6,000 per year on July 1 of the year you turned 49. You took the last one on July 1 of the year you turned 54. Then you stopped the payments altogether. Because you were required to continue payments until you reached age 59½, the substantially equal periodic payment exception became invalid in the year you turned 55 when you failed to take a payment. When you file the tax return for that year, you must report all distributions received and pay the early distribution tax with your tax return. The tax is 10% of all distributions that would have been subject to the early distribution tax if you had not been using the substantially equal periodic payment exception. The total of all distributions is $36,000 (six payments multiplied by $6,000). The early distribution tax is $3,600 ($36,000 x 0.10).

In addition, you will owe interest retroactively on the early distribution tax itself, as if the tax had been imposed on the due date of the tax return for the year in which you received the early distribution. In this example, your early distribution tax for each year was $600. You didn't pay any of it until the year you turned 55. For the distribution you took during the year you were 49, you owe six years of interest on the $600. For the distribution you took during the year you were 50, you owe five years of interest on $600. You get the idea. The rate used to compute the interest you owe is the IRS's standard rate on underpayment of tax. The rate is based on the applicable federal short-term rate and therefore changes from time to time. As of the second quarter of 2007, the rate for underpayment of tax was 8%.

EXAMPLE TWO: Your birthday is August 1. You began taking substantially equal periodic payments of $6,000 per year on December 31 of the year you turned 58. You took an identical payment every December 31 through the year you turned 61 and then stopped. Because you were required to continue payments for five full years, you will be subject to an early distribution tax of 10% on distributions that would have been subject to the tax if you had never invoked the substantially equal periodic payment exception. You took four payments of $6,000, the last one in December of the year you turned 61. However, if you had not been using the substantially equal period payment exception, only the distributions you took in the years you turned 58 and 59

would have been subject to an early distribution tax. All other distributions occurred after age 59½ and thus would not have been subject to penalty. (Note that because your birthday is August 1, you didn't turn 59½ until the same year you turned 60, so the distribution you took in December of the year you turned 59 was an early distribution, because you weren't yet 59½.)

Your early distribution tax will be $1,200 ($6,000 x 2 years x 0.10), plus interest.

Key Tax Code Sections, Regulations, and Notices

§ 72(t)(2)(A)(iv)
Substantially Equal Period Payment Exception

§ 72(t)(3)(B)
Separation From Service Requirement for Age 55 Exception

§ 1.72-9
IRS Life Expectancy Tables

§ 402(c)(4)
Prohibition Against Rollover of Periodic Payment

§ 1.401(a)(9)
Regulations for Minimum Distribution Calculation

Revenue Ruling 2002-62
IRS Guidelines for Computing Substantially Equal Payments

Required Distributions:
Taking Money Out When You Have To

Required Distributions During Your Lifetime 101

Death Before Required Beginning Date 102

Death After Required Beginning Date 103

Special Rules for Tax-Deferred Annuities 104

Special Rules for Roth IRAs 105

Penalty 106

    Innocent Blunders 106

    Chronic Errors 107

    Ineligible Rollovers 107

    Excess Contributions 110

Reporting the Penalty 110

Waiver 111

    Terms of the Waiver 112

    Requesting a Waiver 112

Who Should Read Chapter 5

 SKIP AHEAD

This chapter gives an overview of situations in which you are required to take money out of your retirement plan or IRA. Chapter 6 provides the details you will need to compute required distributions during your lifetime. Chapters 7 and 8 provide the information your heirs will need to compute distributions after your death.

Someone once said that the government's strategy for encouraging people to use their retirement money is a lot like herding cattle through a gate. If a cow heads off to the left of the gate, a cattle prod nudges her back on track. Similarly, if you wander off the retirement trail and withdraw your funds too early, you're brought up short with an early distribution tax. If our proverbial cow meanders too far to the right, she receives another painful poke, just as you are hit with another penalty if you wait too long to withdraw your retirement money. That penalty—for waiting too long—is the focus of this chapter.

CAUTION

Required Distributions Waived for 2009. For 2009 only, Congress has waived the requirement that you must take a minimum amount from your retirement plan. So, if you have reached age 70½ (the age you generally must start required distributions), or you have inherited a plan, you will not be required to take a distribution in 2009. However, you must resume required distributions in 2010. This temporary suspension applies to IRAs, defined contribution plans, 403(b) plans, 403(a) plans, and 457 plans. (See Chapter 1 for more information about these plans.)

To avoid being penalized for delaying distributions, you must comply with what are called the required distribution rules. Those rules mandate that you take a minimum amount from your retirement plan each year, beginning in the year you turn 70½ or, under certain circumstances, in the year you retire if you work past age 70½. The minimum amount is calculated according to a formula in the income tax regulations. You may take more than the minimum, but you may not take less. If you do take less, you will be fined 50% of the amount that should have come out of your plan but didn't—the shortfall, in penalty parlance.

The required distribution rules evolved from Congress's desire that you use up your retirement funds during your own retirement, instead of passing the assets on to your heirs. The law presents you with a date by which you must start withdrawing money from your retirement plan. It also answers questions such as the following: What happens if you die before the date you are supposed to begin distributions? Does the law provide income tax relief to

Helpful Terms

Beneficiary. The person or entity entitled to receive the benefits from insurance or from trust property, such as a retirement plan or IRA, usually after the insured or the owner of the property dies.

Deferral period. The number of years over which distributions from a retirement plan or IRA can be spread.

Distribution. A payout of property (such as shares of stock) or cash from a retirement plan or IRA to the participant or a beneficiary.

Grandfather provision. A part of a new law that exempts an individual or entity from the new law and allows the individual or entity to use the old law or special transitional laws.

TDA or tax-deferred annuity. Many university professors and public school employees are covered by a TDA, which is a retirement annuity plan for public charities or public schools. These retirement plans are usually funded with individual annuity contracts purchased from an insurance company. Retirement benefits are frequently paid as a monthly annuity for life.

Waiver. Intentional dismissal, as of a penalty.

your heirs? Is your beneficiary allowed to defer distributions from your plan even though the funds were never intended for his or her retirement? Does your spouse have special privileges?

As if those issues didn't complicate matters enough, there is a flip side to the premature death issue: What happens if you die after you have started receiving required distributions but before you have used up all your retirement money? Does this change anything? Are your heirs given relief in this situation? And, again, does your spouse have special privileges?

The required distribution rules attempt to address all of these questions and more. In this chapter we offer a summary of these rules.

Required Distributions During Your Lifetime

You don't have to worry about taking required distributions from your own retirement plan until the year in which you turn 70½. At that time, however, you must start taking distributions under one of the following two scenarios:

- You may withdraw everything by your required beginning date, or RBD, which for most people is April 1 of the year after turning 70½, but for some people will be April 1 of the year after they retire. (See Chapter 6 for more information about determining your RBD.)

- Alternatively, you may distribute your retirement plan money over a period of years. Most people will use the Uniform Lifetime Table (see Table III in Appendix B) to determine the number of years over which they may spread distributions. If your spouse is your beneficiary and is more than ten years younger than you are, however, you will use a different and more favorable table called the Joint Life and Last Survivor Table. (See Table II in Appendix B.)

When faced with those two distribution options, few people would choose the first—to distribute the entire amount of their retirement plan at once—because of the income tax implications. A whopping distribution all in one year could put you in the top tax bracket for that year, allowing the government to take a huge tax bite out of your nest egg.

In contrast, the second option allows people to spread distributions over a period of years, thereby keeping their tax burden lower. As an added bonus, the second option is flexible: If people want to take only the minimum required amount, they can, but they also have the option of taking more money out when they need it.

Chapter 6 describes the steps involved in determining your required distributions during your lifetime.

Death Before Required Beginning Date

If you die before your RBD, your beneficiary generally may spread distributions from your retirement plan over his or her life expectancy.

If your retirement plan requires or permits it, your beneficiary might also take distributions according to the five-year rule. This is almost always a less favorable method, so if your beneficiary has a choice, he or she should probably choose another method.

Under the five-year rule, your retirement plan assets must be completely distributed by December 31 of the year containing the fifth anniversary of your death. The law does not prescribe a distribution method. In order to mitigate the tax impact, your beneficiary might choose to take money out of the plan in annual installments over that five-year period. This strategy is perfectly acceptable as long as the plan administrator will allow it. But the plan has the authority to determine the distribution method during the five-year period. Some plans will permit installment payments; others will require a lump sum payment.

If you have no beneficiary, the five-year rule is mandatory.

If your beneficiary is someone other than your spouse, upon your death your beneficiary generally will have the option to transfer your retirement plan assets into a new inherited IRA and spread distributions over his or her own life expectancy. However, the new IRA must be in your name, as the original owner, and distributions to the beneficiary must begin in the year after your death.

Your nonspouse beneficiary might also have the option to transfer your retirement plan assets to a new inherited Roth IRA in your name. This is called a conversion. If your beneficiary chooses this option, he or she must first pay taxes on the converted amounts, and must take distributions over his or her life expectancy beginning in the year after your death. Note that this strategy works only for conversions from an inherited retirement plan to an inherited Roth IRA. Beneficiaries may not convert inherited traditional IRAs to Roth IRAs.

If your beneficiary is your spouse, he or she has some additional privileges. After your death, your spouse may defer distributions from your retirement plan until you would have been 70½. At that point, the distributions will be spread over your spouse's own life expectancy. Alternatively, your spouse can roll over your retirement plan (whether a qualified plan or an IRA) into an IRA or plan of his or her own. Your spouse would then name new beneficiaries and begin distributions in the year he or she turns 70½. If your spouse rolls the plan into a Roth IRA, taxes will be due in the year of the rollover but no distributions will be required during your spouse's lifetime.

CAUTION

If there are multiple beneficiaries. If your spouse is not the sole beneficiary but is instead one of several, then he or she might lose some of these special privileges.

Chapter 7 describes the effect of premature death on your retirement distributions, and it includes a detailed explanation of the life expectancy rule, the five-year rule, and the special privileges accorded a surviving spouse.

Death After Required Beginning Date

If you survive to your RBD, you must begin taking required distributions as described above. If there is still some money in your retirement plan when you die, your beneficiary must continue to take distributions every year—generally based on his or her life expectancy. Your beneficiary can elect to receive more than the prescribed amount, but not less.

As is the case when you die before your RBD, your nonspouse beneficiary may transfer the assets from your retirement plan into an inherited IRA in your name, and then take distributions over his or her life expectancy. Alternatively, your beneficiary may convert your retirement plan to an inherited Roth IRA in your name. Again, distributions from the Roth IRA must begin in the year after your death.

If you did not name a beneficiary, the assets will generally be distributed to your estate over your own remaining life expectancy as of the year of your death.

Some special rules apply if your spouse is your sole beneficiary. For example, your spouse may take distributions as though he or she were a nonspouse beneficiary. Alternatively, your spouse can roll over your retirement plan into an IRA or plan of his or her own. After the rollover, the retirement assets belong to the spouse, and the required distribution rules apply as though the spouse had been the original owner.

Chapter 8 explains your beneficiary's options if you die after you begin receiving required distributions.

Special Rules for Tax-Deferred Annuities

If you were a participant in a tax-deferred annuity (also known as a TDA or 403(b) plan) established before 1987, some special required distribution rules apply. Specifically, all contributions and earnings added to your account after 1986 are subject to the same required distribution rules described above.

However, the amount in your account on December 31, 1986 was grandfathered under an older set of rules and is not subject to the current required distribution rules.

Because of this grandfathering, when it comes time for you to start required distributions from your TDA, you may subtract your pre-1987 balance and compute your required distribution on the difference. You may continue to subtract the pre-1987 balance when computing required distributions every year until you reach age 75, at which time your entire account, including the pre-1987 balance, will be subject to current required distribution rules.

CAUTION

Grandfathering rules are strict. Although you may exclude the pre-1987 balance when computing required distributions, you may not exclude any subsequent earnings attributable to the grandfathered amount. The grandfathered portion is a fixed dollar amount—the precise balance of your account on December 31, 1986.

EXAMPLE: On December 31, 1986 the balance in your TDA was $130,000. You are now retired and will turn 70½ this year. The total value of your account is $220,000. Because you are not yet 75, you may exclude $130,000 (your pre-1987 balance) when you compute your first required distribution, which means the required distribution will be based on an account balance of $90,000 ($220,000 – $130,000). You may use this approach until the year you turn 75. From that year forward, you must use the total value of your account when computing your required distribution.

All required distributions you take before age 75 are deemed to come from your post-1986 accumulation. Any amount you withdraw in excess of the required amount, however, is deemed to come from the pre-1987 portion.

EXAMPLE: As in the previous example, your pre-1987 account balance is $130,000, and your post-1986 accumulation is $90,000. You compute your first required distribution to be $5,625, but decide to take an extra $5,000 to pay some unexpected medical expenses. Your total distribution for the year is $10,625. The minimum required amount of $5,625 is deemed to come from your post-1986 account (the $90,000 portion). The remaining $5,000 is deemed to come from your pre-1987 accumulation. Therefore, next year when you subtract your pre-1987 balance before computing your required distribution, you will subtract $125,000 (which is $130,000 – $5,000), instead of $130,000.

CAUTION

Be careful not to forfeit your option to defer. If at any time before you reach age 75 you roll over your entire TDA into an IRA, then you forfeit the option to defer until age 75 distributions on your pre-1987 accumulation. Similarly, if you roll over your TDA assets to another TDA (that is, you, yourself, take the money from one TDA and move it to another),

you lose the deferral option. To avoid this, simply transfer the funds (trustee to trustee) from the first TDA to the second. Transfers to an IRA don't work, though.

In addition, if the trustee or custodian of your TDA at any time ceases to keep accurate records of the year-end balances of your grandfathered and nongrandfathered portions, the entire balance of your TDA will be subject to current required distribution rules and you will no longer have the option of deferring distributions on your pre-1987 accumulation.

Special Rules for Roth IRAs

Roth IRAs conform to some of the required distribution rules described above, but not to others. Specifically, you are not required to take lifetime distributions. But if you die leaving a balance in your Roth IRA, the post-death rules introduced above, and described fully in Chapter 7, will apply whether you die before or after your RBD. Chapter 9 contains a detailed discussion of the Roth IRA rules.

CAUTION

Roth 401(k) plans are hybrids. A Roth 401(k) plan is treated like a traditional 401(k) plan for purposes of lifetime required distributions. In other words, Roth 401(k) plans are not exempt from lifetime required distributions. However, if you roll over your Roth 401(k) plan into a Roth IRA, either at retirement or when you leave your job, then once the assets are in the Roth IRA (and no longer in the Roth

401(k) plan), the Roth IRA rules would apply and no distributions would be required during your lifetime. See Chapter 10 for more information about Roth 401(k) plans.

Penalty

The penalty for failing to take a required distribution is one of the worst in all the Tax Code: 50% of the shortfall. Some call it onerous, others call it Draconian, but everyone calls it punitive. If you were required to take a $10,000 distribution but took only $4,000, you would owe the IRS $3,000 for your mistake—50% of the $6,000 you didn't take.

And don't think your failure to take a distribution will go unnoticed. The IRS requires trustees and custodians of IRAs to identify on IRS Form 5498 those IRAs for which a minimum distribution is required.

When meting out punishment for failure to comply with a rule or regulation, enforcers of the law sometimes attempt to discern your intent so that the punishment better fits the crime. For example, in the case of a required distribution violation, did you make an inadvertent error? A once-in-a-blue-moon blunder? Or are your failures chronic? Perhaps you attempted to cash in on a perceived loophole? The more egregious the violation, the more severe the penalty is likely to be. Some scenarios are discussed in the following sections.

Innocent Blunders

If you simply forget to take your required distribution one year, the 50% penalty is probably the worst you'll face. And as painful as it is, at least it hits only once. So even if you don't correct the shortfall the next year, the excise tax will not be assessed again with respect to the first transgression.

> **EXAMPLE:** You forgot to take your required distribution of $6,000 for the year 2006. In 2007 you computed your required distribution for 2007 and withdrew it, but you still hadn't discovered your error for the year 2006. Your mind cleared sometime in the year 2008 and you withdrew the $6,000 for 2006 along with your distribution for the year 2008. You must pay a penalty of $3,000 (50% of $6,000) plus interest for the year 2006 mistake. However, you only have to pay it once, even though the mistake remained uncorrected through 2007. (See below for information on how to report the distribution and penalty.)

Once you stumble and are faced with an unavoidable penalty, you might think there is nothing to be gained by distributing the required amount. But here are two good reasons to withdraw it:

- Only if you correct your mistake can you hope to obtain an official waiver of the penalty. (See below for more information about waivers.)

- If you don't correct the shortfall, you risk disqualifying the plan, which would force a total distribution of the account and loss of all future tax-deferred growth. The Tax Code states that a plan will not be a qualified plan unless it complies with the required distribution rules. Arguably you will not be in compliance for as long as a shortfall remains uncorrected.

Chronic Errors

Make no mistake, the IRS will look askance at the taxpayer who habitually fails to take proper required distributions, whether those distributions are late, incorrect, or nonexistent. Once a problem becomes chronic, not only will the IRS's sympathy wane, but plan disqualification becomes a serious risk.

Ineligible Rollovers

There is one more way for you or the trustee of your retirement plan to mess up your required distribution. You might roll it over. Required distributions from plans and IRAs are not eligible for rollover. (See Chapter 2 for more information about rollovers.) If they were, you would be able to withdraw your required distribution each year and roll what you don't need into another plan or IRA. That strategy might fit in with your financial and estate planning goals, but it flies in the face of Congressional intent, which is to encourage you to deplete your retirement account during your retirement, instead of preserving the assets for your heirs.

When Congress enacted the no-rollover rule, lawmakers recognized the rule would be difficult to enforce without help. Consequently, income tax regulations were fashioned to push the rule a step further, tacking on penalties for ineligible rollovers and requiring trustees of qualified plans to lend a hand in enforcement. The regulations for IRAs and TDAs are slightly different from those for qualified plans and qualified annuities.

Qualified Plans and Qualified Annuities

If you decide to roll over an amount from one qualified plan to another qualified plan or to an IRA during a year you are required to take a distribution, then only the amount that exceeds the required distribution is eligible for rollover. The amount of the required distribution itself must be distributed to you, and if it is not, it must be included in your taxable income for the year anyway.

> **EXAMPLE:** When you retired, you left your 401(k) assets with your employer. When you turned 70½ several years ago, your employer began distributing your minimum required distributions to you. On January 1 of this year, you decide to roll over your remaining 401(k) account balance into an IRA so that you can manage your own

investments. The balance of your 401(k) is $500,000. Your minimum distribution for the current year is $40,000. When you receive your 401(k) distribution, you are permitted to roll over only $460,000, because your required distribution for the current year is not eligible for rollover. If you roll over the entire $500,000 anyway, you must still report $40,000 of income on your tax return as though you had not rolled over the required distribution. And there could be other penalties, as well.

If you roll over an ineligible amount into an IRA, the consequences extend beyond including the ineligible portion in your income for the year. The ineligible amount is considered an excess contribution to the IRA. If it is not promptly withdrawn, it will be subject to excess contribution penalties in the year of the contribution (rollover) and again each year the excess remains uncorrected. (See below for more about excess contributions.)

To help ensure that the required distribution is not rolled over, the regulations require trustees of retirement plans to compute required distributions for all participants. There is good reason for placing this burden on a trustee: The portion of any distribution that exceeds the participant's required distribution is eligible for rollover. When a trustee distributes any amount that is eligible for rollover, the trustee must comply with a host of

procedural rules and regulations related to withholding, disclosure, and participant notification of tax options. In order to comply with these administrative rules, the trustee must determine whether or not some or all of a distribution is eligible for rollover. That in turn requires computation of the required distribution.

 CAUTION

Required distributions are not only ineligible for rollover, they are also ineligible for transfer. This means that a trustee must compute the minimum required distribution not only during a rollover, but also when benefits are being transferred by the trustee directly to a new plan. Consequently, the trustee must distribute the required amount to the participant either at the time of transfer or segregate the amount and distribute it before the required distribution deadline for the year.

IRAs and TDAs

Required distributions from IRAs and TDAs also are ineligible for rollover, but compliance can be a little tricky. If you have more than one IRA (whether traditional, SEP, or SIMPLE IRA), you must compute the required distribution for each one. You are then permitted to withdraw the total required amount from one or more of the IRAs. This aggregation rule applies to TDAs as well. So if you have more than one TDA, you may calculate the required distribution for each and withdraw the total from only one. Note, however, that you may not mix and match. You may not calculate a required distribution from your IRA and withdraw it from your TDA, or vice versa.

EXAMPLE: You have two IRAs and a TDA. Your required distribution from IRA #1 is $3,000 and from IRA #2 is $2,500. Your required distribution from your TDA is $4,000. You may total the required distributions from your two IRAs and withdraw the entire $5,500 from either IRA #1 or IRA #2 (or part from both). But the $4,000 required distribution from the TDA must be distributed from the TDA, not from one of the IRAs.

CAUTION

Inherited IRAs and inherited TDAs. You are not permitted to aggregate inherited IRAs and inherited TDAs with your own IRAs and TDAs for required distribution purposes. For example, assume you have an IRA to which you have made contributions over the years. You also have an IRA that you inherited from your father. When the time comes to take required distributions, you must compute the distribution for each IRA separately and withdraw the required amount from the respective IRA.

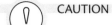

CAUTION

Aggregation does not apply to qualified plans or qualified annuities. For example, if you have more than one 401(k) plan, you must compute the distribution for each and withdraw the required amount from the respective plan.

Because of this aggregation option for IRAs, the IRS cannot really require IRA custodians to distribute to you the required amount before moving the funds. After all, what if you had already computed and withdrawn the requisite amount from another IRA—or you intend to do so? Because of this potential problem, the IRS relaxed the IRA transfer rules a little. But just a little. If you transfer your funds from one IRA to another in a direct custodian-to-custodian transfer, then the IRS will not require the custodian to withhold (and distribute to you) a required distribution from that IRA. The entire IRA can be transferred.

But if you roll over the funds instead (that is, you, yourself, take the funds out of one IRA and deposit them in another IRA), it is a different story. The law says required amounts cannot be rolled over. Therefore, the custodian would have to withhold a computed required distribution from the IRA funds you want to roll over, even though you intend to take—or already did take—the required amount from another IRA.

Excess Contributions

One of the most intimidating characteristics of the tax law is that penalties sometimes seem to come out of nowhere. One small mistake can turn a manageable tax liability into a financial albatross.

A rollover into a plan or IRA of an amount that is not permitted to be rolled over can lead to catastrophe. Unless the mistake is corrected promptly, usually by the filing deadline for the tax return, the IRS will consider the rollover an excess contribution to the plan or IRA. Excess contributions are subject to a penalty—6% for excess contributions to an IRA or 10% for excess contributions to a qualified plan. This penalty is assessed in addition to any other penalties or taxes that might apply, and it will be imposed every year until the excess is removed.

> **EXAMPLE:** In 2007 you received a required distribution of $6,000 from your 401(k) plan and rolled it over into an IRA. Because required distributions are ineligible for rollover, the $6,000 is an excess contribution. You were unaware of the problem until the IRS audited your 2007 tax return in late 2009. You removed the $6,000 in December 2009. The $6,000 must be reported as income on your tax return for the year 2009. In addition, you will owe an excess contribution penalty of $360 (6% of $6,000) for each of the years 2007 and 2008. Because you

distributed the excess before filing your 2009 tax return, you will owe no penalty for the year 2009.

Reporting the Penalty

If you owe a penalty for failing to take your required distribution, you must complete IRS Form 5329 (you can find a copy of this form in Appendix A) and include it when you file your tax return. If you have already filed your tax return for the year, then you must file an amended tax return for the year of the error and pay the penalty plus interest.

> **EXAMPLE:** You began taking required distributions from your IRA in 2005 and took them regularly until 2008. In 2009, you inherited some money, so you didn't need to draw on the IRA for living expenses as you had in the past. Consequently, you simply forgot to take your required distribution of $6,000. In fact, you forgot to take your 2008 distribution, too, which would have been $6,500. Finally, in February of 2010, you realized your error.
>
> For 2009, you must file an amended tax return and include a completed Form 5329. You must also pay a penalty of $3,000 (50% of $6,000), plus interest, for which the IRS will bill you.
>
> For 2010, because you have not yet passed the filing deadline for your tax return, you may simply file as usual by

April 15, 2011 and include a completed Form 5329. Along with any regular income tax you owe, you will owe a penalty of $3,250 (50% of $6,500). You will not have to pay interest, though, as long as the tax return and payment are filed on time.

Finally, you should correct the distribution errors by withdrawing the required amounts for both 2009 and 2010. If you correct the problem in 2011, you must report the distributions of $6,000 (for 2009) and $6,500 (for 2010) on your 2011 tax return. In addition, you will have to take a required distribution for 2011 and include it as income on your tax return.

In general, you have until December 31 to take your required distribution for any given year. If you miss the deadline, you must pay the penalty when you file your tax return (or pay the penalty with an amended return). The one exception to the December 31 deadline is the first year of required distributions. A grace period gives you until April 1 of the following year to withdraw your first required distribution. (See Chapter 6 for more information about when distributions must begin.) Thus, if you don't take a distribution by December 31 of the first year of required distributions, you won't owe a penalty unless you miss the April 1 deadline as well. If you happen to miss that one, too, you must pay the penalty, but you would pay it when you file

your tax return for the year containing the April 1 distribution deadline.

EXAMPLE: You turned 70½ in 2008, so your required beginning date (with the grace period) was April 1, 2009, although your first distribution year is officially 2008. This means that you were supposed to take your first required distribution by April 1, 2009, and your second distribution by December 31, 2009. Unfortunately, you forgot to take any distribution at all until January 2010. You will owe penalties for 2008 and 2009, because you missed the deadline for both required distributions. But because both distribution deadlines were in 2009, you can simply complete a Form 5329 and attach it to your tax return for the 2009 tax year (which is due by April 15, 2010). At that time, you must pay the 50% penalty on the required distribution shortfalls for both 2008 and 2009. You do not have to file an amended return for 2008, because the distribution for 2008 did not have to be made until April 1, 2009.

Waiver

Mistakes happen. Even Congress knows it. That's why a waiver has been written into the penalty provisions of the required distribution law.

Terms of the Waiver

There are four short paragraphs in the Tax Code section that assesses a penalty for delaying distributions from your retirement plan. But the entire fourth paragraph is devoted to a waiver of the penalty. It says that if you demonstrate that your failure to withdraw the proper amount was due to reasonable error and you are taking steps to correct the shortfall, the penalty may be waived. "May" is the operative word, though. The IRS is not required to waive the penalty; it simply has the authority to do so.

 TIP

Sometimes, the penalty will be waived automatically. Remember: The required distribution rules apply to inherited plans and IRAs, too. If a beneficiary inherits a retirement plan, he or she must generally take distributions over his or her life expectancy beginning in the year after the original participant's death (the life expectancy rule). But if the beneficiary fails to take the first distribution on time, he or she can fall back on the five-year rule to avoid a penalty. The five-year rule requires that all assets be distributed by December 31 of the year containing the fifth anniversary of the participant's death. To fall back on the five-year rule, the plan must permit the five-year rule as an option. If it does and if the beneficiary chooses to use it, the penalty for failing to take a distribution under the life expectancy rule will be waived automatically. (See Chapter 7 for more information about the life expectancy rule and the five-year rule.)

Requesting a Waiver

To request a waiver, you must first explain how the mistake came about. Perhaps you didn't understand the computation formula. Or maybe you wrote a letter to the custodian of your plan requesting a distribution, but you broke your leg on the way to the post office to mail the letter and forgot to drop the letter in a mail box after you were released from the hospital.

Your excuse must accompany a description of the steps you have taken to correct the mistake. For example, you might report that as soon as you discovered you didn't take the appropriate amount from your IRA, you asked the custodian to distribute the funds, which the custodian did the following week.

These explanations must be attached to a completed Form 5329 and filed along with the rest of your return at tax time. If you are submitting an amended return, send it in right away.

The IRS has been generous with these waivers, so don't assume your excuse is too lame to pass muster. For example, taxpayers have argued that they didn't understand the formula for computing the required distribution or that they made an arithmetic error. One taxpayer claimed that he signed the request for a distribution but forgot to mail it to his custodian. In all of those cases, the taxpayers had corrected their mistakes by the time they reported the error to the IRS, and they were all granted waivers.

If you have a plausible explanation for your error and you have taken steps to correct it, you stand a good chance of obtaining a waiver. Even the IRS is aware that 50% is a stiff penalty and is more interested in curbing abuse than punishing the computationally challenged. But if you consistently fail to take appropriate distributions, or if the IRS discovers your mistake during an audit, the IRS is likely to be less forgiving.

Key Tax Code Sections
§ 401(a)(9) Required Distributions From Qualified Plans
§ 402(e)(4) Eligible Rollover From Qualified Plan
§ 408(d)(3)(E) Ineligible Rollover From IRA
§ 4974 50% Excise Tax on Required Distributions
§ 1.403(b)-2 Treatment of Pre-1987 Accumulation in TDA

Required Distributions During Your Lifetime

Required Beginning Date 117

    First Year 118

    Second Year and Beyond 119

Computing the Required Amount 120

    Determining the Account Balance 120

    Determining the Applicable Distribution Period 121

    Computing the Required Distribution 123

    Special Aggregation Rule for IRAs and TDAs 124

    Reporting Distributions From IRAs 124

Designating a Beneficiary 125

    Definition of Designated Beneficiary 125

    Multiple Beneficiaries 127

Special Rules for Annuities 128

    Form of Payment 128

    Required Beginning Date 129

    Starting Early 129

    Young Beneficiaries 130

Divorce or Separation 131

    Separate Account 132

    No Separate Account 133

    Income Taxes and Penalties 133

    Rollovers 134

Who Should Read Chapter 6

SKIP AHEAD

Everyone will need to read this chapter. It tells you precisely when you are required to begin taking money out of your own retirement plan or IRA, how you compute the amount to withdraw, and what other decisions you must make at that time.

Comedians and accountants have long pondered the origin of the numbers that appear in the Tax Code—the ones that don't seem to make any sense. Why must we start taking money out of our retirement plans at age 70½? Why not 70? Or even 71? Some of us like to think Congress has a sense of humor, although cynics believe there's a conspiracy to keep the Tax Code complex. More likely, it's the result of a compromise.

Whatever its history, 70½ has become an important milestone; it's the age when most people must crack open their retirement nest eggs, even if they don't want to. Before age 59½, you have to worry about penalties for tapping your retirement money too early. (See Chapter 3 for information on the early distribution penalty.) Age 59½ to 70½ is the penalty-free zone. You can take distributions any time you want—or not—without penalty. But once you reach 70½, you are required to begin taking distributions.

CAUTION

Required Distributions Waived for 2009. For 2009 only, Congress has waived the requirement that you must take a minimum amount from your retirement plan. So, if you have reached age 70½ (the age you generally must start required distributions), or you have inherited a plan, you will not be required to take a distribution in 2009. However, you must resume required distributions in 2010. This temporary suspension applies to IRAs, defined contribution plans, 403(b) plans, 403(a) plans, and 457 plans. (See Chapter 1 for more information about these plans.)

Some or all of your retirement plan nest egg might be paid to you as an annuity after you retire, which means you will receive your money in installments—usually in the form of monthly payments. The payments might continue for a fixed number of years (a term certain) but more often will be spread over your lifetime. Annuities are a common form of payment if you were covered by your employer's defined benefit plan while you were working.

Annuity payments must also satisfy the required distribution rules described in this chapter. Annuity plan administrators are aware of the distribution rules, and the plans are generally structured to ensure that your payments satisfy the requirements; however, ultimately the responsibility is yours.

Helpful Terms	
Annuity. A contract, sold by an insurance company, that promises to make monthly, quarterly, semiannual, or annual payments for life or for a specified period of time.	**Applicable distribution period (ADP).** The divisor used for determining a required distribution. An account balance is divided by an ADP to arrive at the required distribution for a given year.
Contingent beneficiary. A person or entity who is entitled to receive the benefits of a retirement plan or IRA only if and when a specific event occurs, such as the death of a primary beneficiary.	**Primary beneficiary.** A person or entity entitled to receive benefits from a retirement plan or IRA upon the death of the original participant.
Distribution. A payout of property (such as shares of stock) or cash from a retirement plan or IRA to the participant or a beneficiary.	**Revocable trust.** A trust whose terms allow the creator of the trust to alter its provisions, cancel it, or remove some or all of the property from the trust and return the property to the creator.
Irrevocable trust. A trust that cannot be changed or terminated by the person who created it. Once assets are transferred to an irrevocable trust, the assets are subject to the terms of trust for as long as the trust exists.	**Term certain or period certain.** A fixed, identifiable period, such as a specific number of years. For example, a retirement plan that is distributable over a term certain of 20 years must be completely liquidated (distributed) after 20 years.

If, instead of an annuity, some or all of your nest egg is in an IRA or another type of retirement plan account, then when it is time for you to begin required distributions it is your responsibility to compute and withdraw the appropriate amount each year.

In this chapter, we discuss in detail the rules governing required distributions that you must take during your lifetime.

Required Beginning Date

The absolute deadline for taking your first required distribution (withdrawal) from your retirement plan is called your "required beginning date," or RBD. If you are the original owner of your retirement plan (as opposed to the beneficiary of someone else's plan), then your RBD is April 1 of the year after you turn 70½.

EXAMPLE: You were born January 15, 1938. You will turn 70½ on July 15, 2008. Your RBD is April 1, 2009.

Your RBD marks the deadline for taking the required distribution for your first distribution year only. For all subsequent years, the deadline is December 31.

You can defer your RBD for an employer plan if you work past age 70½. In that case, your RBD for that particular plan is April 1 of the year after you retire, no matter what age you are.

CAUTION

Self-employed people beware.
This special deferral option is not available if you own 5% or more of the business that sponsors the retirement plan, which of course includes virtually all self-employed individuals.

You generally cannot defer your RBD for any IRAs you have. There are exceptions for people who are covered by a federal or state government plan or by a church plan. (A church plan is one maintained by a church for church employees. This would include any type of religious organization or house of worship, as long as the organization qualifies as a tax-exempt organization.) If neither of those situations applies, the RBD for an IRA is April 1 of the year after you turn 70½, even if you continue to work.

As you can see, it's possible to have more than one RDB if you work beyond age 70½—one for an employer plan and one for an IRA.

RESOURCE

If you inherit a retirement plan.
You must use a different set of rules to determine your RBD for plans that you inherit. We discuss those rules in Chapters 7 and 8.

Because April 1 of the year after age 70½ is the RBD for most people, that is the date we will use for discussion purposes in this chapter.

First Year

You must withdraw at least the required minimum amount from your retirement plan account by your RBD or you will face a stiff penalty. To satisfy this requirement, you may count all distributions that take place between January 1 of the year you turn 70½ and April 1 of the following year (which is your RBD). In other words, you have 15 months to complete your first distribution.

Although you are permitted to take the required distribution in one big chunk, you don't have to. You can take it out as you need it, for example in monthly installments, as long as you have removed the minimum required amount for the first year by your RBD.

It is important to remember that amounts distributed before January 1 of the year you turn 70½ do not count toward your first required distribution, nor do amounts distributed after your RBD.

EXAMPLE ONE: You turn 70½ in 2009, and 2009 is your first distribution year. Although you were not required to take money out of your IRA in 2008, you took $20,000 on October 1, 2008, to buy a car. In 2009, your required minimum distribution is $10,000. You may not count the $20,000 you took in 2008 toward your 2009 required distribution.

EXAMPLE TWO: You turn 70½ in 2009, and your RBD is April 1, 2009. Your required distribution for 2008 is $10,000. You decide to wait until 2009 to take the distribution for your first year. You take $9,000 on March 1, 2009, and another $1,000 on May 1, 2009. Because the $1,000 that you took on May 1 is after your RBD, you cannot use it as part of your required distributions. Because you are $1,000 short of the amount required to be distributed, you will owe the IRS penalties on the $1,000 shortfall.

Second Year and Beyond

For the second and all future distribution years, you must take at least the required amount out of your retirement account between January 1 and December 31. There are no more three-month grace periods.

! CAUTION

Waiting can be costly. If you decide to wait until your RBD (which is April 1 of your second distribution year) to take your first required distribution, you must still take the full required distribution for the second year by December 31. That means you would have to take two required distributions in the same year, which could push you into a higher income tax bracket. For example, let's say you turn 70½ in 2008, which is your first distribution year, and your RBD is April 1, 2009. Your required distribution for your first distribution year is $20,000 and for the second year is $22,000. You are single and have no other taxable income. You also use the standard deduction. If you take your first distribution in 2008 and the second in 2009, the tax rate for both distributions is 15%. If you take both distributions in the same year, however, your gross income will be $42,000. At that level, some of your distributions will be taxed at a 28% rate.

Again, you may take the distribution in bits and pieces during the 12-month period, or you may take the entire amount on December 31. If you happen to take more than the required amount in one year, which is permissible, you may not count the excess toward your required distributions for the next year (or beyond).

EXAMPLE: Your required distribution for your second distribution year is $10,000 and for your third distribution year is $12,000. If you take $16,000 in your second distribution year, you may not apply the extra $6,000 to your third distribution year and withdraw only $6,000. Instead you must withdraw the full $12,000 during the third year.

Computing the Required Amount

To compute your required distribution for a given year, simply divide your account balance by what the IRS calls the "applicable distribution period," or ADP. The resulting number is the minimum amount you must withdraw from the account for that year. The sections that follow give detailed instructions on computing the required distribution.

Determining the Account Balance

According to tax regulations, the account balance for computing your required distribution each year is determined as of "the last valuation date in the calendar year before the distribution calendar year." For the vast majority of people who are computing their own required distributions, this would be December 31 of the year before the distribution year.

If your retirement assets are in a qualified plan when you begin required distributions instead of in an IRA, however, it is possible that the plan itself specifies a date other than December 31 for valuing the plan assets and computing required distributions. Nevertheless, we will use December 31 for discussion purposes in this book.

> **EXAMPLE:** You turn 70½ in 2009. To compute the required distribution for your first distribution year (2009), you use your account balance as of December 31, 2008. To compute the required distribution for the year 2010, you look at your account balance as of December 31, 2009, and so on.

Recall that you are permitted to take your first required distribution in the year after you turn 70½, as long as you take it on or before your RBD (which is April 1 of the year after you turn 70½). Deferring your first distribution, however, does not alter the date for determining the appropriate account balance. For example, if you turn 70½ in 2009 and decide to take your first distribution in March of 2010, you must still use your account balance as of December 31, 2008 to compute the amount of your first distribution.

What If You Fail to Take Your Required Distribution?

Almost without exception, you will use the prior year's December 31 balance of your retirement account to compute the required distribution for the current year. But one important exception crops up when you fail to take some or all of your required distribution one year. To avoid penalties, you will want to correct this error as soon as possible for each year you failed to take the appropriate amount out of the account.

When determining the appropriate account balance for each year's calculation, the IRS has indicated that you may reduce the actual account balance by the amount of any required distribution that should have been distributed by that date but was not.

> **EXAMPLE:** You forgot to take your required distributions for the years 2007 and 2008. Now, in 2009, you want to correct the errors and take all require distributions for prior years. To calculate the 2007 required distribution, you will use the actual December 31, 2006 account balance. To calculate the 2008 distribution, you will use the December 31, 2007 balance, reduced by the required distribution for 2007 (which you failed to take). For your 2009 distribution, you will use the December 31, 2008 account balance, reduced by the required distributions for 2007 and 2008 (which you failed to take).

Determining the Applicable Distribution Period

Once you have determined the appropriate account balance to use for a particular distribution year, you must divide it by the applicable distribution period, or ADP, to arrive at your required distribution.

First Year

To find your ADP for your first distribution year, you must use one of two tables provided by the IRS. Most people will use what the IRS calls the Uniform Lifetime Table (Table III in Appendix B), but some people will be able to use the Joint Life and Last Survivor Table (Table II in Appendix B). The table you use depends on whom you designate as your beneficiary.

General Rule

The vast majority of people will use the Uniform Lifetime Table to find their ADP. The only time you would not do so is when your spouse is the sole beneficiary of your retirement account and is more than ten years younger than you are.

In all other cases, you will use the Uniform Lifetime Table. Thus, if your beneficiary is a child, grandchild, friend, charity, your estate, or a spouse who is not more than ten years younger than you are, you will use the Uniform Lifetime Table. And if you haven't yet named a beneficiary, you will still use the Uniform Lifetime Table.

To find the ADP for your first distribution year, you determine your age as of your birthday in the year you turn 70½. If that age is 70, then find the ADP next to age 70 in the Uniform Lifetime Table (Table III in Appendix B). That number is 27.4.

If your age is 71 on your birthday in the year you turn 70½, the ADP from the table is 26.5.

CAUTION

It depends on when your birthday is. You are not always age 70 in your first distribution year. If your birthday falls after June 30, you will turn 70½ in the same year in which you turn 71. In that case, you must use age 71 when looking up the ADP for your first distribution year.

Spouse More Than Ten Years Younger

If your beneficiary is your spouse and he or she is more than ten years younger than you are, the rules are slightly more favorable. You do not use the Uniform Lifetime Table. Instead, you use the Joint Life and Last Survivor Table (Table II in Appendix B) to find your ADP—the actual joint life expectancy of you and your spouse.

To determine your ADP, look up the number that corresponds to your age and your spouse's age on your respective birthdays in your first distribution year. For example, if you are age 70 on your birthday in your first distribution year (the year you turn 70½) and your spouse is age 55 in that year, your ADP from Table II is 31.1.

Be careful, though. In order to use Table II for your ADP, you must satisfy both of the following requirements:

- your spouse must be more than ten years younger than you are, and
- your spouse must have been the sole designated beneficiary of your retirement account for the entire year.

For purposes of this last requirement, your marital status is determined as of January 1 of the distribution year. For example, if you would have been eligible to use Table II except for the fact that your spouse died during the year—or that you and your spouse divorced during the year—you would still be able to use Table II in the year of the death or divorce. However, in the following year, you would use the Uniform Lifetime Table (assuming you were still single on January 1 of that following year).

Second Year and Beyond

Determining the ADP for the second and future distribution years is done in precisely the same way you determined the ADP for the first year.

General Rule

In your second distribution year, you will again use the Uniform Lifetime Table, or Table III, to find your ADP—unless your spouse-beneficiary is more than ten years younger than you are. (In that case, see just below.) For the second year calculation, use your age as of your birthday in the second year. If your age in that year is 71, find the ADP next to age 71 in Table III. That number is 26.5. For the third year, assuming you are age 72 on your birthday, your ADP is 25.6, and so on.

Spouse More Than Ten Years Younger

If your spouse is more than ten years younger than you are, and if he or she was the sole designated beneficiary of your retirement plan or IRA for the entire year, then you use Table II to find the ADP for your second distribution year. Look up the number that corresponds to your age and your spouse's age on your respective birthdays in your second distribution year. For example, if you are age 71 on your birthday in your second distribution year and your spouse is age 56 in that year, Table II indicates that your joint life expectancy—your ADP—for the second year is 30.1.

EXAMPLE: You turned 70½ in 2008. At that time, your brother was the beneficiary of your IRA. In November of 2008, you married someone 20 years younger than you and changed the beneficiary designation of your IRA to your new spouse. For 2008 you must use the Uniform Lifetime Table—Table III—to compute your first required distribution. For 2009, you may use Table II to find your ADP, as long as your new spouse remains the beneficiary for all of 2009.

Computing the Required Distribution

Once you have determined the appropriate account balance and ADP, you simply divide the account balance by the ADP

to arrive at your required minimum distribution. You can withdraw more than the required amount each year, but you may not withdraw less without incurring a penalty. (See Chapter 5 to learn more about the penalty.)

EXAMPLE: You turn 70 on March 1, 2009 and your IRA account balance on December 31, 2008 is $50,000. Your niece is the beneficiary of your IRA. Your ADP for your first distribution year is 27.4 (from Table III). Therefore, your first required distribution is $1,824 ($50,000 ÷ by 27.4).

 TIP

Special opportunity for after-tax contributions. If you retire and receive a lump sum distribution from your employer's plan, your distribution might include after-tax contributions that you made to the plan. Because these amounts are not taxable, you have an interesting planning opportunity if your retirement date is in the year you turn 70½ or later. Specifically, you may count the distribution of after-tax amounts as part of your required distribution from the plan for that particular year. By doing so you can reduce your income tax while leaving additional pretax amounts in the account to grow for another year.

EXAMPLE: You retire in 2009, which is also the year you turn 70½. Over the years, you created quite a nest egg of pretax dollars inside your employer's qualified retirement plan. You have also made $10,000 in after-tax contributions. Your required distribution for your first distribution year is $19,000. When you retire in 2009, your employer distributes your retirement benefits to you as a lump sum. You decide to take your first required distribution by December 31, 2009. Your intention is to roll over into an IRA all but your required distribution for 2009. You keep out your after-tax contributions of $10,000 and an additional $9,000. You then roll over the remainder of the lump sum into an IRA. Thus, you have distributed from your retirement plan the entire amount of your first required distribution ($19,000), but only $9,000 of it is taxable.

Special Aggregation Rule for IRAs and TDAs

If you have more than one IRA, you must compute the required distribution for each IRA separately, but then you may add up all the computed amounts and take the total from only one or several IRAs, as long as the aggregate or total amount is distributed before the deadline.

This strategy also works if you have more than one TDA (tax deferred annuity) plan. You may compute the required distribution for each plan, and then distribute the total from just one plan or more. You may not mix and match IRAs and TDAs, however. If

you have one IRA and one TDA, you must calculate and distribute the required amount from each separately.

> **CAUTION**
>
> **You are not permitted to aggregate either inherited IRAs or inherited TDAs with your own IRAs or TDAs for required distribution purposes.** For example, let's assume you have an IRA to which you have made contributions over the years. You also have an IRA that you inherited from your father. Your required distribution must be computed separately for each IRA and withdrawn from the respective account.

> **CAUTION**
>
> **No aggregation for other types of plans.** You are allowed to use the aggregation rule only for IRAs and TDAs. If you have another type of plan (such as an employer plan or Keogh), you must compute the required amount separately for each plan and take the computed amount from the respective plan account.

Reporting Distributions From IRAs

It's up to you to compute the correct required distribution and report it on your tax return. However, in the case of an IRA, help is available. The law requires IRA custodians to tell IRA owners who have reached age 70½ either the amount of the required distribution or the fact that a distribution is required. If the custodian simply gives notice of the required distribution, the custodian must offer to calculate the amount for the IRA owner.

Custodians also must identify those IRAs for which a minimum distribution must be made. They must do this each year. They do not, however, have to report the amount of the required distribution.

Designating a Beneficiary

In the old days, if you did not name a person as beneficiary of your IRA or retirement plan, you would feel the impact of that decision as soon as you reached age 70½. That was because, without a designated beneficiary, you would have been required to distribute your retirement plan a lot faster than you would have if you had named a designated beneficiary.

In 2001, however, the IRS relaxed that requirement. Now it doesn't matter who your beneficiary is when you start taking required distributions. You are permitted to use the Uniform Lifetime Table even if you fail to name any beneficiary at all.

But even though the IRS won't punish you for not naming a beneficiary by your RBD, naming a designated beneficiary is still important. First, if your spouse is more than ten years younger than you are and you want to use Table II to compute required distributions, you can do so only if your spouse is your designated beneficiary.

Second, if you die without a designated beneficiary of your retirement plan or IRA, the distribution of the plan or IRA assets could be accelerated after your death, possibly leaving your heirs with significant tax problems. (See Chapters 7 and 8 for more information about what happens if you die without a designated beneficiary.)

Bear in mind that you may name any person or entity as the beneficiary of your retirement plan. But not all beneficiaries are "designated" beneficiaries. If you choose a beneficiary who does not fall within the definition of designated beneficiary, you are deemed to have no beneficiary at all for required distribution purposes. (To find out who is, and who is not, a designated beneficiary, see immediately below.)

Definition of Designated Beneficiary

A designated beneficiary must be a natural person, as opposed to an entity such as a charity or a corporation. There is one exception to this natural person rule: a trust that has certain qualifications (known as a qualified trust—see below) can be a designated beneficiary.

If you fail to name a natural person or a qualified trust as your beneficiary and instead name your estate, a charity, a corporation, or a nonqualified trust, then you are deemed to have no designated beneficiary for required distribution purposes.

CAUTION

Just because you do not complete a beneficiary designation form and record the name of a beneficiary does not necessarily mean that you have no designated beneficiary.

Some plans provide for a default beneficiary, usually a spouse, when the owner does not name a beneficiary. Be sure to find out if your plan has such a default provision. If it does not, then you are deemed to have no designated beneficiary even if the laws of your state dictate who should receive your assets. Similarly, some plans or IRAs automatically revoke the designation of a spouse as beneficiary if you divorce. Again, be sure to check the plan provisions to ensure that your retirement plan assets will go to the beneficiaries you intend.

Designated beneficiaries fall into the following three categories:

- spouse
- nonspouse natural person, and
- qualified trust.

We look at each category in the following sections.

Spouse

If your spouse is your designated beneficiary, your spouse will have certain privileges after your death—such as a rollover option—that other beneficiaries will not have. (See Chapters 7 and 8.)

Nonspouse Natural Person

Any human being—what the Tax Code calls a "natural person"—qualifies as a designated beneficiary. For example, your designated beneficiary could be a friend, relative, or a nonmarital partner.

Qualified Trust

A trust can be a designated beneficiary if it meets all of the following requirements:

- The trust must be valid under state law, meaning the terms must be enforceable.
- The trust must be either irrevocable while you are alive (meaning you cannot change its terms or cancel it) or irrevocable upon your death.
- The beneficiaries of the trust must be natural persons (humans) and must be identifiable. They don't have to be identified by name, however. For example, you may use the terms "spouse" or "children."
- You must provide a copy of the trust to the trustee or custodian of your retirement plan or IRA. If the trust is revocable (meaning you can change or amend it), you must give the trustee or custodian a copy of any subsequent amendments. As an alternative to submitting the entire trust agreement, you may also provide a list of beneficiaries with a description of the amount each is to receive and the conditions, if any, under which they will receive benefits.

If the trust meets all of the above qualifications, then the beneficiary of the trust is treated as the designated beneficiary for purposes of computing your required distributions. If your spouse is sole beneficiary of the trust and is more than ten years younger than you are, you can use Table II to find your ADP each year when computing required distributions. If there is more than one beneficiary of the trust, however, the multiple beneficiary rules discussed below will apply.

The trust must satisfy all of the above for any period during which the trust is named beneficiary and during which the beneficiary of the trust is being used to determine required distributions.

So, for example, if you want to use the joint life expectancy of you and your spouse to compute required distributions when you turn 70½, then in order to satisfy the fourth requirement (the fourth bullet point, above), you must provide the custodian with a copy of the trust document by your RBD.

Multiple Beneficiaries

If you want to name more than one person as the beneficiary of your retirement plan, you should be aware of the consequences.

Primary Beneficiaries

You can name several primary beneficiaries of your retirement plan who may or may not share equally in the plan assets after your death. If any one of the primary beneficiaries fails to qualify as a designated beneficiary, then you are deemed to have no designated beneficiary at all. This is true even if all other beneficiaries would qualify as designated beneficiaries. For example, if you name your sister to receive 50% of your IRA and a charity to receive

the rest, you are deemed to have no designated beneficiary (because the charity is not a natural person).

You can avoid this problem by setting up a separate IRA for each beneficiary. For example, you can direct the custodian of the IRA, in writing, to set up a second IRA and transfer half of your existing IRA assets into the new IRA. You would name the charity as sole beneficiary of the new IRA and your sister as sole beneficiary of the old IRA.

TIP

Sometimes, your heirs can cure the problem. If you die having named multiple beneficiaries of your retirement plan and if one of those beneficiaries is not a designated beneficiary, all is not lost. Your heirs might be able to cure the problem by splitting the account or by distributing assets to one or more beneficiaries by December 31 of the year after your death. For more information about these strategies, see the "Multiple Beneficiaries, One Account" sections of Chapters 7 and 8.

Contingent Beneficiaries

A contingent beneficiary is a beneficiary you name to receive your retirement plan assets in the event your primary beneficiary does not qualify to receive the benefits. Usually a primary beneficiary fails to qualify because he or she has already died. If you name a primary beneficiary and then name a contingent beneficiary who will receive the retirement benefits only if the primary beneficiary predeceases you, then the contingent beneficiary has no effect on required distributions.

If the contingent beneficiary could become the primary beneficiary for any reason other than the death of the original primary beneficiary, then the contingent beneficiary is treated as one of multiple beneficiaries (along with the primary beneficiary) when determining required distributions.

> **EXAMPLE:** You have instructed the custodian of your IRA in writing that you name your spouse, who is 15 years younger than you, as primary beneficiary of your IRA, but only if you are married at the time of your death. In the event you and your spouse divorce, your father will become the primary beneficiary of your IRA. Because your father's interest is not contingent solely on the death of your spouse, both your spouse and your father are considered beneficiaries of your retirement plan. Consequently, because your spouse is not the sole designated beneficiary, you may not use Table II to compute required distributions. Instead you must use the Uniform Lifetime Table—Table III.

Special Rules for Annuities

If you are taking some or all of your retirement plan benefits in the form of an annuity, those annuity payments must also satisfy the required distribution rules described in this chapter.

Although the required distribution rules for annuities are essentially the same as those for IRAs and other retirement plans, there are some differences worth noting.

Form of Payment

To satisfy the required distribution rules, annuity payments must come at regular intervals of at least once a year. For example, you can receive payments monthly, quarterly, semiannually, or annually, but not every 18 months.

The payments may be in the form of either a life annuity or a term certain.

If you choose a life annuity, the payments must last for your lifetime or the joint lifetime of you and your beneficiary.

If you choose a term certain, the term must satisfy one of the following:

- it must be no longer than the ADP for your age (from Table III), or
- it must be no longer than the joint life expectancy of you and your spouse beneficiary (from Table II), if your spouse beneficiary is more than ten years younger than you are.

Once payments begin, the term certain may not be lengthened and payments generally must be level, although they might be increased to reflect changes in cost of living or benefit increases under the plan.

Required Beginning Date

When you receive your retirement benefits as an annuity, the first payment must be made on or before your RBD to satisfy the required distribution rules. The amount of the first required payment is simply your regular annuity payment for that period. For example, if the terms of your annuity require that you be paid $2,000 per month for life, then you must receive your first $2,000 payment on or before your RBD.

You are not required to receive any payments before that date.

Starting Early

If you elect to start receiving your annuity before your RBD, and if you comply with the form of payment rules described above, then the start date of your annuity becomes your RBD for all purposes. For example, the designated beneficiary is

---

Types of Annuities

In order to understand how the required distribution rules apply to your annuity, you must first know what type of annuity you have:

Life annuity: A life annuity makes payments to you or to you and your beneficiary for your entire life. You might have a single life annuity or a joint and survivor annuity. Payments from a single life annuity continue throughout your lifetime and stop when you die, regardless of how much has been paid. No further payments are made to any heirs or to your estate. In the case of a joint and survivor annuity, payments continue until your death or the death of your beneficiary—whichever occurs later—and then the payments stop. No additional payments are made to any other heirs or to your estate.

Term certain annuity: A term certain annuity makes payments for a fixed number of years regardless of when you die or when your beneficiary dies. If you die before the term is over, payments will be made to your beneficiary, your estate, or your heirs for the remainder of the term.

Life annuity with term certain: A life annuity with a term certain will make payments for your lifetime or for a term certain if you die before the term is up. For example, assume you are taking a single life annuity with a term certain of ten years. If you live more than ten years, the annuity payments will continue throughout your life and stop when you die. If you die after five years, the annuity will continue payments for five more years. Similarly, if you have a joint and survivor annuity with a term certain, and both you and your beneficiary die before the term is up, the annuity will continue to be paid to your heirs for the remainder of the term.

determined as of your annuity start date. And distributions must continue according to the established schedule even if you die before turning 70½.

Young Beneficiaries

If the beneficiary of your annuity is more than ten years younger than you are (and is not your spouse), then you must use special tables to determine whether or not your annuity satisfies the required distribution rules. You will need to know what type of annuity you have in order to determine which table to use.

If You Have a Term Certain Annuity

If you have elected to take your annuity over a term certain and have named a nonspouse beneficiary who is more than ten years younger than you are, you may still use Table II to find your joint life expectancy, but only until your RBD. Once you reach your RBD, you must satisfy the required distribution rules, which means the term certain may not exceed the period found in Table III (see Appendix B) beginning in the year you turn 70½ and for all subsequent years.

> **EXAMPLE:** You retire and begin taking your annuity when you are age 65. You name your grandson as beneficiary. He is 35 years old and your joint life expectancy, according to Table II, was 48.9 years. You elected to begin taking

distributions over a term certain of 48.9 years. Five years later, when you turn 70½, the remaining term certain is 43.9 years (48.9 − 5). According to Table III, however, which you must use when you reach age 70½, the remaining term certain may not exceed 27.4 years. In order to satisfy required distribution rules, your annuity plan must automatically adjust your payments beginning in the year you turn 70½ so that the annuity is paid out over 27.4 years (instead of 43.9 years).

Joint and Survivor Annuity

If you elect to receive a life annuity (without a term certain) over the joint life of you and a nonspouse beneficiary who is more than ten years younger than you are, then at all times from and after your first distribution year (the year you turn 70½), the projected payment to your beneficiary cannot exceed a certain percentage of the payment you are currently receiving. The percentage is based on the difference in your ages and is determined from Table IV (see Appendix B).

As in the case of a term certain annuity, if you begin receiving payments before your RBD and they do not satisfy the required distribution rules, the payments must be adjusted beginning in the year you turn 70½.

EXAMPLE: You are taking your retirement benefits as a joint and survivor annuity over the joint life of you and your daughter. The year you turn 70½, your monthly payment is $3,000. The age difference between you and your daughter is 21 years. From Table IV, you see that your daughter's projected benefit when you die cannot exceed 72% of your current benefit—that is, it cannot exceed $2,160 per month ($3,000 x 0.72). So when you die, the payment to your daughter must drop from $3,000 per month to no more than $2,160 per month.

If you name more than one beneficiary of your annuity, then you must use the youngest beneficiary to determine the percentage from Table IV. And similarly, if you change your beneficiary to a younger beneficiary (for any reason other than the death of a primary beneficiary), your payments may need to be adjusted so that projected payments to the beneficiary satisfy the percentage requirements from Table IV.

Joint and Survivor Annuity With Term Certain

If you have a life annuity with a term certain, you must satisfy both the term certain requirements and the survivor benefit limitations described above. In other words, the term of your annuity may not exceed the number corresponding to your age in Table III, and the projected

payments to your beneficiary after your death may not exceed the percentage in Table IV.

TIP

It's not always this difficult. Although the annuity rules seem (and can be) complex, most people's annuities take the form of a single life annuity or a joint life annuity with a spouse. If you have selected either of these forms of payment, then you should not have to make new computations every year. It is only when you use a much younger nonspouse beneficiary or when you change beneficiaries that your situation could become more complicated.

Divorce or Separation

If you are divorced or separated, part of your qualified plan, qualified annuity, or TDA might be payable to an "alternate payee" (such as a spouse, former spouse, or child) under the terms of a QDRO—a court-approved divorce or maintenance agreement. (See Chapter 2 for more information about QDROs.)

When you reach your RBD, the required distribution rules will apply to the alternate payee's portion, as well as to your own. And because you are the plan participant, it is your RBD that determines when distributions must begin. Furthermore, if the required amount is not withdrawn in timely fashion, you, not the alternate payee, must pay the penalty. As for other required distribution rules, the way in which they are applied will depend on whether or not the alternate payee's portion is in a separate account.

CAUTION

Alternate payee must wait. The terms of your QDRO might provide that the alternate payee is to receive immediate and total distribution of his or her share of the plan. Unless the plan itself permits such a distribution, however, the alternate payee must wait to receive his or her share until the time when you distribute assets from the plan, either at your retirement or when you begin required distributions or at some other time specified by the plan.

Separate Account

A QDRO might require that an alternate payee's portion be divided and separately accounted for. If so, the following variations in the required distribution rules apply:

- The alternate payee's separate share is not to be combined, or aggregated, with the rest of your plan benefits when you compute required distributions. In other words, you would separately compute the required distribution amount for your portion and the alternate payee's portion. You would then distribute the alternate payee's portion from his or her share.
- In computing the required distribution from the alternate payee's portion,

you may use one of the following to determine the ADP:

- the Uniform Lifetime Table (Table III) based on your age
- the joint life of you and the alternate payee, if the alternate payee is your ex-spouse and is more than ten years younger than you are, or
- the alternate payee's single life expectancy.

The decision about which ADP to use belongs to you—not to the alternate payee —even though the distribution will come from the alternate payee's portion and will be distributed to the alternate payee.

CAUTION

If the alternate payee dies. Although you have several options for selecting a distribution period to compute required distributions from the alternate payee's portion, one option that you do not have is to use the joint life expectancy of the alternate payee and his or her beneficiary. If the alternate payee dies before your RBD, however, the alternate payee's beneficiary will be treated as the beneficiary for required distribution purposes.

EXAMPLE: Your ex-husband is entitled to half of your pension plan under the terms of your QDRO. The pension plan administrator separated your ex-husband's share into a separate account, and your ex-husband named his sister as beneficiary of his separate share of the pension. The plan provides that no distributions can be made until you retire or reach your RBD. If your ex-husband dies before your RBD, then your ex-husband's sister becomes the designated beneficiary when computing distributions from your ex-husband's portion of the pension.

Even if a QDRO mandates dividing the retirement benefit between you and the alternate payee, the terms of the plan might not permit physically separating the shares. The plan administrator can get around this using a reasonable method to separately account for the alternate payee's portion. For example, a reasonable method would be to allocate on a *pro rata* basis all investment gains and losses, as well as contributions and forfeitures (if applicable).

No Separate Account

In some instances, you will not physically separate your share from the alternate payee's share. Some QDROs do not require an actual separation of the alternate payee's share, and some plans don't permit actual separation.

In either case, the retirement plan remains undivided, and a portion of each distribution goes to the alternate payee. Under this scenario, the alternate payee's portion does not have to separately satisfy the minimum distribution requirement. Instead, it is combined, or aggregated, with your other plan assets for purposes

of determining the account balance and calculating your required distribution for the year.

Thus, aggregation means that the required distribution rules work as though there was no alternate payee. When calculating required distributions, you may use either the uniform table or Table II (if your spouse-beneficiary is more than ten years younger than you are). But you may not use the alternate payee's single life expectancy.

Income Taxes and Penalties

Generally speaking, the rules governing the payment of taxes and penalties on QDRO distributions are essentially the same whether the alternate payee is a spouse, former spouse, or child.

There are, however, two exceptions to that general rule. We explain those in the following sections.

Spouse or former spouse alternate payee. If the alternate payee named in the QDRO is your spouse or former spouse, the alternate payee must pay all income taxes on distributions he or she receives. But you are responsible for penalties on any shortfall in required distributions, even though the alternate payee is receiving a portion.

Nonspouse alternate payee. If the alternate payee is someone other than your spouse or former spouse (for example, your child), you must pay all income taxes, as well as any penalties that might apply. This is true even though the distribution actually goes to the alternate payee.

Rollovers

The option to roll over a distribution from a qualified plan into an IRA or another qualified plan is a big tax benefit. Traditionally, the benefit has been reserved for plan participants, and occasionally the participant's spouse. Under the QDRO rules, the privilege is extended to a former spouse.

Spouse or former spouse alternate payee. A spouse or former spouse may roll over any distributed portion of his or her interest in your plan if there is a QDRO in place. This is the case whether or not the spouse or former spouse's portion was held in a separate account. Once the spouse or former spouse completes the rollover to an account in his or her name, the account belongs to the spouse or former spouse in every way, and the required distribution rules apply to that account as though the alternate payee were the original owner.

CAUTION

The plan has the final word. Although the QDRO rules permit your spouse or former spouse to roll over an interest in your retirement plan, some plans will not permit it. Furthermore, some plans will not make any distribution at all until you have reached a certain retirement age—one that is specified in the plan. Because the plan rules ultimately

govern distributions, spouses and former spouses often have little control over how they receive QDRO payments.

Nonspouse alternate payee. Nonspouse alternate payees may not roll over their interest in your retirement plan under any circumstances. The law does not allow it.

CAUTION

When the rules don't apply. Remember: The special rules described in this section apply only to qualified plans, qualified annuities, and TDAs, and they apply only if there is a QDRO in place. If there is no QDRO, your retirement plan is treated as though it is entirely yours for required distribution purposes. If your divorce agreement states that your former spouse is to share in your plan, you must generally give your former spouse his or her share as it is distributed from the plan. In other words, a portion of each distribution would go to your former spouse and you would keep your share. As for IRAs, there are no corresponding QDRO rules. As long as the IRA remains in your name, the required distribution rules apply as though your former spouse had no interest in the IRA. But if some or all of your IRA is transferred into your former spouse's name as a result of a written divorce or separation agreement, then from the time the transfer is complete, the transferred portion belongs to your former spouse in every respect. That means the required distribution rules apply as though your former spouse were the original owner. (See Chapter 2 for more information about IRAs and divorce.)

Key Tax Code and Regulation Sections

§ 401(a)(9)

Required Distributions From Qualified Plans

§ 1.401(a)(9)

Required Distribution Regulations

§ 1.408-8

Required Distribution Rules for IRAs

Distributions to Your Beneficiary If You Die Before Age 70½

Determining the Designated Beneficiary 139

    Deadline for Determining Designated Beneficiary 140

    Changing Beneficiaries Before the Deadline... 140

Distribution Methods 141

    Life Expectancy Rule.. 141

    Five-Year Rule... 142

    Spousal Rollover... 143

    Effect of the Retirement Plan's Rules.. 143

Spouse Beneficiary 144

    Life Expectancy Rule.. 144

    Rollover 146

    Convert to Roth IRA 148

    Death of Spouse Beneficiary 148

Nonspouse Beneficiary 150

    Life Expectancy Rule.. 150

    Rollover 151

    Convert to a Roth IRA 153

    Death of Nonspouse Beneficiary 153

No Designated Beneficiary 154

    Five-Year Rule... 154

    No Life Expectancy Rule.. 154

Multiple Beneficiaries, Separate Accounts 155

Multiple Beneficiaries, One Account.. 155

    Life Expectancy Rule.. 156

    Five-Year Rule... 157

    Splitting Accounts After Death.. 157

When a Spouse Is One of the Beneficiaries 160

Designated and Nondesignated Beneficiaries 160

Trust Beneficiary 161

Nonspouse Beneficiary of Trust 161

Spouse Beneficiary of Trust 161

Multiple Beneficiaries of Trust 163

Trust Beneficiary and Spousal Rollovers 163

Estate as Beneficiary 164

Annuities 165

Start Date 165

Form of Payment 165

Irrevocable Annuity 165

Divorce or Separation 166

Separate Account 166

No Separate Account 167

Reporting Distributions From IRAs 167

Who Should Read Chapter 7

SKIP AHEAD

Read this chapter if you want to know what happens to your own retirement plan after you die or if you inherit a retirement plan or IRA from someone who died before reaching age 70½. This chapter describes how the account must be distributed and explains other administrative procedures to help avoid unnecessary penalties and taxes.

The law says you must start taking money out of your retirement plan by a certain date—your "required beginning date" (RBD). But what if you never make it to that date? What would your premature death mean for your beneficiaries (other than the obvious sadness), and how can you prepare for it?

In this chapter, we look at the answers to those questions, paying particular attention to the ways you can help your beneficiaries avoid onerous taxes and penalties.

CAUTION

Required Distributions Waived for 2009. For 2009 only, Congress has waived the requirement that you must take a minimum amount from your retirement plan. So, if you have reached age 70½ (the age you generally must start required distributions), or you have inherited a plan, you will not be required to take a distribution in 2009. However, you must resume required distributions in 2010. This temporary suspension applies to IRAs, defined contribution plans, 403(b) plans, 403(a) plans, and 457 plans. (See Chapter 1 for more information about these plans.)

Determining the Designated Beneficiary

If you die before your RBD, which for most people is April 1 of the year after they turn 70½ (see Chapter 6 for information about determining your RBD), your designated beneficiary (if you have one) generally must begin taking distributions from your retirement plan in the year after your death, with some exceptions. Just how rapidly the assets must be distributed and according to what schedule depends primarily on who the designated beneficiary is. So before we look at distribution methods, let's see how the IRS will determine who your designated beneficiary is.

Recall that you can name any person or organization you want as the beneficiary of your retirement plan or IRA. However, when determining how your retirement plan assets should be distributed after your death, only designated beneficiaries are taken into account. (See Chapter 6 for more information about designated beneficiaries.) If one or more of your named beneficiaries is not a designated beneficiary, you are deemed to have no designated beneficiary and distributions must be accelerated.

Helpful Terms

Annuity. A contract, sold by an insurance company, that promises to make monthly, quarterly, semiannual, or annual payments for life or for a specified period of time.

Contingent beneficiary. A person or entity who is entitled to receive the benefits of a retirement plan or IRA only if and when a specific event occurs, such as the death of a primary beneficiary.

Deferral period. The number of years over which distributions from a retirement plan or IRA can be spread.

Disclaimer. A renunciation of or a refusal to accept property to which a person is entitled by gift, by law, or under the terms of a will or a trust.

Distribution. A payout of property (such as shares of stock) or cash from a retirement plan or IRA to the participant or a beneficiary.

Estate. All property that a person owns.

Irrevocable trust. A trust that cannot be changed or terminated by the person who created it. Once assets are transferred to an irrevocable trust, the assets are subject to the terms of the trust for as long as the trust exists.

Primary beneficiary. A person or entity entitled to receive benefits from a retirement plan or IRA upon the death of the original participant.

Revocable trust. A trust whose terms allow the creator of the trust to alter its provisions, cancel it, or remove some or all of the property from the trust and return the property to the creator.

Term certain. A fixed, identifiable period, such as a specific number of years. For example, a retirement plan that is distributable over a term certain of 20 years must be completely liquidated after 20 years.

Deadline for Determining Designated Beneficiary

The designated beneficiary of your retirement plan is determined as of September 30 of the year after your death. Although the determination date occurs after you die, this doesn't mean that someone can come along and name beneficiaries of your retirement plan after your death. If you fail to name any beneficiary of your retirement plan, you generally will be deemed to have no designated beneficiary.

But if nobody can add a beneficiary after your death, why, you might ask, is the deadline for determining the beneficiary so long after your death? That's the issue that we address in the following section.

Changing Beneficiaries Before the Deadline

Even though no one can add beneficiaries to your retirement plan after you die, your beneficiary could change after your death.

For example, suppose you name your spouse as primary beneficiary and your children as contingent beneficiaries. After your death, your spouse decides she has enough money to live on for the rest of her life without using any of your retirement plan assets. She might disclaim (renounce) her interest in your retirement plan. In that case, the plan assets would go to your children as contingent beneficiaries.

The IRS inserted this extended deadline into the regulations as a relief provision. It gives beneficiaries an opportunity to do some postmortem planning, whether to make administration of distributions easier or to clean up a disadvantageous situation you left behind.

For example, suppose you named your wife and your favorite charity as equal beneficiaries of your retirement account. When you die, if the charity and your spouse are still equal beneficiaries on September 30 of the year after your death, you are deemed to have no designated beneficiary (because the charity isn't a designated beneficiary) and distributions to all beneficiaries must be accelerated. This could have disastrous tax consequences for your spouse.

As a cleanup measure, however, the charity can receive its entire distribution before September 30 of the year after death, leaving only your spouse as beneficiary. Then the post-death rules apply as though your spouse were sole beneficiary of the account. This would produce a much more favorable result.

Distribution Methods

If you die before your RBD, your retirement plan benefits will be distributed using one of three methods: the life expectancy rule, the five-year rule, or a spousal rollover. Read on to learn more about each of these methods.

Life Expectancy Rule

The life expectancy rule allows your beneficiary to spread distributions over his or her life expectancy after your death, if both of the following conditions are met:

- the beneficiary of your plan or IRA as of September 30 of the year after your death is a designated beneficiary, and
- the plan itself either permits the life expectancy rule or is silent (meaning it doesn't indicate one way or another which rule should be used).

TIP

What if the plan specifies the five-year rule? Even if the plan specifies that the retirement plan assets must be distributed to the beneficiary according to the five-year rule, you might be able escape that provision of the plan by transferring the assets into an IRA. But this will work only if the plan allows such a transfer, and you complete the transfer in timely fashion. For more information about this strategy, see "Nonspouse Beneficiaries Might Not Be Stuck With the Five-Year Rule," below.

Distributions under the life expectancy rule generally must begin in the year after your death and continue until the entire account has been depleted. (Some unusual twists apply if your spouse is your beneficiary. See "Spouse Beneficiary," below.)

Five-Year Rule

The five-year rule is mandatory in cases where both of the following are true:

- you die before your RBD, and
- your retirement plan or IRA is deemed to have no designated beneficiary as of September 30 of the year after your death. (See Chapter 6 for more information about which beneficiaries qualify as designated beneficiaries.)

If the five-year rule applies, all of your retirement plan assets must be distributed within five years after your death.

TIP

Actually, it's five years plus. Practically speaking, your beneficiary has a little more than five years to withdraw the assets when the five-year rule applies. This is because the official distribution deadline is December 31 of the year containing the fifth anniversary of your death. For example, if you die on March 3 in the year 2008, your retirement plan need not be completely distributed until December 31, 2013—five years and almost ten months later.

Required Beginning Date

The five-year rule applies only if you die before your RBD. If you live past that milestone, a different set of rules will apply when you die without a designated beneficiary. If you have passed your RBD, you can forget about the five-year rule (and you should be reading Chapter 8). But be careful: It is your RBD that counts—not the year you turn 70½. For example, if your RBD is April 1, 2009, but you die on March 15, 2009, the five-year rule will apply even though you have already passed age 70½ and even if you have already taken a distribution for your first distribution year. Technically, you have not begun required distributions until you pass your RBD.

EXAMPLE: You turned 70½ in June 2008, which makes your RBD April 1, 2009. On December 30, 2008 you withdrew $6,000 from your IRA, which was the amount of your first required distribution. But then you died on March 15, 2009, before reaching your RBD. Because you died before your RBD, the five-year rule will apply even though you had already withdrawn an amount that would have satisfied your first required distribution.

Distributing the Account

The five-year rule mandates that all assets be distributed from your retirement plan by December 31 of the year containing the fifth anniversary of your death, but it places no restriction on the form of payment. This means, for example, that your beneficiary could receive the entire amount as a lump sum in the month after your death, monthly installments spread over the five-year period, or perhaps nothing at all until the December 31 deadline in the fifth year.

Although the IRS would accept any of those approaches, the retirement plan itself might have more stringent distribution requirements—and the plan controls how payments will be made. (See below for more about plan rules.) Some plans allow beneficiaries to receive installment payments or to leave the funds in the plan until the five-year period is up. If the plan requires immediate distribution of the entire account, however, then that's what your beneficiary will be stuck with.

Spousal Rollover

If your beneficiary is your spouse and if he or she is the beneficiary of your retirement plan, your spouse will generally have an alternative to the life expectancy rule or the five-year rule. That alternative is to roll over your retirement plan into an IRA in the spouse's own name. (See below for more information about spousal rollovers.)

Effect of the Retirement Plan's Rules

Although the law provides a framework for required distributions within which

retirement plans may operate, the plan's own rules can be—and usually are—more restrictive. In that case, the plan's rules govern. For example, even though the law allows a designated beneficiary to use the life expectancy rule and take distributions over his or her life expectancy, the plan itself might require that even designated beneficiaries use the five-year rule. Or sometimes the plan will allow the designated beneficiary to choose a method of distribution.

Optional Provisions

Sometimes, plans give beneficiaries a choice of which rule to use. For example, in the best of all worlds (from the taxpayer's perspective), plans would allow beneficiaries to choose between the five-year rule and the life expectancy rule. And if a beneficiary didn't have a choice and was saddled with the five-year rule, the beneficiary would certainly like to be able to choose how the assets were distributed over that five-year period.

TIP

If you do get to choose. Generally, a beneficiary who has the option to use the life expectancy rule would choose it and not the five-year rule. However, if a beneficiary failed to take a timely distribution under the life expectancy rule, he or she might want to fall back on the five-year rule to avoid the hefty penalty for failing to take a required distribution.

But this isn't the best of worlds, and plan administrators don't always put taxpayers' needs first. In fact, some plans offer no options at all to beneficiaries, instead mandating distribution of the entire plan in the year of death. At the other extreme, some plans might distribute nothing at all until the end of the fifth year.

Furthermore, many plans have different policies for different beneficiaries. For example, the terms of a plan might require that nonspouse beneficiaries receive a distribution of the entire plan immediately following the participant's death (without the five-year grace period), but allow a spouse beneficiary to use the life expectancy rule.

Default Provisions

If the plan is resolutely silent on how distributions will occur after the death of the plan participant, certain default provisions kick in by law. Specifically, if the plan has a designated beneficiary, the life expectancy rule applies by default.

Spouse Beneficiary

If your spouse is the beneficiary of your retirement plan, he or she has two options for taking distributions from your retirement plan after your death. Your spouse can:

- leave the account in your name and use the life expectancy rule to take distributions over his or her own life

expectancy beginning in the year you would have been 70½—or the year after your death if that is later, or
- roll over the plan or IRA into a plan or an IRA in his or her own name.

Read the section immediately below to learn more about these options.

CAUTION

For purposes of this section, we assume that the spouse was the sole beneficiary of the retirement plan. The rules change if a spouse is one of several beneficiaries. (See "Multiple Beneficiaries, One Account," below.)

Life Expectancy Rule

If your spouse is the beneficiary of your retirement account, your spouse can wait until the year you would have turned 70½ to begin receiving required distributions. This additional deferral—until the deceased participant would have turned 70½—is available only to a spouse. Your spouse can choose this option even if he or she has already turned 70½ as long as he or she leaves the account in your name.

If your spouse chooses the life expectancy rule, he or she would use the following steps to compute the first required distribution from your account:

Step One: Determine the account balance. Your spouse must use your retirement account balance as of December 31 of the year before you would have turned 70½ to compute the first required distribution.

Step Two: Determine the ADP.

Using his or her age in the year you would have turned 70½, your spouse must look up the appropriate life expectancy factor in Table I (see Appendix B). That factor is the applicable distribution period—or ADP— for the first year.

Step Three: Calculate the required distribution.

To determine the first required distribution, your spouse divides the account balance by the ADP—which is Step One divided by Step Two. The resulting amount must be distributed by December 31 of the year you would have turned 70½.

> **EXAMPLE:** Ed was born March 15, 1939 and died on June 1, 2006, at age 67—before reaching his RBD. His wife, Bertha, is the beneficiary of his retirement plan. Bertha intends to use the life expectancy rule to determine required distributions from the plan. She wants to defer distributions until 2009—the year Ed would have turned 70½. To calculate the first required distribution, she must do the following:

> Step One: To compute the required distribution, Bertha must use the account balance as of December 31, 2008—the year before Ed would have turned 70½. That amount is $100,000.

> Step Two: Bertha will be age 68 on her birthday in 2009—the year Ed would have turned 70½. Her single life expectancy at age 68 (from Table I in Appendix B) is 18.6 years.

> Step Three: Bertha's first required distribution is $100,000 ÷ 18.6 (Step One ÷ Step Two), or $5,376. Bertha must withdraw at least that amount by December 31, 2009.

For the second and future years, your spouse would find the ADP from Table I each year, using his or her age for the current year. Your spouse would then divide the account balance as of December 31 of the previous year by the new ADP.

> **EXAMPLE:** Continuing the example, above, for the year 2010, Bertha will use the December 31, 2009 balance of Ed's retirement account and divide it by her ADP. The ADP for age 69 (from Table I) is 17.8.

 TIP

If you turned 70½ in the year of your death. Remember, if you turned 70½ (or would have turned 70½) in the same year that you died, your spouse does not have to begin distributions that same year. Instead, he or she can delay the start of distributions until the year after your death. In that case, your spouse would use the account balance as of December 31 of the year of your death and his or her age in the year after your death to compute the first required distribution.

Rollover

If a spouse is the beneficiary of a retirement plan or IRA, the spouse has another quite valuable deferral option. The spouse can roll over the plan assets into a plan or IRA of his or her own. (Note: This option is available only to a spouse.)

If your plan is not an IRA, the only way your spouse can make the plan his or her own is by rolling the plan assets over into an IRA or plan in the spouse's own name.

But if your retirement plan is an IRA, your spouse has several ways to make your IRA her own. Your spouse can do so by:

- rolling over the assets into a new or preexisting IRA or plan in the spouse's own name
- failing to take one of your post-death required distributions at the proper time, or
- contributing additional amounts of his or her own to your IRA.

Convert to Spouse's Plan or IRA by Rollover

A spouse can roll over a deceased participant's IRA into a plan or IRA in the spouse's own name. This method is the cleanest because there is a clear record of what happened and when.

Once the account becomes the spouse's own, it belongs to the spouse in every way —as though he or she were the original owner. Required distributions will begin when the spouse reaches his or her own RBD and will be based on the ADP for the spouse's age at that time.

EXAMPLE: Grace died in 2003 at the age of 69. Her husband, George, was the beneficiary of her IRA, and he turned 64 on February 14, 2003. At the end of 2003, George rolled over Grace's IRA into an IRA in his own name. George will not need to begin required distributions until his own RBD, which is April 1 of the year after he turns 70½, or April 1, 2010.

If a surviving spouse rolls over a deceased participant's IRA into a new IRA in the spouse's name, the spouse may name a new beneficiary of his or her own choosing.

EXAMPLE: Your husband is the primary beneficiary of your IRA, and your brother will inherit the plan if your husband dies before you do. But let's say you predecease your husband and he decides to roll over your IRA into an IRA in his own name. He completes the rollover and names his sister as primary beneficiary. His action is completely legal under the rollover rules. Once he rolls over your IRA, the assets are his. His sister will receive the IRA assets; your brother will not.

Your spouse may roll over your retirement plan and name a new beneficiary after you die, even if your spouse has passed his or her RBD at the time of the rollover. In that case, your spouse's RBD for purposes of the new IRA is December 31 of the year of the rollover, and required distributions must begin at that time.

EXAMPLE: You died in 2007 at the age of 69. Your wife turned 72 in 2007. In March 2008, she rolled over your retirement plan into an IRA in her name and designated your children as beneficiaries. Your wife must take her first required distribution by December 31, 2008.

Convert to Spouse's IRA by Failing to Take Required Distribution

If you die before your RBD, and your spouse fails to take a required distribution under the life expectancy rule—either by December 31 of the year after your death or by December 31 of the year you would have been 70½—your spouse is deemed to have made an election to treat your IRA as his or her own. The IRA becomes your spouse's own on December 31 of the year of the failure, and your spouse will not be required to take a distribution until his or her own RBD.

EXAMPLE: Your wife died in the year 2004 at age 63. You were the beneficiary of her IRA. You did not take any distributions in 2005, nor had you taken any distributions by December 31, 2011—the year your wife would have been 70½. Therefore, by missing all of the deadlines for taking a distribution from your wife's retirement account, the account is deemed to be your own as of December 31, 2011.

Timing

The IRS imposes no deadline for a spouse to roll over a deceased participant's retirement plan into the spouse's own plan or IRA. That means a spouse can begin taking distributions as a beneficiary under the life expectancy rule and then some years later roll over the assets into a plan or IRA of the spouse's own.

As a practical matter, if a spouse is past age 59½ and intends to roll over a participant's retirement plan, there is nothing to be gained from waiting. If the spouse needs money, the spouse can take it freely from the IRA even after rolling it over, because there is no penalty for taking distributions after age 59½.

If the spouse is younger than 59½, however, free use of the IRA funds could be dicey. Recall that one of the exceptions to the early distribution tax is a distribution to a beneficiary after the death of the original participant. (See Chapter 3 for more information on the early distribution tax.) But that particular exception is not available to a spouse after the spouse rolls over the deceased person's plan into a plan or IRA in the spouse's name. Once it is rolled over, it is the spouse's, and because the spouse is still alive, the after-death exception does not apply. Thus, the spouse must generally postpone distributions until age 59½ to avoid the early distribution tax.

Consequently, if the spouse is younger than 59½ and needs to use the retirement plan money to live on, the spouse might be better off leaving the plan or IRA in the name of the deceased so that the after-death exception can be used. The one disadvantage of this approach is that, according to at least one IRS private letter ruling, once a spouse invokes the after-death exception to the early distribution tax, the spouse forever forfeits the right to roll over the account into a plan or IRA of the spouse's own.

Convert to Roth IRA

If a spouse qualifies, he or she may also convert the retirement plan (but not an IRA) directly to a Roth IRA in the spouse's own name. If this option is chosen, the spouse will generally pay income tax on the pretax converted amounts in the year of conversion, but because the Roth IRA will be in the spouse's name, no further distributions will be required during the spouse's lifetime. When the spouse dies, the assets will be distributed to the beneficiaries that the spouse designated when the Roth IRA was established. See

Chapter 9 for more information about converting to a Roth IRA and taking distributions from Roth IRAs.

If the spouse is the beneficiary of a traditional IRA (rather than an employer's plan, for example), in order to convert the traditional IRA to a Roth IRA, the spouse must first roll over the plan assets to a traditional IRA in his or her own name. Once the assets are in the spouse's IRA, he or she may convert them to a Roth IRA, also in the spouse's name.

Death of Spouse Beneficiary

If a spouse beneficiary inherits a retirement plan or IRA and begins taking required distributions on December 31 of the year after the participant's death (or December 31 of the year the deceased participant would have turned 70½) but dies before all assets of the retirement account are distributed, the spouse's beneficiary must take distributions in the following way:

- In the year of the spouse's death, the spouse's beneficiary will divide the account balance as of December 31 of the year before the spouse's death by the ADP for the spouse in the year of the spouse's death (using the spouse's age on his or her birthday in the year of death and looking up the respective ADP in Table I in Appendix B).
- In the second year and beyond, the spouse's beneficiary will reduce the ADP determined in the previous

paragraph by one and divide it into the account balance as of the previous December 31. The computation continues in this way each year until the entire account is depleted.

EXAMPLE: You died in 2005 at age 69. Your wife was the beneficiary of your IRA and began taking required distributions from your IRA in 2006. She died in 2008. She would have been 64 on her birthday. Her sister is the sole beneficiary of her estate. On December 31, 2007 the balance in the IRA was $60,000. Your wife's ADP in 2008 (for age 64) is 21.8 (from Table I). The required distribution for 2008 is $2,752 ($60,000 ÷ 21.8).

In the second year—2009—the ADP will be reduced by one. On December 31, 2008 the balance in the IRA was $63,000. The ADP for 2009 is 20.8 (which is 21.8 – 1). Therefore, the sister's required distribution for 2009 is $3,029 ($63,000 ÷ 20.8).

If a spouse beneficiary dies after the participant, but before beginning required distributions under the life expectancy rule (and before rolling over the account into an IRA in the spouse's own name), then the following rules apply:

- In general, the life expectancy rule or the five-year rule will apply to the spouse's beneficiary as though the spouse had been the original participant. Specifically, the age of the spouse's beneficiary will determine how required distributions are computed under the life expectancy rule. (If the spouse remarries and names his or her new spouse as beneficiary, however, the new spouse will be treated as a nonspouse beneficiary. See the next bullet point.)

EXAMPLE: You die in 2005 at age 65. Your wife is the beneficiary of your retirement plan account and therefore is not required to begin distributions until you would have been age 70½ (in the year 2010). Her sister is the sole beneficiary of your wife's estate. Your wife died in 2008 before beginning required distributions from your retirement account. The life expectancy rule will apply to distributions to her sister, the beneficiary. Under the life expectancy rule, your wife's sister must begin distributions by December 31, 2009, and take them over her life expectancy. For her first distribution, she would use her age in 2009 and find the ADP in Table I. For subsequent years, she would reduce the ADP by one.

- If your spouse remarried and named his or her new spouse as beneficiary, the special additional deferral option, described above, is not available to the new spouse beneficiary. Specifically, the spouse's new wife or husband is not permitted to wait until the spouse would have been 70½ to begin required distributions. The spouse's beneficiary is simply treated as a nonspouse and is subject to the rules in the previous bullet point.

EXAMPLE: You die in 2005 at age 65. Your wife is the beneficiary of your retirement plan account and therefore is not required to begin distributions until you would have been age 70½ (in 2010). Your wife remarried in 2007 and named her new husband as beneficiary of her entire estate. She died in 2008 before beginning required distributions from your retirement account. The life expectancy rule applies and your wife's new husband must begin distributions by December 31, 2009, and take them over his life expectancy. He is not entitled to use the special deferral option of a spouse, however. He may not wait until his spouse (your wife) would have been 70½ to begin distributions.

Nonspouse Beneficiary

As a participant in a retirement plan, or as the spouse of a participant, it is easy to take for granted the special privileges, exceptions, and additional distribution options the Tax Code offers. But when the beneficiary is a nonspouse beneficiary, that person typically has only one option—the life expectancy rule.

CAUTION

If there is more than one beneficiary. The rules in this section apply if there is only one beneficiary named on the account. If there is more than one beneficiary, a different set of rules applies. The multiple beneficiary rules are discussed later in this chapter.

Life Expectancy Rule

The law allows a nonspouse beneficiary to use the life expectancy rule to calculate required distributions after the plan participant's death. Those distributions must begin no later than December 31 of the year after the participant's death. No additional deferral is permitted.

Don't forget, however, to check the plan to see what it says. Remember: When the plan rules are more restrictive than the law, the plan controls. For example, the plan can require that benefits be paid out according to the five-year rule, in which case the beneficiary is stuck with it. But see the tip, below, for a possible escape hatch. On the other hand, if the plan is silent on post-death distributions, the life expectancy rule applies by default.

EXAMPLE: You died on March 15, 2008, before reaching your RBD. Your son is the beneficiary of your retirement plan, and he turns 48 in 2009. Your account was valued at $100,000 on December 31, 2008. Your son will use the life expectancy rule to compute required distributions.

Step One: To compute the first payment, your son must use the account balance as of December 31, 2008 the year of your death. That amount is $100,000.

Step Two: Your son will be age 48 on his birthday in the year after your death (2009). His single life expectancy—or ADP—at age 48 (from Table I in Appendix B) is 36.0 years.

Step Three: Your son's first required distribution is $100,000 ÷ 36.0 (Step One ÷ Step Two) or $2,778. Your son must withdraw at least that amount by December 31, 2009.

For distributions in years after the first year, a nonspouse beneficiary must reduce the previous ADP by one. A nonspouse beneficiary is not permitted to use Table I for any year but the first year of required distributions.

EXAMPLE: Continuing the above example, for the year 2010, your son will use the December 31, 2009 balance of your retirement account and divide it by the new ADP, which is 35.0 (36.0 – 1).

Remember, too, that a beneficiary can always take more than the minimum amount each year, but not less.

Rollover

The law also allows a nonspouse beneficiary to transfer the assets of an inherited retirement plan into a new inherited IRA, as long as the retirement plan itself permits the transfer. The new inherited IRA must be established in the name of the deceased and the assets must be transferred directly from the plan trustee to the custodian of the new IRA. The beneficiary may not take possession of the funds at any time or those funds will be deemed distributed and taxable.

A nonspouse beneficiary is never permitted to roll over a deceased person's retirement plan or IRA into the beneficiary's own IRA. If the beneficiary attempts to do so, the entire rollover could be considered a taxable distribution and an excess contribution to an IRA—and it would be subject to penalties. Even if the excess contribution is corrected, the retirement plan assets cannot be redeposited into the deceased participant's account. Consequently, the beneficiary will owe income tax on the entire amount, whether or not penalties are assessed.

A nonspouse beneficiary must leave the retirement account in the name of the deceased participant (or transfer the account into an IRA in the name of the deceased) until the account is completely

Nonspouse Beneficiaries Might Not Be Stuck With the Five-Year Rule

Generally, nonspouse beneficiaries may use the life expectancy rule when taking distributions from an inherited retirement plan. However, if the plan itself requires that distributions to nonspouse beneficiaries be paid out according to the five-year rule, the beneficiary will be bound by the rules of the plan—unless the plan documents contain a provision that allows the beneficiary to transfer the plan's assets into an inherited IRA. If so, the beneficiary might be able to get out from under the five-year rule, depending on when the transfer actually occurs. Specifically,

- If the beneficiary transfers the assets in the year of death into an inherited IRA in the decedent's name, the beneficiary may transfer all of the assets and then begin taking distributions over the beneficiary's life expectancy beginning in the year after death.
- If the transfer to the inherited IRA occurs in the year after death, the beneficiary may transfer all but the required distribution amount for the year after death. In subsequent years, the beneficiary will take distributions based on his or her life expectancy in the year after death reduced by one each subsequent year (as described under the life expectancy rule, above).
- In the second, third, and fourth years after the year of death, the transfer might be permitted, but the five-year rule will still apply. In other words, the transfer must be completed by December 31 of the year after death in order for the beneficiary to be able to use the life expectancy rule. If the transfer is completed in the second through fourth years, the beneficiary may transfer the entire amount (without taking any required distributions), but then the inherited IRA to which the assets were transferred must be distributed in its entirety by December 31 of the fifth year after death.
- And finally, no transfer will be permitted during the fifth year after the year of death. Instead, the retirement plan must be distributed to the beneficiary by December 31 of that year and the beneficiary must pay income tax on the entire distribution.

distributed under the life expectancy rule (or more rapidly).

Convert to a Roth IRA

The same rule, described above, that would allow a nonspouse beneficiary to transfer an inherited retirement plan (an employer plan) into an IRA in the decedent's name would also allow the beneficiary to transfer the plan assets into a new inherited Roth IRA in the decedent's name. If the beneficiary chooses this action, the transfer constitutes a conversion from a retirement plan to a Roth IRA, and the following rules would apply:

- The beneficiary may take this action only if the plan itself permits such a transfer.
- The beneficiary may convert the plan to a Roth IRA only if the beneficiary qualifies. For 2009, that means the beneficiary's modified AGI cannot exceed $100,000. And if the beneficiary is married, he or she must file jointly with his or her spouse in the year of the conversion. For 2010 and beyond, there are no income or filing status restrictions on converting to a Roth IRA.
- The beneficiary must accomplish the conversion by means of a trustee-to-trustee transfer, which means the funds must go directly from the trustee of the decedent's retirement plan to the custodian of the new inherited IRA.

- The new inherited IRA must be in the name of the decedent, for the benefit of the beneficiary (see "Name on Account," below).
- The beneficiary must pay income tax on the pretax portion of the amount that is transferred from the retirement plan to the new inherited Roth IRA. The income tax will generally be due with the tax return for the year of the conversion. (For conversions that occur in 2010 only, you will be able to pay the tax liability over two years, beginning in 2011.)
- The beneficiary must take required distributions from the inherited Roth IRA according to the same schedule that would apply to an inherited retirement plan or to an inherited traditional IRA.

Note that if a nonspouse beneficiary inherits an IRA instead of a retirement plan (an employer plan), the beneficiary does not have the option to convert the traditional inherited IRA into a Roth IRA.

For more information about converting retirement plan assets to a Roth IRA and taking distributions from Roth IRAs, see Chapter 9.

Death of Nonspouse Beneficiary

If a nonspouse beneficiary dies after the participant has died, but before the retirement plan has been completely distributed, the distribution method remains the same. For example, if distributions were made under the life expectancy rule, distributions will still be made over the life expectancy of the deceased beneficiary, using the beneficiary's age on his or her birthday in the year after the participant's death, reduced by one in each subsequent year.

> **EXAMPLE:** Sara named her brother, Archie, as beneficiary of her retirement plan. She died in 2009 at the age of 68. Archie intended to begin taking distributions over his life expectancy beginning in 2010. He would have turned 55 on March 1, 2010, but he died on February 15, 2010. Nonetheless, distributions will be made to his beneficiary as though he were still alive. Archie's ADP at age 55 would have been 29.6 years (from Table I). The ADP will be reduced by one each year until the entire account is distributed.

If the plan had required the beneficiary to use the five-year rule, the entire account must still be distributed by December 31 of the year containing the fifth anniversary of the original participant's death, even though the beneficiary has since died.

TIP

Who is the beneficiary's beneficiary? When a primary beneficiary dies after the original participant has died but before all the retirement plan assets have been distributed, where does the remainder go? The answer depends on the laws of your state. If the primary beneficiary had designated a beneficiary, the path is clear. If not, typically, the retirement plan will be distributed according to the terms of the primary beneficiary's will. In the absence of a will, the assets would be distributed to the heirs of the primary beneficiary according to state law.

No Designated Beneficiary

If you have no designated beneficiary for your retirement account, then payout options at your death are restricted. Recall that a designated beneficiary must usually be a natural person, although it may also be a special type of trust. (See Chapter 6 for more information about designated beneficiaries.) And although you are permitted to name any beneficiary you choose, whether a person or an entity, some privileges are reserved for beneficiaries that qualify as designated beneficiaries.

Five-Year Rule

If the beneficiary of your retirement plan is not a designated beneficiary and if you die before your RBD, the five-year rule applies and the entire account must be distributed by December 31 of the year containing the fifth anniversary of your death.

No Life Expectancy Rule

If your beneficiary is not a designated beneficiary, the life expectancy rule is never an option under any circumstances.

The five-year rule is mandatory, and all of the assets in the plan must be distributed by December 31 of the year containing the fifth anniversary of your death.

 TIP

The law allows installments. Even if the life expectancy rule is not an option, it is still permissible for the beneficiary to take distributions in installments over the five-year period, if the plan will allow it.

Multiple Beneficiaries, Separate Accounts

If you have several IRAs or retirement plans, each with a different beneficiary, then each plan is treated separately for purposes of the required distribution rules. You are not considered to have multiple beneficiaries.

Even if you do name multiple beneficiaries of a single retirement plan, your beneficiaries might still be deemed to have separate accounts. If the plan administrator or custodian agrees to do so, he or she can segregate each beneficiary's share and treat each as a separate account payable to one beneficiary. And even if the administrator does not segregate the shares, the shares may be treated as separate accounts if the administrator or custodian sets up separate accounting procedures (under which, for example, investment gains and losses are allocated to beneficiaries on a *pro rata* basis). Under either of these scenarios,

each beneficiary could take distributions over his or her own life expectancy after your death without being subject to the multiple beneficiary rules. (See below for more information about multiple beneficiaries with one account.)

 CAUTION

Don't count on administrators allowing separate accounting. As a practical matter, many qualified plan administrators are reluctant to shoulder the burden of separate accounting or even to physically split the account. Consequently, the beneficiaries may be stuck with the multiple beneficiary/one account rules described in the next section. IRA custodians, too, are often unwilling to provide a separate accounting for each beneficiary when multiple beneficiaries are named on one account. In the case of an IRA, however, there is nothing to prevent you from splitting the account during your lifetime into separate IRAs, one for each beneficiary. And in most cases, the account can be split after your death, as well.

Multiple Beneficiaries, One Account

The rules change significantly if there is more than one beneficiary of a single retirement account. Bear in mind, the date for determining the beneficiaries is September 30 of the year following your death. If on that date all beneficiaries are designated beneficiaries, then they have until December 31 to split the account so that each beneficiary gets his or her separate share. (See below for more about splitting accounts.) If the accounts are split in timely fashion, the required distribution rules apply separately to each share or account. Then, for example, each beneficiary could use his or her own life expectancy to compute required distributions.

 CAUTION

This won't work if one or more beneficiaries is not a designated beneficiary. Splitting accounts in this manner will work only if all beneficiaries are designated beneficiaries as of September 30 of the year after your death. If on that date there are multiple beneficiaries named on the account and even one of them fails to qualify as a designated beneficiary, then you are deemed to have no designated beneficiary and the five-year rule will apply.

But let's assume that multiple designated beneficiaries remain on the account through December 31 of the year after your death. What are the consequences?

First of all, the beneficiaries are not free to use their own life expectancies to take distribution of their respective shares. Also, a spouse might lose some special privileges if both your spouse and child are beneficiaries of a single account.

When you have multiple beneficiaries, for purposes of the life expectancy rule and the five-year rule, all beneficiaries are treated as nonspouse beneficiaries, even if

one of them is your spouse. As a result, the most restrictive rules—those that generally produce the worst result—will apply to all beneficiaries. For example, if you name your spouse and your children, the beneficiaries must choose from the options available to your children because children have fewer options than spouses.

Life Expectancy Rule

The life expectancy rule still applies when there are multiple beneficiaries on a single account (as long as the plan does not require accelerated payments). But the least favorable distribution period is the one your beneficiaries must use: The account must be distributed over the single life expectancy of the oldest beneficiary. This will yield the largest distribution and deplete the account most rapidly—exactly what Congress wants. The oldest beneficiary's life expectancy is determined (from Table I) as of his or her age in the first distribution year—the year after your death. Once the distribution amount is calculated and withdrawn, it is divided among the beneficiaries in proportion to their interest in the account.

EXAMPLE: You name your mother and your three children as equal beneficiaries of your retirement plan. You die in 2009. Under the terms of the plan, your beneficiaries are permitted to use the life expectancy rule when distributing your retirement account. Because your mother is the oldest beneficiary, the account must be distributed over her life expectancy. She will turn 85 in 2010, the first distribution year. Her life expectancy—or ADP—at that time will be 7.6 years (from Table I). To compute the first distribution, your beneficiaries must divide the December 31, 2009 account balance by 7.6. That amount will then be distributed and divided equally among your mother and your three children. Each will get a fourth. The ADP will drop by one each subsequent year, and the account will be completely distributed in just eight years.

Five-Year Rule

Again, it's important to remember that the plan can require that distributions be made according to the five-year rule. If the plan provides that the five-year rule applies to nonspouse beneficiaries, but the life expectancy rule is available for a spouse, the spouse is nonetheless prohibited from using the life expectancy rule if the spouse is one of multiple beneficiaries.

Splitting Accounts After Death

If you die before your required beginning date having named multiple beneficiaries of your single retirement account, and as of September 30 of the year after your death all beneficiaries are designated beneficia-ries, your beneficiaries have until December 31 of the year after your death to separate their respective shares. If they complete the separation in time, the distribution rules will apply separately to each beneficiary and his or her respective share.

As we explained above, the biggest benefit will be that each beneficiary will be able to use his or her own life expectancy to calculate distributions from his or her share. Furthermore, the separation will give each beneficiary autonomy over investment decisions and will also simplify accounting and other record keeping. As long as the plan itself permits the separation, the law won't prevent it.

One cautionary note: Beneficiaries may use their own life expectancies beginning in the year after the accounts are separated. So if the accounts are separated in the year after death, the required distribution for that year must be based on the life expectancy of the oldest beneficiary (presumably because there were, in fact, multiple beneficiaries named on the account for part of the year). Confused? Here's an example.

> **EXAMPLE:** You named your mother, Josephine, and your three children, Holly, Herman, and Hank, as equal beneficiaries of your retirement plan. You died in 2009. In March 2010, your mother and the three children instructed the custodian to split your IRA into four separate but equal IRAs. All of the new IRAs remain in your name, but one

names your mother as beneficiary, one names Holly, one names Herman, and one names Hank. For the year 2010 (the year of the split), the beneficiaries must use your mother's life expectancy to compute required distributions. But then beginning in 2011 (the year after the split), each beneficiary can take required distributions from his or her share of the IRA over his or her own life expectancy.

TIP

Splitting the account in the year of death. If, in the above example, the account were split in 2009 (the year of death), each beneficiary could use his or her own life expectancy to compute the 2010 required distribution (as well as future distributions) from his or her share.

CAUTION

If you name a trust as beneficiary. Splitting the account will not work when a trust is named beneficiary of your retirement account and the trust itself has multiple beneficiaries. (See "Trust Beneficiary," below, for more information.)

Transfer

When separating each beneficiary's share into a separate account after your death, assets must be transferred directly from the trustee or custodian of the original single plan account to the trustee or custodian of each separate account. The beneficiary must not have control of the funds at any time. If the beneficiary is deemed to have control, the IRS will consider the assets fully distributed and fully taxable in the current year.

Furthermore, in the case of nonspouse beneficiaries, the account must remain in the name of the deceased, so it cannot be transferred to one or more of the beneficiaries' existing retirement plans or even into a new retirement account in a beneficiary's name. If a spouse is one of the beneficiaries, however, the spouse could presumably separate his or her share and roll it over to either an existing or a new IRA in the spouse's name.

Name on Account

When transferring a portion of the plan assets to a new account, the IRS requires that the new account also be in the original participant's name. But financial institutions generally do not like to maintain accounts, let alone set up new ones, in the name of a deceased person. To accommodate both the IRS requirements and their own internal accounting procedures, many custodians construct account titles that identify both the original participant (now deceased) and the beneficiary who is to receive distributions.

> **EXAMPLE:** Joe Corpus died leaving a substantial IRA equally to his three children, Dan, Irwin, and Bruce. The children want to split the IRA into three separate IRAs so that each can manage his own investments. The IRA custodian set up three new IRA

accounts in Joe's name and transferred a third of Joe's original IRA into each one. The title on Dan's account reads: "Joe Corpus, Deceased, for the benefit of (or FBO) Dan Corpus." The other two accounts are titled "Joe Corpus, Deceased, FBO Irwin Corpus" and "Joe Corpus, Deceased, FBO Bruce Corpus."

Reporting Requirements

The IRS has issued what is called a "revenue procedure" outlining a set of reporting requirements that IRA custodians must adhere to after an IRA participant dies. The custodian must file IRS Form 5498 (you can find a sample in Appendix A) for each beneficiary. The form reports the name of the original owner, the name of the beneficiary, the beneficiary's tax ID or Social Security number, and the value of the beneficiary's share of the IRA as of the end of the year.

With this information, the IRS can trace the source of the IRA for income tax purposes and determine who is liable for the deferred tax. The form must be filed every year until the account is depleted.

CAUTION

Nonspouse beneficiaries, beware! Some nonspouse beneficiaries and, unfortunately, even some custodians are under the mistaken impression that a beneficiary may roll over a deceased participant's retirement plan into an IRA in the beneficiary's own name. This option, however, is available only to a spouse beneficiary. Nonspouse beneficiaries are never permitted to roll over retirement plan assets into a new or existing IRA in their own names.

Choosing a Distribution Option

As we explained above, the effect of naming multiple beneficiaries of one retirement plan account (assuming the account is not split by December 31 of the year after death) is to limit the deferral period to the life expectancy of the oldest beneficiary. As long as the plan permits, however, there is nothing to prevent one beneficiary from accelerating distributions of his or her share while the remaining beneficiaries use the life expectancy rule. The remaining beneficiaries' deferral period would be limited to the life expectancy of the oldest, even if the oldest had already withdrawn some or all of his or her share.

> **EXAMPLE:** Mary, Paul, and Peter inherited an IRA from their father, Jake. The children had not split the account by December 31 of the year after Jake's death. Now, Mary, the oldest child, wants to take her share and use it to buy a house. The boys don't need the money right now and want to take their portions out slowly, spreading distributions over as many years as possible. Mary may take her

share outright, and the boys may continue to spread distribution of their shares over Mary's life expectancy.

When a Spouse Is One of the Beneficiaries

If your spouse is one of multiple beneficiaries of your retirement account, your spouse loses the option to defer distributions until you would have been 70½. Also, even if your spouse is the oldest beneficiary, your spouse would not be permitted to look up his or her ADP in the Single Life Table (Table I) each year. Instead, your spouse would look up his or her ADP in the year after death (using Table I), but in subsequent years, would reduce the ADP by one each year.

If the account is an IRA, your spouse also would lose the option to make the IRA her own by failing to take a required distribution or by making a contribution of her own. However, she can still roll over any distribution she receives into an IRA in her own name, whether or not she is the sole beneficiary of your retirement account.

A spouse is the sole beneficiary of your retirement account if he or she is the sole beneficiary on September 30 of the year after your death. If your spouse is one of several designated beneficiaries (see immediately below) as of September 30, all is not lost. If your spouse's share is then separated on or before December 31 of the year after death, making your spouse the sole beneficiary of his or her share, then your spouse is deemed to be the sole

beneficiary of his or her share, and all the special privileges accorded a spouse-beneficiary would apply to that separate share.

Designated and Nondesignated Beneficiaries

If as of September 30 of the year after your death any one of the beneficiaries of your retirement account is not a designated beneficiary, the account is deemed to have no designated beneficiary, even if one or more of the other beneficiaries on the account would otherwise be a designated beneficiary. If the account is deemed to have no designated beneficiary, the life expectancy rule is not available. Instead, the assets must be distributed under the five-year rule. Many a charitably inclined taxpayer, wanting to leave a portion of his or her retirement plan to charity and a portion to a spouse or child, has been blindsided by this unfavorable application of the rules.

> **EXAMPLE:** Paul named his son and the American Cancer Society as equal beneficiaries of his IRA. Paul died in 2008. The beneficiaries did not get around to splitting the account or paying out the charity's portion by September 30, 2009. Because the American Cancer Society is not a natural person or a qualified trust, it is not considered a designated beneficiary. Therefore, the IRA is deemed to have no designated

beneficiary, even though Paul's son would have qualified had he been the sole beneficiary. As a result, the entire account must be distributed by December 31, 2012, with half going to Paul's son and half to the American Cancer Society.

Remember, though, this problem can be cured by separating the account or by distributing the charity's share before September 30 of the year after death.

CAUTION

All beneficiaries must be designated beneficiaries. The December 31 deadline for splitting accounts applies only if all beneficiaries are designated beneficiaries as of September 30 of the year after death.

Trust Beneficiary

Generally, a beneficiary must be a natural person to qualify as a designated beneficiary and be eligible for the life expectancy rule. The exception to this general rule applies when the beneficiary is a trust that meets certain stringent requirements. As explained in Chapter 6, if the trust satisfies all of those requirements, then the beneficiaries of the trust will be treated as designated beneficiaries for purposes of the life expectancy rule. In other words, the trustee or custodian of the retirement plan may look through the trust to find the designated beneficiary whose

life expectancy can be used to compute required distributions.

One of those requirements is to provide a copy of the trust to the trustee or custodian of your retirement plan. For purposes of post-death distributions, the trust document must be in the hands of the trustee or custodian by October 31 of the year after death.

Nonspouse Beneficiary of Trust

If you do name a trust as beneficiary and if it meets the requirements of a designated beneficiary (see Chapter 6), distributions under the life expectancy rule or the five-year rule will be computed as though there were no trust in place—as though the beneficiary of the trust had been named beneficiary of the retirement plan. Therefore, if the beneficiary of the trust is not your spouse, the life expectancy rule would apply and the beneficiary may spread required distributions over the beneficiary's life expectancy beginning in the year after your death. In any case, all distributions would go into the trust and become subject to the terms of the trust, which may or may not call for an immediate distribution to the beneficiary.

Spouse Beneficiary of Trust

If your spouse is sole beneficiary of the trust, your spouse will be treated as the designated beneficiary for purposes of the life expectancy rule. That means your

Bypass Trusts and Estate Planning

You must jump through a raft of hoops to name a trust as beneficiary of a retirement plan and feel confident that you have accomplished what you intended. Sometimes, you never do achieve a high level of confidence. So with all the risk and uncertainty, why would anyone bother?

People name trusts as beneficiaries for all kinds of reasons, and one of the most significant of those is to fund what is called a bypass trust to minimize estate taxes.

The use of trusts in estate planning to minimize estate taxes and other costs is complex, but here's a brief summary of what it means to use a retirement plan to fund a bypass trust.

The law allows each individual to leave a certain amount, called an "exclusion amount," to his or her heirs free of estate taxes. (The exclusion amount for 2009 is $3.5 million.) In addition, an individual may leave an unlimited amount to a spouse. If an individual leaves everything outright to a spouse, however, some or all of the individual's exclusion amount could be wasted.

For example, assume a husband and wife have a combined net worth of $7 million. The husband dies in January 2009 and leaves everything to his wife, never using his $3.5 million exclusion amount. Although there will be no estate taxes when the husband dies, when the wife dies, she can leave only her own exclusion amount tax free to the children. The remainder will be subject to estate taxes. If the wife dies in December 2009 and the estate is still worth $7 million, she leaves $3.5 million tax free to the children, but the remaining $3.5 million is subject to estate taxes. If the husband had given his $3.5 million to the children when he died, instead of to his spouse, the entire estate could have passed to the children tax free.

Many people choose not to give large amounts to their children outright because they don't want to risk leaving a spouse strapped for cash. That's where the bypass trust concept comes in. When the husband dies, he can direct his exclusion amount to a trust which is accessible to the wife during her lifetime and which flows to the children upon her death. Technically, the assets in the trust do not belong to the wife, so when she dies, she can give additional amounts equal to the exclusion to the children—all of it tax free.

Now, what role does the IRA or retirement plan play in all of this? For many people, a retirement plan is their most substantial asset, and a bypass trust couldn't be fully funded unless the plan assets were used. In other words, many people don't have enough assets outside the plan to put the exclusion amount into a bypass trust. But the law won't allow a trust to "own" a retirement plan, which means it is not possible to simply transfer the plan into the trust. To fund the trust, a person would have to name the trust as beneficiary so that after-death distributions from the plan would be directed into the trust every year until the trust is fully funded. The spouse could then have access to the funds once they have been distributed from the retirement plan to the trust.

spouse could take distributions over his or her life expectancy either beginning on December 31 of the year you would have been 70½ or beginning the year after your death if that is later. In either case, your spouse would use his or her age each year to find the corresponding ADP in Table I.

TIP

Your spouse cannot make your IRA her own. If you name a trust as beneficiary of your IRA, IRS regulations state that even if your spouse is the sole beneficiary of your trust, she cannot make the IRA her own, either by failing to take a required distribution or by making additional contributions. However, she might be able to receive a distribution of IRA assets from the trust and then roll them over into her own IRA. See "Trust Beneficiary and Spousal Rollovers," below.

Multiple Beneficiaries of Trust

If a trust has multiple beneficiaries and meets the criteria for looking through the trust for a designated beneficiary, then for purposes of applying the life expectancy rule, the multiple beneficiary rules described above will apply as though the individuals themselves were named beneficiaries of the retirement plan.

CAUTION

Splitting the account won't work if a trust is the beneficiary. If you have named a trust as beneficiary of your retirement plan and there are multiple beneficiaries of the trust, splitting the retirement plan into separate accounts for each beneficiary of the trust—whether it is done before or after your death—won't allow beneficiaries to use their own life expectancies to compute required distributions. The multiple beneficiary rules would still apply, and distributions would have to be taken over the life expectancy of the oldest beneficiary of the trust.

Trust Beneficiary and Spousal Rollovers

Recall that a trust is often named the beneficiary of a retirement plan in order to fund a bypass trust. Assuming the spouse is the beneficiary of the trust, distributions from the plan go into the trust when the participant dies, and then the trust makes distributions to the spouse.

But sometimes the surviving spouse discovers after the participant dies that the retirement plan assets are not needed to fund the bypass trust after all. In that case, the surviving spouse might prefer to simply roll over the retirement plan assets into his or her own IRA, name his or her own beneficiary, and begin a new schedule of required distributions.

Unfortunately, the law says that only a spouse beneficiary (and not a trust) may roll over retirement plan assets—and then only if the spouse acquires the assets directly from and by reason of the participant's death.

But taxpayers have argued that if the spouse is the sole beneficiary of the trust and can distribute all of the assets without interference from any third party, then the assets essentially pass directly from the deceased to the spouse—making the rollover within the spirit of the law.

Between 1987 and 2001, the IRS established a pattern of approving such actions in private letter rulings—despite the lack of explicit legal approval.

In final regulations issued in April 2002, however, the IRS stated specifically that a spouse cannot make a deceased participant's IRA her own if a trust is named primary beneficiary of the IRA—even if the spouse is the sole beneficiary of the trust.

Nonetheless, some practitioners believe that if the spouse has the power to distribute all assets of the trust, he or she could distribute the IRA assets to the trust and then distribute the assets from the trust to the spouse. Having done so, the spouse could then roll over the assets into an IRA of his or her own. Although this strategy is not specifically sanctioned by the IRS, some practitioners believe it will pass muster, even under the current regulations.

We think you should proceed with caution. If you name a trust as beneficiary of your retirement plan with the expectation that the spouse can fall back on a rollover, you are taking a risk.

As an alternative to taking this risk, consider naming your spouse as primary beneficiary (thus preserving the rollover opportunity) and your trust as contingent beneficiary. After your death, your spouse would have the option of disclaiming some or all of his or her interest in your retirement plan, allowing it to flow to the bypass trust. Ultimately, however, no strategy involving a trust is completely simple or safe.

Estate as Beneficiary

In cases in which an estate was named beneficiary of a retirement plan, private letter rulings issued before 2001 closely paralleled those in which a trust was named beneficiary. If the participant's spouse was the sole beneficiary of the estate, and no one had the authority to restrict the spouse's access to the estate, several IRS private letter rulings permitted the spouse to take a distribution of the plan assets and roll them over into an IRA in the spouse's name.

It is still unclear, however, how much weight these old private letter rulings will carry under the newer regulations. We believe it is safest to avoid using this strategy.

 CAUTION

Think twice before naming your estate as beneficiary. Although many people name their estate as beneficiary of their retirement plan or IRA, there is little advantage to doing so and some significant disadvantages. For example, because your estate is not a designated beneficiary, you are deemed to have no designated beneficiary for required distribution purposes. As a result, distributions could be accelerated after your death unless your spouse is the sole beneficiary of your estate and is permitted to roll over the plan assets. Relying on such an option for your spouse is risky business, however, given that the strategy has thin support from only a few IRS private letter rulings. Whatever it is you want to accomplish by naming your estate as beneficiary of your retirement plan can almost certainly be achieved through another strategy.

Annuities

If your retirement plan benefits are to be paid in the form of an annuity, whether to you or to your beneficiary, the required distribution rules must still be satisfied.

Start Date

If you die before your RBD, the date by which payments to your beneficiary must begin (the start date) depends on whether or not your beneficiary is your spouse.

If you have named a nonspouse beneficiary, the start date is December 31 of the year after your death.

If your beneficiary is your spouse, however, the start date is the later of December 31 of the year after your death or December 31 of the year you would have turned 70½.

If you had already started receiving your annuity payments and died before your RBD, payments still must satisfy the required distribution rules described below as of the start date.

Form of Payment

In order to satisfy required distribution rules, payments must be in a particular form, although the form varies with the type and terms of the annuity. (See Chapter 6 for more information about types of annuities.) After your death, your beneficiary must take his or her first payment by one of the start dates described above. That payment, however, can be a normal payment. For example, if your beneficiary intends to take monthly payments over his or her life expectancy, the first monthly payment can be paid in December of the year after your death and monthly thereafter. Your beneficiary need not take the full annual amount in December of that first year.

Irrevocable Annuity

If you had already begun receiving payments under an irrevocable annuity at the time of your death, your beneficiary must continue to receive payments with no break in the distribution schedule.

Divorce or Separation

If you were divorced or separated at some time during your life, part of your qualified plan, qualified annuity, or TDA may be payable to an alternate payee (such as a spouse, former spouse, or child) under the terms of a QDRO—a court-approved divorce or maintenance agreement. (See Chapter 2 for more information about QDROs.)

If the alternate payee's entire share has not yet been paid at the time of your death, then the alternate payee's distribution options are determined by whether or not the alternate payee's interest was held in a separate account or aggregated with the rest of your benefit.

Separate Account

If an alternate payee's share is segregated or separately accounted for (see Chapter 6 for more information about separate accounts), then the life expectancy rule applies to that share, and the alternate payee may take distributions over his or her own life expectancy, beginning no later than December 31 of the year after your death. Remember, though, the plan itself could require application of the five-year rule, in which case the alternate payee's share must be distributed by December 31 of the year containing the fifth anniversary of your death.

Spouse or Former Spouse Alternate Payee

A spouse or former spouse alternate payee has all the rights and privileges of a surviving spouse beneficiary as long as the alternate payee's share is in a separate account. The life expectancy rule would apply unless it is prohibited under the plan. Distributions may be made over the ex-spouse's life expectancy, and must begin by the later of December 31 of the year following the death of the participant or December 31 of the year the participant would have turned 70½.

And if the plan permits, the spouse or former spouse alternate payee may roll over his or her share distribution into a retirement plan or IRA in his or her own name.

Death of Alternate Payee

If the alternate payee dies before his or her interest has been completely distributed, the alternate payee's beneficiary will be treated as the designated beneficiary of the alternate payee's portion for purposes of the life expectancy rule and the five-year rule.

> **EXAMPLE:** Your former wife is entitled to one-half of your retirement plan benefits under the terms of a QDRO. Your former wife has named her brother as beneficiary of her share of the retirement plan. Your ex-wife died when you were age 60, before she had

received any portion of your retirement plan. You die a year later at the age of 62. Your beneficiary may take distribution of his or her share of the account over his or her own life expectancy. At the same time, your ex-wife's brother can receive your ex-wife's portion over his own life expectancy.

No Separate Account

If the plan administrator has not maintained a separate account for the alternate payee of your retirement plan, the beneficiary designation will determine how distributions will be made after your death. Specifically, the multiple beneficiary rules, described above, will apply. The distribution would then be divided among the alternate payee and the beneficiaries in proportion to their interests.

EXAMPLE: Your former husband is entitled to one-half of your retirement plan benefits under the terms of a QDRO. You have named your father as beneficiary of the other half. Your former husband's share has not been segregated or separately accounted for. You die an untimely death at the age of 56. Under the terms of the plan, your beneficiary will use the life expectancy rule. Because the interests of your father and your former husband are aggregated in one account, your father, as beneficiary, is the one whose life

expectancy must be used to determine required distributions. Each distribution will be split equally between your former husband and your father.

Reporting Distributions From IRAs

If you are the beneficiary of an IRA, it is up to you to compute the required distribution each year and report it on your tax return. If you were the original owner of the IRA, the custodian would be required to help you compute the proper amount. However, the law does not currently extend this benefit to beneficiaries. As a beneficiary, you will still receive a Form 5498, reporting the value of the IRA each year, but when it comes to calculating the required distribution, you're on your own.

Key Tax Code and Regulation Sections

§ 401(a)(9)

Required Distributions From Qualified Plans

§ 1.401(a)(9)

Required Distribution Regulations

§ 402(c)

Rollovers From Qualified Plans

§ 408

Individual Retirement Accounts

§ 1.408-8, A-5

Election by Spouse to Treat Decedent's
IRA as Own

Rev. Proc. 89-52

After-Death IRA Reporting Requirements

Distributions to Your Beneficiary If You Die After Age 70½

Administrative Details 171

    Name on the Account 171

    Timing of Distributions 172

    Designated Beneficiary 172

    Reporting Distributions 173

Spouse Beneficiary 173

    Year of Death 174

    Second Year and Beyond 174

    Rollover 176

    Convert to a Roth IRA 178

    Death of Spouse Beneficiary 178

Nonspouse Beneficiary 180

    Year of Death 180

    Second Year and Beyond 180

    Death of Nonspouse Beneficiary 181

    Rollover 181

    Convert to a Roth IRA 182

No Designated Beneficiary 183

Multiple Beneficiaries, Separate Accounts 183

Multiple Beneficiaries, One Account 183

    Determining the Designated Beneficiary 184

    Computing the Required Distribution 184

    Splitting Accounts 185

    When a Spouse Is One of the Beneficiaries 186

Trust Beneficiary.. 187

    Nonspouse Beneficiary of Trust 187

    Spouse Beneficiary of Trust... 187

    Multiple Beneficiaries of Trust 188

    Trust Beneficiary and Spousal Rollovers 188

Estate as Beneficiary.. 189

Annuities 190

Divorce or Separation.. 190

Who Should Read Chapter 8

SKIP AHEAD

Read this chapter if you want to know what happens to your own retirement plan after you die or if you inherit a retirement plan or IRA from someone who died after reaching age 70½ and who had already begun mandatory distributions from the plan or IRA. This chapter describes how the remainder of the account must be distributed.

Even though you are required to start taking money out of your retirement account on your required beginning date (which, for most people, is April 1 of the year after they turn 70½), the account might not be empty when you die. It might even be quite large, especially if you had been withdrawing only the minimum required amount each year—or if you die soon after your RBD. So what happens to the leftovers? The answer to that question is the subject of this chapter.

Administrative Details

Although the rules for computing required distributions after your death might vary depending on who your beneficiary is, the following administrative procedures apply almost across the board.

Name on the Account

Unless your beneficiary is your spouse, your retirement account must remain in your name until the account is entirely depleted. If a beneficiary other than your spouse attempts to change the name on the retirement plan account to his or her own name, the action could be deemed a distribution of the entire account. Worse, if the beneficiary attempts to roll over your account into the beneficiary's own IRA, not only will it be deemed a distribution, but penalties for contributing more to an IRA than is allowed may be assessed as well.

Despite the above rule, the trustee or custodian might want to retitle the account to show that you have died. This is permissible as long as the custodian complies with certain procedures for titling the account and reporting distributions. (See Chapter 7 for more information about titling accounts.)

The account can also be transferred to a new IRA as long as the new IRA is titled in the name of the deceased and the funds are transferred directly from the trustee or custodian of the original plan to the trustee or custodian of the new IRA. (See "Nonspouse Beneficiary," below, for more information.)

A special rule allows your spouse to treat your retirement plan account as his or her own. See "Spouse Beneficiary," below, to learn how this can be done.

Helpful Terms

Annuity. A contract, sold by an insurance company, that promises to make monthly, quarterly, semiannual, or annual payments for life or for a specified period of time.

Beneficiary. The person or entity entitled to receive the benefits from insurance or from trust property, such as a retirement plan or IRA.

Deferral period. The number of years over which distributions from a retirement plan or IRA can be spread.

Distribution. A payout of property (such as shares of stock) or cash from a retirement plan or IRA to the participant or a beneficiary.

Estate. All property that a person owns.

Primary beneficiary. A person or entity entitled to receive benefits from a retirement plan or IRA upon the death of the original participant.

Term certain. A fixed, identifiable period, such as a specific number of years. For example, a retirement plan that is distributable over a term certain of 20 years must be completely liquidated after 20 years.

Timing of Distributions

Once you pass your RBD, distributions from your account must continue, even after your death. There can be no hiatus in distributions. If you failed to take some or all of your required distribution in the year of your death, your beneficiary must take the remainder before the end of the year. Then your beneficiary must continue to take distributions in all subsequent years until the account is depleted.

The only exception to this rule occurs if your spouse elects to treat the account as his or her own. In that case, required distributions from the account (after the spouse makes it his or her own) will be determined as if the spouse had been the original owner of the account. (See "Spouse Beneficiary," below, for more about this strategy.)

Designated Beneficiary

Recall that you can name any person or organization you choose as the beneficiary of your retirement plan or IRA. When determining how your retirement assets should be distributed after your death, however, only designated beneficiaries are taken into account. (See Chapter 6 for more information about designated beneficiaries.) If one or more of your beneficiaries is not a designated beneficiary, you are deemed to have no designated beneficiary.

Deadline for Determining Designated Beneficiary

For purposes of computing post-death required distributions, your designated beneficiary is determined as of September 30 of the year after your death. That doesn't mean someone else can name a new beneficiary of your retirement plan after you die. In fact, no new beneficiaries can be added. Therefore, it is important that you carefully consider and then formally select a beneficiary before you die (using the plan's Designation of Beneficiary form). Not only will that beneficiary receive the assets of your plan, but his or her life expectancy will determine how quickly assets must be distributed after your death.

Changing Beneficiaries Before the Deadline

The IRS allows this extended deadline for determining beneficiaries specifically to give those beneficiaries an opportunity to do some postmortem planning—to make administration of the retirement plan easier or to clean up a disadvantageous situation you left behind. For example, suppose you name your spouse as primary beneficiary and your daughter as contingent beneficiary. After your death, your spouse might decide she has no need for the assets in your retirement plan. She might disclaim (renounce) her interest in those assets. If she does, the plan assets would go to your daughter, and your daughter's life expectancy would determine the period over which your retirement plan assets are ultimately distributed.

Reporting Distributions

If you are the beneficiary of an IRA or other retirement plan, it is up to you to compute the required distribution each year and report it on your tax return. In the case of an IRA, the custodian will send you a Form 5498, reporting the value of the IRA each year, but you are responsible for the calculation. If you had been the original owner of the IRA, the law would require the custodian to help you compute the proper amount. (See Chapter 6.) However, the law does not extend this benefit to beneficiaries.

Spouse Beneficiary

If your spouse is the beneficiary of your retirement account, he or she may take distributions under the rules described in this section.

CAUTION

For sole beneficiaries only. For purposes of this section, we assume that the spouse was the sole beneficiary of the retirement plan. The rules change if a spouse is one of several beneficiaries. (See "Multiple Beneficiaries, One Account," below, for the multiple beneficiary rules.)

Year of Death

The minimum required distribution for the year of your death will be computed in exactly the same way you would have computed it if you had lived to the end of the year. If you did not take a distribution of the required amount before your death, your spouse beneficiary must do so on your behalf by December 31 of the year of your death. In other words, your spouse would use the Uniform Lifetime Table and find the ADP for your age on your birthday in the year of your death. Then your spouse would divide the account balance as of December 31 of the previous year by the ADP.

If your spouse is more than ten years younger than you are, and if you had been using Table II (Joint and Last Survivor Table) to compute lifetime distributions, your spouse would use Table II to find the ADP in the year of your death, as well.

 CAUTION

Spouse must take required distribution for year of death. A spouse beneficiary has the option to treat a deceased participant's retirement plan as the spouse's own. Nonetheless, if you die after your RBD, your spouse must take your required distribution for the year of your death (if you had not already done so) before your spouse can make the

account his or her own. Once the account is in the spouse's name, all the required distribution rules apply as though the spouse were the original owner. (See "Rollover," below, to learn what happens when the account is rolled over or placed in the name of a surviving spouse.)

Second Year and Beyond

If your spouse is younger than you are, beginning in the second year (and assuming your spouse does not roll over the account into a retirement account in his or her own name), your spouse will use his or her own age and Table I (Single Life Table) to look up the ADP each year.

EXAMPLE: Richard died on October 14, 2007, at the age of 75. Richard's wife, Pat, was the sole beneficiary of his IRA. She was 74 in 2007. Richard had been computing required distributions using the Uniform Lifetime Table (Table III). Richard withdrew his required distribution for 2007 before he died.

To compute the required distribution for 2008, Pat uses Table I to find her ADP for her age in 2008. Pat turned 75 in 2008, so her ADP from Table I is 13.4. Pat will divide the December 31, 2007 balance of Richard's IRA by 13.4 to determine the required distribution for 2008.

In 2009, Pat turns 76. Her ADP (from Table I) is 12.7. Pat will divide the December 31, 2008 balance of Richard's IRA by 12.7 to determine the required distribution for 2009.

If your spouse is older than you, your spouse will compute required distributions using the greater of:

- your remaining life expectancy at the time of your death, reduced by one each subsequent year, or
- your spouse's life expectancy, redetermined each year using his or her age and looking up the ADP in the Single Life Table.

Because you are permitted to use the most favorable (larger) ADP, it is quite possible that your surviving spouse will start out using your life expectancy and then switch to his or her own once the ADP surpasses your remaining life expectancy. (To find your remaining life expectancy, see the life expectancy tables in Appendix B.)

EXAMPLE: You died in 2008 at age 73, after having taken your required distribution from your IRA for the year. Your spouse, who was the sole beneficiary of your IRA, turned 74 in 2008.

For 2009, the ADP is the greater of:

- your life expectancy (from the Single Life Table) in 2008, reduced by one, which is 13.8 (14.8 − 1), or
- your spouse's life expectancy in 2009 at age 75 (from the Single Life Table), which is 13.4.

Because your remaining life expectancy of 13.8 exceeds your surviving spouse's life expectancy of 13.4 in 2009, your spouse would use 13.8 to compute the required distribution for 2009.

For 2010, the ADP is the greater of:

- your life expectancy as of the year of your death reduced by one for each subsequent year, which is 12.8 (14.8 − 2), or
- your spouse's life expectancy in 2010 at age 76 (from the Single Life Table), which is 12.7.

Because your remaining life expectancy of 12.8 exceeds your surviving spouse's life expectancy in 2010, your spouse would use 12.8 to compute the required distribution for 2010.

For 2011, the ADP is the greater of:

- your life expectancy as of the year of your death reduced by one for each subsequent year, which is 11.8 (14.8 − 3), or
- your spouse's life expectancy in 2011 at age 77 (from the Single Life Table), which is 12.1.

Because your surviving spouse's life expectancy of 12.1 in 2011 now exceeds your remaining life expectancy of 11.8, your spouse would switch to using his or her own life expectancy to compute the required distribution for 2011 and beyond.

Rollover

When you die, your spouse may choose to leave your retirement plan or IRA in your name, applying all the distribution rules described above until the account has been completely liquidated.

Fortunately for your spouse, however, there is another, usually more favorable, option. Your spouse can roll over the plan assets into a plan or IRA of his or her own. (Note that this option is available only to a spouse beneficiary.)

If your plan is not an IRA, a rollover to a plan in the spouse's name is the only way to make the plan the spouse's own.

But if the retirement plan is an IRA, your spouse has several ways to make the IRA his or her own. Your spouse can do so by:

- rolling over the assets into a new or preexisting IRA or plan in the spouse's own name (see below)
- failing to take your post-death required distribution at the proper time (see below), or
- contributing additional amounts of the spouse's own to your IRA.

The following sections look at each of these in more detail.

Convert to Spouse's Plan or IRA by Rollover

Most spouses choose the rollover method because it is convenient and because it leaves a clear trail. Once the rollover is complete, the account belongs to your spouse in every way. Not only can your spouse name a new beneficiary, but your

spouse's RBD will determine when future required distributions must begin.

If your surviving spouse is not 70½ or older when he or she rolls over your retirement plan or IRA, required distributions may be discontinued until your spouse reaches his or her RBD. Then on your spouse's RBD, your spouse must begin required distributions anew, using the Uniform Lifetime Table to determine the ADP—or using Table II if your spouse has since married someone else and if the new spouse is more than ten years younger.

 CAUTION

Spouse must take a distribution in the year of death. As mentioned above, if you had not withdrawn your required distribution before your death and if your spouse wants to roll over the account into his or her own name, your spouse must withdraw the required amount for the year of your death before he or she can complete the rollover.

After you die, your spouse may roll over your retirement plan or IRA even if your spouse has passed his or her own RBD. In this case, however, there can be no hiatus in required distributions. If your spouse rolls over your IRA in the year of your death, he or she must take a distribution on your behalf (if you had not done so). The following year, your spouse must take a distribution on his or her own behalf (because it is now your spouse's IRA and his or her RBD has passed).

EXAMPLE: Richard died on October 14, 2008 at the age of 75. Richard's wife, Pat, was the sole beneficiary of his IRA. She was 74 in 2008. Richard had already withdrawn the required distribution for 2008.

On January 19, 2009 Pat opened an IRA in her own name and rolled over Richard's IRA into her new account. She named her daughter Tash as beneficiary of the new account. To determine her required distribution for 2009, Pat will use the December 31, 2008 IRA balance. She will divide that balance by the ADP for her age in 2009, which is 75. Her ADP (from the Uniform Lifetime Table—Table III), is 22.9.

Convert to Spouse's IRA by Failing to Take a Required Distribution

If you die after your RBD, and if your spouse fails to take a required distribution on your behalf in any year after the year of your death, your spouse is deemed to have made an election to treat your IRA as his or her own. (Remember that because you are past your required beginning date, your spouse must take your required distribution for the year of your death if you had not already done so.) The IRA becomes the spouse's own on December 31 of the year of the failure, and the spouse will not be required to take a distribution until his or her own RBD.

If your spouse has passed his or her own RBD, then your spouse must take a distribution in the year your spouse makes the IRA his or her own. The distribution will be based on your spouse's age in that year, and the ADP will be determined from the Uniform Lifetime Table. If your spouse has remarried by that time someone who is more than ten years younger, the ADP will be determined from Table II, using the surviving spouse's and his or her new spouse's ages.

Timing of Rollover

The income tax regulations give your spouse no deadline for converting or rolling over your retirement account to his or her own IRA after your death. Your spouse should be able to make the election at any time—even years after your death—as long as he or she continues to take timely required distributions on your behalf for as long as the account remains in your name.

As a practical matter, if a spouse is past age 59½ and intends to roll over a participant's retirement plan into the spouse's own IRA, there is nothing to be gained from waiting. If the spouse needs money, the spouse can take it freely from his or her own IRA even after rolling it over, because there is no penalty for taking distributions after age 59½.

If the spouse is younger than age 59½, however, free use of the IRA funds could be dicey. Recall that one of the exceptions to the early distribution tax is a distribution to a beneficiary after the death of the original participant. (See Chapter 3 for more information on the early distribution tax.) But that particular exception is not available to a spouse after the spouse rolls over the deceased person's plan into the spouse's own plan or IRA. Once it is rolled over, it is the spouse's IRA. Because the spouse is still alive, the after-death exception does not apply. Thus, the spouse must generally postpone distributions until age 59½ to avoid the early distribution tax.

Consequently, if the spouse is younger than age 59½ and needs to use the retirement plan money to live on, the spouse might be better off leaving the plan in the name of the deceased so that the after-death exception can be used. The one disadvantage of this approach is that, according to at least one IRS private letter ruling, once a spouse invokes the after-death exception to the early distribution tax, the spouse forever forfeits the right to roll over the account into an IRA in the spouse's own name.

Convert to a Roth IRA

If a spouse qualifies, he or she may also convert the retirement plan (but not an IRA) directly to a Roth IRA in the spouse's own name. If this option is chosen, the spouse will generally pay income tax on the pretax converted amounts in the year of conversion, but because the Roth IRA will be in the spouse's name, no further distributions will be required during the spouse's lifetime. When the spouse dies, the assets will be distributed to the beneficiaries that the spouse designated when the Roth IRA was established. See Chapter 9, for more information about converting to a Roth IRA and taking distributions from Roth IRAs.

If the spouse is beneficiary of a traditional IRA (rather than an employer's plan, for example), in order to convert the traditional IRA to a Roth IRA, the spouse must first roll over the plan assets to a traditional IRA in his or her own name. Once the assets are in the spouse's IRA, he or she may convert them to a Roth IRA, also in the spouse's name.

Death of Spouse Beneficiary

When your spouse dies, assuming your spouse did not roll over your retirement plan into a plan or IRA of his or her own, the spouse's beneficiary must continue to take distributions according to the rules discussed in this section.

Year of Spouse's Death

The spouse's beneficiary must take a distribution in the year of the spouse's death. The beneficiary will use Table I to find the ADP that corresponds to the spouse's age on his or her birthday in the year of death, and then the beneficiary will divide the account balance as of December 31 of the year before the spouse's death by the ADP for the year of death.

Second Year and Beyond

For subsequent years, the ADP is reduced by one each year. The account balance for the previous December 31 is divided by the ADP for the current year to determine the required distribution. This calculation method continues until the account is completely distributed, regardless of whether or not the spouse's beneficiary survives until the account is empty.

> **EXAMPLE:** Pierre was born on January 10, 1934 and turned 70½ in 2004. Pierre's wife, Zoe, was his designated beneficiary. She turned 68 in 2004. To compute his required distribution for 2004, Pierre used an ADP of 27.4, which he found in the Uniform Lifetime Table next to his age of 70.

2004 Distribution:

Pierre's December 31, 2003, IRA account balance was $100,000. Thus, Pierre's first required distribution (for 2004) was $3,650 ($100,000 ÷ 27.4.).

2005 Distribution:

Pierre died in 2005 before taking his required distribution. Zoe found Pierre's ADP of 26.5 (for age 71) from the Uniform Lifetime Table (Table III in Appendix B). The IRA account balance on December 31, 2004 was $106,000. The required distribution for 2005, the year of Pierre's death, was $4,030 ($106,000 ÷ 26.3).

2006 Distribution:

Zoe decided not to roll over Pierre's IRA into an IRA in her own name. The required distribution for 2006 was based on Zoe's single life expectancy. Therefore, she used Table I. Zoe turned 70 in 2006. The ADP for age 70 is 16. The December 31, 2005 IRA balance was $111,000. Therefore, the 2006 required distribution was $6,938 ($111,000 ÷ 16).

2007 Distribution:

Zoe died in 2007 before taking her required distribution. Her beneficiaries will again use Table I to find Zoe's ADP for 2007, the year of her death. The ADP for Zoe's age that year, which was 71, is 16.3. The December 31, 2006 balance of the IRA was $115,000. The required distribution is $7,055 ($115,000 ÷ 16.3).

2008 Distribution:

For the year after Zoe's death and each subsequent year, Zoe's beneficiaries must reduce the ADP for the previous year by one. Therefore, the ADP for 2008 is 15.3 (16.3 − 1). The December 31, 2007 balance of the IRA was $120,000. The required distribution is $7,843 ($120,000 ÷ 15.3).

Nonspouse Beneficiary

If the beneficiary of your retirement plan or IRA is not your spouse, distributions after your death are computed according to the rules described in this section.

 CAUTION

If there is more than one beneficiary. The rules in this section apply if there is only one beneficiary named on the account. If there is more than one beneficiary, a different set of rules applies. Those rules are discussed in the multiple beneficiary sections later in this chapter.

Year of Death

In the year of your death, if you had not yet taken your required distribution for the year, your beneficiary must do so before the end of the year. Your beneficiary will use the Uniform Lifetime Table (Table III in Appendix B) one last time, looking up the ADP for your age on your birthday in the year of your death. If you had already taken your required distribution, your beneficiary need not take another distribution in the year of your death.

Second Year and Beyond

Beginning in the year after your death, required distributions are calculated differently depending on whether you were younger or older than your beneficiary. First, let's assume that your beneficiary was younger than you. In that case, your beneficiary would compute required distributions for the second year and beyond using the beneficiary's single life expectancy in the year after your death (from Table I). In subsequent years, the beneficiary will reduce the ADP by one each year.

EXAMPLE: You turned 70½ in 2002 and began taking required distributions from your IRA at that time. Your designated beneficiary was your daughter, Prudence, who turned 45 in 2002. You had been using the Uniform Lifetime Table (Table III, Appendix B).

You died in the year 2006 after having taken your required distribution for the year. In 2007, the year after your death, Prudence must take a distribution based on her own single life expectancy, determined as of her birthday in 2007. Prudence turned 50 in 2007, and her single life expectancy, or ADP (from Table I), was 34.2. To determine the required distribution for 2007, Prudence divides the December 31, 2006 IRA balance by 34.2.

In 2008, Prudence will reduce the ADP by 1 and divide the December 31, 2007 balance by 33.2 (34.2 − 1). In future years, the ADP will be reduced by one until the entire IRA is depleted.

Second, let's assume you were younger than your beneficiary. In that case, your beneficiary would calculate the required distribution for the year after your death using your single life expectancy (from Table I) in the year of your death, reduced by one (that is, the ADP for the year after your death). In subsequent years, your beneficiary will reduce the ADP by one each year.

EXAMPLE: You turned 70½ in 1996 and began taking required distributions from your IRA at that time. Your designated beneficiary was your brother Ernest, who turned 73 in 1996. You had been using the Uniform Lifetime Table (Table III, Appendix B).

You died in 2006 after taking your required distribution for the year. In 2007, the year after your death, Ernest must take a distribution based on your single life expectancy. He must determine your life expectancy in 2006 (the year of death) and reduce it by one. In 2006, you would have been 80 on your birthday. Your single life expectancy in that year (from Table I) was 10.2. Therefore, Ernest must use an ADP of 9.2 (10.2 − 1) to compute the required distribution for the year 2007. He will divide the December 31, 2006 balance by 9.2.

In 2008, Ernest will reduce the ADP by one. Therefore, he must divide the December 31, 2007 balance by 8.2 (9.2 − 1). In future years, he will reduce the ADP by one until the entire account is depleted.

Death of Nonspouse Beneficiary

If your nonspouse beneficiary dies after you do but before the account is completely empty, the computation method for required distributions will not change at the beneficiary's death. Distributions will be made to the beneficiary's beneficiary according to the schedule established at your death, using the original beneficiary's life expectancy (or yours if you were younger) as the ADP in the year after your death and reducing the ADP by one each subsequent year. Bear in mind, however, that beneficiaries are always permitted to take more than the minimum required distribution.

Rollover

The law also allows a nonspouse beneficiary to transfer the assets of an inherited retirement plan into a new inherited IRA, as long as the retirement plan itself permits the transfer. The new inherited IRA must be established in the name of the deceased and the assets must be transferred directly from the plan trustee to the custodian of the new IRA. The beneficiary may not take possession of the funds at any time or those funds will be deemed distributed and taxable.

On the other hand, a nonspouse beneficiary is never permitted to roll over a deceased participant's retirement plan or IRA into the beneficiary's own IRA. Furthermore, the consequences are the same whether or not the deceased had passed his or her RBD at the time of death. Any rollover attempt will be deemed a distribution, and if the assets are actually deposited into an IRA in the beneficiary's name, the deposit will be considered an excess contribution to an IRA and will be subject to penalties if not withdrawn in a timely fashion.

Convert to a Roth IRA

The same rule, described above, that would allow a nonspouse beneficiary to transfer an inherited retirement plan (an employer plan) into an IRA in the decedent's name would also allow the beneficiary to transfer the plan assets into a new inherited Roth IRA in the decedent's name. If the beneficiary chooses this action, the transfer constitutes a conversion from a retirement plan to a Roth IRA, and the following rules would apply:

- The beneficiary may take this action only if the plan itself permits such a transfer.
- The beneficiary may convert the plan to a Roth IRA only if the beneficiary qualifies. For 2009, that means the beneficiary's modified AGI cannot exceed $100,000. And if the beneficiary is married, he or she must file jointly with his or her spouse in the year of the conversion. For 2010 and beyond, there are no income or filing status restrictions on converting to a Roth IRA.

- The beneficiary must accomplish the conversion by means of a trustee-to-trustee transfer, which means the funds must go directly from the trustee of the decedent's retirement plan to the custodian of the new inherited IRA.
- The new inherited IRA must be in the name of the decedent, for the benefit of the beneficiary (see "Name on Account," below).
- The beneficiary must pay income tax on the pretax portion of the amount that is transferred from the retirement plan to the new inherited Roth IRA. The income tax will generally be due with the tax return for the year of the conversion. (For conversions that occur in 2010 only, you will be able to pay the tax liability over two years, beginning in 2011.)
- The beneficiary must take required distributions from the inherited Roth IRA according to the same schedule that would apply to an inherited retirement plan or to an inherited traditional IRA.

Note that if a nonspouse beneficiary inherits an IRA instead of a retirement plan (an employer plan), the beneficiary does not have the option to convert the traditional inherited IRA into a Roth IRA.

For more information about converting retirement plan assets to a Roth IRA and taking distributions from Roth IRAs see Chapter 9.

No Designated Beneficiary

If you did not name a beneficiary of your retirement plan or if the beneficiary does not qualify as a designated beneficiary, then distributions are based on your own single life expectancy in the year of your death, reduced by one for each subsequent year until the account is depleted.

> **EXAMPLE:** You turned 70½ in 2005. You named your estate as beneficiary and never got around to changing the designation before your death.
>
> You died in the year 2009 before taking your required distribution for the year. Your beneficiary (that is, the beneficiary of your estate) must use the Uniform Lifetime Table (Table III in Appendix B) and your age in 2009 to compute the required distribution for 2009. The ADP for age 74 is 23.8.
>
> For 2010, your beneficiary must find your single life expectancy (from Table I) for your age in 2009 (the year of your death) and reduce it by one. Your single life expectancy for age 74 is 14.1. Therefore, the ADP for the 2010 required distribution is 13.1 (14.1 – 1). In the future, the ADP will be reduced by one each year.

Multiple Beneficiaries, Separate Accounts

If you have several IRAs or retirement plans, each with a single beneficiary, then the required distribution rules are applied separately to each plan. You are not considered to have multiple beneficiaries.

Multiple Beneficiaries, One Account

If you name more than one designated beneficiary of a single retirement account, then you have multiple beneficiaries for that account, and required distributions after your death will be computed as though the beneficiary with the shortest life expectancy were your sole beneficiary.

For example, if you name your sister and your children as equal beneficiaries of your IRA, and your sister is the oldest beneficiary, then distributions are computed after your death as though your sister were your sole beneficiary. But once calculated and withdrawn, the distribution will be divided equally among the beneficiaries.

Note, however, that if the beneficiary with the shortest life expectancy is older than you are, your beneficiaries will use your remaining single life expectancy to compute required distributions after your death. This is the same exception that applies if you die on or after your RBD having named a person who is older than you as your only beneficiary.

Determining the Designated Beneficiary

As is the case if you die before your RBD, the date for determining the beneficiaries is September 30 of the year following your death. If you had more than one beneficiary as of your date of death, your beneficiaries would still have time to make some changes. For example, one or more beneficiaries could disclaim an interest. Or perhaps the interests of one or more beneficiaries could be distributed by September 30 of the year after your death. (See Chapter 7 for more information about changes that can be made after your death.)

There's one other cure for multiple beneficiaries. If on September 30 of the year after your death all beneficiaries are designated beneficiaries, then they have until December 31 of that year to split the account so that each beneficiary has his or her separate share. (See below for more about splitting accounts.) If the accounts are split in timely fashion, the required distribution rules would apply separately to each share or account. Then, for example, each beneficiary could use his or her own life expectancy to compute required distributions.

CAUTION

If one or more beneficiaries is not a designated beneficiary. If on September 30 of the year after death there are multiple beneficiaries named on the account and one of them is not a designated beneficiary, then you are deemed to have no designated beneficiary. Splitting the account after September 30 will not cure the problem.

Computing the Required Distribution

If there are multiple beneficiaries named on your retirement account and they do not cure the problem, as described above, distributions must be spread over the life expectancy of the oldest beneficiary. In other words, the ADP is determined as though the oldest beneficiary were the sole beneficiary. Once the distribution is calculated, each beneficiary will receive his or her proportionate share.

EXAMPLE: You have only one IRA, and you name your three children, Tanya, Durf, and Trina, as equal beneficiaries. You die in 2008 at age 74 after having taken your required distribution for the year. As of December 31, 2009 your children were all still named equal beneficiaries of the account. In 2009 Tanya was 40, Durf was 30, and Trina was 22. Because Tanya is the oldest, distributions must be spread over her single life expectancy in the year after your death, reduced by one each subsequent year. In 2009, the ADP for Tanya's age 40 (from Table I) is 43.6. Each child receives one-third of the distribution. In the future, the ADP will be reduced by one each year.

Splitting Accounts

Accountants and taxpayers alike rejoiced when the IRS simplified matters by allowing accounts to be split among beneficiaries after the original owner died, whether the owner died before or after the required beginning date.

If you die having named multiple beneficiaries of your single retirement account, and if all beneficiaries are designated beneficiaries as of September 30 of the year after death, your beneficiaries have until December 31 of the year after your death to separate their respective shares. If they complete the separation in time, the distribution rules will apply separately to each beneficiary and his or her respective share.

The biggest benefit of timely separation is that each beneficiary can use his or her own life expectancy to calculate distributions from his or her share. Furthermore, the separation gives each beneficiary autonomy over investment decisions and simplifies accounting and other record keeping. As long as the plan itself permits the separation, the law won't prevent it.

A word of caution, however. Beneficiaries may use their own life expectancies to compute required distributions beginning in the year after the accounts were separated. So if the accounts are separated in the year after death, the required distribution for that year must be based on the life expectancy of the oldest beneficiary (presumably because there were, in fact, multiple beneficiaries named on the account for part of the year).

EXAMPLE: You name your brother, Joseph, and your three children, Holly, Herman, and Hank, as equal beneficiaries of your retirement plan. You die in 2008 at the age of 72 after taking your required distribution for the year. In March 2009, your brother and the three children instructed the custodian to split your IRA into four separate but equal IRAs. All of the new IRAs remain in your name, but one names only your brother as beneficiary, one names Holly, one names Herman, and one names Hank. Because your IRA was split into separate IRAs for each beneficiary before December 31, 2009 (the year after your death), each beneficiary can take required distributions from his or her share of the IRA over his or her own life expectancy—beginning in 2010.

However, for the year 2009 (the year the IRA was split), each beneficiary must use your brother's life expectancy to compute his or her required distribution, because your brother is the oldest beneficiary.

 TIP

Splitting in the year of death. If, in the above example, the account were split in 2008 (the year of death), each beneficiary could use his or her own life expectancy to compute the 2009 required distribution (as well as future distributions) from his or her share.

CAUTION

When a trust is beneficiary.
Splitting the account will not work when you name a trust as beneficiary of your retirement account and the trust itself has multiple beneficiaries. (See below for more information.)

Transfer

When separating each beneficiary's share into a separate account after your death, assets must be transferred directly from the trustee or custodian of the original single account to the trustee or custodian of each separate account. The beneficiary must not have control of the funds at any time. If the beneficiary is deemed to have control, the IRS will consider the assets fully distributed and fully taxable in the current year.

Furthermore, in the case of nonspouse beneficiaries, the account must remain in the name of the deceased, so it cannot be transferred to one or more of the beneficiaries' existing retirement plans or even into a new retirement account in a beneficiary's name. If a spouse is one of the beneficiaries, however, the spouse can separate his or her share and roll it over to an existing or a new IRA in the spouse's name.

Name on Account

When transferring a portion of the plan assets to a new account, the IRS requires that the new account also be in the original participant's name. But financial institutions generally do not like to maintain accounts,

let alone set up new ones, in the name of a deceased person. To accommodate both the IRS requirements and their own internal accounting procedures, many custodians construct account titles that identify both the original participant (now deceased) and the beneficiary who is to receive distributions.

Choosing a Distribution Option

As we explained above, the effect of naming multiple beneficiaries of one retirement plan account (assuming the account is not split by December 31 of the year after death) is to limit the deferral period to the life expectancy of the oldest beneficiary. As long as the plan permits, however, there is nothing to prevent one beneficiary from accelerating the distribution of his or her share while the remaining beneficiaries use the life expectancy rule. The remaining beneficiaries' deferral period would be limited to the life expectancy of the oldest, even if the oldest had already withdrawn some or all of his or her share.

When a Spouse Is One of the Beneficiaries

If your spouse is one of several beneficiaries of your retirement account, he or she can still roll over future distributions from the account into an IRA in his or her own name, whether or not your spouse was the sole beneficiary of your retirement account. However, even if your spouse is the oldest beneficiary, your spouse would not be permitted to look up the ADP in the Single Life Table (Table I) each year. Instead, your spouse would look up the ADP in the year after death (using Table I) and reduce it by one in each subsequent year.

If your account was an IRA and your spouse was not the sole beneficiary, your spouse loses the option to make the IRA his or her own by failing to take a required distribution or by making a contribution of his or her own.

A spouse is the sole beneficiary of your retirement account if he or she is the sole beneficiary on September 30 of the year after your death. If your spouse is one of several designated beneficiaries as of September 30 but separates his or her share on or before December 31 of the year after death (making your spouse the sole beneficiary of his or her share), then your spouse is deemed to be the sole beneficiary of his or her share, and your spouse gets all the special privileges accorded a spouse-beneficiary.

Trust Beneficiary

If you name a trust as beneficiary of your retirement plan or IRA and if that trust meets certain requirements (see Chapter 6 for a discussion of those requirements), then you are permitted to look through the trust to find the beneficiary of the trust. The trust beneficiary can then be treated as a designated beneficiary for purposes of computing required distributions.

All of the retirement plan distributions would go into the trust and become subject to the terms of the trust.

Nonspouse Beneficiary of Trust

A nonspouse beneficiary of the trust will use the required distribution rules described above. This means the beneficiary may spread required distributions over his or her life expectancy. The beneficiary would find the ADP (from Table I) corresponding to his or her age in the year after your death. The ADP would then be reduced by one each subsequent year.

 TIP

Older nonspouse beneficiary. If your nonspouse beneficiary is older than you, he or she may use your remaining life expectancy to compute required distributions after your death.

Spouse Beneficiary of Trust

If your spouse is sole beneficiary of the trust, your spouse will be treated as the designated beneficiary for purposes of computing post-death distributions. That means your spouse can take distributions over his or her single life expectancy beginning on December 31 of the year after your death and looking up the ADP for his or her age each year in Table I.

TIP

Older spouse beneficiary. As is the case when you name your spouse directly as beneficiary of your retirement plan, if your spouse is older than you, he or she would use your remaining life expectancy to compute required distributions after your death.

CAUTION

Your spouse cannot make your IRA his or her own. If you name a trust as beneficiary of your IRA, IRS regulations state that even if your spouse is the sole beneficiary of your trust, your spouse cannot make the IRA his or her own, either by failing to take a required distribution or by making additional contributions. However, your spouse might be able to receive a distribution of IRA assets from the trust and then roll them over into his or her own IRA. See below.

Multiple Beneficiaries of Trust

If a trust has multiple beneficiaries, then for purposes of post-death required distributions, the multiple beneficiary rules described above apply as though the individuals themselves were named beneficiaries of the retirement plan.

CAUTION

Splitting the account won't work if a trust is the beneficiary. If you name a trust as beneficiary of your retirement plan and there are multiple beneficiaries of the trust, splitting

the retirement plan into separate accounts for each beneficiary of the trust—whether it is done before or after your death—won't allow beneficiaries to use their own life expectancies to compute required distributions. The multiple beneficiary rules still apply, requiring your beneficiaries to take distributions over the life expectancy of the oldest beneficiary of the trust.

Trust Beneficiary and Spousal Rollovers

Recall that a trust is often named the beneficiary of a retirement plan in order to fund a bypass trust. Assuming the spouse is the beneficiary of the trust, distributions from the plan go into the trust and then the trust makes distributions to the spouse.

But sometimes the surviving spouse discovers after the participant dies that the retirement plan assets are not needed to fund the bypass trust after all. In that case, the surviving spouse might prefer to simply roll over the retirement plan assets into his or her own IRA, name his or her own beneficiary, and begin a new schedule of required distributions.

Unfortunately, the law says that only a spouse beneficiary (and not a trust) may roll over retirement plan assets—and then only if the spouse acquires the assets directly from and by reason of the participant's death.

But taxpayers have argued that if the spouse is the sole beneficiary of the trust and can distribute all of the assets without interference from any third party, then the assets essentially pass directly from the deceased to the spouse—making the rollover within the spirit of the law.

Between 1987 and 2001, the IRS established a pattern of approving such actions in private letter rulings—despite the lack of explicit legal approval.

In final regulations issued in April 2002, however, the IRS stated specifically that a spouse cannot make a deceased participant's IRA her own if a trust is named primary beneficiary of the IRA—even if the spouse is the sole beneficiary of the trust.

Nonetheless, some practitioners believe that if the spouse has the power to distribute all assets of the trust, he or she could distribute the IRA assets to the trust and then distribute the assets from the trust to him or herself. Having done so, the spouse could then roll over the assets into an IRA of his or her own. Although this strategy is not specifically sanctioned by the IRS, some practitioners believe it will pass muster, even under the newer regulations.

We think you should proceed with caution. If you name a trust as beneficiary of your retirement plan with the expectation that the spouse can fall back on a rollover, you are taking a risk.

As an alternative to taking this risk, consider naming your spouse as primary beneficiary (thus preserving the rollover opportunity) and your trust as contingent beneficiary. After your death, your spouse would have the option of disclaiming some or all of his or her interest in your retirement plan, allowing it to flow to the bypass trust. Ultimately, however, no strategy involving a trust is completely simple or safe.

Estate as Beneficiary

Recall that an estate does not qualify as a designated beneficiary. If an estate is named beneficiary, then the plan assets must be distributed over the original participant's life expectancy. The ADP for the year after death is the participant's single life expectancy (from Table I) in the year of death, reduced by one. The ADP is reduced by one for each subsequent year, as well. This is true even if the participant's spouse or child is beneficiary of the estate. There is no look-through rule for an estate as there is for certain qualified trusts. Consequently, if a participant was elderly at death, the plan might have to be entirely distributed in a short time.

 TIP

Rollover risky. The IRS has frequently allowed a spouse to roll over the assets of a retirement plan into an IRA in the spouse's own name when an estate is named beneficiary of the plan and when the spouse is the sole beneficiary of the estate. But the strategy is not sanctioned by the Tax Code or by tax regulations, so it remains risky.

Annuities

If you die on or after your RBD and if you had been receiving your retirement benefits as an annuity, the form of the annuity determines how the remaining benefits will be paid to your beneficiary. (See Chapter 6 for more information about types of annuities.)

For example, the annuity might have been a joint and survivor annuity that must continue to pay your beneficiary the same benefits you were receiving. Or the annuity might have been a term certain annuity; if you survive only part of the term, your beneficiary receives payments for the remainder of the term.

Divorce or Separation

If you were divorced or separated during your lifetime, some or all of your retirement plan might be distributable to an alternate payee such as a spouse, former spouse, or child, under the terms of a QDRO—a court-approved divorce or maintenance agreement. (See Chapter 2 for more information about QDROs.)

In such cases, some portion of each distribution during your lifetime was payable to the alternate payee (unless, of course, the alternate payee's share was distributed outright). That doesn't change when you die.

If you die after your RBD, payments from your account will continue to be computed using your beneficiary's ADP in the year

after death, reduced by one each subsequent year. If an alternate payee has been receiving a portion of each distribution, the alternate payee is entitled to his or her share of post-death distributions, as well.

> **EXAMPLE:** On September 30 of the year after your death, the designated beneficiary of your retirement plan was your sister. Under the terms of a QDRO, your former spouse is entitled to half of your retirement plan, and you have been giving your former spouse 50% of each distribution. You died in 2008 after taking your required distribution for the year. In 2009, your sister will take a distribution from your retirement plan using the ADP (from Table I) for her age in 2009. Half of the distribution will go to your sister and half to your former spouse.
>
> In 2010 and beyond, your sister will reduce the previous year's ADP by one when computing required distributions. Half of all distributions must go to your former spouse.

If the alternate payee is a nonspouse, he or she may never roll over a distribution from your retirement plan. However, a spouse or former spouse with an interest in your retirement plan under the terms of a QDRO has all the rights of a surviving spouse beneficiary. When you die, your former spouse may roll over any distribution he or she receives from your plan into an IRA or a retirement plan in his or her own name, provided the former spouse first takes a required distribution on your behalf in the year of your death. If your former spouse has not yet reached his or her RBD, future required distributions may be deferred until that time.

Key Tax Code and Regulation Sections, IRS Pronouncements
§ 401(a)(9) Required Distributions From Qualified Plans
§ 1.401(a)(9) Required Distribution Regulations
§ 402(c) Rollovers From Qualified Plans
§ 408 Individual Retirement Accounts
§ 1.408-8, A-5 Election by Spouse to Treat Decedent's IRA as Own
Rev. Proc. 89-52 After-Death IRA Reporting Requirements
Ann. 95-99 Employee Plans Examination Guidelines

Roth IRAs

Taxation of Distributions... 196

    Distribution of Nondeductible Contributions.. 196

    Distribution of Investment Returns 197

    Conversions and Rollovers.. 200

    Correcting Errors: Recharacterizing 204

Early Distribution Tax.. 205

    Qualified Distributions.. 205

    Nonqualified Distributions 205

Ordering of Distributions... 207

Required Distributions.. 209

    During Your Lifetime 209

    After Your Death, Before Your RBD 209

    After Your Death, After Your RBD 210

Who Should Read Chapter 9

SKIP AHEAD

Read this chapter if you have a Roth IRA, if you are considering opening one, or if you would like to convert another retirement plan to a Roth IRA.

In its eternal quest for the most effective way to encourage people to save for retirement, Congress created in 1997 one of the biggest sugarcoated carrots we've ever seen: the Roth IRA.

Congress designed the Roth IRA to be much like a traditional IRA, but with a few attractive modifications. When the modifications began to fill pages rather than paragraphs, the new creature was given its own section in the Tax Code—Section 408A. The section begins with the statement that all the traditional IRA rules apply to Roth IRAs except as noted. This chapter focuses on the exceptions, with special attention to the unusual treatment of distributions.

The lure of the Roth IRA is powerful. Although contributions are not deductible (meaning they are made with after-tax dollars), all distributions, including the earnings on contributions, are potentially tax free—as will be explained below.

Unfortunately, Roth IRAs don't work for everyone. Here's a summary of the key differences between traditional IRAs and Roth IRAs:

Calculating Your Modified Adjusted Gross Income

You are not permitted to make a Roth IRA contribution if your modified adjusted gross income (modified AGI) exceeds a certain amount. When calculating your modified AGI, you make the following adjustments to your regular AGI:

- exclude the converted amount from income
- exclude any distributions from traditional IRAs or other retirement plans that you were required to withdraw because of being older than 70½
- add back income from U.S. savings bonds used for higher education expenses
- add back employer-paid adoption expenses
- add back excluded foreign earned income and payments received for foreign housing
- add back any deduction claimed for a traditional IRA contribution, and
- add back the deduction for educational loan interest.

- You may make a contribution to a traditional IRA no matter how high your income is, as long as you (or your spouse, if you are married and filing a joint return) have earned income (income from employment) and are younger than 70½. But in the case of a Roth IRA, you may not make any contribution if your income exceeds a certain level. If you are married filing

Helpful Terms

Adjusted gross income (AGI). Total taxable income reduced by certain expenses such as qualified plan contributions, IRA contributions, and alimony payments.

After-tax dollars. The amount of income left after all income taxes have been withheld or paid.

Beneficiary. The person or entity entitled to receive the benefits from insurance or from trust property, such as a retirement plan or IRA.

Deferral period. The number of years over which distributions from a retirement plan or IRA can be spread.

Distribution. A payout of property (such as shares of stock) or cash from a retirement plan or IRA to the participant or a beneficiary.

Earned income. Income received for providing goods or services. Earned income might be wages or salary or net profit from a business.

Nondeductible contribution. A contribution to a retirement plan or IRA that may not be used as a business expense or an adjustment to offset taxable income on an income tax return.

Traditional IRA. Any contributory or rollover IRA that is not a Roth IRA or a SIMPLE IRA.

a joint return, the amount that you are allowed to contribute to a Roth IRA is gradually reduced when your modified AGI exceeds $166,000 (for tax year 2009). You may not make any contribution at all once your income reaches $176,000. If you are single, the phaseout begins at $105,000 and is complete when your income reaches $120,000. If you are married filing separate returns, the phaseout begins with your first dollar of income and is complete when your income reaches $10,000. (Note: These numbers will increase for inflation from time to time.)

- No contribution to a traditional IRA is permitted after age 70½. However, you may continue to make contributions to a Roth IRA after age 70½, as long as you or your spouse have earned income and your modified AGI doesn't exceed the limits described above.

- A contribution to a traditional IRA is always deductible if neither you nor your spouse is covered by a qualified plan. If even one of you is covered by a plan, the deduction is phased out as your income increases. On the other hand, no contribution to a Roth IRA is ever deductible, whether or not you are covered by another plan.

- Earnings that accumulate inside a traditional IRA are always subject to income tax when withdrawn. But earnings in a Roth IRA can be completely tax free when distributed if certain requirements are satisfied.

- If you have a traditional IRA, you must begin required distributions on or before your required beginning date—your RBD. If you have a Roth IRA, you are not required to withdraw any amount during your lifetime.

CAUTION

Roth 401(k) plans are different from Roth IRAs. Roth 401(k) plans are not exempt from the lifetime required distribution rules. See Chapter 10 for more information about Roth 401(k) plans.

The contrast between traditional IRAs and Roth IRAs is most stark in the treatment of distributions. The differences turn up not only in the ordinary income tax rules, but also in the application of the early distribution tax and the required distribution rules.

Taxation of Distributions

The income tax rules for traditional IRAs are straightforward. Generally, distributions are taxed as ordinary income unless they are rolled over into another retirement plan or IRA. If you made nondeductible (after-tax) contributions to your traditional IRA over the years, those amounts are not subject to tax when distributed. That's the good news. The bad news is that those after-tax contributions are deemed to come out *pro rata*—not all at once. In other words, the

nondeductible portion of a traditional IRA comes out as only a part of each distribution you ever take from the IRA. Consequently, only a percentage of each distribution is tax free. (See Chapter 2 for more information about calculating the nontaxable portion of a distribution from a traditional IRA.)

The basic rule for Roth IRAs is similar: The taxable portion of any distribution must be reported on your income tax return, and it will be taxed as ordinary income unless you roll it over. But that's where the similarity ends.

The key to squeezing the maximum benefit from a Roth IRA is to be aware of which distributions are taxable and which are not. Maintaining that vigilance is not difficult; you must simply view your Roth IRA as the sum of two distinct parts. One part consists of the contributions you have made. The second part consists of the earnings on those contributions, such as interest earned on bond investments or gains from stock sales.

Distribution of Nondeductible Contributions

The portion of your Roth IRA that consists of your contributions is never subject to income tax when it comes out. Never. Even if you take it out the day after you put it in. That's because all contributions you made were nondeductible, which means you have already paid tax on the money. You don't have to pay tax a second time when you take it out. Fair is fair.

Furthermore, any distribution you take from a Roth IRA is presumed to be a return of your contributions until you have withdrawn all contributions you made to it over the years (or to all Roth IRAs, if you have more than one). In other words, all contributions are recovered before earnings are recovered. This simple rule gives the Roth IRA an advantage over a traditional IRA. It means you may retrieve your contributions whenever you want without incurring any income tax. In this way, the contributions can serve as an emergency fund.

> **EXAMPLE:** Dain began making contributions to a Roth IRA three years ago. By the beginning of this year, the Roth IRA had grown to $8,000. Of that amount, $6,000 was from Dain's annual contributions and $2,000 was from investment returns. In February of this year, Dain had an auto accident and totaled his car. Dain needed to purchase a new car but didn't have any resources other than his Roth IRA. He decided to withdraw $6,000 from his Roth IRA. The $6,000 is not subject to tax because Dain's distribution is deemed to be a return of his contributions.

Distribution of Investment Returns

When you contribute to an IRA, you ordinarily use the contributed funds to purchase investments that will earn money for you. For example, you might invest in

bonds or CDs to generate interest. Or you might buy stock, hoping the price will shoot up so you can make a bundle on a later sale. As long as those earnings—the interest and the stock proceeds—stay inside the IRA, they are not taxed. But what happens when they come out? In the case of a traditional IRA, all of the earnings are subject to ordinary income tax. The advantage of the Roth IRA is that when you distribute earnings, they are tax free—even though they have never been taxed before—as long as the distribution is considered a qualified distribution.

Qualified Distributions

It will pay you handsomely to nail down the tax-free advantage a Roth IRA offers. All you have to do is follow a few simple rules. First, don't take a distribution of your investment returns for five years. A distribution within five calendar years of when you first establish a Roth IRA can never be a qualified distribution.

 CAUTION

If you die before the five years are up. If you die before satisfying the five-year holding period, your beneficiary must wait until you would have satisfied it, or the distribution will not be qualified.

So, counting the year of your first contribution as year one, you will satisfy the five-year requirement if you wait until the sixth year before withdrawing any earnings.

EXAMPLE: Jessica opened a Roth IRA in June 2005. At the end of 2006, her account was worth $15,000, of which $8,000 was from contributions and $7,000 was from investment earnings. In June 2009, Jessica withdrew $10,000 to pay for a trip to China. Of that amount, $8,000 is deemed to be from contributions and will not be subject to income tax. The remaining $2,000 is deemed to come from earnings. Because the distribution did not satisfy the five-year holding requirement, the $2,000 will be subject to income tax. (It might also be subject to an early distribution penalty.).

Although you are permitted to make a contribution to a Roth IRA after the end of the year (until April 15), the five-year holding period for a qualified distribution begins on the first day of the calendar year to which your very first contribution relates, which might be an earlier year than the one during which the contribution was actually made.

EXAMPLE: Soren wanted to set up a Roth IRA and make a contribution for 2008. He finally got around to doing so in February 2009, well before the April 15, 2009 deadline. Because the contribution is for 2008, Soren will count 2008 as year one when computing the five-year holding period, even though he didn't actually make the contribution until 2009.

Simply satisfying the five-year requirement will not automatically make a distribution qualified. It must also be at least one of the following:

- a distribution you take after reaching age 59½
- a distribution you take after becoming disabled
- a distribution to your beneficiary or your estate after your death, or
- a distribution you take to purchase a first home (up to a lifetime withdrawal limit of $10,000).

If your distribution satisfies the five-year requirement and falls into one of the above categories, it will be qualified and thus entirely tax free.

 CAUTION

Remember, contributions are never subject to income tax when they come out of a Roth IRA. So even if they are part of a nonqualified distribution, they are tax free. Only the earnings will be taxed if they are part of a nonqualified distribution.

EXAMPLE: Lara began making contributions to a Roth IRA in 2007. By June 2009, she had accumulated $7,500. Of that amount, $7,000 was from contributions she made in the years 2007, 2008, and 2009. The remaining $500 was from earnings on her investments. In December 2009, Lara withdrew $7,200 from the IRA. The distribution is a nonqualified

Municipal Bonds Offer Another Form of Tax-Free Investment

Typically, when you purchase municipal bonds, all of the interest you earn on the bonds is tax free. As an investment vehicle, a Roth IRA has two distinct advantages over a municipal bond. First, inside a Roth IRA, money can be invested in stocks and other diverse investments that are likely to yield a greater return over the long term than do municipal bonds. Second, although the interest on municipal bonds is tax free, you must be diligent about reinvesting the interest or you will soon have taxable income. For example, if you invest $10,000 in a municipal bond that pays 5% interest, you receive $500 of tax-free interest during the year. But if you place that interest in a regular interest-bearing account or another investment that generates taxable income, the earnings on the $500 will be taxable. To ensure that all future earnings are tax free, you must reinvest in more municipal bonds, which might be difficult with only $500 of cash. Municipal bonds are rarely sold in increments of $500.

In contrast, all distributions from a Roth IRA are potentially tax free, whether you invest in stocks, corporate bonds, or CDs. Thus, not only can you invest in a variety of securities, but also you won't have the same reinvestment concerns you would have if municipal bonds were your only investment option. For example, if you invest in a CD that generates $500 of interest income, you could reinvest in stocks, bonds, or another CD.

distribution because it occurred within five years of her initial contribution. Only $200 is subject to tax, however, because her contributions, which total $7,000, are deemed to come out first—they are never subject to tax.

Nonqualified Distributions

Any distribution from a Roth IRA that does not satisfy the requirements of a qualified distribution is automatically nonqualified. Nonqualified distributions are treated very much like traditional IRA distributions. The contributions you made will come out tax free, but the earnings are taxable. There is one critical difference, however: As mentioned above, the contributions you make to the Roth IRA (which were made with after-tax dollars) are presumed to come out first—before any earnings. This means if you must take a nonqualified distribution, some or all of it will escape income tax, as long as you have not previously withdrawn all of your contributions.

EXAMPLE: JJ has contributed to a Roth IRA in each of the years 2006, 2007, and 2008. By June 2008, he had accumulated $10,000, of which $9,000 was from contributions and $1,000 was from earnings. In December, JJ withdrew $9,000 from his IRA. Although the distribution was non-qualified, the $9,000 was nontaxable because it was all attributable to his contributions. In April 2009, JJ contributed another $4,000 to his Roth IRA. By December, he had a total of $5,200 in the IRA. Only $4,000 was attributable to contributions because he had already withdrawn all contributions for prior years. The remaining $1,200 represented earnings. JJ decided to withdraw $5,000. The entire distribution is nonqualified, but the $4,000 attributable to contributions would be tax free. Only $1,000 of the distribution is attributable to earnings, and that portion will be subject to income tax.

Conversions and Rollovers

When you have a Roth IRA, your rollover opportunities are limited. You can roll over assets from a Roth IRA to another Roth IRA, or if you qualify, you can roll over—or convert—assets from a traditional IRA or a SEP IRA or SIMPLE IRA to a Roth IRA.

CAUTION

SEPs and SIMPLEs. This section applies to SEPs in exactly the same way it applies to traditional IRAs. In other words, a SEP can be converted to a Roth IRA. In the case of a SIMPLE IRA, you may convert to a Roth IRA only after two years from the date you first established a SIMPLE IRA. Before the two years have expired, the SIMPLE IRA is ineligible for conversion.

Beginning in 2008, you will also be able to convert other types of retirement plans to a Roth IRA, if you would otherwise qualify to convert. Specifically, you will be able to convert qualified plans (such as 401(k) plans), tax-deferred annuities (403(b) plans), or government plans (457 plans).

Although you might be permitted to roll over assets from a retirement plan or IRA to a Roth IRA, you may not do the reverse. You are not permitted to roll over assets from a Roth IRA to any other type of plan or IRA. A Roth IRA may only be rolled over to another Roth IRA.

As explained in the paragraphs below, some special rules apply to amounts that have been converted or rolled over to a Roth IRA.

Rollover From Roth IRA

If you take a distribution from a Roth IRA with the intention of rolling it over, you may roll it over only to another Roth IRA. This is logical when you think about it. Distributions from Roth IRAs are all potentially tax free, whereas most, if not all, distributions from a traditional IRA or a qualified plan are taxable. If you were allowed to mix plans indiscriminately, the IRS would have a hard time tracking the source of the various distributions to determine which funds are taxable.

Except for the fact that you may only roll a Roth IRA to another Roth IRA, all the rules governing rollovers between IRAs apply to rollovers between Roth IRAs. (See

Chapter 2 for more about IRA rollovers.) Among the most important of those rules are the following:

- Once you take a distribution from a Roth IRA, you have only 60 days to complete the rollover to another Roth IRA.
- You are permitted only one Roth-to-Roth rollover per year.
- Rollover distributions between IRAs are not subject to income tax withholding.

Rollover to Roth IRA

Rollovers to a Roth IRA may come from another Roth IRA, a traditional IRA, a qualified plan, tax deferred annuity, or a government plan.

A Roth IRA may be rolled into another Roth IRA without any restrictions other than those that apply to rollovers between traditional IRAs, as described in the previous section. A rollover from a traditional IRA or from another retirement plan is called a conversion and is more complex. (See immediately below for more information.)

Conversion to Roth IRA

If you want to convert assets from a traditional IRA or other retirement plan to a Roth IRA, you must be eligible and you must face the consequences. First the consequences.

Consequences

If you determine that you are eligible to convert your retirement plan or IRA to a Roth IRA (see immediately below), and if you elect to do so, you must pay the piper. Specifically, the entire pretax amount of the conversion will be subject to income tax at ordinary rates. (If you made nondeductible contributions to your plan or IRA, those amounts will not be taxed a second time when you convert to a Roth IRA.) Congress wasn't about to wipe out all of those deferred taxes with one stroke of the pen. Once you've ponied up the money and converted the assets, however, all future distributions of the converted amounts will be free of income tax. Furthermore, distributions of future earnings on converted amounts will be tax free as long as those distributions satisfy the five-year holding period and are qualified.

> **EXAMPLE:** In 2003, you converted your $20,000 traditional IRA to a Roth IRA. On your tax return for 2003, you included the $20,000 and paid tax on it. By 2009, your Roth IRA has grown to $35,000, and you withdraw $30,000 to throw yourself a 65th birthday party. The entire $30,000 distribution is tax free because you are older than 59½ and you have satisfied the five-year holding period.

TIP

Can you find separate funds to pay the tax? The conversion of a retirement plan or IRA to a Roth IRA can be a real boon to young investors who can pay the tax from funds outside of the retirement plan or IRA. These folks have years of tax-free compounding ahead of them. However, if the tax is paid out of retirement plan or IRA funds, the advantage of the conversion declines and may even disappear altogether.

As a practical matter, it may be difficult for people with sizable retirement plans or IRAs to convert the entire account to a Roth IRA unless they have large amounts of cash outside the IRA. Imagine paying regular income tax on a $100,000 IRA. One way around this problem would be to convert the retirement plan or IRA to a Roth IRA in bits and pieces over a number of years to keep the tax at a manageable level. Nothing in the law prevents you from converting part of your retirement plan or IRA instead of the whole thing. Furthermore, there is no time limit on conversion. As long as the law doesn't change, you can simply wait and convert some or all of your retirement funds when it makes the most sense for you.

For older IRA participants, converting to a Roth IRA is not necessarily the correct decision. If you must include a large retirement plan or IRA in income, some or all of it could easily be taxed at the maximum tax rate, and you might not recover from that financial outlay (through tax-free compounded growth) before your death. If your primary concern is passing wealth to your beneficiaries, however, a conversion could save estate taxes and also give your beneficiaries an opportunity for additional tax-free growth after your death.

The decision to convert or not to convert can involve some complex calculations. You must factor in age, health, income and estate tax rates, Social Security benefits, and investment returns. If you are young, healthy, and able to pay the taxes with separate money, the conversion is likely to pay off for you.

CAUTION

If you are younger than 59½ and you elect to use some of the converted amounts to pay the tax, the portion that goes to taxes could be subject to the early distribution tax. (See below.)

Eligibility

Even if it makes sense for you to convert a traditional IRA or retirement plan to a Roth IRA, for 2009 you must determine whether you are eligible to do so. (Beginning in 2010, eligibility restrictions are eliminated. See Tip, below, for more information.) You are not eligible if either of the following is true.

If your modified adjusted gross income (modified AGI) exceeds $100,000, you may not convert a plan or IRA to a Roth IRA. This income cap applies whether you are married or single. (See the introduction to this chapter for a definition of modified AGI.)

Note that modified AGI is used only to determine if you qualify to convert. It is not used to compute your tax liability.

> **EXAMPLE:** Tyson's modified AGI for the year is $90,000. He has accumulated $25,000 in a traditional IRA and would like to convert it to a Roth IRA before the end of the year. Because Tyson's modified AGI (not including the $25,000 in his IRA) is under $100,000, he qualifies to convert his traditional IRA to a Roth IRA. On his tax return, he will report income of $115,000 (which is $90,000 + $25,000).

Another part of the Roth IRA law, which took effect in the year 2005, allows you to exclude from your modified AGI the distributions you are required to take from your retirement plans because you have passed age 70½. (See Chapter 5 for a summary of the required distribution rules.) But the required distribution may be excluded only for purposes of computing whether or not you qualify to convert your retirement plan or IRA to a Roth IRA. You must still pay tax on it.

> **EXAMPLE:** Nolan's income for the year 2009 includes $80,000 from interest and dividends and $30,000 in required distributions he must withdraw from his traditional IRA. Nolan plans to convert another $20,000 of his tradi-

tional IRA to a Roth IRA. Although the total income he must report on his tax return is $130,000 (which is $80,000 + $30,000 + $20,000), he still qualifies to convert the $20,000 from his traditional IRA because his income is less than $100,000 when he excludes the required distribution and the converted amount.

CAUTION

You are not permitted to roll over or convert a required distribution. Therefore, in the above example, Nolan's $30,000 required distribution must be placed in a regular account, not an IRA account of any kind. The $20,000 conversion amount must be an additional distribution from his traditional IRA—over and above the required amount of $30,000.

You cannot convert any portion of a retirement plan or IRA to a Roth IRA if you are a married person using the "married filing separately" status on your tax return (instead of "married filing jointly"). Any person using the married filing separately status is automatically ineligible to convert any amount to a Roth IRA.

TIP

Restrictions Disappear in 2010. For 2009, you are not permitted to convert a retirement plan or IRA to a Roth IRA if your modified AGI exceeds $100,000 or if you file your tax return as married filing separately. Both of those restrictions will be eliminated for years after 2009. Furthermore, if you elect to convert amounts to a Roth IRA in 2010, you will be permitted to report half of the conversion income on your 2011 tax return and the remainder on your return for tax year 2012. That "averaging" benefit is available only for 2010 conversions.

Related Rules

If you decide to proceed with the conversion of a retirement plan or IRA to a Roth IRA, you will find that Congress has built in a little tax relief for you.

- The conversion is ignored for purposes of the one-rollover-per-year rule. (See Chapter 2 for more information about this rule.)
- Even if you are younger than 59½, the converted amount will not be subject to the early distribution tax, as long as the entire taxable amount is rolled over. (Beware of using part of the rollover to pay income tax, though. See below.)
- For income tax purposes, later distributions of converted amounts from your Roth IRA are treated like distributions of nondeductible contributions. The converted portion will not be subject to income tax when it is distributed in future years, but the earnings will be subject to tax unless they are part of a qualified distribution. (See above for the definition of a qualified distribution.)

Correcting Errors: Recharacterizing

If you convert funds to a Roth IRA during the year and discover at the end of the year that your modified AGI was too high, you won't be in serious trouble. The law allows you to transfer the funds back out of the Roth IRA and into a traditional IRA before the due date of your tax return (or the extended due date). This is called a recharacterization.

In fact, you can recharacterize after April 15, even if you have already filed your tax return and did not request an extension. You always have until October 15 of the year after the conversion to recharacterize your Roth IRA. However, if you recharacterize after filing your return, you must file an amended return to report the recharacterization.

The proper method for recharacterizing your Roth IRA is to have the custodian of the Roth IRA transfer the errant funds plus any investment earnings on those funds directly to the custodian of the traditional IRA. If this is all done in timely fashion, there will be no income tax or penalties.

If you recharacterize a converted amount—meaning you undo a conversion to a Roth IRA by redirecting the money back into a traditional IRA—you may not reconvert those funds to a Roth IRA until the following tax year or until 30 days have passed, if that period of time is longer. For example, if you recharacterize in June, you must wait until the next January to reconvert. If you recharacterize on December 31, you can reconvert on January 30 of the next year.

> 💡 **TIP**
>
> **Roth IRA waiting periods.** The waiting period for reconverting was added to the Roth IRA laws somewhat belatedly to quash a tax-saving maneuver that was spreading like wildfire. Smart taxpayers were converting and recharacterizing several times during a year to take advantage of dips in the market. When the market dips, the value of a retirement plan drops—and so does the tax cost of conversion.

> **EXAMPLE:** You converted your $100,000 traditional IRA to a Roth IRA in June. By November, the value of the assets had declined to $75,000. So under the old rules, you would be able to recharacterize the Roth IRA to a traditional IRA (transfer the assets back) and then reconvert before the end of the year. You would then pay tax on $75,000 instead of on $100,000.

Early Distribution Tax

Understanding how the early distribution tax applies to Roth IRAs is complicated by the fact that there are two types of distributions (qualified and nonqualified) and a special set of rules for converted amounts. (Early distribution tax rules for traditional IRAs and other retirement plans are discussed in Chapter 3.)

Qualified Distributions

Qualified distributions from Roth IRAs are not subject to the early distribution tax. It's as simple as that. This rule, too, has some logic to it. The early distribution tax applies only to distributions that are included in income—those that are required to be reported on your tax return. Because all qualified distributions from Roth IRAs are tax free, they are all exempt from the early distribution tax.

Nonqualified Distributions

Nonqualified distributions from Roth IRAs are treated in most respects like distributions from traditional IRAs. Any portion of the distribution that is required to be included on your income tax return is subject to the early distribution tax, unless the distribution qualifies for an exception. The exceptions for nonqualified distributions from Roth IRAs are the same as those for traditional IRA distributions. (See Chapter 3 for a detailed description of all the exceptions to the early distribution tax.) The key exceptions to the early distribution tax include distributions:

- after you reach age 59½
- because of your death or disability
- that are substantially equal periodic payments
- for certain medical expenses
- for certain health insurance
- for higher education expenses, or
- for a first home purchase (limited to $10,000).

Distributions of Nondeductible Contributions

Bear in mind that all of your nondeductible contributions to a Roth IRA will come out before any earnings. Because the contributions are nondeductible, they are not subject to tax when distributed, even if they are part of a nonqualified distribution. And because they are tax free and not includable on your income tax return, they automatically escape the early distribution tax. Any earnings that are distributed as part of a nonqualified distribution are subject to the early distribution tax, unless an exception applies.

Again, for planning purposes, this means you can take your contributions out of a Roth IRA at any time, and they will be subject neither to income tax nor to the early distribution tax.

> **EXAMPLE:** In 2006, you established a Roth IRA. You contributed $3,000 in 2006, 2007, and 2008. By November of the year 2009, the account had grown to $9,600. Finding yourself a little strapped for cash, you withdraw $6,000 from the account in late November. Because the distribution is less than your total contributions of $9,000, the $6,000 will not be subject to either income tax or the early distribution tax.

Distribution of Converted Amounts

A special rule exempts converted amounts from the early distribution tax in the year of the conversion, as long as the entire amount of the conversion goes into the Roth IRA. There are two ways to get caught by an early distribution tax when you convert to a Roth IRA. You might use some of the converted amount to pay the income tax you owe on the conversion, or you might withdraw the converted amount too soon. But remember, the early distribution tax would never apply if you were older than 59½ at the time of the distribution (or if another exception, described in Chapter 3, applies).

Paying Income Tax With Converted Amounts

If you qualify to convert a retirement plan or IRA to a Roth IRA, the amount actually deposited into the Roth IRA will not be subject to an early distribution tax. Even though it is included on your tax return and you pay income tax on the converted amount, you are spared the early distribution tax if you roll over everything. But if you use some of the money from the plan or IRA to pay the income tax liability instead of rolling it over, the portion used for taxes will be subject to the early distribution tax—unless you are older than 59½ or another exception applies. (See Chapter 3 for more information about the early distribution tax and exceptions to the tax.)

Withdrawing Converted Amounts Too Soon

Even though converted amounts in a Roth IRA are after-tax amounts (because you paid tax in the year of conversion), if you withdraw any converted dollars within five years, that portion of the distribution will be treated as though it is taxable—but only for purposes of determining the early distribution tax. (Recall that the early distribution tax generally does not apply to amounts that are excluded from your income for tax purposes. This is an exception to that rule.)

> **EXAMPLE:** You have a traditional IRA to which you have been making deductible contributions each year. By the time you are 50, the account has grown to $15,000. You convert the IRA to a Roth IRA, paying tax on the entire $15,000. The following year, you withdraw $10,000 from the Roth IRA to bail your son out of jail. Because you are younger than 59½ and you withdrew the $10,000 within five years of converting your traditional IRA to a Roth IRA, you must pay an early distribution tax of $1,000 ($10,000 x 10%). You will not owe regular income tax on the $10,000.

The portion of a distribution that is subject to the early distribution tax is limited to the amount that you included in your taxable income and reported on your tax return in the year of conversion.

> **EXAMPLE:** You have a traditional IRA to which you have made deductible contributions of $4,000 and non-deductible (after-tax) contributions of $6,000. By the time you are 51, the account has grown to $17,000. You convert the IRA to a Roth IRA, paying tax on $11,000. (You don't have to pay tax on the $6,000 of nondeductible contributions.) The next year, when you are 52, you withdraw $17,000 to help your daughter start a new business. You must pay an early distribution tax on the $11,000, because that is the amount that was included on your income tax return in the year of conversion. The early distribution tax is $1,100 ($11,000 x 10%).

 TIP

How the earnings are treated. The earnings on converted amounts are treated exactly the same as earnings on contributory amounts. Only qualified distributions of earnings escape the early distribution tax, unless another early distribution tax exception applies.

Ordering of Distributions

You might think you should be able to pick and choose which amounts come out of your Roth IRA first. For example, if you take a distribution before the five-year holding period is up, you would want to take your contributions first, because they are not subject to tax or penalties. Or if you converted one of your traditional IRAs six years ago and another two years ago, you would want to take a distribution from the one that was converted six years ago, because those converted amounts satisfy the five-year holding period and would not be subject to an early distribution tax.

Sadly, you cannot pick and choose the origin of each distribution you take. But serendipitously, the ordering rules you are required to use are quite favorable. Distributions are deemed to come out in the following order:

- Regular Roth IRA contributions are distributed first.
- Next come converted amounts, starting with the amounts first converted. If you converted a traditional IRA containing both taxable and nontaxable amounts (for example, if you had made deductible and nondeductible contributions), the taxable portion is deemed to come out first.
- Earnings come out last.

The benefits can be dramatic. For example, if you take a distribution before the five-year holding period is up or if you fail to satisfy the other requirements of a qualified distribution, the withdrawal still won't be subject to the early distribution tax as long as you have taken less than the total amount of all contributions you have made to all your Roth IRAs. Note that for purposes of these ordering rules, all Roth IRAs are considered a single Roth IRA.

EXAMPLE: You have two traditional IRAs: IRA #1 and IRA #2. In 2001, you converted IRA #1, then valued at $10,000, to a Roth IRA. In 2005, you converted IRA #2, valued at $20,000, to a Roth IRA. You also have a separate contributory Roth IRA, which you established in 2001 and to which you have been making annual contributions. By 2009, the contributory Roth IRA has grown to $15,000, of which $8,000 is contributions and $7,000 is earnings. In November 2009, on your 40th birthday, you withdraw $25,000 to pay for your trip to India. The source of the distribution is deemed to be:

- $8,000 from Roth IRA contributions
- $10,000 from the oldest converted amount (IRA #1), and
- $7,000 from the next oldest converted amount (IRA #2).

The $8,000 of contributions are not subject to either income tax or the early distribution tax because they are all from nondeductible after-tax contributions. The $10,000 deemed to be from IRA #1 is also not subject to either income tax (which you already paid in the year of conversion) or the early distribution tax (because the conversion occurred more than five years before). The remaining $7,000 will not be subject to income tax, because it was converted from a traditional IRA and you already paid tax on it in 2005.

However, it will be subject to an early distribution tax of $700 (10% of $7,000), because it was distributed within five years of the conversion and you are younger than 59½.

Required Distributions

The required distribution rules—those that will eventually force you to start taking money out of your retirement plan or your traditional IRA—have a broad reach. (See Chapter 5 for a summary of the required distribution rules.) They apply to IRAs, qualified plans, plans that behave like qualified plans, and even some nonqualified plans. But as broad as that reach is, a significant exception has been carved out for Roth IRAs.

During Your Lifetime

During your lifetime, you are not required to take distributions from a Roth IRA. Ever. In fact, you could die without ever having removed a cent. This rule, which allows Roth IRA participants to accumulate a tax-favored nest egg and then simply pass it on to another generation, seems to conflict with the government's long-standing policy to ensure that tax-favored retirement plans primarily benefit the original participant.

But there is a logical, if cynical, explanation. Because the Roth IRA was structured to allow all qualified distributions to be tax free, the government has no real incentive

to force distributions. There are no deferred taxes to collect. So much for public policy.

After Your Death, Before Your RBD

Once you die, the distribution rules for Roth IRAs again merge with those for traditional IRAs. All of the post-death required distribution rules apply to Roth IRAs in the same way they apply to traditional IRAs. Thus, if you die before your RBD, the life expectancy rule or the five-year rule will apply. Those rules, as well as other required distribution rules that kick in if you die before your RBD, are explained in Chapter 7.

TIP

Roth IRAs can be a boon to your beneficiaries. Although the post-death required distribution rules for traditional IRAs are essentially the same as those for Roth IRAs, the planning implications could be quite different. Because distributions to beneficiaries from a Roth IRA are not subject to income tax, beneficiaries have access to 100% of the funds when the IRA participant dies (unless some of it must be used to pay estate taxes). For this reason, there will undoubtedly be a real temptation for beneficiaries to take distribution of their shares immediately upon the participant's death. Free money. But because assets inside the Roth IRA could continue to grow tax free, it is usually to the beneficiary's advantage to defer distributions for as long as possible.

After Your Death, After Your RBD

If you have a traditional IRA, you must begin required distributions when you reach your required beginning date or RBD. If you die after your RBD, a special set of distribution rules applies. (See Chapter 8.) But because you are not required to take distributions from a Roth IRA during your lifetime, you have no RBD for that purpose. In other words, you are always deemed to have died before your RBD.

Key Tax Code and Regulation Sections
§ 72(t) Early Distribution Tax and Exceptions
§ 72(t)(2)(F) First-Home-Purchase Exception to Early Distribution Tax
§ 401(a)(9) Required Distributions From Qualified Plans
§ 1.401(a)(9) Required Distribution Regulations
§ 408A Roth IRAs
§ 1.408A Roth IRA Regulations

Roth 401(k) Plans

Taxation of Distributions..212

    Distribution of After-Tax Salary Deferral Contributions.......................................213

    Distribution of Pretax Earnings 214

    Conversions and Rollovers...215

Early Distribution Tax..216

    Qualified Distributions...217

    Nonqualified Distributions 217

Ordering of Distributions...217

Required Distributions..217

    Required Distributions During Your Lifetime...217

    Required Distributions After Your Death 218

Who Should Read Chapter 10

 SKIP AHEAD

Read this chapter if you are younger than 59½ and want to withdraw money from your retirement plan or IRA. If you are older than 59½, this chapter does not apply to you.

The Roth 401(k) plan is a bit of a hybrid. Although it is technically a type of 401(k) plan, it has some of the features of a Roth IRA. Sorting out which 401(k) plan rules and which Roth IRA rules apply to the Roth 401(k) can be tricky. The safest approach is to assume that the 401(k) plan rules apply unless you can find a particular exception.

To start with, a Roth 401(k) plan is simply an option that can be added to a traditional 401(k) plan. A Roth 401(k) plan cannot exist on its own. So if your employer wants to establish a Roth 401(k) plan, it must establish a regular 401(k) plan and then add a provision to the plan documents that would establish a separate Roth 401(k) account. Employees would then be able to contribute part of their salaries to either the regular 401(k) plan or the Roth 401(k) plan—or perhaps split the contribution between the two accounts.

Only after-tax salary deferral contributions may be deposited in the Roth 401(k) account. No employer contributions and no pretax employee contributions are permitted. Therefore, the entire account will contain only after-tax contributions from your salary plus pretax earnings on those contributions.

Because the Roth 401(k) is actually just part of a regular 401(k) plan, most of the rules that apply to a regular 401(k) plan also apply to a Roth 401(k) plan. For example, the vesting rules and the contribution limits are the same. But there are significant differences in how the contributions will be taxed when they come out of the plan.

Taxation of Distributions

If you have been participating in a Roth 401(k) plan at work and you leave your job, you will generally have three options (assuming you do not simply take the money and spend it):

- You may transfer your Roth 401(k) plan into the Roth 401(k) plan of your new employer, if your new employer has such a plan. If you choose this option, the rules that you must follow are the same as the rules for transferring a traditional 401(k) plan to a new employer's 401(k) plan. (See Chapter 2.) Just remember: The only employer plan to which you may transfer your Roth 401(k) plan is another Roth 401(k) plan.

- You may roll over or transfer your Roth 401(k) plan to a Roth IRA. If you choose this option, once your Roth 401(k) plan assets have been

---

Helpful Terms

After-tax contribution. A contribution to a retirement plan on which income taxes have already been paid. Those contributions will be tax free when distributed from the plan.

Beneficiary. The person or entity entitled to receive the benefits from insurance or from trust property, such as a retirement plan or IRA.

Distribution. A payout of property, such as shares of stock or cash, from a retirement plan or IRA to the participant or a beneficiary.

401(k) Plan. A type of qualified profit-sharing plan that allows employees to contribute a portion of their salary to the plan instead of receiving that portion in cash.

Pretax earnings. The investment returns earned on retirement plan contributions. Those earnings will be taxable when they are distributed from the retirement plan.

Salary deferral contribution. A contribution to a retirement plan that is paid from salary that would otherwise be paid to the employee in cash.

Pro rata. Proportionately. For example, an amount distributed *pro rata* over four years is distributed evenly over those four years. Property that is distributed *pro rata* to its owners is distributed according to the percentage of each owner's interest.

---

deposited into the Roth IRA, the Roth IRA rules will apply to all of the assets as though they had always been part of the Roth IRA. Bear in mind that the rules described in Chapter 2 for rolling over qualified plans into IRAs will also apply to rollovers from Roth 401(k) plans to Roth IRAs.

- You may leave your Roth 401(k) plan assets with your employer. If you choose this option, the distribution rules described in the remainder of this chapter will apply when you eventually take money out of the plan.

Distribution of After-Tax Salary Deferral Contributions

The portion of your Roth 401(k) plan that consists of your salary deferral contributions is never subject to income tax when it comes out. That's because those contributions were subject to income tax in the year they were contributed to the plan. You don't have to pay tax a second time when you take the money out.

However, when you take money out of a Roth 401(k) plan, a portion of the distribution is deemed to be from your contributions and a portion from earnings.

In other words, your after-tax contributions come out *pro rata*.

> **EXAMPLE:** Ricky has $10,000 in his Roth 401(k) plan. Of that amount, $9,000, or 90%, is attributable to after-tax salary deferral contributions and $1,000 (10%) is from earnings on his contributions. If Ricky takes $3,000 out of his account, $300 (which is 10% of $3,000) will be attributable to earnings and will be subject to income tax, while $2,700 will be attributable to after-tax contributions and will be free of income tax.

 CAUTION

Roth IRA rules are different. Note that this distribution rule is different from the rule that applies to Roth IRAs. When you take money out of a Roth IRA, all of your contributions come out first. Earnings come out last.

Distribution of Pretax Earnings

As is the case with Roth IRAs, the contributions you make to a Roth 401(k) plan are invested and earn money for you. Those earnings—the interest and stock gains—will not be subject to income tax while they reside inside the plan. When it comes time to take money out of the Roth 401(k) plan, the earnings portion, as well as the contributions, will be tax free, as long as the distribution is considered a qualified distribution.

Qualified Distributions

Remember that when you take a distribution from a Roth 401(k) plan, a portion of that distribution will be from your after-tax contributions and a portion will be from the earnings on those contributions. The after-tax portion of the distribution will never be subject to income tax, because you already paid the tax. However, the earnings will be subject to tax unless the distribution is a qualified distribution. The first requirement of a qualified distribution is a five-year holding period. If you take a distribution within five calendar years of when you first contribute to your Roth 401(k) plan, the distribution will not be a qualified distribution.

As with a Roth IRA, if you count the year of your first contribution as year one, you satisfy the five-year requirement if you wait until the sixth year before taking money out of the plan. The five-year holding period begins on the first day of the calendar year for which your contribution was made.

However, unlike its application to Roth IRAs, the five-year holding period applies to each Roth 401(k) plan separately. So if you have more than one Roth 401(k) plan, a distribution will not be a qualified distribution if it is taken from a plan that has not been in place for at least five years.

CAUTION

Roth IRA rules are different. This five-year holding period rule for Roth 401(k) plans is different from the five-year holding period rule for Roth IRAs. If you hold multiple Roth IRAs, you satisfy the five-year holding period for all such IRAs once you have held any Roth IRA for five years.

CAUTION

Five-year holding period applies to beneficiaries. As is the case with a Roth IRA, if you die before satisfying the five-year holding period, your beneficiary must wait until you would have satisfied it, or the distribution will not be qualified.

Simply satisfying the five-year requirement will not automatically make a distribution qualified. It must also be at least one of the following:

- a distribution you take after reaching age 59½
- a distribution you take after becoming disabled, or
- a distribution to your beneficiary or your estate after your death.

If your distribution satisfies the five-year requirement and falls into one of the above categories, it will be qualified and thus entirely tax free.

Nonqualified Distributions

Any distribution from a Roth 401(k) plan that does not satisfy the requirements of a qualified distribution described above is automatically nonqualified. Although the portion of your nonqualified distributions that are attributable to your contributions will not be taxable, the portion that is attributable to earnings will be subject to income tax and perhaps penalties, as well. (See below for information about penalties that might apply.)

Conversions and Rollovers

When you have a Roth 401(k) plan, your rollover opportunities are limited, and your conversion opportunities are nonexistent. Although you are permitted to convert a traditional IRA to a Roth IRA, there is no symmetrical rule for converting a traditional 401(k) plan—or any other type of retirement plan—to a Roth 401(k) plan.

The sections that follow take a closer look at your rollover options.

Rollover to Another Roth 401(k)

You are permitted to transfer your Roth 401(k) plan to another Roth 401(k) plan if you change jobs and your new employer has a Roth 401(k) plan. If you decide to move the assets of your old plan, you must transfer them directly from the trustee of your old plan to the trustee of your new plan. You are not permitted to take possession of the funds yourself.

Technically, this is a trustee-to-trustee transfer, rather than a rollover. If you do not transfer the entire amount to the new plan, the earnings are presumed to be transferred first. (Note: This is an exception to the *pro rata* rule described above.)

Once you have transferred the assets from your old Roth 401(k) plan to the new one and the assets for both plans have been commingled, a new and favorable rule kicks in. Specifically, the five-year holding period requirement for qualified distributions will be based on the oldest plan. So for example, if you had satisfied the five-year holding period for your old plan but not the new one, once the old plan's assets have been commingled with the new plan's assets, all are deemed to satisfy the five-year holding period.

Rollover to a Roth IRA

You are also permitted to roll over your Roth 401(k) plan assets into a Roth IRA. If you choose to do this, the assets can be transferred in a trustee-to-trustee transfer (also known as a direct rollover) to avoid mandatory income tax withholding on the earnings. Alternatively, you can take the funds yourself and roll them over within 60 days to a Roth IRA.

Once the assets of the Roth 401(k) plan have been deposited in your Roth IRA account, all the Roth IRA rules apply to the combined assets. None of the Roth 401(k) plan rules will apply once the funds have been commingled with the Roth IRA assets. This applies also to the five-year

holding period requirement for qualified distributions. All of the assets in the Roth IRA will be subject to the original Roth IRA holding period even if the Roth 401(k) plan had been in place for more than five years and the Roth IRA had not.

No Rollover from a Roth IRA to a Roth 401(k) Plan

Although you are permitted to roll over the assets of a Roth 401(k) plan to a Roth IRA, you may not do the reverse—that is, you are not permitted to roll over the assets of a Roth IRA to a Roth 401(k) plan.

 CAUTION

Traditional IRAs are different. This rule is different from the rollover rules for traditional IRAs. You are permitted to roll over a traditional IRA into a qualified plan, if the plan allows it.

Early Distribution Tax

When making decisions about retirement plans, it is important to take into consideration both income taxes and penalties. The early distribution tax is an income tax that functions like a penalty. The penalty is for taking money out of a retirement plan too soon. The beginning of this chapter discussed income taxes. Now it's time to look at those situations in which an early distribution penalty might apply.

Qualified Distributions

All distributions from Roth 401(k) plans are either qualified distributions or non-qualified distributions. If the distribution is a qualified distribution as described above, the early distribution tax does not apply. The early distribution tax applies only to those distributions that are subject to income tax. Because all qualified distributions from Roth 401(k) plans are tax free, they are all exempt from the early distribution tax as well.

Nonqualified Distributions

Any portion of a nonqualified distribution from your Roth 401(k) plan that is required to be included on your income tax return is subject to the early distribution tax, unless an exception applies. The exceptions to the early distribution tax are the same as those that apply to a regular 401(k) plan distribution. Those exceptions can be found in Chapter 3. Because nonqualified distributions typically comprise after-tax contributions and earnings, only the earnings portion will be subject to the early distribution tax, unless an exception applies.

Ordering of Distributions

The special ordering rules for Roth IRAs that allow you to take your after-tax contributions out first do not apply to Roth 401(k) plans. Consequently, when you take a distribution from your Roth 401(k) plan, the distribution will comprise after-tax contributions and pretax earnings on those contributions in proportion to the total amount of each in your account. (See the example at the beginning of this chapter.)

Required Distributions

The required distribution rules that force you to begin taking money out of your retirement plans and traditional IRAs during your lifetime also apply to Roth 401(k) plans. The required distribution rules also force your beneficiaries to take distributions from the account after your death, whether they need the money or not. The following sections discuss both sets of distribution rules.

Required Distributions During Your Lifetime

The lifetime required distribution rules described in Chapter 6 also apply to distributions from your Roth 401(k) plan. Note that the rules for a Roth 401(k) plan are different from those for a Roth IRA. If you have a Roth 401(k) plan, you must begin taking distributions from the account when you reach age 70½, or after you retire, if that is later.

TIP

A rollover to a Roth IRA might be a good strategy. Recall that if you roll over your Roth 401(k) plan into a Roth IRA, once the assets are commingled, the Roth IRA rules will apply to all the assets in the account. Because you are not required to take distributions from a Roth IRA during your lifetime, if you roll over your Roth 401(k) plan into a Roth IRA, you will be able to bypass the lifetime required distribution rules that would otherwise apply to your Roth 401(k) plan.

Required Distributions After Your Death

All of the post-death required distribution rules apply to Roth 401(k) plans in the same way they apply to other qualified plans and traditional IRAs. Thus, if you die before your RBD, the life expectancy rule or the five-year rule will apply. Chapter 7 explains those rules in detail. If you die after your RBD, the rules described in Chapter 8 will apply.

Key Tax Code Sections and IRS Pronouncements

§ 72(t)
Early Distribution Tax and Exceptions

§ 401(a)(9)
Required Distributions From Qualified Plans

§ 1.401(a)(9)
Required Distribution Regulations

§ 1.401(k)-1(f)
401(k) Regulations Related to Roth 401(k) Contributions

§ 1.402A
Roth 401(k) Regulations

IRS Forms, Notices, and Schedules

Form 4972, *Tax on Lump-Sum Distributions* 220

Tax Rate Schedule for 1986 224

Form 5329, *Additional Taxes on Qualified Plans (Including IRAs)*
   and Other Tax-Favored Accounts 225

Form 5330, *Return of Excise Taxes Related to Employee Benefit Plans* 233

Form 5498, *IRA Contribution Information* 252

Form 8606, *Nondeductible IRAs* 253

Revenue Ruling 2002-62 264

Form **4972**

Department of the Treasury
Internal Revenue Service (99)

Tax on Lump-Sum Distributions

(From Qualified Plans of Participants Born Before January 2, 1936)

▶ Attach to Form 1040, Form 1040NR, or Form 1041.

OMB No. 1545-0193

2008

Attachment
Sequence No. **28**

Name of recipient of distribution | Identifying number

Part I	Complete this part to see if you can use Form 4972			
			Yes	No
1	Was this a distribution of a plan participant's entire balance (excluding deductible voluntary employee contributions and certain forfeited amounts) from all of an employer's qualified plans of one kind (pension, profit-sharing, or stock bonus)? If "No," **do not** use this form	1		
2	Did you roll over any part of the distribution? If "Yes," **do not** use this form	2		
3	Was this distribution paid to you as a beneficiary of a plan participant who was born before January 2, 1936?	3		
4	Were you **(a)** a plan participant who received this distribution, **(b)** born before January 2, 1936, **and (c)** a participant in the plan for at least 5 years before the year of the distribution?	4		
	If you answered "No" to both questions 3 **and** 4, **do not** use this form.			
5a	Did you use Form 4972 after 1986 for a previous distribution from your own plan? If "Yes," **do not** use this form for a 2008 distribution from your own plan	5a		
b	If you are receiving this distribution as a beneficiary of a plan participant who died, did you use Form 4972 for a previous distribution received for that participant after 1986? If "Yes," **do not** use the form for this distribution	5b		

Part II	Complete this part to choose the 20% capital gain election (see instructions)		
6	Capital gain part from Form 1099-R, box 3	6	
7	Multiply line 6 by 20% (.20) . . . . ▶	7	
	If you also choose to use Part III, go to line 8. Otherwise, include the amount from line 7 in the total on Form 1040, line 44, Form 1040NR, line 41, or Form 1041, Schedule G, line 1b, whichever applies.		

Part III	Complete this part to choose the 10-year tax option (see instructions)		
8	Ordinary income from Form 1099-R, box 2a minus box 3. If you did not complete Part II, enter the taxable amount from Form 1099-R, box 2a	8	
9	Death benefit exclusion for a beneficiary of a plan participant who died before August 21, 1996	9	
10	Total taxable amount. Subtract line 9 from line 8	10	
11	Current actuarial value of annuity from Form 1099-R, box 8. If none, enter -0-	11	
12	Adjusted total taxable amount. Add lines 10 and 11. If this amount is $70,000 or more, **skip** lines 13 through 16, enter this amount on line 17, and go to line 18	12	
13	Multiply line 12 by 50% (.50), but **do not** enter more than $10,000 . [13]		
14	Subtract $20,000 from line 12. If line 12 is $20,000 or less, enter -0- . . . . . [14]		
15	Multiply line 14 by 20% (.20) . . . . [15]		
16	Minimum distribution allowance. Subtract line 15 from line 13	16	
17	Subtract line 16 from line 12	17	
18	Federal estate tax attributable to lump-sum distribution	18	
19	Subtract line 18 from line 17. If line 11 is zero, **skip** lines 20 through 22 and go to line 23 . .	19	
20	Divide line 11 by line 12 and enter the result as a decimal (rounded to at least three places) . . . . [20] .		
21	Multiply line 16 by the decimal on line 20 . . . . . . [21]		
22	Subtract line 21 from line 11 . . . . [22]		
23	Multiply line 19 by 10% (.10)	23	
24	Tax on amount on line 23. Use the Tax Rate Schedule in the instructions	24	
25	Multiply line 24 by ten (10). If line 11 is zero, **skip** lines 26 through 28, enter this amount on line 29, and go to line 30	25	
26	Multiply line 22 by 10% (.10) . . . . [26]		
27	Tax on amount on line 26. Use the Tax Rate Schedule in the instructions . . . . . . [27]		
28	Multiply line 27 by ten (10)	28	
29	Subtract line 28 from line 25. Multiple recipients, see instructions . . . . ▶	29	
30	**Tax on lump-sum distribution.** Add lines 7 and 29. Also include this amount in the total on Form 1040, line 44, Form 1040NR, line 41, or Form 1041, Schedule G, line 1b, whichever applies . ▶	30	

For Paperwork Reduction Act Notice, see instructions.   Cat. No. 13187U   Form **4972** (2008)

Section references are to the Internal Revenue Code.

General Instructions

Purpose of Form

Use Form 4972 to figure the tax on a qualified lump-sum distribution (defined below) you received in 2008 using the 20% capital gain election, the 10-year tax option, or both. These are special formulas used to figure a separate tax on the distribution that may result in a smaller tax than if you reported the taxable amount of the distribution as ordinary income.

You pay the tax only once, for the year you receive the distribution, not over the next 10 years. The separate tax is added to the regular tax figured on your other income.

Related Publications

Pub. 575, Pension and Annuity Income.

Pub. 721, Tax Guide to U.S. Civil Service Retirement Benefits.

Pub. 939, General Rule for Pensions and Annuities.

What Is a Qualified Lump-Sum Distribution?

It is the distribution or payment in 1 tax year of a plan participant's entire balance from all of an employer's qualified plans of one kind (for example, pension, profit-sharing, or stock bonus plans) in which the participant had funds. The participant's entire balance does not include deductible voluntary employee contributions or certain forfeited amounts. The participant must have been born before January 2, 1936.

Distributions upon death of the plan participant. If you received a qualifying distribution as a beneficiary after the participant's death, the participant must have been born before January 2, 1936, for you to use this form for that distribution.

Distributions to alternate payees. If you are the spouse or former spouse of a plan participant who was born before January 2, 1936, and you received a qualified lump-sum distribution as an alternate payee under a qualified domestic relations order, you can use Form 4972 to make the 20% capital gain election and use the 10-year tax option to figure your tax on the distribution.

See *How To Report the Distribution* on this page.

Distributions That Do Not Qualify for the 20% Capital Gain Election or the 10-Year Tax Option

The following distributions are not qualified lump-sum distributions and do not qualify for the 20% capital gain election or the 10-year tax option.

• The part of a distribution not rolled over if the distribution is partially rolled over to another qualified plan or an IRA.

• Any distribution if an earlier election to use either the 5- or 10-year tax option had been made after 1986 for the same plan participant.

• U.S. Retirement Plan Bonds distributed with the lump sum.

• A distribution made during the first 5 tax years that the participant was in the plan, unless it was paid because the participant died.

• The current actuarial value of any annuity contract included in the lump sum (Form 1099-R, box 8, should show this amount, which you use only to figure tax on the ordinary income part of the distribution).

• A distribution to a 5% owner that is subject to penalties under section 72(m)(5)(A).

• A distribution from an IRA.

• A distribution from a tax-sheltered annuity (section 403(b) plan).

• A distribution of the redemption proceeds of bonds rolled over tax free to a qualified pension plan, etc., from a qualified bond purchase plan.

• A distribution from a qualified plan if the participant or his or her surviving spouse previously received an eligible rollover distribution from the same plan (or another plan of the employer that must be combined with that plan for the lump-sum distribution rules) and the previous distribution was rolled over tax free to another qualified plan or an IRA.

• A distribution from a qualified plan that received a rollover after 2001 from an IRA (other than a conduit IRA), a governmental section 457 plan, or a section 403(b) tax-sheltered annuity on behalf of the plan participant.

• A distribution from a qualified plan that received a rollover after 2001 from another qualified plan on behalf of that plan participant's surviving spouse.

• A corrective distribution of excess deferrals, excess contributions, excess aggregate contributions, or excess annual additions.

• A lump-sum credit or payment from the Federal Civil Service Retirement System (or the Federal Employees' Retirement System).

How To Report the Distribution

If you can use Form 4972, attach it to Form 1040 (individuals), Form 1040NR (nonresident aliens), or Form 1041 (estates or trusts). The payer should have given you a Form 1099-R or other statement that shows the amounts needed to complete Form 4972. The following choices are available.

20% capital gain election. If there is an amount in Form 1099-R, box 3, you can use Form 4972, Part II, to apply a 20% tax rate to the capital gain portion. See *Capital Gain Election* on page 3.

10-year tax option. You can use Part III to figure your tax on the lump-sum

distribution using the 10-year tax option whether or not you make the 20% capital gain election.

Where to report. Report amounts from your Form 1099-R either directly on your tax return (Form 1040, 1040NR, or 1041) or on Form 4972.

1. If you do not use Form 4972, and you file:

a. **Form 1040.** Report the entire amount from box 1 (Gross distribution) of Form 1099-R on line 16a, and the taxable amount on line 16b. If your pension or annuity is fully taxable, enter the amount from box 2a (Taxable amount) of Form 1099-R on line 16b; do not make an entry on line 16a.

b. **Form 1040NR.** Report the entire amount from box 1 (Gross distribution) of Form 1099-R on line 17a, and the taxable amount on line 17b. If your pension or annuity is fully taxable, enter the amount from box 2a (Taxable amount) of Form 1099-R on line 17b; do not make an entry on line 17a.

c. **Form 1041.** Report the amount on line 8.

2. If you do not use Part III of Form 4972, but use Part II, report only the ordinary income portion of the distribution on Form 1040, lines 16a and 16b, on Form 1040NR, lines 17a and 17b, or on Form 1041, line 8. The ordinary income portion is the amount from box 2a of Form 1099-R, minus the amount from box 3 of that form.

3. If you use Part III of Form 4972, do not include any part of the distribution on Form 1040, lines 16a and 16b, on Form 1040NR, lines 17a and 17b, or on Form 1041, line 8.

The entries in other boxes on Form 1099-R may also apply in completing Form 4972.

• Box 6 (Net unrealized appreciation in employer's securities). See *Net unrealized appreciation (NUA)* on page 3.

• Box 8 (Other). Current actuarial value of an annuity.

If applicable, get the amount of federal estate tax paid attributable to the taxable part of the lump-sum distribution from the administrator of the deceased's estate.

How Often You Can Use Form 4972

After 1986, you can use Form 4972 only once for each plan participant. If you receive more than one lump-sum distribution for the same participant in 1 tax year, you must treat all those distributions the same way. Combine them on a single Form 4972.

If you make an election as a beneficiary of a deceased participant, it does not affect any election you can make for qualified lump-sum distributions from your own plan. You can also make an election as the beneficiary of more than one qualifying person.

Example. Your mother and father died and each was born before January 2, 1936. Each had a qualified plan of which

Form 4972 (2008)   Page **3**

you are the beneficiary. You also received a qualified lump-sum distribution from your own plan and you were born before January 2, 1936. You can make an election for each of the distributions; one for yourself, one as your mother's beneficiary, and one as your father's. It does not matter if the distributions all occur in the same year or in different years. File a separate Form 4972 for each participant's distribution.

 An earlier election on Form 4972 or Form 5544 for a distribution before 1987 does not prevent you from making an election for a distribution after 1986 for the same participant, provided the participant was under age 59½ at the time of the pre-1987 distribution.

When To File Form 4972

You can file Form 4972 with either an original or amended return. Generally, you have 3 years from the later of the due date of your tax return or the date you filed your return to choose to use any part of Form 4972.

Capital Gain Election

If the distribution includes a capital gain, you can (a) make the 20% capital gain election in Part II of Form 4972 or (b) treat the capital gain as ordinary income.

Only the taxable amount of distributions resulting from pre-1974 participation qualifies for capital gain treatment. The capital gain amount should be shown in Form 1099-R, box 3. If there is an amount in Form 1099-R, box 6 (net unrealized appreciation (NUA)), part of it will also qualify for capital gain treatment. Use the NUA Worksheet on this page to figure the capital gain part of NUA if you make the election to include NUA in your taxable income.

You can report the ordinary income portion of the distribution on Form 1040, line 16b, Form 1040NR, line 17b, or Form 1041, line 8 or you can figure the tax using the 10-year tax option. The ordinary income portion is the amount from Form 1099-R, box 2a, minus the amount from box 3 of that form.

Net unrealized appreciation (NUA). Normally, NUA in employer securities received as part of a lump-sum distribution is not taxable until the securities are sold. However, you can elect to include NUA in taxable income in the year received.

The total amount to report as NUA should be shown in Form 1099-R, box 6. Part of the amount in box 6 will qualify for capital gain treatment if there is an amount in Form 1099-R, box 3. To figure the total amount subject to capital gain treatment including the NUA, complete the NUA Worksheet on this page.

Specific Instructions

Name of recipient of distribution and identifying number. At the top of Form 4972, fill in the name and identifying number of the recipient of the distribution.

If you received more than one qualified distribution in 2008 for the same plan participant, add them and figure the tax on the total amount. If you received qualified distributions in 2008 for more than one participant, file a separate Form 4972 for the distributions of each participant.

If you and your spouse are filing a joint return and each has received a lump-sum distribution, complete and file a separate Form 4972 for each spouse's election, combine the tax, and include the combined tax in the total on Form 1040, line 44.

If you are filing for a trust that shared the distribution only with other trusts, figure the tax on the total lump sum first. The trusts then share the tax in the same proportion that they shared the distribution.

Multiple recipients of a lump-sum distribution. If you shared in a lump-sum distribution from a qualified retirement plan when not all recipients were trusts (a percentage was shown in Form 1099-R, boxes 8 and/or 9a), figure your tax on Form 4972 as follows. (Box numbers used below are from Form 1099-R.)

Step 1. Complete Form 4972, Parts I and II. If you made the 20% capital gain election in Part II and also elect to include NUA in taxable income, complete the NUA Worksheet below to determine the amount of NUA that qualifies for capital gain treatment. Then, skip Step 2 and go to Step 3.

Step 2. Use this step only if you do not elect to include NUA in your taxable income or if you do not have NUA.

- If you are not making the capital gain election, divide the amount in box 2a by your percentage of distribution in box 9a. Enter this amount on Form 4972, line 8.

- If you are making the capital gain election, subtract the amount in box 3 from the amount in box 2a. Divide the result by your percentage of distribution in box 9a. Enter the result on Form 4972, line 8.

- Divide the amount in box 8 by the percentage in box 8. Enter the result on Form 4972, line 11. Then, skip Step 3 and go to Step 4.

Step 3. Use this step only if you elect to include NUA in your taxable income.

- If you are not making the capital gain election, add the amount in box 6 to the amount in box 2a. Divide the result by your percentage of distribution in box 9a. Enter the result on Form 4972, line 8.

- If you are making the capital gain election, subtract the amount in box 3 from the amount in box 2a. Add to the result the amount from line F of your NUA Worksheet. Then, divide the total by your percentage of distribution in box 9a. Enter the result on Form 4972, line 8.

- Divide the amount in box 8 by the percentage in box 8. Enter the result on Form 4972, line 11.

Step 4. Complete Form 4972 through line 28.

Step 5. Complete the following worksheet to figure the entry for Form 4972, line 29:

A. Subtract line 28 from line 25 .	_____
B. Enter your percentage of the distribution from box 9a . .	_____
C. Multiply line A by line B. Enter here and on Form 4972, line 29. Also, write "MRD" on the dotted line next to line 29 .	_____

NUA Worksheet (keep for your records)

A.	Enter the amount from Form 1099-R, box 3	**A.** _____
B.	Enter the amount from Form 1099-R, box 2a	**B.** _____
C.	Divide line A by line B and enter the result as a decimal (rounded to at least three places)	**C.** __.__
D.	Enter the amount from Form 1099-R, box 6	**D.** _____
E.	Capital gain portion of NUA. Multiply line C by line D	**E.** _____
F.	Ordinary income portion of NUA. Subtract line E from line D .	**F.** _____
G.	Total capital gain portion of distribution. Add lines A and E. Enter here and on Form 4972, line 6. On the dotted line next to line 6, write "NUA" and the amount from line E above.	**G.** _____

Death Benefit Worksheet (keep for your records)

A.	Enter the amount from Form 1099-R, box 3, or, if you are including NUA in taxable income, the amount from line G of the NUA Worksheet	**A.** _____
B.	Enter the amount from Form 1099-R, box 2a, plus, if you are including NUA in taxable income, the amount from Form 1099-R, box 6 .	**B.** _____
C.	Divide line A by line B and enter the result as a decimal (rounded to at least three places)	**C.** __.__
D.	Enter your share of the death benefit exclusion*	**D.** _____
E.	Multiply line D by line C	**E.** _____
F.	Subtract line E from line A. Enter here and on Form 4972, line 6 .	**F.** _____

*Applies only for participants who died before August 21, 1996. If there are multiple recipients of the distribution, the allowable death benefit exclusion must be allocated among the recipients in the same proportion that they share the distribution.

Form 4972 (2008)   Page **4**

Part II

See *Capital Gain Election* on page 3 before completing Part II.

Line 6. Leave this line blank if your distribution does not include a capital gain amount or you are not making the 20% capital gain election, and go to Part III.

Generally, enter on line 6 the amount from Form 1099-R, box 3. However, if you elect to include NUA in your taxable income, use the NUA Worksheet on page 3 to figure the amount to enter on line 6. If you are taking a death benefit exclusion (for a participant who died before August 21, 1996), use the Death Benefit Worksheet on page 3 to figure the amount to enter on line 6. The remaining allowable death benefit exclusion should be entered on line 9 if you choose the 10-year tax option.

If any federal estate tax was paid on the lump-sum distribution, you must decrease the capital gain amount by the amount of estate tax applicable to it. To figure this amount, you must complete the Death Benefit Worksheet on page 3 through line C, even if you do not take the death benefit exclusion. Multiply the total federal estate tax paid on the lump-sum distribution by the decimal on line C of the Death Benefit Worksheet. The result is the portion of the federal estate tax applicable to the capital gain amount. Then, use that result to reduce the amount in Form 1099-R, box 3, if you do not take the death benefit exclusion, or reduce line F of the Death Benefit Worksheet if you do. Enter the remaining capital gain on line 6. If you elected to include NUA in taxable income, subtract the portion of federal estate tax applicable to the capital gain amount from the amount on line G of the NUA Worksheet. Enter the result on line 6. Enter the remainder of the federal estate tax on line 18.

 If you take the death benefit exclusion and federal estate tax was paid on the capital gain amount, the capital gain amount must be reduced by both the procedures discussed above to figure the correct entry for line 6.

Part III

Line 8. If Form 1099-R, box 2a, is blank, you must first figure the taxable amount. For details on how to do this, see Pub. 575.

If you made the 20% capital gain election, enter only the ordinary income portion of the distribution on this line. The ordinary income portion is the amount from Form 1099-R, box 2a, minus the amount from box 3 of that form. Add the amount from line F of the NUA Worksheet if you included NUA capital gain in the 20% capital gain election.

If you did not make the 20% capital gain election and did not elect to include NUA in taxable income, enter the amount from Form 1099-R, box 2a. If you did not make the 20% capital gain election but did elect to include NUA in your taxable income, add the amount from Form 1099-R, box 2a, to the amount from Form 1099-R, box 6. Enter the total on line 8. On the dotted line next to line 8, write "NUA" and the amount of NUA included.

 Community property laws do not apply in figuring tax on the amount you report on line 8.

Line 9. If you received the distribution because of the plan participant's death and the participant died before August 21, 1996, you may be able to exclude up to $5,000 of the lump sum from your gross income. If there are multiple recipients of the distribution not all of whom are trusts, enter on line 9 the full remaining allowable death benefit exclusion (after the amount taken against the capital gain portion of the distribution by all recipients—see the instructions for line 6) without allocation among the recipients. (The exclusion is in effect allocated among the recipients through the computation under *Multiple recipients of a lump-sum distribution* on page 3.) This exclusion applies to the beneficiaries or estates of common-law employees, self-employed individuals, and shareholder-employees who owned more than 2% of the stock of an S corporation.

Enter the allowable death benefit exclusion on line 9. But see the instructions for line 6 if you made a capital gain election.

Line 18. A beneficiary who receives a lump-sum distribution because of a plan participant's death must reduce the taxable part of the distribution by any federal estate tax paid on the lump-sum distribution. Do this by entering on line 18 the federal estate tax attributable to the lump-sum distribution. Also see the instructions for line 6 if you made a capital gain election.

Lines 24 and 27. Use the following Tax Rate Schedule to complete lines 24 and 27.

Tax Rate Schedule

If the amount on line 23 or 26 is:		Enter on line 24 or 27:	
Over	But not over—		Of the amount over—
$ 0	$1,190	- - - - 11%	$ 0
1,190	2,270	$130.90 + 12%	1,190
2,270	4,530	260.50 + 14%	2,270
4,530	6,690	576.90 + 15%	4,530
6,690	9,170	900.90 + 16%	6,690
9,170	11,440	1,297.70 + 18%	9,170
11,440	13,710	1,706.30 + 20%	11,440
13,710	17,160	2,160.30 + 23%	13,710
17,160	22,880	2,953.80 + 26%	17,160
22,880	28,600	4,441.00 + 30%	22,880
28,600	34,320	6,157.00 + 34%	28,600
34,320	42,300	8,101.80 + 38%	34,320
42,300	57,190	11,134.20 + 42%	42,300
57,190	85,790	17,388.00 + 48%	57,190
85,790	- - - - -	31,116.00 + 50%	85,790

Paperwork Reduction Act Notice. We ask for the information on this form to carry out the Internal Revenue laws of the United States. You are required to give us the information. We need it to ensure that you are complying with these laws and to allow us to figure and collect the right amount of tax.

You are not required to provide the information requested on a form that is subject to the Paperwork Reduction Act unless the form displays a valid OMB control number. Books or records relating to a form or its instructions must be retained as long as their contents may become material in the administration of any Internal Revenue law. Generally, tax returns and return information are confidential, as required by section 6103.

The time needed to complete this form will vary depending on individual circumstances. The estimated burden for individual taxpayers filing this form is approved under OMB control number 1545-0074 and is included in the estimates shown in the instructions for their individual income tax return. The estimated burden for all other taxpayers who file this form is shown below.

Recordkeeping	19 min.
Learning about the law or the form	1 hr., 31 min.
Preparing the form . . .	2 hr., 7 min.
Copying, assembling, and sending the form to the IRS .	20 min.

If you have comments concerning the accuracy of these time estimates or suggestions for making this form simpler, we would be happy to hear from you. See the instructions for the tax return with which this form is filed.

Tax Rate Schedule for 1986

If the amount on line 30 or 33 is:		Enter on line 31 or 34:		
over—	But not Over—	Amount	Plus percentage	Of the amount over—
$0	$1,190	- - - - - -	11%	$0
1,190	2,270	$130.90	+ 12%	1,190
2,270	4,530	260.50	+ 14%	2,270
4,530	6,690	576.90	+ 15%	4,530
6,690	9,170	900.90	+ 16%	6,690
9,170	11,440	1,297.70	+ 18%	9,170
11,440	13,710	1,706.30	+ 20%	11,440
13,710	17,160	2,160.30	+ 23%	13,710
17,160	22,880	2,953.80	+ 26%	17,160
22,880	28,600	4,441.00	+ 30%	22,880
28,600	34,320	6,157.00	+ 34%	28,600
34,320	42,300	8,101.80	+ 38%	34,320
42,300	57,190	11,134.20	+ 42%	42,300
57,190	85,790	17,388.00	+ 48%	57,190
85,790	- - - - -	31,116.00	+ 50%	85,790

Form **5329**	**Additional Taxes on Qualified Plans (Including IRAs) and Other Tax-Favored Accounts**	OMB No. 1545-0074
Department of the Treasury Internal Revenue Service (99)	▶ Attach to Form 1040 or Form 1040NR. ▶ See separate instructions.	**2008** Attachment Sequence No. **29**

Name of individual subject to additional tax. If married filing jointly, see instructions.

Your social security number

Fill in Your Address Only If You Are Filing This Form by Itself and Not With Your Tax Return ▶

Home address (number and street), or P.O. box if mail is not delivered to your home

Apt. no.

City, town or post office, state, and ZIP code

If this is an amended return, check here ▶ ☐

If you **only** owe the additional 10% tax on early distributions, you may be able to report this tax directly on Form 1040, line 59, or Form 1040NR, line 54, without filing Form 5329. See the instructions for Form 1040, line 59, or for Form 1040NR, line 54.

Part I   Additional Tax on Early Distributions

Complete this part if you took a taxable distribution (other than a qualified disaster recovery assistance or qualified recovery assistance distribution), before you reached age 59½, from a qualified retirement plan (including an IRA) or modified endowment contract (unless you are reporting this tax directly on Form 1040 or Form 1040NR—see above). You may also have to complete this part to indicate that you qualify for an exception to the additional tax on early distributions or for certain Roth IRA distributions (see instructions).

1	Early distributions included in income. For Roth IRA distributions, see instructions	1
2	Early distributions included on line 1 that are not subject to the additional tax (see instructions). Enter the appropriate exception number from the instructions: _____	2
3	Amount subject to additional tax. Subtract line 2 from line 1	3
4	**Additional tax.** Enter 10% (.10) of line 3. Include this amount on Form 1040, line 59, or Form 1040NR, line 54	4

Caution: *If any part of the amount on line 3 was a distribution from a SIMPLE IRA, you may have to include 25% of that amount on line 4 instead of 10% (see instructions).*

Part II   Additional Tax on Certain Distributions From Education Accounts

Complete this part if you included an amount in income, on Form 1040 or Form 1040NR, line 21, from a Coverdell education savings account (ESA) or a qualified tuition program (QTP).

5	Distributions included in income from Coverdell ESAs and QTPs	5
6	Distributions included on line 5 that are not subject to the additional tax (see instructions) . .	6
7	Amount subject to additional tax. Subtract line 6 from line 5	7
8	**Additional tax.** Enter 10% (.10) of line 7. Include this amount on Form 1040, line 59, or Form 1040NR, line 54	8

Part III   Additional Tax on Excess Contributions to Traditional IRAs

Complete this part if you contributed more to your traditional IRAs for 2008 than is allowable or you had an amount on line 17 of your 2007 Form 5329.

9	Enter your excess contributions from line 16 of your 2007 Form 5329 (see instructions). If zero, go to line 15		9
10	If your traditional IRA contributions for 2008 are less than your maximum allowable contribution, see instructions. Otherwise, enter -0-	10	
11	2008 traditional IRA distributions included in income (see instructions)	11	
12	2008 distributions of prior year excess contributions (see instructions)	12	
13	Add lines 10, 11, and 12		13
14	Prior year excess contributions. Subtract line 13 from line 9. If zero or less, enter -0-		14
15	Excess contributions for 2008 (see instructions)		15
16	Total excess contributions. Add lines 14 and 15		16
17	**Additional tax.** Enter 6% (.06) of the **smaller** of line 16 **or** the value of your traditional IRAs on December 31, 2008 (including 2008 contributions made in 2009). Include this amount on Form 1040, line 59, or Form 1040NR, line 54		17

Part IV   Additional Tax on Excess Contributions to Roth IRAs

Complete this part if you contributed more to your Roth IRAs for 2008 than is allowable or you had an amount on line 25 of your 2007 Form 5329.

18	Enter your excess contributions from line 24 of your 2007 Form 5329 (see instructions). If zero, go to line 23		18
19	If your Roth IRA contributions for 2008 are less than your maximum allowable contribution, see instructions. Otherwise, enter -0-	19	
20	2008 distributions from your Roth IRAs (see instructions)	20	
21	Add lines 19 and 20		21
22	Prior year excess contributions. Subtract line 21 from line 18. If zero or less, enter -0- . . .		22
23	Excess contributions for 2008 (see instructions)		23
24	Total excess contributions. Add lines 22 and 23		24
25	**Additional tax.** Enter 6% (.06) of the **smaller** of line 24 **or** the value of your Roth IRAs on December 31, 2008 (including 2008 contributions made in 2009). Include this amount on Form 1040, line 59, or Form 1040NR, line 54		25

For Privacy Act and Paperwork Reduction Act Notice, see page 6 of the instructions.   Cat. No. 13329Q   Form **5329** (2008)

Form 5329 (2008)   Page **2**

Part V   Additional Tax on Excess Contributions to Coverdell ESAs

Complete this part if the contributions to your Coverdell ESAs for 2008 were more than is allowable or you had an amount on line 33 of your 2007 Form 5329.

26	Enter the excess contributions from line 32 of your 2007 Form 5329 (see instructions). If zero, go to line 31	**26**
27	If the contributions to your Coverdell ESAs for 2008 were less than the maximum allowable contribution, see instructions. Otherwise, enter -0- **27**	
28	2008 distributions from your Coverdell ESAs (see instructions) **28**	
29	Add lines 27 and 28	**29**
30	Prior year excess contributions. Subtract line 29 from line 26. If zero or less, enter -0-	**30**
31	Excess contributions for 2008 (see instructions)	**31**
32	Total excess contributions. Add lines 30 and 31	**32**
33	**Additional tax.** Enter 6% (.06) of the **smaller** of line 32 **or** the value of your Coverdell ESAs on December 31, 2008 (including 2008 contributions made in 2009). Include this amount on Form 1040, line 59, or Form 1040NR, line 54 **33**	

Part VI   Additional Tax on Excess Contributions to Archer MSAs

Complete this part if you or your employer contributed more to your Archer MSAs for 2008 than is allowable or you had an amount on line 41 of your 2007 Form 5329.

34	Enter the excess contributions from line 40 of your 2007 Form 5329 (see instructions). If zero, go to line 39	**34**
35	If the contributions to your Archer MSAs for 2008 are less than the maximum allowable contribution, see instructions. Otherwise, enter -0- **35**	
36	2008 distributions from your Archer MSAs from Form 8853, line 10 . **36**	
37	Add lines 35 and 36	**37**
38	Prior year excess contributions. Subtract line 37 from line 34. If zero or less, enter -0-	**38**
39	Excess contributions for 2008 (see instructions)	**39**
40	Total excess contributions. Add lines 38 and 39	**40**
41	**Additional tax.** Enter 6% (.06) of the **smaller** of line 40 **or** the value of your Archer MSAs on December 31, 2008 (including 2008 contributions made in 2009). Include this amount on Form 1040, line 59, or Form 1040NR, line 54 **41**	

Part VII   Additional Tax on Excess Contributions to Health Savings Accounts (HSAs)

Complete this part if you, someone on your behalf, or your employer contributed more to your HSAs for 2008 than is allowable or you had an amount on line 49 of your 2007 Form 5329.

42	Enter the excess contributions from line 48 of your 2007 Form 5329. If zero, go to line 47 . .	**42**
43	If the contributions to your HSAs for 2008 are less than the maximum allowable contribution, see instructions. Otherwise, enter -0- **43**	
44	2008 distributions from your HSAs from Form 8889, line 16 **44**	
45	Add lines 43 and 44	**45**
46	Prior year excess contributions. Subtract line 45 from line 42. If zero or less, enter -0-	**46**
47	Excess contributions for 2008 (see instructions)	**47**
48	Total excess contributions. Add lines 46 and 47	**48**
49	**Additional tax.** Enter 6% (.06) of the **smaller** of line 48 **or** the value of your HSAs on December 31, 2008 (including 2008 contributions made in 2009). Include this amount on Form 1040, line 59, or Form 1040NR, line 54	**49**

Part VIII   Additional Tax on Excess Accumulation in Qualified Retirement Plans (Including IRAs)

Complete this part if you did not receive the minimum required distribution from your qualified retirement plan.

50	Minimum required distribution for 2008 (see instructions)	**50**
51	Amount actually distributed to you in 2008	**51**
52	Subtract line 51 from line 50. If zero or less, enter -0-	**52**
53	**Additional tax.** Enter 50% (.50) of line 52. Include this amount on Form 1040, line 59, or Form 1040NR, line 54	**53**

Sign Here Only If You Are Filing This Form by Itself and Not With Your Tax Return

Under penalties of perjury, I declare that I have examined this form, including accompanying attachments, and to the best of my knowledge and belief, it is true, correct, and complete. Declaration of preparer (other than taxpayer) is based on all information of which preparer has any knowledge.

▶ _____ Your signature   ▶ _____ Date

Paid Preparer's Use Only	Preparer's signature ▶		Date	Check if self-employed ☐	Preparer's SSN or PTIN
	Firm's name (or yours if self-employed), address, and ZIP code ▶			EIN	
				Phone no. ( )	

Form **5329** (2008)

20**08**

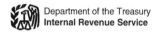

Department of the Treasury
Internal Revenue Service

Instructions for Form 5329

Additional Taxes on Qualified Plans (Including IRAs) and Other Tax-Favored Accounts

Section references are to the Internal Revenue Code unless otherwise noted.

General Instructions

What's New

Rollovers from qualified retirement plans to Roth IRAs. Beginning in 2008, you can roll over (convert) amounts from a qualified retirement plan to a Roth IRA. Generally, the 10% tax on early distributions does not apply to these rollovers. See *Rollover* on page 2 for more information.

Economic stimulus payments. If your economic stimulus payment was directly deposited into a tax-favored account (such as your individual retirement arrangement (IRA), Coverdell education savings account (ESA), Archer MSA, health savings account (HSA), or qualified tuition program (QTP) account), you can withdraw all or part of the payment. The amount withdrawn will not be considered as contributed to or distributed from the account and is not subject to any additional tax or penalty. The withdrawal must be made by the due date (including extensions) for filing your 2008 tax return. For a Coverdell ESA, the withdrawal can be made by the later of the above date or June 1, 2009.

Midwestern disaster relief. The additional tax on early distributions does not apply to qualified disaster recovery assistance distributions. See Form 8930, Qualified Disaster Recovery Assistance Retirement Plan Distributions and Repayments, for more information.

Kansas storms and tornadoes. The additional tax on early distributions does not apply to qualified recovery assistance distributions. See Pub. 4492-A, Information for Taxpayers Affected by the May 4, 2007, Kansas Storms and Tornadoes, for more information.

Required minimum distributions for 2009. For 2009, you are not required to take a minimum distribution from your employer-provided qualified retirement plan or IRA. For more information, see Pub. 575, Pension and Annuity Income, or Pub. 590, Individual Retirement Arrangements (IRAs).

Purpose of Form

Use Form 5329 to report additional taxes on:
- IRAs,
- Other qualified retirement plans,
- Modified endowment contracts,
- Coverdell ESAs,
- QTPs,
- Archer MSAs, or
- HSAs.

Who Must File

You must file Form 5329 if any of the following apply, except you do not have to file Form 5329 to report a qualified disaster recovery assistance distribution, a qualified recovery assistance distribution, or the timely withdrawal of an economic stimulus payment that was directly deposited into your tax-favored account (see *Economic stimulus payments* on this page).

- You received an early distribution from a Roth IRA, the amount on line 23 of Form 8606, Nondeductible IRAs, is more than zero, and you are required to enter an amount that is more than zero on Form 5329, line 1 (see *Exception for Roth IRA Distributions* on page 2).
- You received an early distribution from a qualified retirement plan (other than a Roth IRA) and distribution code 1 is not shown in box 7 of Form 1099-R, Distributions From Pensions, Annuities, Retirement or Profit-Sharing Plans, IRAs, Insurance Contracts, etc.

Note. You do not have to file Form 5329 if distribution code 1 is correctly shown in box 7 of all Forms 1099-R and you owe the additional tax on each Form 1099-R. Instead, see the instructions for Form 1040, line 59, or Form 1040NR, line 54, for how to report the additional 10% tax directly on that line.

- You meet an exception to the tax on early distributions and distribution code 1 is shown in box 7 of Form 1099-R.
- You meet an exception to the tax on early distributions from the list on page 3 but box 7 of your Form 1099-R does not indicate an exception or the exception does not apply to the entire distribution.
- You received taxable distributions from Coverdell ESAs or QTPs.
- The contributions for 2008 to your traditional IRAs, Roth IRAs, Coverdell ESAs, Archer MSAs, or HSAs exceed your maximum contribution limit, or you

had a tax due from an excess contribution on line 17, 25, 33, 41, or 49 of your 2007 Form 5329.
- You did not receive the minimum required distribution from your qualified retirement plan.

TIP *If you rolled over part or all of a distribution from a qualified retirement plan, the part rolled over is not subject to the additional tax on early distributions. See the instructions for Form 1040, lines 15a and 15b or lines 16a and 16b; Form 1040A, lines 11a and 11b or 12a and 12b; or Form 1040NR, lines 16a and 16b or 17a and 17b, for how to report the rollover.*

When and Where To File

File Form 5329 with your 2008 Form 1040 or Form 1040NR by the due date, including extensions, of your Form 1040 or Form 1040NR.

If you do not have to file a 2008 income tax return, complete and file Form 5329 by itself at the time and place you would be required to file Form 1040 or Form 1040NR. Be sure to include your address on page 1 and your signature and the date on page 2. Enclose, but do not attach, a check or money order payable to "United States Treasury" for any taxes due. Write your SSN and "2008 Form 5329" on the check.

Prior tax years. If you are filing Form 5329 for a prior year, you must use that year's version of the form. If you do not have other changes and have not previously filed a federal income tax return for that year, file Form 5329 by itself (discussed earlier). If you have other changes, file Form 5329 for that year with Form 1040X, Amended U.S. Individual Income Tax Return.

Definitions

Qualified retirement plan. A qualified retirement plan includes:
- A qualified pension, profit-sharing, or stock bonus plan (including a 401(k) plan),
- A tax-sheltered annuity contract,
- A qualified annuity plan, and
- An IRA.

For purposes of the additional tax on early distributions, an eligible governmental section 457 deferred compensation plan is treated as a qualified retirement plan, but only to the extent that a distribution is attributable

Cat. No. 13330R

to an amount transferred from a qualified retirement plan (defined on page 1).

Note. Modified endowment contracts are not qualified retirement plans.

Traditional IRAs. For purposes of Form 5329, a traditional IRA is any IRA, including a simplified employee pension (SEP) IRA, other than a SIMPLE IRA or Roth IRA.

Early distribution. Generally, any distribution from your IRA, other qualified retirement plan, or modified endowment contract before you reach age 59½ is an early distribution.

Rollover. Generally, a rollover is a tax-free distribution of assets from one qualified retirement plan that is reinvested in another plan or the same plan. Generally, you must complete the rollover within 60 days of receiving the distribution. Any taxable amount not rolled over must be included in income and may be subject to the additional tax on early distributions.

Beginning in 2008, you can roll over (convert) amounts from a qualified retirement plan to a Roth IRA. Any amount rolled over to a Roth IRA is subject to the same rules for converting a traditional IRA to a Roth IRA. You must include in your gross income distributions from a qualified retirement plan that you would have had to include in income if you had not rolled them into a Roth IRA. Generally, the 10% tax on early distributions does not apply. For more information, see *Rollover From Employer's Plan Into a Roth IRA* in chapter 2 of Pub. 590.

The IRS may waive the 60-day requirement if failing to waive it would be against equity or good conscience, such as situations where a casualty, disaster, or other events beyond your reasonable control prevented you from meeting the 60-day requirement. Also, the 60-day period may be extended if you had a frozen deposit. See Pub. 590 for details.

Compensation. Compensation includes wages, salaries, tips, bonuses, and other pay you receive for services you perform. It also includes sales commissions, commissions on insurance premiums, and pay based on a percentage of profits. It includes net earnings from self-employment, but only for a trade or business in which your personal services are a material income-producing factor.

For IRAs, treat nontaxable combat pay and all taxable alimony received under a decree of divorce or separate maintenance as compensation.

Compensation does not include any amounts received as a pension or annuity and does not include any amount received as deferred compensation.

Taxable compensation is your compensation that is included in gross income reduced by any deductions on Form 1040, lines 27 and 28, or on Form

1040NR, line 27, but not by any loss from self-employment.

Additional Information

See Pub. 590; Pub. 560, Retirement Plans for Small Business; Pub. 575; Pub. 969, Health Savings Accounts and Other Tax-Favored Health Plans; Pub. 970, Tax Benefits for Education; Pub. 4492-A; and Pub. 4492-B.

Specific Instructions

Joint returns. If both you and your spouse are required to file Form 5329, complete a separate form for each of you. Include the combined tax on Form 1040, line 59.

Amended returns. If you are filing an amended 2008 Form 5329, check the box at the top of page 1 of the form. Do not use the 2008 Form 5329 to amend your return for any other year. Instead, see *Prior tax years* on page 1.

Part I—Additional Tax on Early Distributions

In general, if you receive an early distribution (including an involuntary cashout) from an IRA, other qualified retirement plan, or modified endowment contract, the part of the distribution included in income generally is subject to an additional 10% tax. But see *Exception for Roth IRA Distributions* on this page.

The additional tax on early distributions does not apply to any of the following:

- A qualified disaster recovery assistance distribution. See Form 8930 for more details.
- A qualified recovery assistance distribution. See Pub. 4492-A for more details.
- An economic stimulus payment directly deposited into your IRA and withdrawn by the due date of your tax return (including extensions).
- A qualified HSA funding distribution from an IRA (other than a SEP or SIMPLE IRA). See Pub. 969 for details.
- A distribution from a traditional or SIMPLE IRA that was converted to a Roth IRA.
- A rollover from a qualified retirement plan to a Roth IRA.
- A distribution of certain excess IRA contributions (see the instructions for lines 15 and 23 on page 4).

Note. Any related earnings withdrawn with excess contributions are subject to the additional tax on early distributions if you were under age 59½ at the time of the distribution.

- A distribution of excess contributions from a qualified cash or deferred arrangement.
- A distribution of excess aggregate contributions to meet nondiscrimination requirements for employee contributions and matching employer contributions.

- A distribution of excess deferrals.
- A distribution from an eligible governmental section 457 deferred compensation plan to the extent the distribution is not attributable to an amount transferred from a qualified retirement plan (excluding an eligible section 457 deferred compensation plan).

See the instructions for line 2 on page 3 for other distributions that are not subject to the tax.

Line 1

Enter the amount of early distributions included in income that you received from:

- A qualified retirement plan, including earnings on withdrawn excess contributions to your IRAs included in income in 2008, or
- A modified endowment contract entered into after June 20, 1988.

Certain prohibited transactions, such as borrowing from your IRA or pledging your IRA assets as security for a loan, are considered to be distributions and may also cause you to owe the additional tax on early distributions. See Pub. 590 for details.

Exception for Roth IRA Distributions

If you received an early distribution from a Roth IRA, first allocate the amount on your 2008 Form 8606, line 19 (not including any qualified disaster recovery assistance distributions or qualified recovery assistance distributions), in the order shown, to the amounts on the lines listed below (to the extent a prior year distribution was not allocable to the amount).

- Your 2008 Form 8606, line 20.
- Your 2008 Form 8606, line 22*.
- Your 1998 Form 8606, line 16.
- Your 1998 Form 8606, line 15.
- Your 1999 Form 8606, line 16.
- Your 1999 Form 8606, line 15.
- Your 2000 Form 8606, line 16.
- Your 2000 Form 8606, line 15.
- Your 2001 Form 8606, line 18.
- Your 2001 Form 8606, line 17.
- Your 2002 Form 8606, line 18.
- Your 2002 Form 8606, line 17.
- Your 2003 Form 8606, line 18.
- Your 2003 Form 8606, line 17.
- Your 2004 Form 8606, line 18.
- Your 2004 Form 8606, line 17.
- Your 2005 Form 8606, line 18.
- Your 2005 Form 8606, line 17.
- Your 2006 Form 8606, line 18.
- Your 2006 Form 8606, line 17.
- Your 2007 Form 8606, line 18.
- Your 2007 Form 8606, line 17.
- Your 2008 Form 8606, line 18.
- Your 2008 Form 8606, line 17.
- Your 2008 Form 8606, line 25c.

*If applicable, reduce this amount by any amounts attributable to qualified disaster recovery assistance distributions or qualified recovery assistance distributions.

Then, include on line 1 of Form 5329 the amount from your 2008 Form 8606, line 25c, plus the amount, if any, allocated to the amount on your 2008 Form 8606, line 20, and the amount, if any, allocated to line 18 of your 2004 through 2008 Forms 8606. Also include the amount, if any, from your 2008 Form 8606, line 20, on Form 5329, line 2, and enter exception number 09.

Example. You converted $20,000 from a traditional IRA to a Roth IRA in 2004 and converted $10,000 in 2005. Your 2004 Form 8606 had $5,000 on line 17 and $15,000 on line 18 and your 2005 Form 8606 had $3,000 on line 17 and $7,000 on line 18. You made Roth IRA contributions of $2,000 for 2004 and 2005. You did not make any Roth IRA conversions or contributions for 2006 through 2008, or take any Roth IRA distributions before 2008. On July 9, 2008, at age 53, you took a $33,000 distribution from your Roth IRA. Your 2008 Form 8606 shows $33,000 on line 19; $29,000 on line 23 ($33,000 minus $4,000 for your contributions on line 22) and $0 on line 25a ($29,000 minus your basis in conversions of $30,000). First, $4,000 of the $33,000 is allocated to your 2008 Form 8606, line 22; then $15,000 to your 2004 Form 8606, line 18; $5,000 to your 2004 Form 8606, line 17; and $7,000 to your 2005 Form 8606, line 18. The remaining $2,000 is allocated to the $3,000 on your 2005 Form 8606, line 17. On line 1, enter $22,000 ($15,000 allocated to your 2004 Form 8606, line 18, plus the $7,000 that was allocated to your 2005 Form 8606, line 18). If you take a Roth IRA distribution in 2009, the first $1,000 will be allocated to the $1,000 remaining from your 2005 Form 8606, line 17, and will not be subject to the additional tax on early distributions.

Additional information. For more details, see *Are Distributions Taxable?* in Pub. 590.

Line 2
The additional tax on early distributions does not apply to the distributions described below. Enter on line 2 the amount that can be excluded. In the space provided, enter the applicable exception number (01-12).

No. Exception

01 Qualified retirement plan distributions (does not apply to IRAs) if you separated from service in or after the year you reach age 55 (age 50 for qualified public safety employees).

02 Distributions made as part of a series of substantially equal periodic payments (made at least annually) for your life (or life expectancy) or the joint lives (or joint life expectancies) of you and your designated beneficiary (if from an employer plan, payments must begin after separation from service).

03 Distributions due to total and permanent disability.

04 Distributions due to death (does not apply to modified endowment contracts).

05 Qualified retirement plan distributions up to (1) the amount you paid for unreimbursed medical expenses during the year minus (2) 7.5% of your adjusted gross income for the year.

06 Qualified retirement plan distributions made to an alternate payee under a qualified domestic relations order (does not apply to IRAs).

07 IRA distributions made to unemployed individuals for health insurance premiums.

08 IRA distributions made for higher education expenses.

09 IRA distributions made for purchase of a first home, up to $10,000.

10 Distributions due to an IRS levy on the qualified retirement plan.

11 Qualified distributions to reservists while serving on active duty for at least 180 days.

12 Other (see *Other*, below). Also, enter this code if more than one exception applies.

Other. The following exceptions also apply.

• Distributions incorrectly indicated as early distributions by code 1, J, or S in box 7 of Form 1099-R. Include on line 2 the amount you received when you were age 59½ or older.

• Distributions from a section 457 plan, which are not from a rollover from a qualified retirement plan.

• Distributions from a plan maintained by an employer if:

1. You separated from service by March 1, 1986;

2. As of March 1, 1986, your entire interest was in pay status under a written election that provides a specific schedule for distribution of your entire interest; and

3. The distribution is actually being made under the written election.

• Distributions that are dividends paid with respect to stock described in section 404(k).

• Distributions from annuity contracts to the extent that the distributions are allocable to the investment in the contract before August 14, 1982.

For additional exceptions that apply to annuities, see Pub. 575.

Line 4
If any amount on line 3 was a distribution from a SIMPLE IRA received within 2 years from the date you first participated in the SIMPLE IRA plan, you must multiply that amount by 25% instead of 10%. These distributions are included in boxes 1 and 2a of Form 1099-R and are designated with code S in box 7.

Part II—Additional Tax on Certain Distributions From Education Accounts

 An economic stimulus payment that was directly deposited into an education account can be fully or partly withdrawn by the due date (including extensions) of your 2008 tax return. For a Coverdell ESA, the withdrawal can be made by the later of the above date or June 1, 2009. The amount withdrawn will not be subject to any additional tax or penalty.

Line 6
This tax does not apply to distributions that are includible in income if:
• Due to the death or disability of the beneficiary;
• Made on account of a tax-free scholarship, allowance, or payment described in section 25A(g)(2);
• Made because of attendance by the beneficiary at a U.S. military academy. This exception applies only to the extent that the distribution does not exceed the costs of advanced education (as defined in title 10 of the U.S. Code) at the academy; or
• Included in income because you used the qualified education expenses to figure the Hope and lifetime learning credit.

Enter on line 6 the portion of line 5 that is excluded.

Part III—Additional Tax on Excess Contributions to Traditional IRAs
If you contributed more for 2008 than is allowable or you had an amount on line 17 of your 2007 Form 5329, you may owe this tax. But you may be able to avoid the tax on any 2008 excess contributions (see the instructions for line 15 on page 4).

 An economic stimulus payment that was directly deposited into an IRA can be fully or partly withdrawn by the due date (including extensions) of your 2008 tax return. The amount withdrawn will not be subject to any additional tax or penalty.

Line 9
Enter the amount from line 16 of your 2007 Form 5329 only if the amount on line 17 of your 2007 Form 5329 is more than zero.

Line 10
If you contributed less to your traditional IRAs for 2008 than your contribution limit for traditional IRAs, enter the difference.

If you are not married filing jointly, your contribution limit for traditional IRAs is the smaller of your taxable compensation (see page 2) or $5,000

($6,000 if age 50 or older at the end of 2008). If you are married filing jointly, your contribution limit is generally $5,000 ($6,000 if age 50 or older at the end of 2008) and your spouse's contribution limit is $5,000 ($6,000 if age 50 or older at the end of 2008). But if the combined taxable compensation for you and your spouse is less than $10,000 ($11,000 if one spouse is 50 or older at the end of 2008; $12,000 if both spouses are 50 or older at the end of 2008), see *How Much Can Be Contributed?* in Pub. 590 for special rules.

TIP *If you participated in a 401(k) plan and the employer who maintained the plan went into bankruptcy in an earlier year, you may be able to contribute up to $8,000 to your traditional IRA. See Pub. 590 for more details.*

Also include on line 11a or 11b of the IRA Deduction Worksheet in the instructions for Form 1040, line 32, the smaller of (a) Form 5329, line 10, or (b) the excess, if any, of Form 5329, line 9, over the sum of Form 5329, lines 11 and 12.

Line 11

Enter on line 11 any withdrawals from your traditional IRAs that are included in your income. Do not include any withdrawn contributions reported on line 12.

Line 12

Enter any excess contributions to your traditional IRAs for 1976 through 2006 that you had returned to you in 2008 and any 2007 excess contributions that you had returned to you in 2008 after the due date (including extensions) of your 2007 income tax return, that are included on line 9, if:

- You did not claim a deduction for the excess contributions and no traditional IRA deduction was allowable (without regard to the modified AGI limitation) for the excess contributions, and
- The total contributions to your traditional IRAs for the tax year for which the excess contributions were made were not more than: (a) $4,000 for 2007 or 2006 ($5,000 if age 50 or older at the end of the year), (b) $4,000 for 2005 ($4,500 if age 50 or older at the end of the year), (c) $3,000 for years after 2001 and before 2005 ($3,500 if age 50 or older at the end of the year), (d) $2,000 for years after 1996 and before 2002, or (e) $2,250 for years before 1997. If the total contributions for the year included employer contributions to a SEP, increase that amount by the smaller of the amount of the employer contributions or $45,000 ($44,000 for 2006, $42,000 for 2005, $41,000 for 2004, $40,000 for 2003 and 2002, $35,000 for 2001, or $30,000 for years before 2001).

Line 15

Enter the excess of your contributions to traditional IRAs for 2008 (unless withdrawn—see below) over your contribution limit for traditional IRAs. See the instructions for line 10 that begin on page 3 to figure your contribution limit for traditional IRAs. Any amount you contribute for the year in which you reach age 70½ or a later year is an excess contribution because your contribution limit is zero. Do not include rollovers in figuring your excess contributions.

You can withdraw some or all of your excess contributions for 2008 and they will not be treated as having been contributed if:

- You make the withdrawal by the due date, including extensions, of your 2008 tax return,
- You do not claim a traditional IRA deduction for the withdrawn contributions, and
- You withdraw any earnings on the withdrawn contribution and include the earnings in gross income (see the Instructions for Form 8606 for details). Also, if you had not reached age 59½ at the time of the withdrawal, include the earnings as an early distribution on line 1 of Form 5329 for the year in which you report the earnings.

If you timely filed your return without withdrawing the excess contributions, you can still make the withdrawal no later than 6 months after the due date of your tax return, excluding extensions. If you do, file an amended return with "Filed pursuant to section 301.9100-2" written at the top. Report any related earnings for 2008 on the amended return and include an explanation of the withdrawal. Make any other necessary changes on the amended return (for example, if you reported the contributions as excess contributions on your original return, include an amended Form 5329 reflecting that the withdrawn contributions are no longer treated as having been contributed).

Part IV—Additional Tax on Excess Contributions to Roth IRAs

If you contributed more to your Roth IRA for 2008 than is allowable or you had an amount on line 25 of your 2007 Form 5329, you may owe this tax. But you may be able to avoid the tax on any 2008 excess contributions (see the instructions for line 23 that begin on this page).

TIP *An economic stimulus payment that was directly deposited into a Roth IRA can be fully or partly withdrawn by the due date (including extensions) of your 2008 tax return. The amount withdrawn will not be subject to any additional tax or penalty.*

Line 18

Enter the amount from line 24 of your 2007 Form 5329 only if the amount on line 25 of your 2007 Form 5329 is more than zero.

Line 19

If you contributed less to your Roth IRAs for 2008 than your contribution limit for Roth IRAs, enter the difference. Your contribution limit for Roth IRAs is generally your contribution limit for traditional IRAs (see the instructions for line 10 that begin on page 3) reduced by the amount you contributed to traditional IRAs. But your contribution limit for Roth IRAs may be further reduced or eliminated if your modified AGI for Roth IRA purposes is over:

- $159,000 if married filing jointly or qualifying widow(er),
- $0 if married filing separately and you lived with your spouse at any time in 2008, or
- $101,000 for any other taxpayer.

See Pub. 590 for details.

Line 20

Generally, enter the amount from Form 8606, line 19, plus any qualified distributions. But if you withdrew the entire balance of all your Roth IRAs, do not enter less than the amount on Form 5329, line 18 (see *Example*).

Example. You contributed $1,000 to a Roth IRA in 2006, your only contribution to Roth IRAs. In 2008, you discovered you were not eligible to contribute to a Roth IRA in 2006. On September 9, 2008, you withdrew $800, the entire balance in the Roth IRA. You must file Form 5329 for 2006 and 2007 to pay the additional taxes for those years. When you complete Form 5329 for 2008, you enter $1,000 (not $800) on line 20, because you withdrew the entire balance.

Line 23

Enter the excess of your contributions to Roth IRAs for 2008 (unless withdrawn—see below) over your contribution limit for Roth IRAs (see the instructions for line 19 on this page).

Any amounts converted (including any amounts rolled over from a qualified retirement plan) to a Roth IRA are excess Roth IRA contributions if your modified AGI for Roth IRA purposes is over $100,000 or your filing status is married filing separately and you lived with your spouse at any time in 2008. See *Recharacterizations* in the Instructions for Form 8606 for details. Do not include rollovers from another Roth IRA or designated Roth account in figuring your excess contributions.

You can withdraw some or all of your excess contributions for 2008 and they will not be treated as having been contributed if:

- You make the withdrawal by the due date, including extensions, of your 2008 tax return, and

• You withdraw any earnings on the withdrawn contributions and include the earnings in gross income (see the Instructions for Form 8606 for details). Also, if you had not reached age 59½ at the time of the withdrawal, include the earnings as an early distribution on line 1 of Form 5329 for the year in which you report the earnings.

Note. A Form 5329 is not required if the excess Roth IRA contributions are not treated as having been contributed and you do not have any earnings to report as early distributions on the form.

If you timely filed your return without withdrawing the excess contributions, you can still make the withdrawal no later than 6 months after the due date of your tax return, excluding extensions. If you do, file an amended return with "Filed pursuant to section 301.9100-2" written at the top. Report any related earnings for 2008 on the amended return and include an explanation of the withdrawal. Make any other necessary changes on the amended return (for example, if you reported the contributions as excess contributions on your original return, include an amended Form 5329 reflecting that the withdrawn contributions are no longer treated as having been contributed).

Part V—Additional Tax on Excess Contributions to Coverdell ESAs

If the contributions to your Coverdell ESAs for 2008 were more than is allowable or you had an amount on line 33 of your 2007 Form 5329, you may owe this tax. But you may be able to avoid the tax on any 2008 excess contributions (see the instructions for line 31 on this page).

 An economic stimulus payment that was directly deposited into a Coverdell ESA can be fully or partly withdrawn by the later of the due date (including extensions) of your 2008 tax return or June 1, 2009. The amount withdrawn will not be subject to any additional tax or penalty.

Line 26

Enter the amount from line 32 of your 2007 Form 5329 only if the amount on line 33 of your 2007 Form 5329 is more than zero.

Line 27

Enter the excess, if any, of the maximum amount that can be contributed to your Coverdell ESAs for 2008 (see the instructions for line 31 on this page) over the amount actually contributed for 2008.

Line 28

Enter your total distributions from Coverdell ESAs in 2008. Do not include rollovers or returned excess contributions.

Line 31

Enter the excess of the contributions to your Coverdell ESAs for 2008 (not including rollovers) over your contribution limit for Coverdell ESAs. Your contribution limit is the smaller of $2,000 or the sum of the maximum amounts allowed to be contributed by the contributor(s) to your Coverdell ESAs. The maximum contribution may be limited based on the contributor's modified AGI. See Pub. 970 for details.

You can withdraw some or all of the excess contributions for 2008 and they will not be treated as having been contributed if:
• You make the withdrawal before June 1, 2009, and
• You also withdraw any income earned on the withdrawn contributions and include the earnings in gross income for the year in which the contribution was made.

If you filed your return without withdrawing the excess contributions, you can still make the withdrawal, but it must be made before June 1, 2009. If you do, file an amended return. Report any related earnings for 2008 on the amended return and include an explanation of the withdrawal. Make any other necessary changes on the amended return (for example, if you reported the contributions as excess contributions on your original return, include an amended Form 5329 reflecting that the withdrawn contributions are no longer treated as having been contributed).

Part VI—Additional Tax on Excess Contributions to Archer MSAs

If you or your employer contributed more to your Archer MSA for 2008 than is allowable or you had an amount on line 41 of your 2007 Form 5329, you may owe this tax. But you may be able to avoid the tax on any 2008 excess contributions (see the instructions for line 39 on this page).

 An economic stimulus payment that was directly deposited into an Archer MSA can be fully or partly withdrawn by the due date (including extensions) of your 2008 tax return. The amount withdrawn will not be subject to any additional tax or penalty.

Line 34

Enter the amount from line 40 of your 2007 Form 5329 only if the amount on line 41 of your 2007 Form 5329 is more than zero.

Line 35

If your contribution limit for your Archer MSAs (the smaller of line 5 or line 6 of Form 8853, Archer MSAs and Long-Term Care Insurance Contracts) is greater than the contributions to your Archer MSAs for 2008, enter the

difference on line 35. Also include on your 2008 Form 8853, line 7, the smaller of:
• Form 5329, line 35, or
• The excess, if any, of Form 5329, line 34, over Form 5329, line 36.

Line 39

Enter the excess of your contributions to your Archer MSA for 2008 (from Form 8853, line 4) over your contribution limit (the smaller of line 5 or line 6 of Form 8853). Also include on line 39 any excess contributions your employer made. See the Instructions for Form 8853 for details.

However, you can withdraw some or all of the excess contributions for 2008 and they will not be treated as having been contributed if:
• You make the withdrawal by the due date, including extensions, of your 2008 tax return, and
• You withdraw any income earned on the withdrawn contributions and include the earnings in gross income for the year in which you receive the withdrawn contributions and earnings.

Include the withdrawn contributions and related earnings on Form 8853, lines 8a and 8b.

If you timely filed your return without withdrawing the excess contributions, you can still make the withdrawal no later than 6 months after the due date of your tax return, excluding extensions. If you do, file an amended return with "Filed pursuant to section 301.9100-2" written at the top. Report any related earnings for 2008 on the amended return and include an explanation of the withdrawal. Make any other necessary changes on the amended return (for example, if you reported the contributions as excess contributions on your original return, include an amended Form 5329 reflecting that the withdrawn contributions are no longer treated as having been contributed).

Part VII—Additional Tax on Excess Contributions to Health Savings Accounts (HSAs)

If you, someone on your behalf, or your employer contributed more to your HSAs for 2008 than is allowable or you had an amount on line 49 of your 2007 Form 5329, you may owe this tax. But you may be able to avoid the tax on any 2008 excess contributions (see the instructions for line 47 on page 6).

 An economic stimulus payment that was directly deposited into an HSA can be fully or partly withdrawn by the due date (including extensions) of your 2008 tax return. The amount withdrawn will not be subject to any additional tax or penalty.

Line 43

If your contribution limit for your HSAs (line 12 of Form 8889, Health Savings

Accounts (HSAs)) is greater than the contributions you made to your HSAs (or those made on your behalf) for 2008 (Form 8889, line 2), enter the difference on line 43. Also include on your 2008 Form 8889, line 13, the smaller of:
• Form 5329, line 43, or
• The excess, if any, of Form 5329, line 42, over Form 5329, line 44.

Line 47

Enter the excess of your contributions (including those made on your behalf) to your HSAs for 2008 (Form 8889, line 2) over your contribution limit (Form 8889, line 12). Also include on line 47 any excess contributions your employer made. See the instructions for Form 8889 for details.

However, you can withdraw some or all of the excess contributions for 2008 and they will not be treated as having been contributed if:
• You make the withdrawal by the due date, including extensions, of your 2008 return, and
• You withdraw any income earned on the withdrawn contributions and include the earnings in gross income for the year in which you receive the withdrawn contributions and earnings.

Include the withdrawn contributions and related earnings on Form 8889, lines 14a and 14b.

If you timely filed your return without withdrawing the excess contributions, you can still make the withdrawal no later than 6 months after the due date of your tax return, excluding extensions. If you do, file an amended return with "Filed pursuant to section 301.9100-2" written at the top. Report any related earnings for 2008 on the amended return and include an explanation of the withdrawal. Make any other necessary changes on the amended return (for example, if you reported the contributions as excess contributions on your original return, include an amended Form 5329 reflecting that the withdrawn contributions are no longer treated as having been contributed).

Part VIII—Additional Tax on Excess Accumulation in Qualified Retirement Plans (Including IRAs)

You owe this tax if you do not receive the minimum required distribution from your qualified retirement plan, including an IRA or an eligible section 457 deferred compensation plan. The additional tax is 50% of the excess accumulation—the difference between the amount that was required to be distributed and the amount that was actually distributed.

Required Distributions

IRA (other than a Roth IRA). You must start receiving distributions from

your IRA by April 1 of the year following the year in which you reach age 70½. At that time, you can receive your entire interest in the IRA or begin receiving periodic distributions. If you choose to receive periodic distributions, you must receive a minimum required distribution each year. You can figure the minimum required distribution by dividing the account balance of your IRAs (other than Roth IRAs) on December 31 of the year preceding the distribution by the applicable life expectancy. For applicable life expectancies, see Pub. 590.

If the trustee, custodian, or issuer of your IRA informs you of the minimum required distribution, you can use that amount.

If you have more than one IRA, you can take the minimum required distribution from any one or more of the individual IRAs.

For more details on the minimum distribution rules (including examples), see Pub. 590.

⚠️ *A qualified charitable distribution will count towards your minimum required distribution. See Pub. 590 for more information.*

Roth IRA. There are no minimum required distributions during the lifetime of the owner of a Roth IRA. Following the death of the Roth IRA owner, required distribution rules apply to the beneficiary. See Pub. 590 for details.

Qualified retirement plans (other than IRAs) and eligible section 457 deferred compensation plans. In general, you must begin receiving distributions from your plan no later than April 1 following the later of (a) the year in which you reach age 70½ or (b) the year in which you retire.

Exception. If you owned more than 5% of the employer maintaining the plan, you must begin receiving distributions no later than April 1 of the year following the year in which you reach age 70½, regardless of when you retire.

Your plan administrator should figure the amount that must be distributed each year.

Waiver of tax. The IRS can waive part or all of this tax if you can show that any shortfall in the amount of distributions was due to reasonable error and you are taking appropriate steps to remedy the shortfall. If you believe you qualify for this relief, attach a statement of explanation and file Form 5329 as follows.

1. Complete lines 50 and 51 as instructed.
2. Enter "RC" and the amount you want waived in parentheses on the dotted line next to line 52. Subtract this amount from the total shortfall you figured without regard to the waiver, and enter the result on line 52.

3. Complete line 53 as instructed. You must pay any tax due that is reported on line 53.

The IRS will review the information you provide and decide whether to grant your request for a waiver.

For more details, see Pub. 590.

💡 *For 2009, you are not required to take a minimum distribution from your employer-provided qualified retirement plan or IRA. For more details, see Pub. 575 or Pub. 590.*

Privacy Act and Paperwork Reduction Act Notice. We ask for the information on this form to carry out the Internal Revenue laws of the United States. We need this information to ensure that you are complying with these laws and to allow us to figure and collect the right amount of tax. You are required to give us this information if you made certain contributions or received certain distributions from qualified plans, including IRAs, and other tax-favored accounts. Our legal right to ask for the information requested on this form is sections 6001, 6011, 6012(a), and 6109 and their regulations. The reason we need your social security number is to secure proper identification in order to gain access to the tax information in our files to properly process the form. If you do not file this information, or provide incomplete or false information, you may be subject to penalties.

You are not required to provide the information requested on a form that is subject to the Paperwork Reduction Act unless the form displays a valid OMB control number. Books or records relating to a form or its instructions must be retained as long as their contents may become material in the administration of any Internal Revenue law. Generally, tax returns and return information are confidential, as required by section 6103. However, we may give this information to the Department of Justice for civil and criminal litigation, and to cities, states, and the District of Columbia to carry out their tax laws. We may also disclose this information to other countries under a tax treaty, to federal and state agencies to enforce federal nontax criminal laws, or to federal law enforcement and intelligence agencies to combat terrorism.

The average time and expenses required to complete and file this form will vary depending on individual circumstances. For the estimated averages, see the instructions for your income tax return.

If you have suggestions for making this form simpler, we would be happy to hear from you. See the instructions for your income tax return.

Form **5330** (Rev. January 2008) Department of the Treasury Internal Revenue Service	**Return of Excise Taxes Related to Employee Benefit Plans** (Under sections 4965, 4971, 4972, 4973(a)(3), 4975, 4976, 4977, 4978, 4979, 4979A, 4980, and 4980F of the Internal Revenue Code)	OMB No. 1545-0575

Filer tax year beginning _____ , **and ending** _____ ,

A Name of filer (see instructions)	B Filer's identifying number (see instructions)
Number, street, and room or suite no. (If a P.O. box, see instructions)	E Plan sponsor's EIN
City or town, state, and ZIP code	F Plan year ending (MM/DD/YYYY)
C Name of plan	G Plan number
D Name and address of plan sponsor	

H   If this is an **amended return,** check here . . . . ▶ ☐

Part I   Taxes. You can only complete one Section of Part I for each Form 5330 filed (see instructions).

	FOR IRS USE ONLY		
Section A—Taxes that are reported by the last day of the 7th month after the end of the tax year of the employer (or other person who must file the return)			
1 Section 4972 tax on nondeductible contributions to qualified plans (from Schedule A, line 12)	161	**1**	
2 Section 4973(a)(3) tax on excess contributions to section 403(b)(7)(A) custodial accounts (from Schedule B, line 12)	164	**2**	
3a Section 4975(a) tax on prohibited transactions (from Schedule C, line 3)	159	**3a**	
b Section 4975(b) tax on failure to correct prohibited transactions	224	**3b**	
4 Section 4976 tax on disqualified benefits for funded welfare plans	200	**4**	
5a Section 4978 tax on ESOP dispositions	209	**5a**	
b The tax on line 5a is a result of the application of: ☐ Sec. 664(g) ☐ Sec. 1042		**5b**	
6 Section 4979A tax on certain prohibited allocations of qualified ESOP securities. . . .	203	**6**	
7 **Total Section A taxes.** Add lines 1 through 6. Enter here and on Part II, line 17 . ▶		**7**	
Section B—Taxes that are reported by the last day of the 7th month after the end of the employer's tax year or 8½ months after the last day of the plan year that ends within the filer's tax year			
8a Section 4971(a) tax on failure to meet minimum funding standards (from Schedule D, line 2).	163	**8a**	
b Section 4971(b) tax for failure to correct minimum funding standards	225	**8b**	
9a Section 4971(f)(1) tax on failure to pay liquidity shortfall (from Schedule E, line 4) . . .	226	**9a**	
b Section 4971(f)(2) tax for failure to correct liquidity shortfall	227	**9b**	
10a Section 4971(g)(2) tax on failure to comply with a funding improvement or rehabilitation plan (see instructions)	450	**10a**	
b Section 4971(g)(3) tax on failure to meet requirements for plans in endangered or critical status (from Schedule F, line 1c)	451	**10b**	
c Section 4971(g)(4) tax on failure to adopt rehabilitation plan (from Schedule F, line 2d) .	452	**10c**	
Section B1—Tax that is reported by the last day of the 7th month after the end of the calendar year in which the excess fringe benefits were paid to the employer's employees			
11 Section 4977 tax on excess fringe benefits (from Schedule G, line 4)	201	**11**	
12 **Total Section B taxes.** Add lines 8a through 11. Enter here and on Part II, line 17 . ▶		**12**	
Section C—Tax that is reported by the last day of the 15th month after the end of the plan year			
13 Section 4979 tax on excess contributions to certain plans (from Schedule H, line 2). Enter here and on Part II, line 17 . . . . ▶	205	**13**	

For Privacy Act and Paperwork Reduction Act Notice, see instructions.   Cat. No. 11870M   Form **5330** (Rev. 1-2008)

Form 5330 (Rev. 1-2008)   Page **2**

Name of Filer:	Filer's identifying number:		

Section D—Tax that is reported by the last day of the month following the month in which the reversion occurred

14	Section 4980 tax on reversion of qualified plan assets to an employer (from Schedule I, line 3). Enter here and on Part II, line 17 . . . . ▶	204	**14**	

Section E—Tax that is reported by the last day of the month following the month in which the failure occurred

15	Section 4980F tax on failure to provide notice of significant reduction in future accruals (from Schedule J, line 5). Enter here and on Part II, line 17 . . . . ▶	228	**15**	

Section F—Taxes reported on or before the 15th day of the 5th month following the close of the entity manager's taxable year during which the plan became a party to a prohibited tax shelter transaction

16	Section 4965 tax on prohibited tax shelter transactions for entity managers (from Schedule K, line 2). Enter here and on Part II, line 17 . . . . ▶	237	**16**	

Part II   Tax Due

17	Enter the amount from Part I, line 7, 12, 13, 14, 15, or 16 (whichever is applicable)	**17**
18	Enter amount of tax paid with Form 5558 or any other tax paid prior to filing this return . . .	**18**
19	**Tax due.** Subtract line 18 from line 17. If the result is greater than zero, enter here, and attach check or money order payable to "United States Treasury." Write your name, identifying number, plan number, and "Form 5330, Section(s) _____" on your payment . . . . ▶	**19**

Sign Here

Under penalties of perjury, I declare that I have examined this return, including accompanying schedules and statements, and to the best of my knowledge and belief, it is true, correct, and complete. Declaration of preparer (other than taxpayer) is based on all information of which preparer has any knowledge.

▶	▶	▶
Your signature	Telephone number	Date

Paid Preparer's Use Only

Preparer's signature ▶	Date	Check if self-employed ☐	Preparer's SSN or PTIN
Firm's name (or yours if self-employed), address, and ZIP code ▶		EIN	
		Phone no. ( )	

Form **5330** (Rev. 1-2008)

Form 5330 (Rev. 1-2008)   Page **3**

Name of Filer: Filer's identifying number:

Schedule A—Tax on Nondeductible Employer Contributions to Qualified Employer Plans (Section 4972)
Reported by the last day of the 7th month after the end of the tax year of the employer (or other person who must file the return)

1	Total contributions for your tax year to your qualified employer plan (under section 401(a), 403(a), 408(k), or 408(p))	**1**		
2	Amount allowable as a deduction under section 404	**2**		
3	Subtract line 2 from line 1	**3**		
4	Enter amount of any prior year nondeductible contributions made for years beginning after 12/31/86 . . . . **4**			
5	Amount of any prior year nondeductible contributions for years beginning after 12/31/86 returned to you in this tax year for any prior tax year . **5**			
6	Subtract line 5 from line 4 . . . . **6**			
7	Amount of line 6 carried forward and deductible in this tax year . . . **7**			
8	Subtract line 7 from line 6	**8**		
9	Tentative taxable excess contributions. Add lines 3 and 8	**9**		
10	Nondeductible section 4972(c)(6) or (7) contributions exempt from excise tax	**10**		
11	Taxable excess contributions. Subtract line 10 from line 9	**11**		
12	Multiply line 11 by 10%. Enter here and on Part I, line 1 . . . . ▶	**12**		

Schedule B—Tax on Excess Contributions to Section 403(b)(7)(A) Custodial Accounts (Section 4973(a)(3))
Reported by the last day of the 7th month after the end of the tax year of the employer (or other person who must file the return)

1	Total amount contributed for current year less rollovers (see instructions)	**1**	
2	Amount excludable from gross income under section 403(b) (see instructions)	**2**	
3	Current year excess contributions. Subtract line 2 from line 1. If zero or less, enter -0- . . .	**3**	
4	Prior year excess contributions not previously eliminated. If zero, go to line 8	**4**	
5	Contribution credit. If line 2 is more than line 1, enter the excess; otherwise, enter -0- . . .	**5**	
6	Total of all prior years' distributions out of the account included in your gross income under section 72(e) and not previously used to reduce excess contributions	**6**	
7	Adjusted prior years' excess contributions. Subtract the total of lines 5 and 6 from line 4 . .	**7**	
8	Taxable excess contributions. Add lines 3 and 7	**8**	
9	Multiply line 8 by 6%	**9**	
10	Enter the value of your account as of the last day of the year	**10**	
11	Multiply line 10 by 6%	**11**	
12	**Excess contributions tax.** Enter the lesser of line 9 or line 11 here and on Part I, line 2 . ▶	**12**	

Form **5330** (Rev. 1-2008)

Form 5330 (Rev. 1-2008)   Page **4**

Name of Filer: Filer's identifying number:

Schedule C—Tax on Prohibited Transactions (Section 4975) *(see instructions)* **Reported by the last day of the 7th month after the end of the tax year of the employer (or other person who must file the return)** *(continued)*

1 Is the excise tax a result of a prohibited transaction that was (box "a" or box "b" must be checked):

   a ☐ discrete   **b** ☐ other than discrete (a lease or a loan)

2 Complete the table below to disclose the prohibited transactions and figure the initial tax (see instructions)

(a) Transaction number	**(b)** Date of transaction (see instructions)	**(c)** Description of prohibited transaction	**(d)** Amount involved in prohibited transaction (see instructions)	**(e)** Initial tax on prohibited transaction (multiply each transaction in column (d) by the appropriate rate (see instructions))
(i)				
(ii)				
(iii)				
(iv)				
(v)				
(vi)				
(vii)				
(viii)				
(ix)				
(x)				
(xi)				
(xii)				

3 Add amounts in column (e); enter here and on Part I, line 3a . . . . ▶

4 Have you corrected all of the prohibited transactions that you are reporting on this return? If "Yes," complete Schedule C, line 5, on the next page. If "No," attach statement (see instructions) . . . . ▶ ☐ **Yes** ☐ **No**

Form **5330** (Rev. 1-2008)

Form 5330 (Rev. 1-2008)   Page **5**

Name of Filer: Filer's identifying number:

Schedule C—Tax on Prohibited Transactions (Section 4975) Reported by the last day of the 7th month after the end of the tax year of the employer (or other person who must file the return) *(continued)*

5   Complete the table below, if applicable, of other participating disqualified persons and description of correction (see instructions).

(a) Item no. from line 2	(b) Name and address of disqualified person	(c) EIN or SSN	(d) Date of correction	(e) Description of correction

Schedule D—Tax on Failure To Meet Minimum Funding Standards (Section 4971(a)) Reported by the last day of the 7th month after the end of the employer's tax year or 8 ½ months after the last day of the plan year that ends within the filer's tax year

1	Aggregate unpaid required contributions (accumulated funding deficiency for multiemployer plans) (see instructions)	**1**	
2	Multiply line 1 by 10% (5% for multiemployer plans). Enter here and on Part I, line 8a . . ▶	**2**	

Form **5330** (Rev. 1-2008)

Form 5330 (Rev. 1-2008)   Page **6**

Name of Filer:	Filer's identifying number:

Schedule E—Tax on Failure To Pay Liquidity Shortfall (Section 4971(f)(1)) Reported by the last day of the 7th month after the end of the employer's tax year or 8 ½ months after the last day of the plan year that ends within the filer's tax year

		(a) 1st Quarter	(b) 2nd Quarter	(c) 3rd Quarter	(d) 4th Quarter	(e) Total Add cols. a-d for line 3
1	Amount of shortfall **1**					
2	Shortfall paid by the due date **2**					
3	Net shortfall amount . . . **3**					
4	Multiply line 3 column (e) by 10% (5% for multiemployer plans). Enter here and on Part I, line 9a . . . . ▶ **4**					

Schedule F—Tax on Multiemployer Plans in Endangered or Critical Status (Section 4971(g)(3), 4971(g)(4)) Reported by the last day of the 7th month after the end of the employer's tax year or 8 ½ months after the last day of the plan year that ends within the filer's tax year

1	Section 4971(g)(3) tax on failure to meet requirements for plans in endangered or critical status	**1**
a	Enter the amount of contributions necessary to meet the applicable benchmarks or requirements . .	**1a**
b	Enter the amount of the accumulated funding deficiency	**1b**
c	Enter the greater of line 1a or line 1b, here and on Part I, line 10b. . . . . ▶	**1c**
2	Section 4971(g)(4) tax on failure to adopt rehabilitation plan	**2**
a	Enter the amount of the excise tax on the accumulated funding deficiency under section 4971(a)(2) from Schedule D, line 2	**2a**
b	Enter the number of days during the tax year which are included in the period beginning on the first day of the 240 day period and ending on the day the rehabilitation plan is adopted ▶ _____	**2b**
c	Multiply line 2b by $1,100	**2c**
d	Enter the greater of line 2a or line 2c, here and on Part I, line 10c . . . . ▶	**2d**

Schedule G—Tax on Excess Fringe Benefits (Section 4977) Reported by the last day of the 7th month after the end of the calendar year in which the excess fringe benefits were paid to the employer's employees

1	Did you make an election to be taxed under section 4977?. . . . . ☐ **Yes** ☐ **No**	
2	If "Yes," enter the calendar year (YYYY) in which the excess fringe benefits were paid ▶ _____	
3	If line 1 is "Yes," enter the excess fringe benefits on this line (see instructions)	**3**
4	Enter 30% of line 3 here and on Part I, line 11 . . . . ▶	**4**

Schedule H—Tax on Excess Contributions to Certain Plans (Section 4979) Reported by the last day of the 15th month after the end of the plan year

1	Enter the amount of an excess contribution under a cash or deferred arrangement that is part of a plan qualified under section 401(a), 403(a), 403(b), 408(k), or 501(c)(18) or excess aggregate contributions . .	**1**
2	Multiply line 1 by 10% and enter here and on Part I, line 13 . . . . ▶	**2**

Schedule I—Tax on Reversion of Qualified Plan Assets to an Employer (Section 4980) Reported by the last day of the month following the month in which the reversion occurred

1	Date reversion occurred . . . . ▶ MM ____ DD ____ YY ____	
2a	Employer reversion amount _____ **b** Excise tax rate _____	
3	Multiply line 2a by line 2b and enter the amount here and on Part I, line 14 . . . . . ▶	**3**
4	Explain below why you qualify for a rate other than 50%:	

Schedule J—Tax on Failure to Provide Notice of Significant Reduction in Future Accruals (Section 4980F) Reported by the last day of the month following the month in which the failure occurred

1	Enter the number of applicable individuals who were not provided ERISA section 204(h) notice ▶ _____	**1**
2	Enter the effective date of the amendment . . . . ▶ MM ____ DD ____ YY ____	**2**
3	Enter the number of days in the noncompliance period ▶ _____	**3**
4	Enter the total number of failures to provide ERISA section 204(h) notice (see instructions)	**4**
5	Multiply line 4 by $100. Enter here and on Part I, line 15 . . . . ▶	**5**
6	Provide a brief description of the failure, and of the correction, if any	

Schedule K—Tax on Prohibited Tax Shelter Transactions (Section 4965) Reported on or before the 15th day of the 5th month following the close of the entity manager's tax year during which the plan became a party to a prohibited tax shelter transaction

1	Enter the number of prohibited tax shelter transactions you caused the same plan to be a party to ▶ _____	**1**
2	Multiply line 1 by $20,000. Enter the result here and on Part I, line 16 . . . . ▶	**2**

Form **5330** (Rev. 1-2008)

Instructions for Form 5330
(Rev. January 2008)

**Department of the Treasury
Internal Revenue Service**

Return of Excise Taxes
Related to Employee Benefit Plans

Section references are to the Internal Revenue Code unless otherwise noted.

General Instructions

What's New

Section 4971(g), Multiemployer Plans in Endangered or Critical Status. For years beginning after 2007, the Pension Protection Act of 2006 states that a failure to comply with a funding improvement or rehabilitation plan, a failure to meet requirements for plans in endangered or critical status, or a failure to adopt a rehabilitation plan may be subject to an excise tax.

Reminders

Section 4965, Prohibited Tax Shelter Transactions. For tax years beginning after May 17, 2006, the Tax Increase Prevention and Reconciliation Act of 2005 provides that an entity manager of a tax-exempt organization may be subject to an excise tax on prohibited tax shelter transactions under section 4965. In the case of a plan entity, an *entity manager* is any person that approves or otherwise causes the tax-exempt entity to be a party to a prohibited tax shelter transaction. The excise tax is $20,000 and is assessed for each approval or other act causing the organization to be a party to the prohibited tax shelter transaction.

Section 4971, Failure to Meet the Minimum Funding Standards. Section 214 of the Pension Protection Act of 2006 provides that, for certain tax years, a multiemployer pension plan with (1) less than 100 participants, (2) an annual normal cost of less than $100,000, and (3) a funding deficiency on August 17, 2006, will not incur the excise tax for an accumulated funding deficiency under section 4971(a)(2) if the employers participated in a Federal Fishery Capacity Reduction Program and the Northeast Fisheries Assistance Program.

Section 4975, Prohibited Transactions. Generally, for purposes of a prohibited transaction described in section 4975(c)(1)(A), (B), (C), or (D), if

a disqualified person enters into a prohibited transaction in connection with the acquisition, holding, or disposition of certain securities or commodities, and the transaction is corrected within the 14-day correction period, it will not be treated as a prohibited transaction and no tax will be assessed.

When calculating the prohibited transaction excise tax where there is a failure to transmit participant contributions (elective deferrals) or amounts that would have otherwise been payable to the participant in cash, the *amount involved* is based on interest on those elective deferrals. See Rev. Rul. 2006-38.

Generally, for financial investment advice provided after December 31, 2006, the prohibited transaction rules of section 4975(c) will not apply to any transaction in connection with investment advice, if the investment advice provided by a fiduciary adviser is provided under an eligible investment advice arrangement under Department of Labor guidelines.

Section 4972, Nondeductible Contributions to Qualified Employer Plans. The deduction limits of section 404(a)(1)(D) were altered for certain tax years beginning after December 31, 2005. The maximum deductible amount is not less than the excess of 150% of a plan's current liability in the instance of a single-employer defined benefit plan (140% for multiemployer plans) over the value of that plan's assets. Where an employer contributes to one or more defined contribution plans, the overall limit applicable to combinations of defined benefit plans and defined contribution plans only applies to the extent that the contributions exceed 6% of the compensation otherwise paid or accrued during the tax year to the beneficiaries under the defined contribution plans. For purposes of determining the excise tax on nondeductible contributions, matching contributions to a defined contribution plan that are nondeductible solely because of the overall deduction limit are disregarded. In addition, where there is a combination of defined benefit and defined contribution plans, multiemployer plans are not taken into

consideration in applying the overall limit on deductions.

Purpose of Form

File Form 5330 to report the tax on:
- A prohibited tax shelter transaction (section 4965(a)(2)).
- A minimum funding deficiency (section 4971(a) and (b)).
- A failure to pay liquidity shortfall (section 4971(f)).
- A failure to comply with a funding improvement or rehabilitation plan (section 4971(g)(2)).
- A failure to meet requirements for plans in endangered or critical status (section 4971(g)(3)).
- A failure to adopt rehabilitation plan (section 4971(g)(4)).
- Nondeductible contributions to qualified plans (section 4972).
- Excess contributions to a section 403(b)(7)(A) custodial account (section 4973(a)(3)).
- A prohibited transaction (section 4975).
- A disqualified benefit provided by funded welfare plans (section 4976).
- Excess fringe benefits (section 4977).
- Certain ESOP dispositions (section 4978).
- Excess contributions to plans with cash or deferred arrangements (section 4979).
- Certain prohibited allocations of qualified securities by an ESOP (section 4979A).
- Reversions of qualified plan assets to employers (section 4980).
- A failure of an applicable plan reducing future benefit accruals to satisfy notice requirements (section 4980F).

Who Must File

A Form 5330 must be filed by:

1. Any plan entity manager of a tax-exempt entity who approves the entity as a party to, or otherwise causes the entity to be a party to, a prohibited tax shelter transaction during the tax year and knows or has reason to know the transaction is a prohibited tax shelter transaction, see section 4965(a)(2).

2. Any employer who is liable for the tax under section 4971 for failure to meet the minimum funding standards

Cat. No. 11871X

under section 412 (liability for tax in the case of an employer who is a party to a collective bargaining agreement, see section 413(b)(6)).

3. Any employer who is liable for the tax under section 4971(f) for a failure to meet the liquidity requirement of section 412(m)(5).

4. Any employer with respect to a multiemployer plan who is liable for the tax under section 4971(g)(2) for failure to comply with a funding improvement or rehabilitation plan under section 432.

5. Any employer with respect to a multiemployer plan who is liable for the tax under section 4971(g)(3) for failure to meet the requirements for plans in endangered or critical status under section 432.

6. Any plan sponsor with respect to a multiemployer plan who is liable for the tax under section 4971(g)(4) for failure to adopt a rehabilitation plan within the time required under section 432.

7. Any employer who is liable for the tax under section 4972 for nondeductible contributions to qualified plans.

8. Any individual who is liable for the tax under section 4973(a)(3) because an excess contribution to a section 403(b)(7)(A) custodial account was made for them and that excess has not been eliminated as specified in sections 4973(c)(2)(A) and (B).

9. Any disqualified person who is liable for the tax under section 4975 for participating in a prohibited transaction (other than a fiduciary acting only as such), or an individual (or his or her beneficiary) who engages in a prohibited transaction with respect to his or her individual retirement account (unless section 408(e)(2)(A) or section 408(e)(4) applies) for each tax year or part of a tax year in the *taxable period* applicable to such prohibited transaction.

10. Any employer who is liable for the tax under section 4976 for maintaining a funded welfare benefit plan that provides a disqualified benefit during any tax year.

11. Any employer who pays excess fringe benefits and has elected to be taxed under section 4977 on such payments.

12. Any employer or worker-owned cooperative (as defined in section 1042(c)(2)) that maintains an ESOP that disposes of the qualified securities (as defined in section 1042(c)(1)) within the specified 3-year period, under section 4978.

13. Any employer who is liable for the tax under section 4979 on excess contributions to plans with a cash or deferred arrangement, etc.

14. Any employer or worker-owned cooperative that made the written statement described in section 664(g)(1)(E) or 1042(b)(3)(B) and made an allocation prohibited under section 409(n) of qualified securities of an ESOP taxable under section 4979A or any employer or worker-owned cooperative who made an allocation of S corporation stock of an ESOP prohibited under section 409(p) taxable under section 4979A.

15. Any employer who receives an employer reversion from a deferred compensation plan that is taxable under section 4980.

16. Any employer or multiemployer plan liable for the tax under section 4980F for failure to give notice of a significant reduction in the rate of future benefit accrual.

A Form 5330 and tax payment is required for:

• Each year you fail to meet the minimum funding standards under section 412 or contribute an excess amount to your section 403(b)(7)(A) custodial account.

• Each year any of the items in 1, 3, 5, 6, 7, or 9 through 14, or 16 under *Who Must File*, beginning on page 1, apply.

• Each failure of the employer to make the required contribution as required by a funding improvement or rehabilitation plan under section 432 with respect to a multiemployer plan.

• A reversion of plan assets from a qualified plan taxable under section 4980.

Table 1. Excise Tax Due Dates

If the taxes due are under section . . .	Then, except for section 4965, file Form 5330 by the last day of the . . . and for section 4965 by the . . .
4965	15th day of the 5th month following the close of the entity manager's tax year during which the tax-exempt entity becomes a party to the transaction.
4971	7th month after the end of the employer's tax year or 8½ months after the last day of the plan year that ends with or within the filer's tax year.
4971(f)	7th month after the end of the employer's tax year or 8½ months after the last day of the plan year that ends with or within the filer's tax year.
4971(g)(2)	7th month after the end of the employer's tax year or 8½ months after the last day of the plan year that ends with or within the filer's tax year.
4971(g)(3)	7th month after the end of the employer's tax year or 8½ months after the last day of the plan year that ends with or within the filer's tax year.
4971(g)(4)	7th month after the end of the employer's tax year or 8½ months after the last day of the plan year that ends with or within the filer's tax year.
4972	7th month after the end of the tax year of the employer or other person who must file this return.
4973(a)(3)	7th month after the end of the tax year of the employer or other person who must file this return.
4975	7th month after the end of the tax year of the employer or other person who must file this return.
4976	7th month after the end of the tax year of the employer or other person who must file this return.
4977	7th month after the end of the calendar year in which the excess fringe benefits were paid to your employees.
4978	7th month after the end of the tax year of the employer or other person who must file this return.
4979	15th month after the close of the plan year to which the excess contributions or excess aggregate contributions relate.
4979A	7th month after the end of the tax year of the employer or other person who must file this return.
4980	month following the month in which the reversion occurred.
4980F	month following the month in which the failure occurred.

If the filing due date falls on a Saturday, Sunday, or legal holiday, the return may be filed on the next business day.

- Each year (or part of a year) in the taxable period applicable to a prohibited transaction, under section 4975. See the instructions for Schedule C, line 2, columns (d) and (e), for a definition of taxable period.

When To File

File one Form 5330 to report excise taxes with the same filing due date. One Form 5330 may be filed to report one or more of these taxes. However, if the taxes are from separate plans, file separate forms for each plan.

Generally, the filing of a Form 5330 starts the statute of limitations running only with respect to the particular excise tax(es) reported on that Form 5330. However, statutes of limitations with respect to the prohibited transaction excise tax(es) are based on the filing of the applicable Form 5500. Use Table 1 to determine the due date of Form 5330.

Extension. File Form 5558, Application for Extension of Time to File Certain Employee Plan Returns, to request an extension of time to file. If approved, you may be granted an extension of up to 6 months after the normal due date of Form 5330.

Caution: Form 5558 does not extend the time to pay your taxes. See the instructions for Form 5558.

Where To File

 File Form 5330 with the: Department of the Treasury, Internal Revenue Service Center, Ogden, UT 84201.

Private delivery services. You can use certain private delivery services designated by the IRS to meet the "timely mailing as timely filing/paying" rule for tax returns and payments. These private delivery services include only the following:
- DHL Express (DHL): DHL Same Day Service, DHL Next Day 10:30 a.m., DHL Next Day 12:00 p.m., DHL Next Day 3:00 p.m., DHL 2nd Day Service.
- Federal Express (FedEx): FedEx Priority Overnight, FedEx Standard Overnight, FedEx 2Day, FedEx International Priority, and FedEx International First.
- United Parcel Service (UPS): UPS Next Day Air, UPS Next Day Air Saver, UPS 2nd Day Air, UPS 2nd Day Air A.M., UPS Worldwide Express Plus, and UPS Worldwide Express.

The private delivery service can tell you how to get written proof of the mailing date.

Interest and Penalties

Interest. Interest is charged on taxes not paid by the due date even if an extension of time to file is granted.

Interest is also charged on penalties imposed for failure to file, negligence, fraud, gross valuation overstatements, and substantial understatements of tax from the due date (including extensions) to the date of payment. The interest charge is figured at a rate determined under section 6621.

Penalty for late filing of return. If you do not file a return by the due date, including extensions, you may have to pay a penalty of 5% of the unpaid tax for each month or part of a month the return is late, up to a maximum of 25% of the unpaid tax. The minimum penalty for a return that is more than 60 days late is the smaller of the tax due or $100. The penalty will not be imposed if you can show that the failure to file on time was due to reasonable cause. If you file late, you must attach a statement to Form 5330 explaining the reasonable cause.

Penalty for late payment of tax. If you do not pay the tax when due, you may have to pay a penalty of ½ of 1% of the unpaid tax for each month or part of a month the tax is not paid, up to a maximum of 25% of the unpaid tax. The penalty will not be imposed if you can show that the failure to pay on time was due to reasonable cause.

Interest and penalties for late filing and late payment will be billed separately after the return is filed.

Claim for Refund or Credit/ Amended Return

File an amended Form 5330 for any of the following:
- To claim a refund of overpaid taxes reportable on Form 5330;
- For a credit for overpaid taxes; or
- To report additional taxes due within the same tax year of the filer if those taxes have the same due date as those previously reported. Check the box in item H on page 1 of the return and report the correct amount of taxes in Schedule A through K, as appropriate, and on lines 1 through 16 of Part I. See instructions for Part II, lines 17 through 19.

If you file an amended return to claim a refund or credit, the claim must state in detail the reasons for claiming the refund. In order for the IRS to promptly consider your claim, you must explain why you are filing the claim and provide the appropriate supporting evidence. See Regulations section 301.6402-2 for more details.

Specific Instructions

Filer tax year. Enter the tax year of the employer, entity, or individual on whom the tax is imposed.

Item A. Name and address of filer. Enter the name and address of the employer, individual, or other entity who is liable for the tax.

Include the suite, room, or other unit numbers after the street number. If the post office does not deliver mail to the street address and you have a P.O. box, show the box number instead of the street address.

Item B. Filer's identifying number. Enter the filer's identifying number of the employer, entity, or individual on whom the tax is imposed. The identifying number of an individual (other than a sole proprietor with an employer identification number (EIN)) is his or her social security number. The identifying number of all others is their EIN.

Item C. Name of plan. Enter the formal name of the plan, group insurance arrangement, or enough information to identify the plan. This should be the same name indicated on the Form 5500 series return/report if required to be filed for the plan.

Item D. Name and address of plan sponsor. The term *plan sponsor* means:

1. The employer, for an employee benefit plan that a single employer established or maintains;
2. The employee organization in the case of a plan of an employee organization;
3. The association, committee, joint board of trustees, or other similar group of representatives of the parties who establish or maintain the plan, if the plan is established or maintained jointly by one or more employers and one or more employee organizations, or by two or more employers.

Include the suite, room, or other unit numbers after the street number. If the post office does not deliver mail to the street address and you have a P.O. box, show the box number instead of the street address.

Item E. Plan sponsor's EIN. Enter the nine-digit EIN assigned to the plan sponsor. This should be the same number used to file the Form 5500 series return/report.

Item F. Plan year ending. Plan year means the calendar or fiscal year on which the records of the plan are kept. Enter eight digits in month/date/year order. This number assists the IRS in properly identifying the plan and time period for which the Form 5330 is being filed. For example, a plan year ended

March 31, 2007, should be shown as 03/31/2007.

Item G. Plan number. Enter the three-digit number that the employer or plan administrator assigned to the plan.

Item H. Amended return. If you are filing an amended Form 5330, check the box on this line, and see the instructions for Part II, lines 17 through 19. Also see *Claim for Refund or Credit/Amended Return*, earlier.

Filer's signature. Please sign and date the form. Also enter a daytime phone number where you can be reached.

Preparer's signature. Anyone who prepares your return and does not charge you should not sign your return. For example, a regular full-time employee or your business partner who prepares the return should not sign.

Generally, anyone who is paid to prepare a return must sign it and fill in the *Paid Preparer's Use Only* area.

The paid preparer must complete the required preparer information and—
• Sign the return by hand, in the space provided for the preparer's signature (signature stamps and labels are not acceptable).
• Give a copy of the return to the filer.

Part I—Taxes

Line 4. Section 4976—Tax on Disqualified Benefits for Funded Welfare Plans. Section 4976 imposes an excise tax on employers who maintain a funded welfare benefit plan that provides a disqualified benefit during any tax year. The tax is 100% of the disqualified benefit.

Generally, a *disqualified benefit* is any one of the following:
• Any post-retirement medical benefit or life insurance benefit provided for a key employee unless the benefit is provided from a separate account established for the key employee under section 419A(d);
• Any post-retirement medical benefit or life insurance benefit unless the plan meets the nondiscrimination requirements of section 505(b) for those benefits; or
• Any portion of the fund that reverts to the benefit of the employer.

Enter on line 4 the total amount of the disqualified benefit.

Line 5a and 5b. Section 4978—Tax on Certain ESOP Dispositions. Section 4978 imposes an excise tax on dispositions of securities acquired in a sale to which section 1042 applied, or in a qualified gratuitous transfer to which section 664(g) applied, if the dispositions take place within 3 years after the date of the acquisition of qualified securities (as defined in

section 1042(c)(1) or a section 664(g) transfer).

The tax is 10% of the amount realized on the disposition of the qualified securities if an ESOP or eligible worker-owned cooperative (as defined in section 1042(c)(2)) disposes of the qualified securities within the 3-year period described above, and either of the following applies:
• The total number of shares held by that plan or cooperative after the disposition is less than the total number of employer securities held immediately after the sale, or
• Except to the extent provided in regulations, the value of qualified securities held by the plan or cooperative after the disposition is less than 30% of the total value of all employer securities as of the disposition (60% of the total value of all employer securities in the case of any qualified employer securities acquired in a qualified gratuitous transfer to which section 664(g) applied).

See section 4978(b)(2) for the limitation on the amount of tax.

The section 4978 tax must be paid by the employer or the eligible worker-owned cooperative that made the written statement described in section 1042(b)(3)(B) on dispositions that occurred during their tax year.

The section 4978 tax does not apply to a distribution of qualified securities or sale of such securities if any of the following occurs:
• The death of the employee;
• The retirement of the employee after the employee has reached age 59½;
• The disability of the employee (within the meaning of section 72(m)(7)); or
• The separation of the employee from service for any period that results in a 1-year break in service (as defined in section 411(a)(6)(A)).

For purposes of section 4978, an exchange of qualified securities in a reorganization described in section 368(a)(1) for stock of another corporation will not be treated as a disposition.

 For section 4978 excise taxes, the amount entered on Part I, line 5a is the amount realized on the disposition of qualified securities multiplied by 10%. Also check the appropriate box on line 5b.

Line 6. Section 4979A—Tax on Certain Prohibited Allocations of Qualified ESOP Securities. Section 4979A imposes a 50% excise tax on allocated amounts involved in:

1. A prohibited allocation of qualified securities by any ESOP or eligible worker-owned cooperative.
2. An allocation described in section 664(g)(5)(A). Section

664(g)(5)(A) prohibits any portion of the assets of the ESOP attributable to securities acquired by the plan in a qualified gratuitous transfer to be allocated to the account of:

a. Any person related to the decedent (within the meaning of section 267(b)) or a member of the decedent's family (within the meaning of section 2032A(e)(2)), or

b. Any person who, at the time of the allocation, or at any time during the 1-year period ending on the date of the acquisition of qualified employer securities by the plan, is a 5% shareholder of the employer maintaining the plan.

3. The accrual or allocation of S corporation shares in an ESOP during a nonallocation year constituting a prohibited allocation under section 409(p).

4. Any synthetic equity owned by a disqualified person in any nonallocation year.

Prohibited allocations for ESOP or worker-owned cooperative. For purposes of items 1 and 2 above, a *prohibited allocation* of qualified securities by any ESOP or eligible worker-owned cooperative is any allocation of qualified securities acquired in a non-recognition-of-gain sale under section 1042 which violates section 409(n); and any benefit that accrues to any person in violation of section 409(n).

Under section 409(n), an ESOP or worker-owned cooperative cannot allow any portion of assets, attributable to employer securities acquired in a section 1042 sale, to accrue or be allocated (directly or indirectly) to the taxpayer involved in the transaction (or any person related to the taxpayer) during the nonallocation period. For purposes of section 409(n), relationship to the taxpayer is defined under section 267(b).

The *nonallocation period* is the period beginning on the date the qualified securities are sold and ends on the later of:
• 10 years after the date of sale; or
• The date on which the final payment is made if acquisition indebtedness was incurred at the time of sale.

The employer sponsoring the plan, or the eligible worker-owned cooperative, is responsible for paying the tax.

Prohibited allocations of securities in an S corporation.

Generally, the prohibited allocation rules for securities in an S corporation are effective for plan years beginning after December 31, 2004; however, these

rules are effective for plan years ending after March 14, 2001, if:
• *The ESOP was established after March 14, 2001, or*
• *The ESOP was established on or before March 14, 2001, and the employer maintaining the plan was **not** an S corporation.*

The rules below apply to the prohibited allocation, identified in items 3 and 4, under line 6. The excise tax on these transactions under section 4979A is 50% of the amount involved. The amount involved includes:

1. The value of any synthetic equity owned by a disqualified person in any nonallocation year. *Synthetic equity* means any stock option, warrant, restricted stock, deferred issuance stock right, or similar interest or right that gives the holder the right to acquire or receive stock of the S corporation in the future. Synthetic equity may also include a stock appreciation right, phantom stock unit, or similar right to a future cash payment based on the value of the stock or appreciation; and nonqualified deferred compensation as described in Regulations section 1.409(p)-1(f)(2)(iv). The value of a synthetic equity is the value of the shares on which the synthetic equity is based or the present value of the nonqualified deferred compensation.

2. The value of any S corporation shares in an ESOP accruing during a nonallocation year or allocated directly or indirectly under the ESOP or any other plan of the employer qualified under section 401(a) for the benefit of a disqualified person. For additional information see Regulations section 1.409(p)-1(b)(2).

3. The total value of all the deemed-owned shares of all disqualified persons.

A *nonallocation year* means a plan year where the ESOP, at any time during the year, holds employer securities in an S corporation, and disqualified persons own at least:
• 50% of the number of outstanding shares of the S corporation (including deemed-owned ESOP shares), or
• 50% of the aggregate number of outstanding shares of stock (including deemed-owned ESOP shares) and synthetic equity in the S corporation.

For purposes of determining a nonallocation year, the attribution rules of section 318(a) will apply; however, the option rule of section 318(a)(4) will not apply. Additionally, the attribution rules defining family member is modified to include the individual's:
• Spouse.
• Ancestor or lineal descendant of the individual or the individual's spouse.

• A brother or sister of the individual or of the individual's spouse and any lineal descendant of the brother or sister.

A spouse of an individual who is legally separated from an individual under a decree of divorce or separate maintenance is not treated as the individual's spouse.

An individual is a *disqualified person* if:
• The total number of shares owned by the person and the members of the person's family (as defined in section 409(p)(4)(D)) is at least 20% of the deemed-owned shares (as defined in section 409(p)(4)(C)) in the S corporation, or
• The person owns at least 10% of the deemed-owned shares (as defined in section 409(p)(4)(C)) in the S corporation.

 Under section 409(p)(7), the Secretary of the Treasury may, through regulations or other guidance of general applicability, provide that a nonallocation year occurs in any case in which the principal purpose of the ownership structure of an S corporation constitutes an avoidance or evasion of section 409(p). For a description of situations where the definition of nonallocation year was considered, see Rev. Rul. 2004-4, 2004-6 I.R.B. 414.

 For section 4979A excise taxes, the amount entered on Part I, line 6 is 50% of the amount involved in the prohibited allocations described in items 1 through 4, under *Line 6. Section 4979A – Tax on Certain Prohibited Allocations of Qualified ESOP Securities*, earlier.

Line 10a. Section 4971(g)(2)—Failure to Comply With a Funding Improvement or Rehabilitation Plan. Failure to comply with a funding improvement or rehabilitation plan will result in an excise tax equal to each failure of each employer to make the required contribution within the time frame under such plan. The tax is paid by each employer responsible for contributing to or under the plan. Include on line 10a the amount of each contribution the employer failed to make in a timely manner.

A funding improvement plan is a plan which consists of the actions, including options or a range of options to be proposed to the bargaining parties, formulated to provide, based on reasonably anticipated experience and reasonable actuarial assumptions, for the attainment by the plan during the funding improvement period.

A rehabilitation plan is a plan which consists of actions, including options or a range of options to be proposed to the bargaining parties, formulated,

based on reasonably anticipated experience and reasonable actuarial assumptions, to enable the plan to cease to be in critical status by the end of the rehabilitation period.

All, or part, of this excise tax may be waived under Section 4971(g)(5).

Line 16. Section 4965—Prohibited Tax Shelter Transactions. For tax years ending after May 17, 2006, if an entity manager of a tax-exempt entity approves or otherwise causes the entity to be a party to a prohibited tax shelter transaction during the year and knows or has reason to know that the transaction is a prohibited tax shelter transaction, then the entity manager must pay the excise tax under section 4965(b)(2).

For purposes of section 4965, plan entities are:
• Qualified pension, profit-sharing, and stock bonus plans described in section 401(a);
• Annuity plans described in section 403(a);
• Annuity contracts described in section 403(b);
• Qualified tuition programs described in section 529;
• Retirement plans described in section 457(b) maintained by a governmental employer;
• Individual retirement accounts within the meaning of section 408(a);
• Individual retirement annuities within the meaning of section 408(b);
• Archer medical savings accounts (MSAs) within the meaning of section 220(d);
• Coverdell education savings accounts described in section 530; and
• Health savings accounts within the meaning of section 223(d).

An *entity manager* is the person who approves or otherwise causes the entity to be a party to a prohibited tax shelter transaction.

The excise tax under section 4965(a)(2) is $20,000 for each approval or other act causing the organization to be a party to a prohibited tax shelter transaction.

A *prohibited tax shelter transaction* is:

1. A Listed transaction within the meaning of section 6707A(c)(2). *Listed transactions* are reportable transactions that are the same as, or substantially similar to, any transactions that have been specifically identified by the Secretary as a tax avoidance transaction for purposes of section 6011.

2. A prohibited reportable transaction is:

a. Any confidential transaction within the meaning of Regulations section 1.6011-4(b)(3); or

-5-

b. Any transaction with contractual protection within the meaning of Regulations section 1.6011-4(b)(4).

Part II—Tax Due

Required disclosure. Lines 17 through 19.

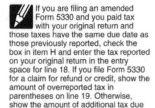 If you are filing an amended Form 5330 and you paid tax with your original return and those taxes have the same due date as those previously reported, check the box in item H and enter the tax reported on your original return in the entry space for line 18. If you file Form 5330 for a claim for refund or credit, show the amount of overreported tax in parentheses on line 19. Otherwise, show the amount of additional tax due on line 19 and include the payment with the amended Form 5330.

Make your check or money order payable to the "United States Treasury" for the full amount due. Attach the payment to your return. Write your name, identifying number, plan number, and "Form 5330, Section _____" on your payment.

Schedule A (Section 4972)

Tax on Nondeductible Employer Contributions to Qualified Employer Plans

Section 4972. Section 4972 imposes an excise tax on employers who make nondeductible contributions to their qualified plans. The excise tax is 10% of the nondeductible contributions in the plan as of the end of the employer's tax year.

A *qualified plan* for purposes of this tax means any plan qualified under section 401(a), any annuity plan qualified under section 403(a), and any simplified employee pension plan qualified under section 408(k) or 408(p). The term qualified plan does not include certain governmental plans and certain plans maintained by tax-exempt organizations.

Nondeductible contributions. For purposes of section 4972, *nondeductible contributions* for the employer's current tax year are the sum of:

1. The excess (if any) of the employer's contribution for the tax year less the amount allowable as a deduction under section 404 for that year, and
2. The total amount of the employer's contributions for each preceding tax year that was not allowable as a deduction under section 404 for such preceding year, reduced by the sum of

a. The portion of such amount that was available for return under the applicable qualification rules and was actually returned to the employer prior to the close of the current tax year and

b. The portion of such amount that became deductible for a preceding tax year or for the current tax year.

Although pre-1987 nondeductible contributions are not subject to this excise tax, they are taken into account to determine the extent to which post-1986 contributions are deductible. See section 4972 and Pub. 560, Retirement Plans for Small Business, for details.

Defined benefit plans exception. Generally, contributions up to the current unfunded liability of a defined benefit plan are deductible, regardless of the number of participants in the plan. In addition, when determining the amount of nondeductible contributions for any tax year, an employer may elect, for that tax year, not to include any contributions to a defined benefit plan except to the extent they exceed the full-funding limitation (as defined in section 412(c)(7), determined without regard to section 412(c)(7)(A)(i)(I)). This election applies to terminated and ongoing plans. An employer making this election cannot also benefit from the exceptions for terminating plans and for certain contributions to defined contribution plans under section 4972(c)(6). When determining the amount of nondeductible contributions, the deductible limits under section 404(a)(7) must be applied first to contributions to defined contribution plans and then to contributions to defined benefit plans.

Defined contribution plans exception. Employer contributions to one or more defined contribution plans that are nondeductible because they exceed the combined plan deduction limits of section 404(a)(7) are not subject to the 10% excise tax. In determining the amount of nondeductible contributions that are subject to the 10% excise tax, do not include:

- Employer contributions to one or more defined contribution plans which are nondeductible solely because of section 404(a)(7) that do not exceed the matching contributions described in section 401(m)(4)(A),
- Contributions to a SIMPLE 401(k) or a SIMPLE IRA that are considered nondeductible because they are not made in connection with the employer's trade or business. However, this provision pertaining to SIMPLEs does

not apply to contributions made on behalf of the employer or the employer's family, or

- Contributions not in excess of 6% of the compensation (as defined in section 404(a) and adjusted in section 404(a)(12)) paid or accrued during the tax year to the beneficiaries under the plans.

For purposes of this exception, the combined plan deduction limits are first applied to contributions to the defined benefit plan and then to the defined contribution plan.

Restorative payments to a defined contribution plan are not considered nondeductible contributions if the payments are made to restore some or all of the plan's losses due to an action (or a failure to act) that creates a reasonable risk of liability for breach of fiduciary duty. Amounts paid in excess of the amount of the loss are not considered restorative payments.

For these purposes, multiemployer plans are not taken into consideration in applying the overall limit on deductions where there is a combination of defined benefit and defined contribution plans.

Schedule B (Section 4973(a)(3))

Tax on Excess Contributions to Section 403(b)(7)(A) Custodial Accounts

Section 4973(c) imposes a 6% excise tax on the excess contributions to 403(b)(7)(A) custodial accounts at the close of the tax year. The tax is paid by the individual account holder.

Line 1. Enter the total current year contributions, less any rollover contributions described in sections 403(b)(8) or 408(d)(3)(A).

Line 2. The amount you will enter on line 2 is the amount excludable under section 415(c) (limit on annual additions).

> To determine the amount excludable for a specific year, see Pub. 571, Tax-Sheltered Annuity (403(b)) Plans, for that year.

The limit on annual additions under section 415(c)(1)(A) is subject to cost-of-living adjustments as described in section 415(d). The dollar limit for a calendar year as adjusted annually is published during the fourth quarter of the prior calendar year in the Internal Revenue Bulletin.

Schedule C (Section 4975)

Tax on Prohibited Transactions

Section 4975 imposes an excise tax on a disqualified person that engages in a prohibited transaction with the plan.

Plan. For purposes of prohibited transactions (section 4975), the term *plan* means any of the following:

• A trust described in section 401(a) that forms part of a plan.
• A plan described in section 403(a), and that trust or plan is exempt from tax under section 501(a).
• An individual retirement account described in section 408(a).
• An individual retirement annuity described in section 408(b).
• An Archer MSA described in section 220(d).
• A Coverdell education savings account described in section 530.
• A Health Savings Account described in section 223(d).
• A trust described in section 501(c)(22).

 If the IRS determined at any time that your plan was a plan as defined above, it will always remain subject to the excise tax on prohibited transactions (section 4975). This also applies to the tax on minimum funding deficiencies (section 4971).

Disqualified person. A *disqualified person* is any person who is:

1. A fiduciary.
2. A person providing services to the plan.
3. An employer, any of whose employees are covered by the plan.
4. An employee organization, any of whose members are covered by the plan.
5. Any direct or indirect owner of 50% or more of:
  a. The combined voting power of all classes of stock entitled to vote, or the total value of shares of all classes of stock of a corporation,
  b. The capital interest or the profits interest of a partnership,
  c. The beneficial interest of a trust or unincorporated enterprise in a, b, or c, which is an employer or an employee organization described in 3 or 4 above. A limited liability company should be treated as a corporation, or a partnership, depending on how the organization is treated for federal tax purposes.
6. A member of the family of any individual described in 1, 2, 3, or 5. A member of a family is the spouse, ancestor, lineal descendant, and any spouse of a lineal descendant.
7. A corporation, partnership, or trust or estate of which (or in which) any direct or indirect owner holds 50% or more of the interest described in 5a,

5b, or 5c of such entity. For purposes of 7, the beneficial interest of the trust or estate is owned directly or indirectly, or held by persons described in 1 through 5.

8. An officer, director (or an individual having powers or responsibilities similar to those of officers or directors), a 10% or more shareholder or highly compensated employee (earning 10% or more of the yearly wages of an employer) of a person described in 3, 4, 5, or 7.
9. A 10% or more (in capital or profits) partner or joint venturer of a person described in 3, 4, 5, or 7.
10. Any disqualified person, as described in 1 through 9 above, who is a disqualified person with respect to any plan to which a section 501(c)(22) trust applies, that is permitted to make payments under section 4223 of the Employee Retirement Income Security Act (ERISA).

Prohibited transaction. A *prohibited transaction* is any direct or indirect:

1. Sale or exchange, or leasing of any property between a plan and a disqualified person; or a transfer of real or personal property by a disqualified person to a plan where the property is subject to a mortgage or similar lien placed on the property by the disqualified person within 10 years prior to the transfer, or the property transferred is subject to a mortgage or similar lien which the plan assumes.
2. Lending of money or other extension of credit between a plan and a disqualified person.
3. Furnishing of goods, services, or facilities between a plan and a disqualified person.
4. Transfer to, or use by or for the benefit of, a disqualified person of income or assets of a plan.
5. Act by a disqualified person who is a fiduciary whereby he or she deals with the income or assets of a plan in his or her own interest or account.
6. Receipt of any consideration for his or her own personal account by any disqualified person who is a fiduciary from any party dealing with the plan connected with a transaction involving the income or assets of the plan.

Exemptions. See sections 4975(d), 4975(f)(6)(B)(ii), and 4975(f)(6)(B)(iii) for specific exemptions to prohibited transactions. Also see section 4975(c)(2) for certain other transactions or classes of transactions that may become exempt.

Line 1. Check the box that best characterizes the prohibited transaction for which an excise tax is being paid. A prohibited transaction is discrete unless it is of an ongoing nature. Transactions

involving the use of money (loans, etc.) or other property (rent, etc.) are of an ongoing nature and will be treated as a new prohibited transaction on the first day of each succeeding tax year or part of a tax year that is within the taxable period.

Line 2, Column (b). List the date of all prohibited transactions that took place in connection with a particular plan during the current tax year. Also list the date of all prohibited transactions that took place in prior years unless either the transaction was corrected in a prior tax year or the section 4975(a) tax was assessed in the prior tax year. A disqualified person who engages in a prohibited transaction must file a separate Form 5330 to report the excise tax due under section 4975 for each tax year.

Line 2, Columns (d) and (e). The *amount involved* in a prohibited transaction means the greater of the amount of money and the fair market value (FMV) of the other property given, or the amount of money and the FMV of the other property received. However, for services described in sections 4975(d)(2) and (10), the amount involved only applies to excess compensation. For purposes of section 4975(a), FMV must be determined as of the date on which the prohibited transaction occurs. If the use of money or other property is involved, the amount involved is the greater of the amount paid for the use or the FMV of the use for the period for which the money or other property is used. In addition, transactions involving the use of money or other property will be treated as giving rise to a prohibited transaction occurring on the date of the actual transaction plus a new prohibited transaction on the first day of each succeeding tax year or portion of a succeeding tax year which is within the taxable period. The *taxable period* is the period of time beginning with the date of the prohibited transaction and ending with the earliest of:

1. The date the correction is completed,
2. The date of the mailing of a notice of deficiency, or
3. The date on which the tax under section 4975(a) is assessed.

See the instructions for *Additional tax for failure to correct the prohibited transaction,* under Schedule C for the definition of correction.

 Temporary Regulations section 141.4975-13 states that, until final regulations are written under section 4975(f), the definitions of amount involved and correction found in Regulations section 53.4941(e)-1 will apply.

-7-

Figure 1. Example for the calendar 2005 plan year used when filing for the 2005 tax year

Schedule C—Tax on Prohibited Transactions (section 4975) Reported by the last day of the 7th month after the end of the tax year of the employer (or other person who must file the return)

(a) Transaction number	(b) Date of transaction (see page 7 of the instructions)	(c) Description of prohibited transaction	(d) Amount involved in prohibited transaction (see page 7 of the instructions)	(e) Initial tax on prohibited transaction (multiply each transaction in column (d) by the appropriate rate (see page 7 of the instructions))
(i)	7-1-05	Loan	$6,000	$900
(ii)				
(iii)				

3. Add amounts in column (e). Enter here and on Part I, line 3a . . . . ▶ $900

Figure 2. Example for the calendar 2006 plan year used when filing for the 2006 tax year

Schedule C—Tax on Prohibited Transactions (Section 4975) Reported by the last day of the 7th month after the end of the tax year of the employer (or other person who must file the return)

(a) Transaction number	(b) Date of transaction (see page 7 of the instructions)	(c) Description of prohibited transaction	(d) Amount involved in prohibited transaction (see page 7 of the instructions)	(e) Initial tax on prohibited transaction (multiply each transaction in column (d) by the appropriate rate (see page 7 of the instructions))
(i)	7-1-05	Loan	$6,000	$900
(ii)	1-1-06	Loan	$12,000	$1,800
(iii)				

3. Add amounts in column (e). Enter here and on Part I, line 3a . . . . ▶ $2,700

Failure to transmit participant contributions. For purposes of calculating the excise tax on a prohibited transaction where there is a failure to transmit participant contributions (elective deferrals) or amounts that would have otherwise been payable to the participant in cash, the amount involved is based on interest on those elective deferrals. See Rev. Rul. 2006-38.

Column (e). The initial tax on a prohibited transaction is 15% of the amount involved in each prohibited transaction for each year or part of a year in the taxable period. Multiply the amount in column (d) by 15%.

Example. The above example of a prohibited transaction does not cover all types of prohibited transactions. For more examples, see Regulations section 53.4941(e)-1(b)(4).

A disqualified person borrows money from a plan in a prohibited transaction under section 4975. The FMV of the use of the money and the actual interest on the loan is $1,000 per month (the actual interest is paid in this example). The loan was made on July 1, 2005, (date of transaction) and repaid on December 31, 2006 (date of correction). The disqualified person's tax year is the calendar year. On July 31, 2007, the disqualified person files a delinquent Form 5330 for the 2005 plan year (which in this case is the calendar

year) and a timely Form 5330 for the 2006 plan year (which in this case is the calendar year). No notice of deficiency with respect to the tax imposed by section 4975(a) has been mailed to the disqualified person and no assessment of such excise tax has been made by the IRS before the time the disqualified person filed the Forms 5330.

Each prohibited transaction has its own separate taxable period which begins on the date the prohibited transaction occurred or is deemed to occur and ends on the date of correction. The taxable period that begins on the date the loan occurs runs from July 1, 2005 (date of loan) through December 31, 2006 (date of correction). When a loan is a prohibited transaction, the loan is treated as giving rise to a prohibited transaction on the date the transaction occurs, and an additional prohibited transaction on the first day of each succeeding tax year (or portion of a tax year) within the taxable period that begins on the date the loan occurs. Therefore, in this example, there are two prohibited transactions, the first occurring on July 1, 2005 and ending on December 31, 2006, and the second occurring on January 1, 2006 and ending on December 31, 2006.

Section 4975(a) imposes a 15% excise tax on the amount involved for

each tax year or part thereof in the taxable period of each prohibited transaction.

The Form 5330 for the year ending December 31, 2005: The amount involved to be reported on Schedule C, line 2, column (d) is $6,000 (6 months x $1,000). The amount of the tax due is $900 ($6,000 x 15%). (See *Figure 1.*) (Any interest and penalties imposed for the delinquent filing of the Form 5330 and the delinquent payment of the excise tax for 2005 will be billed separately to the disqualified person.)

The Form 5330 for the year ending December 31, 2006: The excise tax to be reported would include both the prohibited transaction of July 1, 2005, with an amount involved of $6,000, resulting in a tax due of $900 ($6,000 x 15%) and the second prohibited transaction of January 1, 2006, with an amount involved of $12,000 (12 months x $1,000), resulting in a tax due of $1,800 ($12,000 x 15%). (See *Figure 2.*) The taxable period for the second prohibited transaction runs from January 1, 2006, through December 31, 2006 (date of correction). Because there are two prohibited transactions with taxable periods running during 2006, the section 4975(a) tax is due for the 2006 tax year for both prohibited transactions.

TIP *When a loan from a qualified plan that is a prohibited transaction spans successive tax years, and thus constitutes multiple prohibited transactions, and during those years the first tier prohibited transaction excise tax rate changes, the first tier excise tax liability for each prohibited transaction is the sum of the products resulting from multiplying the amount involved for each year in the taxable period for that prohibited transaction by the excise tax rate in effect at the beginning of that taxable period. For more information see Rev. Rul. 2002-43, 2002-2 I.R.B. 85. Unlike the previous example, the example in Rev. Rul. 2002-43 contains unpaid interest.*

Additional tax for failure to correct the prohibited transaction (Section 4975(b)). To avoid liability for additional taxes and penalties, and in some cases further initial taxes, a correction must be made within the taxable period. The term *correction* is defined as undoing the prohibited transaction to the extent possible, but in any case placing the plan in a financial position not worse than that in which it would be if the disqualified person were acting under the highest fiduciary standards.

If the prohibited transaction is not corrected within the taxable period, an additional tax equal to 100% of the amount involved will be imposed under section 4975(b). Any disqualified person who participated in the prohibited transaction (other than a fiduciary acting only as such) must pay this tax imposed by section 4975(b). Report the additional tax on line 3b of Section A, Form 5330.

Line 4. If the "No" box is checked on line 4, there has not been a correction of all of the prohibited transactions by the end of the tax year for which this Form 5330 is being filed. Attach a statement indicating when the correction has been or will be made.

Schedule C *(continued)*

Schedule of Other Participating Disqualified Persons and Description of Correction

If more than one disqualified person participated in the same prohibited transaction, list on this schedule the name, address, and social security number or employer identification number of each disqualified person, other than the disqualified person who files this return.

Line 5. For all transactions complete columns (a), (b), and (c). If the transaction has been corrected, complete columns (a) through (e). If additional space is needed you may

attach a statement fully explaining the correction and identifying persons involved in the prohibited transaction.

Prohibited Transactions and Investment Advice

For financial investment advice provided after December 31, 2006, the prohibited transaction rules of section 4975(c) will not apply to any transaction in connection with investment advice, if the investment advice provided by a fiduciary adviser is provided under an eligible investment advice arrangement.

For this purpose an *eligible investment advice arrangement* is an arrangement which either:
• Provides that any fees (including any commission or other compensation) received by the fiduciary adviser for investment advice or with respect to the sale, holding, or acquisition of any security or other property for the investment of plan assets do not vary depending on the basis of any investment option selected, or
• Uses a computer model under an investment advice program, described in section 4975(f)(8)(C), in connection with investment advice provided by a fiduciary adviser to a participant or beneficiary.
Additionally, the eligible investment advice arrangement must meet the provisions of section 4975(f)(8)(D), (E), (F), (G), (H), and (I).

For purposes of the statutory exemption on investment advice, a *fiduciary adviser* is defined in section 4975(f)(8)(J).

Correcting certain prohibited transactions. Generally, if a disqualified person enters into a direct or indirect prohibited transaction (listed in items 1 through 4 below) in connection with the acquisition, holding, or disposition of certain securities or commodities, and the transaction is corrected within the correction period, it will not be treated as a prohibited transaction and no tax will be assessed.

1. Sale or exchange, or leasing of any property between a plan and a disqualified person.
2. Lending of money or other extension of credit between a plan and a disqualified person.
3. Furnishing of goods, services, or facilities between a plan and a disqualified person.
4. Transfer to, or use by or for the benefit of, a disqualified person of income or assets of a plan.

However, if at the time the transaction was entered into, the disqualified person knew or had reason to know that the transaction was prohibited, the transaction would be

subject to the tax on prohibited transactions.

For purposes of section 4975(d)(23) the term *correct* means to:
• Undo the transaction to the extent possible and in all cases to make good to the plan or affected account any losses resulting from the transaction, and
• Restore to the plan or affected account any profits made through the use of assets of the plan.

The *correction period* is the 14-day period beginning on the date on which the disqualified person discovers or reasonably should have discovered that the transaction constitutes a prohibited transaction.

Schedule D (Section 4971(a) and (b))

Tax on Failure To Meet Minimum Funding Standards

Section 4971(a) imposes a 10% tax (5% for multiemployer plans) on the amount of the accumulated funding deficiency determined as of the end of the plan year.

If a plan fails to meet the funding requirements of section 412, the employer and all controlled group members will be subject to the excise taxes under section 4971(a) and (b).

Except in the case of a multiemployer plan, all members of a controlled group are jointly and severally liable for this tax. A *controlled group* in this case means a controlled group of corporations (section 414(b)), a group of trades or businesses under common control (section 414(c)), an affiliated service group (section 414(m)), and any other group treated as a single employer under section 414(o).

If the IRS determined at any time that your plan was a plan as defined in Schedule C (section 4975), it will always remain subject to the excise tax on failure to meet minimum funding standards.

Line 1. If your plan has an accumulated funding deficiency as defined in section 412(a) (section 418B if this is a multiemployer plan in reorganization), complete line 1.

Line 2. Multiply line 1 by the applicable tax rate shown below and enter the result on line 2.
• 10% for plans (other than multiemployer plans), or
• 5% for all multiemployer plans.

Additional tax for failure to correct the accumulated funding deficiency. When an initial tax is imposed by section 4971(a) on an accumulated funding deficiency and the accumulated funding deficiency is not corrected within the taxable period, an additional tax equal to 100% of the accumulated funding deficiency to the extent not corrected is imposed by section 4971(b).

The *taxable period* is the period beginning with the end of the plan year where there is an accumulated funding deficiency and ending on the earlier of:
• The date the notice of deficiency for the section 4971(a) excise tax is mailed, or
• The date the section 4971(a) excise tax is assessed.

Report the tax for failure to correct the accumulated funding deficiency on Part I, Section B, line 8b.

Section 214 of the Pension Protection Act of 2006 provides that, for certain tax years ending after August 17, 2006, a multiemployer pension plan with (1) less than 100 participants, (2) an annual normal cost of less than $100,000, and (3) a funding deficiency on August 17, 2006, will not incur the excise tax for an accumulated funding deficiency if its employers participated in a Federal Fishery Capacity Reduction Program and the Northeast Fisheries Assistance Program.

Schedule E (Section 4971(f))

Tax on Failure to Pay Liquidity Shortfall

Section 4971(f)(1). If your plan has a liquidity shortfall for which an excise tax under section 4971(f)(1) is imposed for any quarter of the plan year, complete lines 1 through 4.

Line 1. Include on line 1 the amount of the liquidity shortfall(s) for each quarter of the plan year.

Line 2. Include on line 2 the amount of any contributions made to the plan by the due date of the required quarterly installment(s) which partially corrected the liquidity shortfall(s) reported on line 1.

Line 3. Include on line 3 the net amount of the liquidity shortfall (subtract line 2 from line 1).

Additional tax for failure to correct liquidity shortfall. If the plan has a liquidity shortfall as of the close of any quarter and as of the close of the following 4 quarters, an additional tax will be imposed under section 4971(f)(2) equal to the amount on which tax was imposed by section 4971(f)(1) for such quarter. Report the additional tax on Part I, Section B, line 9b.

Schedule F (Section 4971(g))

For years beginning after 2007, Section 4971(g), which pertains to multiemployer plans, imposes an excise tax for failure to comply with a funding improvement or rehabilitation plan, failure to meet requirements for plans in endangered or critical status, or failure to adopt a rehabilitation plan. See page 5 of the instructions for information on *Section 4971(g)(2), Failure to Comply With A Funding Improvement or Rehabilitation Plan.*

 At the time of the drafting of these instructions, technical correction bills were pending in the Congress that may alter this.

Section 4971(g)(3)—Failure to Meet Requirements for Plans in Endangered or Critical Status

An excise tax is incurred by the failure to meet requirements for plans in endangered or critical status. A plan which is in seriously endangered status that fails to meet the applicable benchmarks by the end of the funding improvement period or a plan which is in critical status and either fails to meet the requirements of section 432 by the end of the rehabilitation period or has received a certification under section 432(b)(3)(A)(ii) for 3 consecutive plan years that the plan is not making the scheduled progress in meeting its requirements under the rehabilitation plan, shall be treated as having an accumulated funding deficiency for the last plan year in such period (and each succeeding plan year until such benchmarks or requirements are met). The accumulated funding deficiency is an amount equal to the greater of the amount of the contributions necessary to meet the benchmarks or requirements or the amount of the accumulated funding deficiency without regard to this rule. The existence of an accumulated funding deficiency triggers the initial 5% excise tax under section 4971(a). A plan is in endangered status if:

• The plan's actuary timely certifies that the plan is not in critical status for that plan year and at the beginning of that plan year the plan's funded percentage for plan year is less than 80 percent, or
• The plan has an accumulated funding deficiency for the plan year or is projected to have such an accumulated funding deficiency for any of the 6 succeeding plan years, taking into account any extension of amortization periods under section 431(d).

A plan is in critical status if it is determined by the multiemployer plan's actuary that one of the four formulas in section 432(b)(2) is met for the applicable plan year.

All, or part, of this excise tax may be waived under section 4971(g)(5).

Section 4971(g)(4)—Failure to Adopt Rehabilitation Plan

An excise tax is incurred by the failure to adopt a rehabilitation plan within the time prescribed under section 432. The amount of the tax, which is imposed on the plan sponsor, is equal to the greater of the amount of the tax imposed under section 4971(a) (determined without regard to section 4971(g)), or the amount equal to $1,100 multiplied by the number of days in the tax year which are included in the period that begins on the first day of the 240-day period that a multiemployer plan has to adopt a rehabilitation plan once it has entered critical status and that ends on the day that the rehabilitation plan is adopted. Liability for this tax is imposed on each plan sponsor.

This excise tax may not be waived.

Schedule G (Section 4977)

Tax on Excess Fringe Benefits

If you made an election to be taxed under section 4977 to continue your nontaxable fringe benefit policy that was in existence on or after January 1, 1984, check the "Yes" box on line 1 and complete lines 2 through 4.

Line 3. The excess fringe benefits are figured by subtracting 1% of the aggregate compensation paid by you to your employees during the calendar year that was includable in their gross income from the aggregate value of the nontaxable fringe benefits under sections 132(a)(1) and 132(a)(2).

Schedule H (Section 4979)

Tax on Excess Contributions to Certain Plans

Section 4979. Any employer who maintains a plan described in section 401(a), 403(a), 403(b), 408(k), or 501(c)(18) may be subject to an excise tax on the excess aggregate contributions made on behalf of highly compensated employees. The employer may also be subject to an excise tax on the excess contributions to a cash or deferred arrangement connected with the plan.

The tax is on the excess contributions and the excess aggregate contributions made to or on behalf of the highly compensated employees (as defined in section 414(q)).

A *highly compensated employee* generally is an employee who:
    1. Was a 5-percent owner at any time during the year or the preceding year, or
    2. For the preceding year had compensation from the employer in excess of a dollar amount for the year ($100,000 for 2006 and for 2007) and,

if the employer so elects, was in the top-paid group for the preceding year.

An employee is in the top-paid group for any year if the employee is in the group consisting of the top 20% of the employees of the employer when ranked on the basis of compensation paid. An employee (who is not a 5% owner) who has compensation in excess of $100,000 is not a highly compensated employee if the employer elects the top-paid group limitation and the employee is not a member of the top-paid group.

The *excess contributions* subject to the section 4979 excise tax are equal to the amount by which employer contributions actually paid over to the trust exceed the employer contributions that could have been made without violating the special nondiscrimination requirements of section 401(k)(3) or section 408(k)(6) in the instance of certain SEPs.

The *excess aggregate contributions* subject to the section 4979 excise tax are equal to the amount by which the aggregate matching contributions of the employer and the employee contributions (and any qualified nonelective contribution or elective contribution taken into account in computing the contribution percentage under section 401(m)) actually made on behalf of the highly compensated employees for each plan year exceed the maximum amount of the contributions permitted in the contribution percentage computation under section 401(m)(2)(A).

However, there is no excise tax liability if the excess contributions or the excess aggregate contributions and any income earned on the contributions are distributed (or, if forfeitable, forfeited) to the participants for whom the excess contributions were made within 2½ months after the end of the plan year.

Schedule I (Section 4980)

Tax on Reversion of Qualified Plan Assets to an Employer

Section 4980 imposes an excise tax on an employer reversion of qualified plan assets to an employer. Generally, the reversion excise tax is 20% of the amount of the employer reversion. The excise tax rate is increased to 50% if the employer does not (1) establish or maintain a qualified replacement plan following the plan termination or (2) provide certain pro-rata benefit increases in connection with the plan termination. See section 4980(d)(1)(A) or (B) for more information.

An *employer reversion* is the amount of cash and the FMV of property received, directly or indirectly, by an

employer from a qualified plan. For exceptions to this definition, see section 4980(c)(2)(B) and section 4980(c)(3).

A *qualified plan* is:
- Any plan meeting the requirements of section 401(a) or 403(a), other than a plan maintained by an employer if that employer has at all times been exempt from federal income tax, or
- A governmental plan within the meaning of section 414(d).

Terminated defined benefit plan. If a defined benefit plan is terminated, and an amount in excess of 25% of the maximum amount otherwise available for reversion is transferred from the terminating defined benefit plan to a defined contribution plan, the amount transferred is not treated as an employer reversion for purposes of section 4980. However, the amount the employer receives is subject to the 20% excise tax. For additional information, see Rev. Rul. 2003-85, 2003-32 I.R.B. 291.

Lines 1 through 4. If you owe the section 4980 tax, enter the date of the reversion on line 1. Enter the reversion amount on line 2a, and the applicable excise tax rate on line 2b. If you use a tax percentage other than 50% on line 2b, explain on line 4 why you qualify to use a rate other than 50%.

Include on line 3 and Part I, Section D, line 14 the section 4980 tax on employer reversions from a qualified plan.

Schedule J (Section 4980F)

Tax on Failure to Provide Notice of Significant Reduction in Future Accruals

Section 4980F imposes on an employer (or, in the case of a multiemployer plan, the plan) an excise tax of $100 per day per each applicable individual and each employee organization representing participants who are applicable individuals for each day of the noncompliance period for the failure to give notice of plan amendments that provide for a significant reduction in the rate of future benefit accrual or the elimination or significant reduction of an early retirement benefit or retirement-type subsidy. This notice is called a *section 204(h) notice* because section 204(h) of ERISA has parallel notice requirements.

An *applicable individual* is a participant in the plan, or an alternate payee of a participant under a qualified domestic relations order, whose rate of future benefit accrual (or early retirement benefit or retirement-type subsidy) under the plan may reasonably be expected to be significantly reduced by a plan

amendment (starting in plan years beginning after December 31, 2007, the requirement to give notice is extended to an employer who has an obligation to contribute to a multiemployer plan).

Whether a participant, alternate payee or an employer, as described in the above paragraph, is an applicable individual is determined on a typical business day that is reasonably approximate to the time the section 204(h) notice is provided (or at the latest date for providing section 204(h) notice, if earlier), based on all relevant facts and circumstances. For more information in determining whether an individual is a participant or alternate payee, see Regulations section 54.4980F-1, Q&A 10.

The *noncompliance period* is the period beginning on the date the failure first occurs and ending on the date the notice of the failure is provided or the failure is corrected.

Exceptions. Section 4980F excise tax will not be imposed for a failure during any period in which:

1. Any person subject to liability for the tax did not know that the failure existed and exercised reasonable diligence to meet the notice requirement. A person is considered to have exercised reasonable diligence, but did not know the failure existed, only if:

a. The responsible person exercised reasonable diligence in attempting to deliver section 204(h) notice to applicable individuals by the latest date permitted. Generally, the section 204(h) notice must be provided at least 45 days before the effective date of the section 204(h) amendment. For exceptions to this rule, see Regulations section 54.4980F-1, Q&A 9.

b. At the latest date permitted for delivery of section 204(h) notice, the person reasonably believes that section 204(h) notice was actually delivered to each applicable individual by that date.

2. Any person subject to liability for the tax exercised reasonable diligence to meet the notice requirement and corrects the failure within 30 days after the employer (or other person responsible for the tax) knew, or exercising reasonable diligence would have known, that the failure existed.

If the person subject to liability for the excise tax exercised reasonable diligence to meet the notice requirement, the total excise tax imposed during a tax year of the employer will not exceed $500,000. Furthermore, in the case of a failure due to reasonable cause and not to willful neglect, the Secretary of the Treasury is authorized to waive the excise tax to the extent that the payment of the tax would be excessive relative to the failure involved. See Rev. Proc. 2007-4, 2007-1 I.R.B. 118 for procedures to follow in applying for a waiver of part or all of the excise tax due to reasonable cause. You can find Rev. Proc. 2007-4 at *www.irs.gov/pub/irs-irbs/irb07-01.pdf.*

Line 4. A failure occurs on any day that any applicable individual is not provided section 204(h) notice.

Example. There are 1,000 applicable individuals (AI). The plan administrator fails to give section 204(h) notice to 100 AIs for 60 days, and to 50 of those AIs for an additional 30 days. In this case there are 7,500 failures ((100 AI x 60 days) + (50 AI x 30 days) = 7,500).

Privacy Act and Paperwork Reduction Act Notice. We ask for the information on this form to carry out the Internal Revenue laws of the United States. This form is required to be filed under sections 4965, 4971, 4972, 4973, 4975, 4976, 4977, 4978, 4979, 4979A, 4980, and 4980F of the Internal Revenue Code. Section 6109 requires you to provide your taxpayer identification number (SSN or EIN). If you fail to provide this information in a timely manner, you may be liable for penalties and interest. Routine uses of this information include giving it to the Department of Justice for civil and criminal litigation, and cities, states, and the District of Columbia for use in administering their tax laws. We may also disclose this information to federal and state or local agencies to enforce federal nontax criminal laws and to combat terrorism.

You are not required to provide the information requested on a form that is subject to the Paperwork Reduction Act unless the form displays a valid OMB control number. Books or records relating to a form or its instructions must be retained as long as their contents may become material in the administration of any Internal Revenue law. Generally, tax returns and return information are confidential, as required by section 6103.

The time needed to complete and file this form will vary depending on individual circumstances. The estimated average time is:

Recordkeeping . . . 30 hr., 22 min.

Learning about the law or the form . . . 15 hr., 45 min.

Preparing and sending the form to the IRS . . . . . . 18 hr., 08 min.

If you have comments concerning the accuracy of these time estimates or suggestions for making this form simpler, we would be happy to hear from you. You can write to the Internal Revenue Service, Tax Products Coordinating Committee, SE:W:CAR:MP:T:T:SP, IR-6526, 1111 Constitution Ave. NW, Washington, DC 20224. Do not send this form to this address. Instead, see *Where To File* on page 3.

Index

A
Amended return 3, 6
Amount involved 5

C
Claim for refund 3

D
Disqualified benefit, funded
  welfare plans 4
Disqualified person 9
Due dates 3

E
Eligible investment advice
  arrangement 9
Employer reversion 11
Entity manager 5
ESOP 4
  Prohibited allocations 4
ESOP dispositions 4
Excess contributions:
  403(b)(7) plans 6
  Section 4979 10
Excise tax due dates 3, 4
Extension 3

F
Form 5558 3
Form 8886-T 6
Funded welfare plans 4

I
Interest 3
Investment advice 9

L
Late filing 3
  Interest 3
  Penalty 3
Late payment 3
Liquidity shortfall 10
  Additional tax 10
Listed transaction 5

M
Minimum funding standards,
  failure 9

N
Nonallocation period 4
Nonallocation year 5
Nondeductible employer
  contributions 6
  Exception, defined benefit
    plan 6
  Exception, defined
    contribution plan 6
  Nondeductible
    contributions 6
  Qualified plan 6
Notice of significant reduction in
  future accruals 11
  Applicable individual 11

P
Payment of taxes 6
Penalty 3
  Late payment 3
Private delivery services 3
Prohibited allocation:
  Disqualified person 5
  ESOP 4

Nonallocation period 4
S corporation 4
Synthetic equity 5
Worker-owned
  cooperative 4
Prohibited reportable
  transaction 5
Prohibited tax shelter
  transaction 5
  Entity manager 5
  Required disclosure 6
Prohibited transaction 7
  Correcting 9
  Correction period 9
  Definition 7
  Disqualified person 7
  Exemptions 7
  Failure to correct 9
  Investment advice 9
Purpose of form 1

Q
Qualified ESOP securities 4

R
Required disclosure:
  Prohibited tax shelter
    transaction 6
Reversion of qualified plan
  assets 11
  Qualified plan 11
  Terminated defined benefit
    plan 11

S
S corporations:
  Prohibited allocations 4

Section 403(b) plan 6
Section 4965 5
Section 4971(a) 9
Section 4971(b) 9
Section 4971(f) 10
Section 4971(g) 10
Section 4971(g)(2) 5
Section 4971(g)(3) 10
Section 4971(g)(4) 10
Section 4972 6
Section 4973(a)(3) 6
Section 4975 7
Section 4976 4
Section 4977 10
Section 4979 10
Section 4979A 4
Section 4980 11
Section 4980F 11
Summary of taxes due 4
Synthetic equity 5
  Amount involved 5

T
Table of due dates 3

W
When to file 3
Where to file 3
Who must file 1
Worker-owned
  cooperative 4

■

☐ VOID   ☐ CORRECTED

TRUSTEE'S or ISSUER'S name, street address, city, state, and ZIP code		**1** IRA contributions (other than amounts in boxes 2–4 and 8–10) $	OMB No. 1545-0747 **20**08 Form **5498**	**IRA Contribution Information**
		2 Rollover contributions $		
TRUSTEE'S or ISSUER'S federal identification no.	PARTICIPANT'S social security number	**3** Roth IRA conversion amount $	**4** Recharacterized contributions $	**Copy C**
PARTICIPANT'S name		**5** Fair market value of account $	**6** Life insurance cost included in box 1 $	**For Trustee or Issuer**
Street address (including apt. no.)		**7** IRA ☐ SEP ☐	SIMPLE ☐ Roth IRA ☐	For Privacy Act and Paperwork Reduction Act Notice, see the
City, state, and ZIP code		**8** SEP contributions $	**9** SIMPLE contributions $	**2008 General Instructions for Forms 1099, 1098, 5498, and W-2G.**
Account number (see instructions)		**10** Roth IRA contributions $	**11** Check if RMD for 2009 ☐	

Form **5498**

Department of the Treasury - Internal Revenue Service

Form **8606**

Department of the Treasury
Internal Revenue Service (99)

Nondeductible IRAs

▶ See separate instructions.

▶ Attach to Form 1040, Form 1040A, or Form 1040NR.

OMB No. 1545-0074

2008

Attachment
Sequence No. **48**

Name. If married, file a separate form for each spouse required to file Form 8606. See page 5 of the instructions.

Your social security number

Fill in Your Address Only If You Are Filing This Form by Itself and Not With Your Tax Return ▶	Home address (number and street, or P.O. box if mail is not delivered to your home)	Apt. no.
	City, town or post office, state, and ZIP code	

Part I Nondeductible Contributions to Traditional IRAs and Distributions From Traditional, SEP, and SIMPLE IRAs

Complete this part only if one or more of the following apply.
- You made nondeductible contributions to a traditional IRA for 2008.
- You took distributions from a traditional, SEP, or SIMPLE IRA in 2008 **and** you made nondeductible contributions to a traditional IRA in 2008 or an earlier year. For this purpose, a distribution does not include a rollover (other than a repayment of a qualified disaster recovery assistance distribution), qualified charitable distribution, one-time distribution to fund an HSA, conversion, recharacterization, or return of certain contributions.
- You converted part, but not all, of your traditional, SEP, and SIMPLE IRAs to Roth IRAs in 2008 (excluding any portion you recharacterized) **and** you made nondeductible contributions to a traditional IRA in 2008 or an earlier year.

1	Enter your nondeductible contributions to traditional IRAs for 2008, including those made for 2008 from January 1, 2009, through April 15, 2009 (see page 5 of the instructions)	1	
2	Enter your total basis in traditional IRAs (see page 6 of the instructions)	2	
3	Add lines 1 and 2	3	

| In 2008, did you take a distribution from traditional, SEP, or SIMPLE IRAs, or make a Roth IRA conversion? | No ──▶ | Enter the amount from line 3 on line 14. Do not complete the rest of Part I. |
| | Yes ──▶ | Go to line 4. |

4	Enter those contributions included on line 1 that were made from January 1, 2009, through April 15, 2009	4	
5	Subtract line 4 from line 3	5	
6	Enter the value of **all** your traditional, SEP, and SIMPLE IRAs as of December 31, 2008, plus any outstanding rollovers. Subtract any repayments of qualified disaster recovery assistance distributions. If the result is zero or less, enter -0- (see page 6 of the instructions) .	6	
7	Enter your distributions from traditional, SEP, and SIMPLE IRAs in 2008. **Do not** include rollovers (other than repayments of qualified disaster recovery assistance distributions), qualified charitable distributions, a one-time distribution to fund an HSA, conversions to a Roth IRA, certain returned contributions, or recharacterizations of traditional IRA contributions (see page 6 of the instructions) . . .	7	
8	Enter the net amount you converted from traditional, SEP, and SIMPLE IRAs to Roth IRAs in 2008. **Do not** include amounts converted that you later recharacterized (see page 7 of the instructions). Also enter this amount on line 16	8	
9	Add lines 6, 7, and 8	9		
10	Divide line 5 by line 9. Enter the result as a decimal rounded to at least 3 places. If the result is 1.000 or more, enter "1.000" . . .	10	× .
11	Multiply line 8 by line 10. This is the nontaxable portion of the amount you converted to Roth IRAs. Also enter this amount on line 17 . . .	11	
12	Multiply line 7 by line 10. This is the nontaxable portion of your distributions that you did not convert to a Roth IRA	12	
13	Add lines 11 and 12. This is the nontaxable portion of all your distributions	13	
14	Subtract line 13 from line 3. This is **your total basis in traditional IRAs for 2008 and earlier years**	14	
15a	Subtract line 12 from line 7	15a	
b	Amount on line 15a attributable to qualified disaster recovery assistance distributions (see page 7 of the instructions). Also enter this amount on Form 8930, line 13	15b	
c	**Taxable amount.** Subtract line 15b from line 15a. If more than zero, also include this amount on Form 1040, line 15b; Form 1040A, line 11b; or Form 1040NR, line 16b	15c	

Note: You may be subject to an additional 10% tax on the amount on line 15c if you were under age 59½ at the time of the distribution (see page 7 of the instructions).

For Privacy Act and Paperwork Reduction Act Notice, see page 9 of the instructions.   Cat. No. 63966F   Form **8606** (2008)

Form 8606 (2008) Page **2**

Part II 2008 Conversions From Traditional, SEP, or SIMPLE IRAs to Roth IRAs

Complete this part if you converted part or all of your traditional, SEP, and SIMPLE IRAs to a Roth IRA in 2008 (excluding any portion you recharacterized).

Caution: *If your modified adjusted gross income is over $100,000 or you are married filing separately and you lived with your spouse at any time in 2008, you cannot convert any amount from traditional, SEP, or SIMPLE IRAs to Roth IRAs for 2008. If you erroneously made a conversion, you must recharacterize (correct) it (see page 7 of the instructions).*

16 If you completed Part I, enter the amount from line 8. Otherwise, enter the net amount you converted from traditional, SEP, and SIMPLE IRAs to Roth IRAs in 2008. **Do not** include amounts you later recharacterized back to traditional, SEP, or SIMPLE IRAs in 2008 or 2009 (see page 7 of the instructions) . . . . | **16** |

17 If you completed Part I, enter the amount from line 11. Otherwise, enter your basis in the amount on line 16 (see page 7 of the instructions) . . . . | **17** |

18 **Taxable amount.** Subtract line 17 from line 16. Also include this amount on Form 1040, line 15b; Form 1040A, line 11b; or Form 1040NR, line 16b . . . . | **18** |

Part III Distributions From Roth IRAs

Complete this part only if you took a distribution from a Roth IRA in 2008. For this purpose, a distribution does not include a rollover (other than a repayment of a qualified disaster recovery assistance distribution), qualified charitable distribution, one-time distribution to fund an HSA, recharacterization, or return of certain contributions (see page 7 of the instructions).

19 Enter your total nonqualified distributions from Roth IRAs in 2008 including any qualified first-time homebuyer distributions (see page 7 of the instructions). . . . . | **19** |

20 Qualified first-time homebuyer expenses (see page 7 of the instructions). **Do not** enter more than $10,000 . . . . | **20** |

21 Subtract line 20 from line 19. If zero or less, enter -0- and skip lines 22 through 25 . . . . | **21** |

22 Enter your basis in Roth IRA contributions (see page 8 of the instructions) . . . . . . | **22** |

23 Subtract line 22 from line 21. If zero or less, enter -0- and skip lines 24 and 25. If more than zero, you may be subject to an additional tax (see page 8 of the instructions) . . . . | **23** |

24 Enter your basis in conversions from traditional, SEP, and SIMPLE IRAs and rollovers from qualified retirement plans to a Roth IRA (see page 8 of the instructions) . . . . | **24** |

25a Subtract line 24 from line 23. If zero or less, enter -0- and skip lines 25b and 25c . . . . . | **25a** |

b Amount on line 25a attributable to qualified disaster recovery assistance distributions (see page 8 of the instructions). Also enter this amount on Form 8930, line 14 . . . . | **25b** |

c **Taxable amount.** Subtract line 25b from line 25a. If more than zero, also include this amount on Form 1040, line 15b; Form 1040A, line 11b; or Form 1040NR, line 16b . . . . | **25c** |

Sign Here Only If You Are Filing This Form by Itself and Not With Your Tax Return

Under penalties of perjury, I declare that I have examined this form, including accompanying attachments, and to the best of my knowledge and belief, it is true, correct, and complete. Declaration of preparer (other than taxpayer) is based on all information of which preparer has any knowledge.

▶ _____ Your signature   ▶ _____ Date

Paid Preparer's Use Only

Preparer's signature ▶	Date	Check if self-employed ☐	Preparer's SSN or PTIN
Firm's name (or yours if self-employed), address, and ZIP code ▶		EIN	
		Phone no. ( )	

Form **8606** (2008)

20**08**

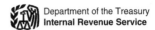

Department of the Treasury
Internal Revenue Service

Instructions for Form 8606

Nondeductible IRAs

Section references are to the Internal Revenue Code unless otherwise noted.

General Instructions

What's New

IRA contribution limit increased. You and your spouse, if filing jointly, each may be able to contribute up to $5,000 ($6,000 if age 50 or older at the end of 2008) to your IRA. See *Overall Contribution Limit for Traditional and Roth IRAs* on page 3.

Modified AGI limit for Roth IRA contributions increased. You can contribute to a Roth IRA for 2008 only if your 2008 modified adjusted gross income (AGI) for Roth IRA purposes is less than:
- $169,000 if married filing jointly or qualifying widow(er),
- $116,000 if single, head of household, or married filing separately and you did not live with your spouse at any time in 2008, or
- $10,000 if married filing separately and you lived with your spouse at any time in 2008.

See *Roth IRAs* on page 2.

Rollovers from qualified retirement plans to Roth IRAs. Beginning in 2008, you can roll over amounts from a qualified retirement plan to a Roth IRA. Any amount rolled over is subject to the same rules for converting a traditional IRA to a Roth IRA. However, do not file Form 8606 solely to report rollovers from qualified retirement plans. For more information, see *Rollover From Employer's Plan Into a Roth IRA* in chapter 2 of Pub. 590, Individual Retirement Arrangements (IRAs).

Tax relief for the Kansas disaster area. Special rules may apply if you received a distribution from your IRA and your main home was located in the Kansas disaster area, and you sustained an economic loss due to the storms and tornadoes that began on May 4, 2007.

Special rules may also apply if you received a distribution to purchase or construct a main home in the Kansas disaster area, but the home was not purchased or constructed because of the storms and tornadoes.

See Pub. 4492-A, Information for Taxpayers Affected by the May 4, 2007, Kansas Storms and Tornadoes, for more information.

Tax relief for the Midwestern disaster areas. Special rules may apply if you received a distribution from your IRA and your main home was located in a Midwestern disaster area on the date the disaster occurred, and you sustained an economic loss due to the severe storms, tornadoes, or flooding.

Special rules may also apply if you received a distribution to purchase or construct a main home in a Midwestern disaster area, but the home was not purchased or constructed because of the severe storms, tornadoes, or flooding.

See Pub. 4492-B, Information for Affected Taxpayers in the Midwestern Disaster Areas, and Form 8930, Qualified Disaster Recovery Assistance Retirement Plan Distributions and Repayments, for more information.

Qualified settlement income. If you received qualified settlement income in connection with the Exxon Valdez litigation, you may be able to roll over some or all of the amount you received to your IRA. For more information on qualified settlement income, see Pub. 590.

Military death gratuities and servicemembers' group life insurance (SGLI) payments. If you received a military death gratuity or SGLI payment with respect to a death from injury that occurred after October 6, 2001, you may be able to roll over some or all of the amount you received to your Roth IRA. For more information on military death gratuities and SGLI payments, see Pub. 590.

Airline payments. If you are a qualified airline employee, you may contribute any portion of an airline payment you receive as a result of an airline carrier bankruptcy to a Roth IRA. For more information on airline payments, see Pub. 590.

Required minimum distributions for 2009. For 2009, you are not required to take a minimum distribution from your IRA. For more information, see Pub. 590.

Purpose of Form

Use Form 8606 to report:
- Nondeductible contributions you made to traditional IRAs,
- Distributions from traditional, SEP, or SIMPLE IRAs, if you have ever made nondeductible contributions to traditional IRAs,
- Distributions from Roth IRAs, and

- Conversions from traditional, SEP, or SIMPLE IRAs to Roth IRAs.

Additional information. See Pub. 590, for more details.

TIP *If you received distributions from a traditional, SEP, or SIMPLE IRA in 2008 and you have never made nondeductible contributions to traditional IRAs, do not report the distributions on Form 8606. Instead, see the instructions for Form 1040, lines 15a and 15b; Form 1040A, lines 11a and 11b; or Form 1040NR, lines 16a and 16b. Also, to find out if any of your contributions to traditional IRAs are deductible, see the instructions for Form 1040, line 32; Form 1040A, line 17; or Form 1040NR, line 31.*

Who Must File

File Form 8606 if any of the following apply.
- You made nondeductible contributions to a traditional IRA for 2008, including a repayment of a qualified reservist distribution.
- Your economic stimulus payment or tax refund was directly deposited into a traditional IRA and you are treating it as a nondeductible contribution.
- You received distributions from a traditional, SEP, or SIMPLE IRA in 2008 and your basis in traditional IRAs is more than zero. For this purpose, a distribution does not include a rollover (other than a repayment of a qualified disaster recovery assistance distribution or a qualified recovery assistance distribution), qualified charitable distribution, a one-time distribution to fund an HSA, conversion, recharacterization, or return of certain contributions.
- You converted an amount from a traditional, SEP, or SIMPLE IRA to a Roth IRA in 2008 (unless you recharacterized the entire conversion—see page 3).
- You received distributions from a Roth IRA in 2008 (other than a rollover, recharacterization, or return of certain contributions—see page 7).
- You made a repayment of a qualified hurricane, disaster recovery assistance, or recovery assistance distribution that is attributable to previously nondeductible contributions.

Note. If you recharacterized a 2008 Roth IRA contribution as a traditional IRA contribution, or vice versa, treat the contribution as having been made to the second IRA, not the first IRA. See page 3.

Cat. No. 25399E

If you received any qualified disaster recovery assistance distributions, complete Part I of Form 8930 before you complete Form 8606. If you received any qualified recovery assistance distributions, see Pub. 4492-A for instructions on completing Part I of the 2006 version of Form 8915 before completing Form 8606.

 You do not have to file Form 8606 solely to report regular contributions to Roth IRAs or rollovers from qualified retirement plans to Roth IRAs. But see What Records Must I Keep? *on page 5.*

When and Where To File

File Form 8606 with your 2008 Form 1040, 1040A, or 1040NR. If you are not required to file an income tax return but are required to file Form 8606, sign Form 8606 and send it to the Internal Revenue Service at the same time and place you would otherwise file Form 1040, 1040A, or 1040NR.

Definitions

Deemed IRAs

A qualified employer plan (retirement plan) can maintain a separate account or annuity under the plan (a deemed IRA) to receive voluntary employee contributions. If in 2008 you had a deemed IRA, use the rules for either a traditional IRA or a Roth IRA depending

on which type it was. See Pub. 590 for more details.

Traditional IRAs

For purposes of Form 8606, a traditional IRA is an individual retirement account or an individual retirement annuity other than a SEP, SIMPLE, or Roth IRA.

Contributions. An overall contribution limit applies to traditional IRAs and Roth IRAs. See *Overall Contribution Limit for Traditional and Roth IRAs* on page 3. Contributions to a traditional IRA may be fully deductible, partially deductible, or completely nondeductible.

Basis. Your basis in traditional IRAs is the total of all your nondeductible contributions and nontaxable amounts included in rollovers made to traditional IRAs minus the total of all your nontaxable distributions, adjusted if necessary (see the instructions for line 2 on page 6). Keep track of your basis to figure the nontaxable part of your future distributions.

SEP IRAs

A simplified employee pension (SEP) is an employer-sponsored plan under which an employer can make contributions to traditional IRAs for its employees. If you make contributions to that IRA (excluding employer contributions you make if you are self-employed), they are treated as contributions to a traditional IRA and

may be deductible or nondeductible. SEP IRA distributions are reported in the same manner as traditional IRA distributions.

SIMPLE IRAs

Your participation in your employer's SIMPLE IRA plan does not prevent you from making contributions to a traditional, SEP, or Roth IRA.

Roth IRAs

A Roth IRA is similar to a traditional IRA, but has the following features.
• Contributions are never deductible.
• Contributions can be made after the owner reaches age 70½.
• No minimum distributions are required during the Roth IRA owner's lifetime.
• Qualified distributions are not includible in income.

Qualified distribution. Generally, a qualified distribution is any distribution made:

• On or after age 59½,
• Upon death,
• Due to disability, or
• For qualified first-time homebuyer expenses.

Exception. Any distribution made during the 5-year period beginning with the first year for which you made a Roth IRA contribution or conversion is not a qualified distribution, and may be taxable.

Contributions. You can contribute to a Roth IRA for 2008 only if your 2008 modified adjusted gross income (AGI) for Roth IRA purposes is less than:
• $10,000 if married filing separately and you lived with your spouse at any time in 2008,
• $169,000 if married filing jointly or qualifying widow(er), or
• $116,000 if single, head of household, or if married filing separately and you did not live with your spouse at any time in 2008.

Use the Maximum Roth IRA Contribution Worksheet on this page to figure the maximum amount you can contribute to a Roth IRA for 2008. If you are married filing jointly, complete the worksheet separately for you and your spouse.

 If you contributed too much, see Recharacterizations *on page 3.*

Modified AGI for Roth IRA purposes.
First, figure your AGI (Form 1040, line 38; Form 1040A, line 22; or Form 1040NR, line 36). Then, refigure it by:
   1. Subtracting the following.
   a. Roth IRA conversions included on Form 1040, line 15b; Form 1040A, line 11b; or Form 1040NR, line 16b.
   b. Roth IRA rollovers from qualified retirement plans included on Form 1040, line 16b; Form 1040A, line 12b; or Form 1040NR, line 17b.
   c. Minimum required distributions from IRAs (for conversions and

---

Maximum Roth IRA Contribution Worksheet (keep for your records)

Caution: *If married filing jointly and the combined taxable compensation (defined on page 3) for you and your spouse is less than $10,000 ($11,000 if one spouse is 50 or older at the end of 2008; $12,000 if both spouses are 50 or older at the end of 2008),* **do not** *use this worksheet. Also,* **do not** *use this worksheet if you or your spouse qualify for the catch-up contributions for certain employer bankruptcies. Instead, see Pub. 590 for special rules.*

   1. If married filing jointly, enter $5,000 ($6,000 if age 50 or older at the end of 2008). All others, enter the **smaller** of $5,000 ($6,000 if age 50 or older at the end of 2008) or your taxable compensation (defined on page 3) . . . . **1.** _____
   2. Enter your total contributions to traditional IRAs for 2008 . . . . . **2.** _____
   3. Subtract line 2 from line 1 . . . . **3.** _____
   4. Enter: $169,000 if married filing jointly or qualifying widow(er); $10,000 if married filing separately and you lived with your spouse at any time in 2008. All others, enter $116,000 . . . . . **4.** _____
   5. Enter your modified AGI for Roth IRA purposes (see this page) **5.** _____
   6. Subtract line 5 from line 4. If zero or less, **stop here;** you may not contribute to a Roth IRA for 2008. See **Recharacterizations** on page 3 if you made Roth IRA contributions for 2008 . . . . **6.** _____
   7. If line 4 above is $116,000, enter $15,000; otherwise, enter $10,000. If line 6 is more than or equal to line 7, skip lines 8 and 9 and enter the amount from line 3 on line 10 . . . . **7.** _____
   8. Divide line 6 by line 7 and enter the result as a decimal (rounded to at least 3 places). If the result is 1.000 or more, enter 1.000 . . . . **8.** _____
   9. Multiply line 1 by line 8. If the result is not a multiple of $10, increase it to the next multiple of $10 (for example, increase $490.30 to $500). Enter the result, but not less than $200 . . . . **9.** _____
   10. **Maximum 2008 Roth IRA Contribution.** Enter the **smaller** of line 3 or line 9. See **Recharacterizations** on page 3 if you contributed more than this amount to Roth IRAs for 2008 . . . . **10.** _____

---

rollovers from qualified retirement plans only).

2. Adding the following.

a. IRA deduction from Form 1040, line 32; Form 1040A, line 17; or Form 1040NR, line 31.

b. Student loan interest deduction from Form 1040, line 33; Form 1040A, line 18; or Form 1040NR, line 32.

c. Tuition and fees deduction from Form 1040, line 34; or Form 1040A, line 19.

d. Domestic production activities deduction from Form 1040, line 35; or Form 1040NR, line 33.

e. Exclusion of interest from Form 8815, Exclusion of Interest From Series EE and I U.S. Savings Bonds Issued After 1989.

f. Exclusion of employer-provided adoption benefits from Form 8839, Qualified Adoption Expenses.

g. Foreign earned income exclusion from Form 2555, Foreign Earned Income, or Form 2555-EZ, Foreign Earned Income Exclusion.

h. Foreign housing exclusion or deduction from Form 2555.

 When figuring modified AGI for Roth IRA purposes, you may have to refigure items based on modified AGI, such as taxable social security benefits and passive activity losses allowed under the special allowance for rental real estate activities. See Can You Contribute to a Roth IRA? *in Pub. 590 for details.*

Distributions. See the instructions for Part III that begin on page 7.

Overall Contribution Limit for Traditional and Roth IRAs

If you are not married filing jointly, your limit on contributions to traditional and Roth IRAs is the smaller of $5,000 ($6,000 if age 50 or older at the end of 2008) or your taxable compensation (defined later). If you are married filing jointly, your contribution limit is generally $5,000 ($6,000 if age 50 or older at the end of 2008) and your spouse's contribution limit is $5,000 ($6,000 if age 50 or older at the end of 2008) as well. But if the combined taxable compensation of both you and your spouse is less than $10,000 ($11,000 if one spouse is 50 or older at the end of 2008; $12,000 if both spouses are 50 or older at the end of 2008), see Pub. 590 for special rules. This limit does not apply to employer contributions to a SEP or SIMPLE IRA.

Catch-up contributions in certain employer bankruptcies. If you participated in a 401(k) plan and the employer who maintained the plan went into bankruptcy in an earlier year, you may be able to contribute an additional $3,000 to your IRA. For more information, see *Catch-up contributions in certain employer bankruptcies* in Pub. 590.

Note. Rollovers, Roth IRA conversions, Roth IRA rollovers from

qualified retirement plans, and repayments of qualified hurricane, disaster recovery assistance, recovery assistance, and reservist distributions do not affect your contribution limit.

 The amount you can contribute to a Roth IRA may also be limited by your modified AGI (see Contributions *and the* Maximum Roth IRA Contribution Worksheet *on page 2).*

Taxable compensation includes the following.

● Wages, salaries, tips, etc. If you received a distribution from a nonqualified deferred compensation plan or nongovernmental section 457 plan that is included in Form W-2, box 1, or in Form 1099-MISC, box 7, do not include that distribution in taxable compensation. The distribution should be shown in (a) Form W-2, box 11, (b) Form W-2, box 12, with code Z, or (c) Form 1099-MISC, box 15b. If it is not, contact your employer for the amount of the distribution.

● Nontaxable combat pay if you were a member of the U.S. Armed Forces.

● Self-employment income. If you are self-employed (a sole proprietor or a partner), taxable compensation is your net earnings from your trade or business (provided your personal services are a material income-producing factor) reduced by your deduction for contributions made on your behalf to retirement plans and the deduction allowed for one-half of your self-employment tax.

● Alimony and separate maintenance. See Pub. 590 for details.

Recharacterizations

Generally, you can recharacterize (correct) an IRA contribution, Roth IRA conversion, or a Roth IRA rollover from a qualified retirement plan by making a trustee-to-trustee transfer from one IRA to another type of IRA. Trustee-to-trustee transfers are made directly between financial institutions or within the same financial institution. You generally must make the transfer by the due date of your return (including extensions) and reflect it on your return. However, if you timely filed your return without making the transfer, you can make the transfer within 6 months of the due date of your return, excluding extensions. If necessary, file an amended return reflecting the transfer (see page 5). Write "Filed pursuant to section 301.9100-2" on the amended return.

Reporting recharacterizations. Any recharacterized conversion or Roth IRA rollover from a qualified retirement plan will be treated as though the conversion or rollover had not occurred. Any recharacterized contribution will be treated as having been originally contributed to the second IRA, not the first IRA. The amount transferred must include related earnings or be reduced by any loss. In most cases, the related

earnings that you must transfer are figured by your IRA trustee or custodian. If you need to figure the related earnings, see *How Do You Recharacterize a Contribution* in Pub. 590. Any earnings or loss that occurred in the first IRA will be treated as having occurred in the second IRA. You cannot deduct any loss that occurred while the funds were in the first IRA. Also, you cannot take a deduction for a contribution to a traditional IRA if the amount is later recharacterized. See below for how to report the four different types of recharacterizations, including the statement that must be attached to your return explaining the recharacterization.

1. You converted an amount from a traditional, SEP, or SIMPLE IRA to a Roth IRA in 2008 and later recharacterized all or part of the amount back to a traditional, SEP, or SIMPLE IRA. If you only recharacterized part of the amount converted, report the amount not recharacterized on Form 8606. If you recharacterized the entire amount, do not report the recharacterization on Form 8606. In either case, attach a statement to your return explaining the recharacterization and include the amount converted from the traditional, SEP, or SIMPLE IRA in the total on Form 1040, line 15a; Form 1040A, line 11a; or Form 1040NR, line 16a. If the recharacterization occurred in 2008, also include the amount transferred back from the Roth IRA on that line. If the recharacterization occurred in 2009, report the amount transferred only in the attached statement, and not on your 2008 or 2009 tax return (a 2009 Form 1099-R should be sent to you by February 1, 2010, stating that you made a recharacterization of an amount converted in the prior year).

Example. You are married filing jointly and converted $20,000 from your traditional IRA to a new Roth IRA on May 20, 2008. On April 7, 2009, you determine that your 2008 modified AGI for Roth IRA purposes will exceed $100,000, and you are not allowed to make a Roth IRA conversion. The value of the Roth IRA on that date is $19,000. You recharacterize the conversion by transferring that entire amount to a traditional IRA in a trustee-to-trustee transfer. You report $20,000 on Form 1040, line 15a. You do not include the $19,000 on line 15a because it did not occur in 2008 (you also do not report that amount on your 2009 return because it does not apply to the 2009 tax year). You attach a statement to Form 1040 explaining that (a) you made a conversion of $20,000 from a traditional IRA on May 20, 2008, and (b) you recharacterized the entire amount, which was then valued at $19,000, back to a traditional IRA on April 7, 2009.

2. You made a contribution to a traditional IRA and later recharacterized part or all of it to a Roth IRA. If you

recharacterized only part of the contribution, report the nondeductible traditional IRA portion of the remaining contribution, if any, on Form 8606, Part I. If you recharacterized the entire contribution, do not report the contribution on Form 8606. In either case, attach a statement to your return explaining the recharacterization. If the recharacterization occurred in 2008, include the amount transferred from the traditional IRA on Form 1040, line 15a; Form 1040A, line 11a; or Form 1040NR, line 16a. If the recharacterization occurred in 2009, report the amount transferred only in the attached statement.

Example. You are single, covered by a retirement plan, and you contributed $4,000 to a new traditional IRA on May 27, 2008. On February 24, 2009, you determine that your 2008 modified AGI will limit your traditional IRA deduction to $1,000. The value of your traditional IRA on that date is $4,400. You decide to recharacterize $3,000 of the traditional IRA contribution as a Roth IRA contribution, and have $3,300 ($3,000 contribution plus $300 related earnings) transferred from your traditional IRA to a Roth IRA in a trustee-to-trustee transfer. You deduct the $1,000 traditional IRA contribution on Form 1040. You are not required to file Form 8606, but you must attach a statement to your return explaining the recharacterization. The statement indicates that you contributed $4,000 to a traditional IRA on May 27, 2008; recharacterized $3,000 of that contribution on February 24, 2009, by transferring $3,000 plus $300 of related earnings from your traditional IRA to a Roth IRA in a trustee-to-trustee transfer; and that all $1,000 of the remaining traditional IRA contribution is deducted on Form 1040. You do not report the $3,300 distribution from your traditional IRA on your 2008 Form 1040 because the distribution occurred in 2009. You do not report the distribution on your 2009 Form 1040 because the recharacterization related to 2008 and was explained in an attachment to your 2008 return.

3. You made a contribution to a Roth IRA and later recharacterized part or all of it to a traditional IRA. Report the nondeductible traditional IRA portion, if any, on Form 8606, Part I. If you did not recharacterize the entire contribution, do not report the remaining Roth IRA portion of the contribution on Form 8606. Attach a statement to your return explaining the recharacterization. If the recharacterization occurred in 2008, include the amount transferred from the Roth IRA on Form 1040, line 15a; Form 1040A, line 11a; or Form 1040NR, line 16a. If the recharacterization occurred in 2009, report the amount transferred only in the attached statement, and not on your 2008 or 2009 tax return.

Example. You are single and contributed $4,000 to a new Roth IRA on June 16, 2008. On December 29, 2008, you determine that your 2008 modified AGI will allow a full traditional IRA deduction. You decide to recharacterize the Roth IRA contribution as a traditional IRA contribution and have $4,200, the balance in the Roth IRA account ($4,000 contribution plus $200 related earnings), transferred from your Roth IRA to a traditional IRA in a trustee-to-trustee transfer. You deduct the $4,000 traditional IRA contribution on Form 1040. You are not required to file Form 8606, but you must attach a statement to your return explaining the recharacterization. The statement indicates that you contributed $4,000 to a new Roth IRA on June 16, 2008; recharacterized that contribution on December 29, 2008, by transferring $4,200, the balance in the Roth IRA, to a traditional IRA in a trustee-to-trustee transfer; and that $4,000 of the traditional IRA contribution is deducted on Form 1040. You include the $4,200 distribution on your 2008 Form 1040, line 15a.

4. You rolled over an amount from a qualified retirement plan to a Roth IRA in 2008 and later recharacterized all or part of the amount to a traditional IRA. Attach a statement to your return explaining the recharacterization and include the amount of the original rollover on Form 1040, line 16a; Form 1040A, line 12a; or Form 1040NR, line 17a. Also, include any taxable amount of the rollover not recharacterized on Form 1040, line 16b; Form 1040A, line 12b; or Form 1040NR, line 17b. If the recharacterization occurred in 2008, also include the amount transferred from the Roth IRA on Form 1040, line 15a; Form 1040A, line 11a; or Form 1040NR, line 16a. If the recharacterization occurred in 2009, report the amount transferred only in the attached statement, and not on your 2008 or 2009 tax return (a 2009 Form 1099-R should be sent to you by February 1, 2010, stating that you made a recharacterization of an amount in the prior year). You do not report these rollovers or recharacterizations on Form 8606.

Example. You are single and you rolled over $50,000 from your 401(k) plan to a new Roth IRA on July 20, 2008. On March 25, 2009, you determine that your 2008 modified AGI for Roth IRA purposes will exceed $100,000, and you are not allowed to make a Roth IRA rollover. The value of the Roth IRA on that date is $49,000. You recharacterize the rollover by transferring that entire amount to a traditional IRA in a trustee-to-trustee transfer. You report $50,000 on Form 1040, line 16a. You do not include the $49,000 on line 15a because it did not occur in 2008 (you also do not report that amount on your 2009 return because it does not apply to the 2009 tax year). You attach a statement to Form 1040 explaining that (a) you

made a rollover of $50,000 from a 401(k) plan to a Roth IRA on July 20, 2008, and (b) you recharacterized the entire amount, which was then valued at $49,000, to a traditional IRA on March 25, 2009.

Return of IRA Contributions

If, in 2008 or 2009, you made traditional IRA contributions or Roth IRA contributions for 2008 and you had those contributions returned to you with any related earnings (or minus any loss) by the due date (including extensions) of your 2008 tax return, the returned contributions are treated as if they were never contributed. Do not report the contribution or distribution on Form 8606 or take a deduction for the contribution. However, you must report the distribution and any related earnings on your 2008 Form 1040, lines 15a and 15b; Form 1040A, lines 11a and 11b; or Form 1040NR, lines 16a and 16b. Attach a statement explaining the distribution. You cannot deduct any loss that occurred (see Pub. 590 for an exception if you withdrew the entire amount in all your traditional or Roth IRAs). Also, if you were under age 59½ at the time of a distribution with related earnings, you generally are subject to the additional 10% tax on early distributions (see Form 5329, Additional Taxes on Qualified Plans (Including IRAs) and Other Tax-Favored Accounts).

If you timely filed your 2008 tax return without withdrawing a contribution that you made in 2008, you can still have the contribution returned to you within 6 months of the due date of your 2008 tax return, excluding extensions. If you do, file an amended return with "Filed pursuant to section 301.9100-2" written at the top. Report any related earnings on the amended return and include an explanation of the withdrawal. Make any other necessary changes on the amended return (for example, if you reported the contributions as excess contributions on your original return, include an amended Form 5329 reflecting that the withdrawn contributions are no longer treated as having been contributed).

In most cases, the related earnings that you must withdraw are figured by your IRA trustee or custodian. If you need to figure the related earnings on IRA contributions that were returned to you, see *Contributions Returned Before Due Date of Return* in Pub. 590. If you made a contribution or distribution while the IRA held the returned contribution, see Pub. 590.

If you made a contribution for 2007 and you had it returned to you in 2008 as described above, do not report the distribution on your 2008 tax return. Instead, report it on your 2007 original or amended return in the manner described above.

Example. On May 28, 2008, you contributed $4,000 to your traditional IRA. The value of the IRA was $18,000 prior to the contribution. On December 29, 2008, when you are age 57 and the value of the IRA is $23,600, you realize you cannot make the entire contribution because your taxable compensation for the year will be only $3,000. You decide to have $1,000 of the contribution returned to you and withdraw $1,073 from your IRA ($1,000 contribution plus $73 earnings). You did not make any other withdrawals or contributions. You are not required to file Form 8606. You deduct the $3,000 remaining contribution on Form 1040. You include $1,073 on Form 1040, line 15a, and $73 on line 15b. You attach a statement to your tax return explaining the distribution. Because you properly removed the excess contribution with the related earnings by the due date of your tax return, you are not subject to the additional 6% tax on excess contributions. However, because you were under age 59½ at the time of the distribution, the $73 of earnings is subject to the additional 10% tax on early distributions. You include $7.30 on Form 1040, line 59.

Return of Excess Traditional IRA Contributions

The return (distribution) in 2008 of excess traditional IRA contributions for years prior to 2008 is not taxable if all three of the following apply.

1. The distribution was made after the due date, including extensions, of your tax return for the year for which the contribution was made (if the distribution was made earlier, see *Return of IRA Contributions* on page 4).

2. The total contributions (excluding rollovers and conversions) to your traditional and SEP IRAs for the year for which the excess contribution was made did not exceed:

a. $4,000 ($5,000 if age 50 or older at the end of the year) for 2007 or 2006,

b. $4,000 ($4,500 if age 50 or older at the end of the year) for 2005,

c. $3,000 ($3,500 if age 50 or older at the end of the year) for years after 2001 and before 2005,

d. $2,000 for years after 1996 and before 2002, or

e. $2,250 for years before 1997.

If your total IRA contributions for the year included employer contributions to a SEP IRA, increase the $4,000 ($5,000 or $4,500, if applicable), $3,000 ($3,500, if applicable), $2,000, or $2,250 by the smaller of the employer contributions or $45,000 ($44,000 for 2006, $42,000 for 2005, $41,000 for 2004, $40,000 for 2003 and 2002, $35,000 for 2001, or $30,000 for years before 2001).

3. No deduction was allowable (without regard to the modified AGI

limitation) or taken for the excess contributions.

Include the total amount distributed on Form 1040, line 15a; Form 1040A, line 11a; or Form 1040NR, line 16a; and attach a statement to your return explaining the distribution. See the example below.

If you meet these conditions and are otherwise required to file Form 8606:
• Do not take into account the amount of the withdrawn contributions in figuring line 2, and
• Do not include the amount of the withdrawn contributions on line 7.

Example. You are single, you retired in 2005, and you had no taxable compensation after 2005. However, you made traditional IRA contributions (that you did not deduct) of $3,000 in 2006 and $4,000 in 2007. In November 2008, a tax practitioner informed you that you had made excess contributions for those years because you had no taxable compensation. You withdrew the $7,000 and filed amended returns for 2006 and 2007 reflecting the additional 6% tax on excess contributions on Form 5329. You include the $7,000 distribution on your 2008 Form 1040, line 15a, enter -0- on line 15b, and attach a statement to your return explaining the distribution, including the fact that you filed amended returns for 2006 and 2007 and paid the additional 6% tax on the excess contributions for those years. The statement indicates that the distribution is not taxable because (a) it was made after the due dates of your 2006 and 2007 tax returns, including extensions, (b) your total IRA contributions did not exceed $4,000 ($5,000 if age 50 or older at the end of the year) for 2006 or 2007, and (c) you did not take a deduction for the contributions, and no deduction was allowable because you did not have any taxable compensation for those years. The statement also indicates that the distribution reduced your excess contributions to -0-, as reflected on your 2008 Form 5329 and it indicates your adjusted basis in nondeductible contributions.

Amending Form 8606

After you file your return, you can change a nondeductible contribution to a traditional IRA to a deductible contribution or vice versa. You also may be able to make a recharacterization (see page 3). If necessary, complete a new Form 8606 showing the revised information and file it with Form 1040X, Amended U.S. Individual Income Tax Return.

Penalty for Not Filing

If you are required to file Form 8606 to report a nondeductible contribution to a traditional IRA for 2008, but do not do so, you must pay a $50 penalty, unless you can show reasonable cause.

Overstatement Penalty

If you overstate your nondeductible contributions, you must pay a $100 penalty, unless you can show reasonable cause.

What Records Must I Keep?

To verify the nontaxable part of distributions from your IRAs, including Roth IRAs, keep a copy of the following forms and records until all distributions are made.
• Page 1 of Forms 1040 (or Forms 1040A, 1040NR, or 1040-T) filed for each year you made a nondeductible contribution to a traditional IRA.
• Forms 8606 and any supporting statements, attachments, and worksheets for all applicable years.
• Forms 5498 or similar statements you received each year showing contributions you made to a traditional IRA or Roth IRA.
• Forms 5498 or similar statements you received showing the value of your traditional IRAs for each year you received a distribution.
• Forms 1099-R or W-2P you receive for each year you received a distribution.

Note. Forms 1040-T and W-2P are forms that were used in prior years.

Specific Instruction

Name and social security number (SSN). If you file a joint return, enter only the name and SSN of the spouse whose information is being reported o Form 8606. If both you and your spouse are required to file Form 8606 file a separate Form 8606 for each of you.

Part I—Nondeductible Contributions to Traditional IRAs and Distributions From Traditional, SEP, and SIMPLE IRAs

Line 1

If you used the IRA Deduction Worksheet in the Form 1040 or 1040A instructions, subtract line 12 (line 10 fo Form 1040A) of the worksheet (or the amount you chose to deduct on Form 1040, line 32, or Form 1040A, line 17, less) from the smaller of line 10 or line 11 (line 8 or line 9 for Form 1040A) of the worksheet. Enter the result on line of Form 8606. You cannot deduct the amount included on line 1.

If you used the worksheet Figuring Your Reduced IRA Deduction for 200 in Pub. 590, enter on line 1 of Form 8606 any nondeductible contributions from the appropriate lines of that worksheet.

If you did not have any deductible contributions, you can make nondeductible contributions up to your contribution limit. Enter on line 1 of Form 8606 your nondeductible contributions.

Include on line 1 any repayment of a qualified reservist distribution. Also, include any repayment of a qualified hurricane, disaster recovery assistance, or recovery assistance distribution that is attributable to previously nondeductible contributions.

Do not include on line 1 contributions that you had returned to you with the related earnings (or less any loss). See page 4.

Line 2

If this is the first year you are required to file Form 8606, enter -0-. Otherwise, use the chart below to find the amount to enter on line 2.

However, you may need to enter an amount other than -0- or adjust the amount from the chart if your basis changed because of any of the following.
• You had a return of excess traditional IRA contributions (see page 5).
• Incident to divorce, you transferred or received part or all of a traditional IRA (see the next to last bulleted item under *Line 7* that begins on this page).
• You rolled over any nontaxable portion of your qualified employer plan to a traditional or SEP IRA. Include the nontaxable portion on line 2.

IF the last Form 8606 you filed was for...	THEN enter on line 2...
2007, 2006, 2005, 2004, 2003, 2002, or 2001	The amount from line 14 of that Form 8606
A year after 1992 and before 2001	The amount from line 12 of that Form 8606
A year after 1988 and before 1993	The amount from line 14 of that Form 8606
1988	The total of the amounts on lines 7 and 16 of that Form 8606
1987	The total of the amounts on lines 4 and 13 of that Form 8606

Line 4

If you made contributions to traditional IRAs for 2008 in 2008 and 2009 and you have both deductible and nondeductible contributions, you can choose to treat the contributions made in 2008 first as nondeductible contributions and then as deductible contributions, or vice versa. But the amount on line 4 cannot be less than

the excess, if any, of the amount on line 1 over the contributions you actually made in 2008.

Example. You made contributions for 2008 of $2,000 in May 2008 and $2,000 in January 2009, of which $3,000 are deductible and $1,000 are nondeductible. You choose $1,000 of your contribution in 2008 to be nondeductible. You enter the $1,000 on line 1, but not line 4, and it becomes part of your basis for 2008.

Although the contributions to traditional IRAs for 2008 that you made from January 1, 2009, through April 15, 2009, can be treated as nondeductible, they are not included in figuring the nontaxable part of any distributions you received in 2008.

Line 6

Enter the total value of all your traditional, SEP, and SIMPLE IRAs as of December 31, 2008, plus any outstanding rollovers. A statement should be sent to you by January 31, 2009, showing the value of each IRA on December 31, 2008. However, if you recharacterized any amounts, enter on line 6 the total value taking into account all recharacterizations, including recharacterizations made after December 31, 2008.

For line 6, a rollover is a tax-free distribution from one traditional, SEP, or SIMPLE IRA that is contributed to another traditional, SEP, or SIMPLE IRA. The rollover must be completed within 60 days of receiving the distribution from the first IRA. An outstanding rollover is any amount distributed in 2008 after November 1, 2008, that was rolled over in 2009, but within the 60-day rollover period.

The IRS may waive the 60-day requirement if failing to waive it would be against equity or good conscience, such as situations where a casualty, disaster, or other events beyond your reasonable control prevented you from meeting the 60-day requirement. Also, the 60-day period may be extended if you had a frozen deposit. See Pub. 590 for details.

Note. Do not include a rollover from a traditional or SEP IRA to a qualified employer plan even if it was an outstanding rollover.

Also include on line 6, any qualified distributions you repaid before March 4, 2009, if the distributions were to be used to purchase or construct a main home in a Midwestern disaster area, but the home was not purchased or constructed because of the severe storms, tornadoes, or flooding. See Pub. 4492-B for more information.

Repayments of qualified disaster recovery assistance distributions and recovery assistance distributions. Subtract the total amount of repayments of qualified disaster recovery assistance distributions or recovery assistance distributions you made in 2008 from the

amount you would otherwise enter on line 6. If the result is zero or less, enter -0-.

Example. You received a $30,000 qualified disaster recovery assistance distribution on August 18, 2008, from your traditional IRA. On December 15, 2008, you made a repayment of $15,000 to your traditional IRA. The value of all your traditional, SEP, and SIMPLE IRAs as of December 31, 2008, was $50,000. You had no outstanding rollovers. You would enter $35,000 ($50,000 minus the $15,000 repayment) on line 6.

Line 7

⚠ **CAUTION** *If you received a distribution in 2008 from a traditional, SEP, or SIMPLE IRA, and you also made contributions for 2008 to a traditional IRA that may not be fully deductible because of the income limits, you must make a special computation before completing the rest of this form. For details, including how to complete Form 8606, see* Are Distributions Taxable? *in chapter 1 of Pub. 590.*

Do not include any of the following on line 7.
• Distributions that you converted to a Roth IRA.
• Recharacterizations.
• Distributions that you rolled over by December 31, 2008, and any outstanding rollovers included on line 6.
• Distributions you rolled over to a qualified employer plan.
• A one-time distribution to fund an HSA. For details, see Pub. 969, Health Savings Accounts and Other Tax-Favored Health Plans.
• Qualified charitable distributions. For details, see the instructions for Form 1040, lines 15a and 15b; Form 1040A, lines 11a and 11b; or Form 1040NR, lines 16a and 16b.
• Distributions that are treated as a return of contributions under *Return of IRA Contributions* on page 4.
• Distributions that are treated as a return of excess contributions under *Return of Excess Traditional IRA Contributions* on page 5.
• Distributions of excess contributions due to incorrect rollover information. If an excess contribution in your traditional IRA is the result of a rollover from a qualified retirement plan and the excess occurred because the information the plan was required to give you was incorrect, the distribution of the excess contribution is not taxable. Attach a statement to your return explaining the distribution and include the amount of the distribution on Form 1040, line 15a; Form 1040A, line 11a; or Form 1040NR, line 16a. See Pub. 590 for more details.
• Distributions that are incident to divorce. The transfer of part or all of your traditional, SEP, or SIMPLE IRA to your spouse under a divorce or

separation agreement is not taxable to you or your spouse. If this transfer results in a change in the basis of the traditional IRA of either spouse, both spouses must file Form 8606 and show the increase or decrease in the amount of basis on line 2. Attach a statement explaining this adjustment. Include in the statement the character of the amounts in the traditional IRA, such as the amount attributable to nondeductible contributions. Also, include the name and social security number of the other spouse.
• Qualified distributions you repaid before March 4, 2009, if the distributions were to be used to purchase or construct a main home in a Midwestern disaster area, but the home was not purchased or constructed because of the severe storms, tornadoes, or flooding. See Pub. 4492-B for more information.

Qualified disaster recovery assistance distributions and qualified recovery assistance distributions. Be sure to include on line 7, all qualified disaster recovery assistance distributions and all recovery assistance distributions you received, even if they were later repaid.

Line 8

If, in 2008, you converted any amounts from traditional, SEP, or SIMPLE IRAs to a Roth IRA, enter on line 8 the net amount you converted. To figure that amount, subtract from the total amount converted in 2008 any portion that you recharacterized back to traditional, SEP, or SIMPLE IRAs in 2008 or 2009 (see *Recharacterizations* that begins on page 3). Do not take into account related earnings that were transferred with the recharacterized amount or any loss that occurred while the amount was in the Roth IRA. See item 1 under *Reporting recharacterizations* on page 3 for details.

Line 15b

If all your distributions are either qualified disaster recovery assistance distributions or qualified recovery assistance distributions, enter the amount from line 15a on line 15b. If you have distributions unrelated to either the Midwestern severe storms, tornadoes, or flooding; or the Kansas storms and tornadoes, as well as qualified disaster recovery assistance distributions or qualified recovery assistance distributions, you will need to multiply the amount on line 15a by a fraction. The numerator of the fraction is your total disaster recovery assistance distributions or recovery assistance distributions. The denominator of the fraction is the amount from Form 8606, line 7. See the example below.

Example. You received a distribution from your traditional IRA (that you did not roll over) in the amount of $30,000 on April 1, 2008, unrelated to the severe storms,

tornadoes, or flooding in the Midwestern disaster areas. On August 18, 2008, your received a qualified disaster recovery assistance distribution (as a result of the severe storms, tornadoes, or flooding in a Midwestern disaster area) from your traditional IRA in the amount of $10,000. You would report $40,000 on Form 8606, line 7. You would then complete lines 8 through 14 as instructed. Form 8606, line 15a shows an amount of $36,000. You would enter $9,000 ($36,000 x $10,000/$40,000) on line 15b. You would also enter $9,000 on Form 8930, line 13.

Line 15c

If you were under age 59½ at the time you received distributions from your traditional, SEP, or SIMPLE IRA, there generally is an additional 10% tax on the portion of the distribution that is included in income (25% for a distribution from a SIMPLE IRA during the first 2 years). See the Instructions for Form 1040, line 59, or the Instructions for Form 1040NR, line 54.

Part II—2008 Conversions From Traditional, SEP, or SIMPLE IRAs to Roth IRAs

Complete Part II if you converted part or all of your traditional, SEP, or SIMPLE IRAs to a Roth IRA in 2008, excluding any portion you recharacterized. See item 1 under *Reporting recharacterizations* on page 3 for details.

Limit on number of conversions. If you converted an amount from a traditional, SEP, or SIMPLE IRA to a Roth IRA in 2008 and then recharacterized the amount back to a traditional, SEP, or SIMPLE IRA, you cannot reconvert that amount until the later of January 1, 2009, or 30 days after the recharacterization. See Pub. 590 for details.

⚠ **CAUTION** *You cannot convert any amount to Roth IRAs in 2008 if (a) your modified AGI for Roth IRA purposes (see page 2) is more than $100,000, or (b) your filing status is married filing separately and you lived with your spouse at any time in 2008. If you erroneously made a conversion, you must recharacterize the converted amount. See* Recharacterizations *that begins on page 3.*

Line 16

If you did not complete line 8, see the instructions for that line. Then, enter on line 16 the amount you would have entered on line 8 had you completed it.

Line 17

If you did not complete line 11, enter on line 17 the amount from line 2 (or the amount you would have entered on line

2 if you had completed that line) plus any contributions included on line 1 that you made before the conversion.

Part III—Distributions From Roth IRAs

Complete Part III to figure the taxable part, if any, of your 2008 Roth IRA distributions.

Line 19

Do not include on line 19 any of the following.
• Distributions that you rolled over, including distributions made in 2008 and rolled over after December 31, 2008 (outstanding rollovers).
• Recharacterizations.
• Distributions that are a return of contributions under *Return of IRA Contributions* on page 4.
• Distributions made on or after age 59½ if you made a contribution (including a conversion) for 2003 or an earlier year.
• A one-time distribution to fund an HSA. For details, see Pub. 969.
• Qualified charitable contributions. For details, see the instructions for Form 1040, lines 15a and 15b; Form 1040A, lines 11a and 11b; or Form 1040NR, lines 16a and 16b.
• Distributions made upon death or due to disability if you made a contribution (including a conversion) for 2003 or an earlier year.
• Distributions that are incident to divorce. The transfer of part or all of your Roth IRA to your spouse under a divorce or separation agreement is not taxable to you or your spouse.
• Qualified distributions you repaid before March 4, 2009, if the distributions were to be used to purchase or construct a main home in a Midwestern disaster area, but the home was not purchased or constructed because of the severe storms, tornadoes, or flooding. See Pub. 4492-B for more information.

Qualified disaster recovery assistance distributions and qualified recovery assistance distributions. Be sure to include on line 19, all qualified disaster recovery assistance distributions and all recovery disaster distributions you received, even if they were later repaid.

If, after considering the items above, you do not have an amount to enter on line 19, do not complete Part III; your Roth IRA distribution(s) is not taxable. Instead, include your total Roth IRA distribution(s) on Form 1040, line 15a; Form 1040A, line 11a; or Form 1040NR, line 16a.

Line 20

If you had a qualified first-time homebuyer distribution from your Roth IRA and you made a contribution (including a conversion) to a Roth IRA for 2003 or an earlier year, enter the amount of your qualified expenses on

Basis in Regular Roth IRA Contributions—Line 22

IF the most recent year prior to 2008 in which you took a Roth IRA distribution* was...	THEN enter on Form 8606, line 22, this amount...	PLUS the total of all your regular contributions** to Roth IRAs for...
2007 (you had an amount on your 2007 Form 8606, line 19)	The excess of your 2007 Form 8606, line 22, over line 19 of that Form 8606.	2008
2006 (you had an amount on your 2006 Form 8606, line 19)	The excess of your 2006 Form 8606, line 22, over line 19 of that Form 8606.	2007 and 2008
2005 (you had an amount on your 2005 Form 8606, line 19)	The excess of your 2005 Form 8606, line 22, over line 19 of that Form 8606.	2006 through 2008
2004 (you had an amount on your 2004 Form 8606, line 19)	The excess of your 2004 Form 8606, line 22, over line 19 of that Form 8606.	2005 through 2008
2003 (you had an amount on your 2003 Form 8606, line 19)	The excess of your 2003 Form 8606, line 20, over line 19 of that Form 8606.	2004 through 2008
2002 (you had an amount on your 2002 Form 8606, line 19)	The excess of your 2002 Form 8606, line 20, over line 19 of that Form 8606.	2003 through 2008
2001 (you had an amount on your 2001 Form 8606, line 19)	The excess of your 2001 Form 8606, line 20, over line 19 of that Form 8606.	2002 through 2008
2000 (you had an amount on your 2000 Form 8606, line 17)	The excess of your 2000 Form 8606, line 18d, over line 17 of that Form 8606.	2001 through 2008
1999 (you had an amount on your 1999 Form 8606, line 17)	The excess of your 1999 Form 8606, line 18d, over line 17 of that Form 8606.	2000 through 2008
1998 (you had an amount on your 1998 Form 8606, line 18)	The excess of your 1998 Form 8606, line 19c, over line 18 of that Form 8606.	1999 through 2008
Did not take a Roth IRA distribution* prior to 2008	$0	1998 through 2008

*Excluding rollovers, recharacterizations, and contributions that you had returned to you.

**Excluding rollovers, conversions, Roth IRA contributions that were recharacterized, and any contributions that you had returned to you.

line 20, but do not enter more than $10,000.

Line 22

Figure the amount to enter on line 22 as follows.
- If you did not take a Roth IRA distribution before 2008 (other than an amount rolled over or recharacterized or a returned contribution), enter on line 22 the total of all your regular contributions to Roth IRAs for 1998 through 2008 (excluding rollovers from other Roth IRAs and any contributions that you had returned to you), adjusted for any recharacterizations.
- If you did take such a distribution before 2008, use the chart on this page to figure the amount to enter.
- Increase the amount on line 22 by any amount rolled in from a designated Roth account that is treated as investment in the contract.
- Increase or decrease the amount on line 22 by any basis transferred or received incident to divorce. Also attach a statement similar to the one

explained in the next to last bulleted item under *Line 7* that begins on page 6.
- Increase the amount on line 22 by the amounts received as a military gratuity or SGLI payment that was rolled over to your Roth IRA.
- Increase the amount on line 22 by any amount received as qualified settlement income in connection with the Exxon Valdez litigation and rolled over to your Roth IRA.

Line 23

Generally, there is an additional 10% tax on 2008 distributions from a Roth IRA that are shown on line 23. The additional tax is figured on Form 5329, Part I. See the instructions for Form 5329, line 1, for details and exceptions.

Note. The additional 10% tax does not apply to any qualified disaster recovery assistance distributions, see Form 8930 for more details. The additional 10% tax also does not apply to any qualified recovery assistance distributions, see Pub. 4492-A for more details.

Line 24

Figure the amount to enter on line 24 as follows.
- If you have never made a Roth IRA conversion or rolled over an amount from a qualified retirement plan to a Roth IRA, enter -0- on line 24.
- If you took a Roth IRA distribution (other than an amount rolled over or recharacterized or a returned contribution) before 2008 in excess of your basis in regular Roth IRA contributions, use the chart on page 9 to figure the amount to enter on line 24.
- If you did not take such a distribution before 2008, enter on line 24 the total of all your conversions to Roth IRAs (other than amounts recharacterized). These amounts are shown on line 14c of your 1998, 1999, and 2000 Forms 8606 and line 16 of your 2001 through 2008 Forms 8606. Also include on line 24 any amounts rolled over from a qualified retirement plan to a Roth IRA for 2008.
- Increase or decrease the amount on line 24 by any basis transferred or received incident to divorce. Also attach a statement similar to the one explained in the next to last bulleted item under *Line 7* that begins on page 6.

Line 25b

If all your distributions are either qualified disaster recovery assistance distributions or qualified recovery assistance distributions, enter the amount from line 25a on line 25b. If you have distributions unrelated to either the Midwestern severe storms, tornadoes, or flooding; or the Kansas storms and tornadoes, as well as qualified disaster recovery assistance distributions or qualified recovery assistance distributions, you will need to multiply the amount on line 25a by a fraction. The numerator of the fraction is your total disaster recovery assistance distributions or recovery assistance distributions. The denominator of the fraction is the amount from Form 8606, line 21. See the example below.

Example. You received a distribution from your Roth IRA (that you did not roll over) in the amount of $30,000 on April 1, 2008, unrelated to the severe storms, tornadoes, or flooding in the Midwestern disaster areas. On August 18, 2008, you received a qualified disaster recovery assistance distribution (as a result of the severe storms, tornadoes, or flooding in a Midwestern disaster area) from your Roth IRA in the amount of $10,000. You would report total distributions of $40,000 on Form 8606, line 19. You have no first-time homebuyer expenses reported on line 20, so you would also enter $40,000 on line 21. Your would then complete lines 22 through 24 as instructed. Form 8606, line 25a shows an amount of $20,000. You would enter $5,000 ($20,000 x $10,000/$40,000) on line

Basis in Roth IRA Conversions and Rollovers From Qualified Retirement Plans to Roth IRAs—Line 24

IF the most recent year prior to 2008 in which you had a distribution* in excess of your basis in contributions was...	THEN enter on Form 8606, line 24, this amount...	PLUS the sum of the amounts*** on the following lines...
2007 (your 2007 Form 8606, line 22, was less than line 19 of that Form 8606)	The excess, if any, of your 2007 Form 8606, line 24, over line 23** of that Form 8606.	Line 16 of your 2008 Form 8606
2006 (your 2006 Form 8606, line 22, was less than line 19 of that Form 8606)	The excess, if any, of your 2006 Form 8606, line 24, over line 23** of that Form 8606.	Line 16 of your 2007 and 2008 Forms 8606
2005 (your 2005 Form 8606, line 22, was less than line 19 of that Form 8606)	The excess, if any, of your 2005 Form 8606, line 24, over line 23** of that Form 8606.	Line 16 of your 2006 through 2008 Forms 8606
2004 (your 2004 Form 8606, line 22, was less than line 19 of that Form 8606)	The excess, if any, of your 2004 Form 8606, line 24, over line 23** of that Form 8606.	Line 16 of your 2005 through 2008 Forms 8606
2003 (you had an amount on your 2003 Form 8606, line 21)	The excess, if any, of your 2003 Form 8606, line 22, over line 21 of that Form 8606.	Line 16 of your 2004 through 2008 Forms 8606
2002 (you had an amount on your 2002 Form 8606, line 21)	The excess, if any, of your 2002 Form 8606, line 22, over line 21 of that Form 8606.	Line 16 of your 2003 through 2008 Forms 8606
2001 (you had an amount on your 2001 Form 8606, line 21)	The excess, if any, of your 2001 Form 8606, line 22, over line 21 of that Form 8606.	Line 16 of your 2002 through 2008 Forms 8606
2000 (you had an amount on your 2000 Form 8606, line 19)	The excess, if any, of your 2000 Form 8606, line 25, over line 19 of that Form 8606.	Line 16 of your 2001 through 2008 Forms 8606
1999 (you had an amount on your 1999 Form 8606, line 19)	The excess, if any, of your 1999 Form 8606, line 25, over line 19 of that Form 8606.	Line 14c of your 2000 Form 8606 and line 16 of your 2001 through 2008 Forms 8606
1998 (you had an amount on your 1998 Form 8606, line 20)	The excess, if any, of your 1998 Form 8606, line 14c, over line 20 of that Form 8606.	Line 14c of your 1999 and 2000 Forms 8606 and line 16 of your 2001 through 2008 Forms 8606
Did not have such a distribution in excess of your basis in contributions	The amount from your 2008 Form 8606, line 16.	Line 14c of your 1998, 1999, and 2000 Forms 8606 and line 16 of your 2001 through 2007 Forms 8606

*Excluding rollovers, recharacterizations, and contributions that you had returned to you.

**Refigure line 23 without taking into account any amount entered on Form 8606, line 20.

*** Including amounts rolled over from qualified retirement plans to a Roth IRA in 2008.

25b. You would also enter $9,000 on Form 8930, line 14.

Privacy Act and Paperwork Reduction Act Notice. We ask for the information on this form to carry out the Internal Revenue laws of the United States. We need this information to ensure that you are complying with these laws and to allow us to figure and collect the right amount of tax. You are required to give us this information if you made certain contributions or received certain distributions from qualified plans, including IRAs, and other tax-favored accounts. Our legal right to ask for the information requested on this form is sections 6001, 6011, 6012(a), and 6109 and their regulations. The reason we need your social security number is to secure proper identification in order to gain access to the tax information in our files to properly process the form. If you do not file this information, or provide incomplete or false information, you may be subject to penalties.

You are not required to provide the information requested on a form that is subject to the Paperwork Reduction Act unless the form displays a valid OMB control number. Books or records relating to a form or its instructions must be retained as long as their contents may become material in the administration of any Internal Revenue law. Generally, tax returns and return information are confidential, as required by section 6103. However, we may give the information to the Department of Justice for civil and criminal litigation, and to cities, states, and the District of Columbia to carry out their tax laws. We may also disclose this information to other countries under a tax treaty, to federal and state agencies to enforce federal nontax criminal laws, or to federal law enforcement and intelligence agencies to combat terrorism.

The average time and expenses required to complete and file this form will vary depending on individual circumstances. For the estimated averages, see the instructions for your income tax return.

If you have suggestions for making this form simpler, we would be happy to hear from you. See the instructions for your income tax return.

Revenue Ruling 2002-62

Part I

Section 72.—Annuities; Certain Proceeds of Endowment and Life Insurance Contracts

SECTION 1. PURPOSE AND BACKGROUND

.01 The purpose of this revenue ruling is to modify the provisions of Q&A-12 of Notice 89-25, 1989-1 C.B. 662, which provides guidance on what constitutes a series of substantially equal periodic payments within the meaning of 72(t)(2)(A)(iv) of the Internal Revenue Code from an individual account under a qualified retirement plan. Section 72(t) provides for an additional income tax on early withdrawals from qualified retirement plans (as defined in 4974(c)). Section 4974(c) provides, in part, that the term "qualified retirement plan" means (1) a plan described in 401 (including a trust exempt from tax under 501(a)), (2) an annuity plan described in 403(a), (3) a tax-sheltered annuity arrangement described in 403(b), (4) an individual retirement account described in 408(a), or (5) an individual retirement annuity described in 408(b).

.02 (a) Section 72(t)(1) provides that if an employee or IRA owner receives any amount from a qualified retirement plan before attaining age 59½, the employee's or IRA owner's income tax is increased by an amount equal to 10-percent of the amount that is includible in the gross income unless one of the exceptions in 72(t)(2) applies.

(b) Section 72(t)(2)(A)(iv) provides, in part, that if distributions are part of a series of substantially equal periodic payments (not less frequently than annually) made for the life (or life expectancy) of the employee or the joint lives (or joint life expectancy) of the employee and beneficiary, the tax described in 72(t)(1) will not be applicable. Pursuant to 72(t)(5), in the case of distributions from an IRA, the IRA owner is substituted for the employee for purposes of applying this exception.

(c) Section 72(t)(4) provides that if the series of substantially equal periodic payments that is otherwise excepted from the 10-percent tax is subsequently modified (other than by reason of death or disability) within a 5-year period beginning on the date of the first payment, or, if later, age 59½, the exception to the 10-percent tax does not apply, and the taxpayer's tax for the year of modification shall be increased by an amount which, but for the exception, would have been imposed, plus interest for the deferral period.

Revenue Ruling 2002-62 (continued)

(d) Q&A-12 of Notice 89-25 sets forth three methods for determining whether payments to individuals from their IRAs or, if they have separated from service, from their qualified retirement plans, constitute a series of substantially equal periodic payments for purposes of 72(t)(2)(A)(iv).

(e) Final Income Tax Regulations that were published in the April 17, 2002, issue of the Federal Register under 401(a)(9) provide new life expectancy tables for determining required minimum distributions.

SECTION 2. METHODS

.01 General rule. Payments are considered to be substantially equal periodic payments within the meaning of 72(t)(2)(A)(iv) if they are made in accordance with one of the three calculations described in paragraphs (a) – (c) of this subsection (which is comprised of the three methods described in Q&A-12 of Notice 89-25).

(a) The required minimum distribution method. The annual payment for each year is determined by dividing the account balance for that year by the number from the chosen life expectancy table for that year. Under this method, the account balance, the number from the

chosen life expectancy table and the resulting annual payments are redetermined for each year. If this method is chosen, there will not be deemed to be a modification in the series of substantially equal periodic payments, even if the amount of payments changes from year to year, provided there is not a change to another method of determining the payments.

(b) The fixed amortization method. The annual payment for each year is determined by amortizing in level amounts the account balance over a specified number of years determined using the chosen life expectancy table and the chosen interest rate. Under this method, the account balance, the number from the chosen life expectancy table and the resulting annual payment are determined once for the first distribution year and the annual payment is the same amount in each succeeding year.

(c) The fixed annuitization method. The annual payment for each year is determined by dividing the account balance by an annuity factor that is the present value of an annuity of $1 per year beginning at the taxpayer's age and continuing for the life of the taxpayer (or the joint lives of the

Revenue Ruling 2002-62 (continued)

individual and beneficiary). The annuity factor is derived using the mortality table ... and using the chosen interest rate. Under this method, the account balance, the annuity factor, the chosen interest rate and the resulting annual payment are determined once for the first distribution year and the annual payment is the same amount in each succeeding year.

.02 Other rules. The following rules apply for purposes of this section.

(a) Life expectancy tables. The life expectancy tables that can be used to determine distribution periods are: (1) the uniform lifetime table in Appendix A*, or (2) the single life expectancy table in 1.401(a) (9)-9, Q&A-1 of the Income Tax Regulations* or (3) the joint and last survivor table in 1.401(a) (9)-9, Q&A-3*. The number that is used for a distribution year is the number shown from the table for the employee's (or IRA owner's) age on his or her birthday in that year. If the joint and survivor table is being used, the age of the beneficiary on the beneficiary's birthday in the year is also used. In the case of the required minimum distribution method, the same life expectancy table that is used for the first distribution year must be used in each following year. Thus, if the taxpayer uses the single life expectancy table for the required minimum distribution method in the first distribution year, the same table must be used in subsequent distribution years.

(b) Beneficiary under joint tables. If the joint life and last survivor table in 1.401(a)(9)-9, Q&A-3, is used, the survivor must be the actual beneficiary of the employee with respect to the account for the year of the distribution. If there is more than one beneficiary, the identity and age of the beneficiary used for purposes of each of the methods described in section 2.01 are determined under the rules for determining the designated beneficiary for purposes of 401(a)(9). The beneficiary is determined for a year as of January 1 of the year, without regard to changes in the beneficiary in that year or beneficiary determinations in prior years. For example, if a taxpayer starts distributions from an IRA in 2003 at age 50 and a 25-year-old and 55-year-old are beneficiaries on January 1, the 55-year-old is the designated beneficiary and the number for the

* You can find these tables in Appendix B of this book.

Revenue Ruling 2002-62 (continued)

taxpayer from the joint and last survivor tables (age 50 and age 55) would be 38.3, even though later in 2003 the 55-year-old is eliminated as a beneficiary. However, if that beneficiary is eliminated or dies in 2003, under the required minimum distribution method, that individual would not be taken into account in future years. If, in any year there is no beneficiary, the single life expectancy table is used for that year.

(c) Interest rates. The interest rate that may be used is any interest rate that is not more than 120 percent of the federal mid-term rate (determined in accordance with 1274(d) for either of the two months immediately preceding the month in which the distribution begins). The revenue rulings that contain the 1274(d) federal mid-term rates may be found at www.irs.gov\tax_regs\fedrates.html.

(d) Account balance. The account balance that is used to determine payments must be determined in a reasonable manner based on the facts and circumstances. For example, for an IRA with daily valuations that made its first distribution on July 15, 2003, it would be reasonable to determine the yearly account balance when using the required minimum distribution method based on the value of the IRA from December 31, 2002 to July 15, 2003. For subsequent years, under the required minimum distribution method, it would be reasonable to use the value either on the December 31 of the prior year or on a date within a reasonable period before that year's distribution.

(e) Changes to account balance. Under all three methods, substantially equal periodic payments are calculated with respect to an account balance as of the first valuation date selected in paragraph (d) above. Thus, a modification to the series of payments will occur if, after such date, there is (i) any addition to the account balance other than gains or losses, (ii) any nontaxable transfer of a portion of the account balance to another retirement plan, or (iii) a rollover by the taxpayer of the amount received resulting in such amount not being taxable.

Revenue Ruling 2002-62 (continued)

.03 Special rules. The special rules described below may be applicable.

  (a) Complete depletion of assets. If, as a result of following an acceptable method of determining substantially equal periodic payments, an individual's assets in an individual account plan or an IRA are exhausted, the individual will not be subject to additional income tax under 72(t)(1) as a result of not receiving substantially equal periodic payments and the resulting cessation of payments will not be treated as a modification of the series of payments.

  (b) One-time change to required minimum distribution method. An individual who begins distributions in a year using either the fixed amortization method or the fixed annuitization method may in any subsequent year switch to the required minimum distribution method to determine the payment for the year of the switch and all subsequent years and the change in method will not be treated as a modification within the meaning of 72(t)(4). Once a change is made under this paragraph, the required minimum distribution method must be followed in all subsequent years. Any subsequent change will be a modification for purposes of 72(t)(4).

SECTION 3. EFFECTIVE DATE AND TRANSITIONAL RULES

The guidance in this revenue ruling replaces the guidance in Q&A-12 of Notice 89-25 for any series of payments commencing on or after January 1, 2003, and may be used for distributions commencing in 2002. If a series of payments commenced in a year prior to 2003 that satisfied 72(t)(2)(A)(iv), the method of calculating the payments in the series is permitted to be changed at any time to the required minimum distribution method described in section 2.01(a) of this guidance, including use of a different life expectancy table.

SECTION 4. EFFECT ON OTHER DOCUMENTS

Q&A-12 of Notice 89-25 is modified.

SECTION 5. REQUEST FOR COMMENTS

The Service and Treasury invite comments with respect to the guidance provided in this revenue ruling. Comments should reference Rev. Rul. 2002-62. Comments may be submitted to CC:ITA:RU (Rev. Rul. 2002-62), room 5226, Internal Revenue Service, POB 7604 Ben Franklin Station,

Revenue Ruling 2002-62 (continued)

Washington, DC 20044. Comments may be hand delivered between the hours of 8:30 a.m. and 5 p.m. Monday to Friday to: CC:ITA:RU (Rev. Rul. 2002-62), Courier's Desk, Internal Revenue Service, 1111 Constitution Avenue NW, Washington, DC. Alternatively, comments may be submitted via the Internet at Notice. Comments@irscounsel.treas.gov. All comments will be available for public inspection and copying.

Drafting Information

The principal author of this revenue ruling is Michael Rubin of the Employee Plans, Tax Exempt and Government Entities Division. For further information regarding this revenue ruling, please contact Mr. Rubin at 1-202-283-9888 (not a toll-free number).

Life Expectancy Tables

Table I: Single Life Expectancy...272

Table II: Joint Life and Last Survivor Expectancy..273

Table III: Uniform Lifetime Table 291

Table IV: Survivor Benefit Limits 292

Table I: Single Life Expectancy

Age	Divisor	Age	Divisor	Age	Divisor	Age	Divisor
0	82.4	29	54.3	58	27.0	87	6.7
1	81.6	30	53.3	59	26.1	88	6.3
2	80.6	31	52.4	60	25.2	89	5.9
3	79.7	32	51.4	61	24.4	90	5.5
4	78.7	33	50.4	62	23.5	91	5.2
5	77.7	34	49.4	63	22.7	92	4.9
6	76.7	35	48.5	64	21.8	93	4.6
7	75.8	36	47.5	65	21.0	94	4.3
8	74.8	37	46.5	66	20.2	95	4.1
9	73.8	38	45.6	67	19.4	96	3.8
10	72.8	39	44.6	68	18.6	97	3.6
11	71.8	40	43.6	69	17.8	98	3.4
12	70.8	41	42.7	70	17.0	99	3.1
13	69.9	42	41.7	71	16.3	100	2.9
14	68.9	43	40.7	72	15.5	101	2.7
15	67.9	44	39.8	73	14.8	102	2.5
16	66.9	45	38.8	74	14.1	103	2.3
17	66.0	46	37.9	75	13.4	104	2.1
18	65.0	47	37.0	76	12.7	105	1.9
19	64.0	48	36.0	77	12.1	106	1.7
20	63.0	49	35.1	78	11.4	107	1.5
21	62.1	50	34.2	79	10.8	108	1.4
22	61.1	51	33.3	80	10.2	109	1.2
23	60.1	52	32.3	81	9.7	110	1.1
24	59.1	53	31.4	82	9.1	111+	1.0
25	58.2	54	30.5	83	8.6		
26	57.2	55	29.6	84	8.1		
27	56.2	56	28.7	85	7.6		
28	55.3	57	27.9	86	7.1		

Table II: Joint Life and Last Survivor Expectancy

AGES	30	31	32	33	34	35	36	37	38	39
30	60.2	59.7	59.2	58.8	58.4	58.0	57.6	57.3	57.0	56.7
31	59.7	59.2	58.7	58.2	57.8	57.4	57.0	56.6	56.3	56.0
32	59.2	58.7	58.2	57.7	57.2	56.8	56.4	56.0	55.6	55.3
33	58.8	58.2	57.7	57.2	56.7	56.2	55.8	55.4	55.0	54.7
34	58.4	57.8	57.2	56.7	56.2	55.7	55.3	54.8	54.4	54.0
35	58.0	57.4	56.8	56.2	55.7	55.2	54.7	54.3	53.8	53.4
36	57.6	57.0	56.4	55.8	55.3	54.7	54.2	53.7	53.3	52.8
37	57.3	56.6	56.0	55.4	54.8	54.3	53.7	53.2	52.7	52.3
38	57.0	56.3	55.6	55.0	54.4	53.8	53.3	52.7	52.2	51.7
39	56.7	56.0	55.3	54.7	54.0	53.4	52.8	52.3	51.7	51.2
40	56.4	55.7	55.0	54.3	53.7	53.0	52.4	51.8	51.3	50.8
41	56.1	55.4	54.7	54.0	53.3	52.7	52.0	51.4	50.9	50.3
42	55.9	55.2	54.4	53.7	53.0	52.3	51.7	51.1	50.4	49.9
43	55.7	54.9	54.2	53.4	52.7	52.0	51.3	50.7	50.1	49.5
44	55.5	54.7	53.9	53.2	52.4	51.7	51.0	50.4	49.7	49.1
45	55.3	54.5	53.7	52.9	52.2	51.5	50.7	50.0	49.4	48.7
46	55.1	54.3	53.5	52.7	52.0	51.2	50.5	49.8	49.1	48.4
47	55.0	54.1	53.3	52.5	51.7	51.0	50.2	49.5	48.8	48.1
48	54.8	54.0	53.2	52.3	51.5	50.8	50.0	49.2	48.5	47.8
49	54.7	53.8	53.0	52.2	51.4	50.6	49.8	49.0	48.2	47.5
50	54.6	53.7	52.9	52.0	51.2	50.4	49.6	48.8	48.0	47.3
51	54.5	53.6	52.7	51.9	51.0	50.2	49.4	48.6	47.8	47.0
52	54.4	53.5	52.6	51.7	50.9	50.0	49.2	48.4	47.6	46.8
53	54.3	53.4	52.5	51.6	50.8	49.9	49.1	48.2	47.4	46.6
54	54.2	53.3	52.4	51.5	50.6	49.8	48.9	48.1	47.2	46.4
55	54.1	53.2	52.3	51.4	50.5	49.7	48.8	47.9	47.1	46.3
56	54.0	53.1	52.2	51.3	50.4	49.5	48.7	47.8	47.0	46.1
57	54.0	53.0	52.1	51.2	50.3	49.4	48.6	47.7	46.8	46.0
58	53.9	53.0	52.1	51.2	50.3	49.4	48.5	47.6	46.7	45.8
59	53.8	52.9	52.0	51.1	50.2	49.3	48.4	47.5	46.6	45.7

Table II: Joint Life and Last Survivor Expectancy (continued)										
AGES	**30**	**31**	**32**	**33**	**34**	**35**	**36**	**37**	**38**	**39**
60	53.8	52.9	51.9	51.0	50.1	49.2	48.3	47.4	46.5	45.6
61	53.8	52.8	51.9	51.0	50.0	49.1	48.2	47.3	46.4	45.5
62	53.7	52.8	51.8	50.9	50.0	49.1	48.1	47.2	46.3	45.4
63	53.7	52.7	51.8	50.9	49.9	49.0	48.1	47.2	46.3	45.3
64	53.6	52.7	51.8	50.8	49.9	48.9	48.0	47.1	46.2	45.3
65	53.6	52.7	51.7	50.8	49.8	48.9	48.0	47.0	46.1	45.2
66	53.6	52.6	51.7	50.7	49.8	48.9	47.9	47.0	46.1	45.1
67	53.6	52.6	51.7	50.7	49.8	48.8	47.9	46.9	46.0	45.1
68	53.5	52.6	51.6	50.7	49.7	48.8	47.8	46.9	46.0	45.0
69	53.5	52.6	51.6	50.6	49.7	48.7	47.8	46.9	45.9	45.0
70	53.5	52.5	51.6	50.6	49.7	48.7	47.8	46.8	45.9	44.9
71	53.5	52.5	51.6	50.6	49.6	48.7	47.7	46.8	45.9	44.9
72	53.5	52.5	51.5	50.6	49.6	48.7	47.7	46.8	45.8	44.9
73	53.4	52.5	51.5	50.6	49.6	48.6	47.7	46.7	45.8	44.8
74	53.4	52.5	51.5	50.5	49.6	48.6	47.7	46.7	45.8	44.8
75	53.4	52.5	51.5	50.5	49.6	48.6	47.7	46.7	45.7	44.8
76	53.4	52.4	51.5	50.5	49.6	48.6	47.6	46.7	45.7	44.8
77	53.4	52.4	51.5	50.5	49.5	48.6	47.6	46.7	45.7	44.8
78	53.4	52.4	51.5	50.5	49.5	48.6	47.6	46.6	45.7	44.7
79	53.4	52.4	51.5	50.5	49.5	48.6	47.6	46.6	45.7	44.7
80	53.4	52.4	51.4	50.5	49.5	48.5	47.6	46.6	45.7	44.7
81	53.4	52.4	51.4	50.5	49.5	48.5	47.6	46.6	45.7	44.7
82	53.4	52.4	51.4	50.5	49.5	48.5	47.6	46.6	45.6	44.7
83	53.4	52.4	51.4	50.5	49.5	48.5	47.6	46.6	45.6	44.7
84	53.4	52.4	51.4	50.5	49.5	48.5	47.6	46.6	45.6	44.7
85	53.3	52.4	51.4	50.4	49.5	48.5	47.5	46.6	45.6	44.7
86	53.3	52.4	51.4	50.4	49.5	48.5	47.5	46.6	45.6	44.6
87	53.3	52.4	51.4	50.4	49.5	48.5	47.5	46.6	45.6	44.6
88	53.3	52.4	51.4	50.4	49.5	48.5	47.5	46.6	45.6	44.6
89	53.3	52.4	51.4	50.4	49.5	48.5	47.5	46.6	45.6	44.6

Table II: Joint Life and Last Survivor Expectancy (continued)

AGES	30	31	32	33	34	35	36	37	38	39
90	53.3	52.4	51.4	50.4	49.5	48.5	47.5	46.6	45.6	44.6
91	53.3	52.4	51.4	50.4	49.5	48.5	47.5	46.6	45.6	44.6
92	53.3	52.4	51.4	50.4	49.5	48.5	47.5	46.6	45.6	44.6
93	53.3	52.4	51.4	50.4	49.5	48.5	47.5	46.6	45.6	44.6
94	53.3	52.4	51.4	50.4	49.5	48.5	47.5	46.6	45.6	44.6
95	53.3	52.4	51.4	50.4	49.5	48.5	47.5	46.5	45.6	44.6
96	53.3	52.4	51.4	50.4	49.5	48.5	47.5	46.5	45.6	44.6
97	53.3	52.4	51.4	50.4	49.5	48.5	47.5	46.5	45.6	44.6
98	53.3	52.4	51.4	50.4	49.5	48.5	47.5	46.5	45.6	44.6
99	53.3	52.4	51.4	50.4	49.5	48.5	47.5	46.5	45.6	44.6
100	53.3	52.4	51.4	50.4	49.5	48.5	47.5	46.5	45.6	44.6
101	53.3	52.4	51.4	50.4	49.5	48.5	47.5	46.5	45.6	44.6
102	53.3	52.4	51.4	50.4	49.5	48.5	47.5	46.5	45.6	44.6
103	53.3	52.4	51.4	50.4	49.5	48.5	47.5	46.5	45.6	44.6
104	53.3	52.4	51.4	50.4	49.5	48.5	47.5	46.5	45.6	44.6
105	53.3	52.4	51.4	50.4	49.4	48.5	47.5	46.5	45.6	44.6
106	53.3	52.4	51.4	50.4	49.4	48.5	47.5	46.5	45.6	44.6
107	53.3	52.4	51.4	50.4	49.4	48.5	47.5	46.5	45.6	44.6
108	53.3	52.4	51.4	50.4	49.4	48.5	47.5	46.5	45.6	44.6
109	53.3	52.4	51.4	50.4	49.4	48.5	47.5	46.5	45.6	44.6
110	53.3	52.4	51.4	50.4	49.4	48.5	47.5	46.5	45.6	44.6
111	53.3	52.4	51.4	50.4	49.4	48.5	47.5	46.5	45.6	44.6
112	53.3	52.4	51.4	50.4	49.4	48.5	47.5	46.5	45.6	44.6
113	53.3	52.4	51.4	50.4	49.4	48.5	47.5	46.5	45.6	44.6
114	53.3	52.4	51.4	50.4	49.4	48.5	47.5	46.5	45.6	44.6
115+	53.3	52.4	51.4	50.4	49.4	48.5	47.5	46.5	45.6	44.6

AGES	40	41	42	43	44	45	46	47	48	49
	Table II: Joint Life and Last Survivor Expectancy (continued)									
40	50.2	49.8	49.3	48.9	48.5	48.1	47.7	47.4	47.1	46.8
41	49.8	49.3	48.8	48.3	47.9	47.5	47.1	46.7	46.4	46.1
42	49.3	48.8	48.3	47.8	47.3	46.9	46.5	46.1	45.8	45.4
43	48.9	48.3	47.8	47.3	46.8	46.3	45.9	45.5	45.1	44.8
44	48.5	47.9	47.3	46.8	46.3	45.8	45.4	44.9	44.5	44.2
45	48.1	47.5	46.9	46.3	45.8	45.3	44.8	44.4	44.0	43.6
46	47.7	47.1	46.5	45.9	45.4	44.8	44.3	43.9	43.4	43.0
47	47.4	46.7	46.1	45.5	44.9	44.4	43.9	43.4	42.9	42.4
48	47.1	46.4	45.8	45.1	44.5	44.0	43.4	42.9	42.4	41.9
49	46.8	46.1	45.4	44.8	44.2	43.6	43.0	42.4	41.9	41.4
50	46.5	45.8	45.1	44.4	43.8	43.2	42.6	42.0	41.5	40.9
51	46.3	45.5	44.8	44.1	43.5	42.8	42.2	41.6	41.0	40.5
52	46.0	45.3	44.6	43.8	43.2	42.5	41.8	41.2	40.6	40.1
53	45.8	45.1	44.3	43.6	42.9	42.2	41.5	40.9	40.3	39.7
54	45.6	44.8	44.1	43.3	42.6	41.9	41.2	40.5	39.9	39.3
55	45.5	44.7	43.9	43.1	42.4	41.6	40.9	40.2	39.6	38.9
56	45.3	44.5	43.7	42.9	42.1	41.4	40.7	40.0	39.3	38.6
57	45.1	44.3	43.5	42.7	41.9	41.2	40.4	39.7	39.0	38.3
58	45.0	44.2	43.3	42.5	41.7	40.9	40.2	39.4	38.7	38.0
59	44.9	44.0	43.2	42.4	41.5	40.7	40.0	39.2	38.5	37.8
60	44.7	43.9	43.0	42.2	41.4	40.6	39.8	39.0	38.2	37.5
61	44.6	43.8	42.9	42.1	41.2	40.4	39.6	38.8	38.0	37.3
62	44.5	43.7	42.8	41.9	41.1	40.3	39.4	38.6	37.8	37.1
63	44.5	43.6	42.7	41.8	41.0	40.1	39.3	38.5	37.7	36.9
64	44.4	43.5	42.6	41.7	40.8	40.0	39.2	38.3	37.5	36.7
65	44.3	43.4	42.5	41.6	40.7	39.9	39.0	38.2	37.4	36.6
66	44.2	43.3	42.4	41.5	40.6	39.8	38.9	38.1	37.2	36.4
67	44.2	43.3	42.3	41.4	40.6	39.7	38.8	38.0	37.1	36.3
68	44.1	43.2	42.3	41.4	40.5	39.6	38.7	37.9	37.0	36.2
69	44.1	43.1	42.2	41.3	40.4	39.5	38.6	37.8	36.9	36.0

Table II: Joint Life and Last Survivor Expectancy (continued)

AGES	40	41	42	43	44	45	46	47	48	49
70	44.0	43.1	42.2	41.3	40.3	39.4	38.6	37.7	36.8	35.9
71	44.0	43.0	42.1	41.2	40.3	39.4	38.5	37.6	36.7	35.9
72	43.9	43.0	42.1	41.1	40.2	39.3	38.4	37.5	36.6	35.8
73	43.9	43.0	42.0	41.1	40.2	39.3	38.4	37.5	36.6	35.7
74	43.9	42.9	42.0	41.1	40.1	39.2	38.3	37.4	36.5	35.6
75	43.8	42.9	42.0	41.0	40.1	39.2	38.3	37.4	36.5	35.6
76	43.8	42.9	41.9	41.0	40.1	39.1	38.2	37.3	36.4	35.5
77	43.8	42.9	41.9	41.0	40.0	39.1	38.2	37.3	36.4	35.5
78	43.8	42.8	41.9	40.9	40.0	39.1	38.2	37.2	36.3	35.4
79	43.8	42.8	41.9	40.9	40.0	39.1	38.1	37.2	36.3	35.4
80	43.7	42.8	41.8	40.9	40.0	39.0	38.1	37.2	36.3	35.4
81	43.7	42.8	41.8	40.9	39.9	39.0	38.1	37.2	36.2	35.3
82	43.7	42.8	41.8	40.9	39.9	39.0	38.1	37.1	36.2	35.3
83	43.7	42.8	41.8	40.9	39.9	39.0	38.0	37.1	36.2	35.3
84	43.7	42.7	41.8	40.8	39.9	39.0	38.0	37.1	36.2	35.3
85	43.7	42.7	41.8	40.8	39.9	38.9	38.0	37.1	36.2	35.2
86	43.7	42.7	41.8	40.8	39.9	38.9	38.0	37.1	36.1	35.2
87	43.7	42.7	41.8	40.8	39.9	38.9	38.0	37.0	36.1	35.2
88	43.7	42.7	41.8	40.8	39.9	38.9	38.0	37.0	36.1	35.2
89	43.7	42.7	41.7	40.8	39.8	38.9	38.0	37.0	36.1	35.2
90	43.7	42.7	41.7	40.8	39.8	38.9	38.0	37.0	36.1	35.2
91	43.7	42.7	41.7	40.8	39.8	38.9	37.9	37.0	36.1	35.2
92	43.7	42.7	41.7	40.8	39.8	38.9	37.9	37.0	36.1	35.1
93	43.7	42.7	41.7	40.8	39.8	38.9	37.9	37.0	36.1	35.1
94	43.7	42.7	41.7	40.8	39.8	38.9	37.9	37.0	36.1	35.1
95	43.6	42.7	41.7	40.8	39.8	38.9	37.9	37.0	36.1	35.1
96	43.6	42.7	41.7	40.8	39.8	38.9	37.9	37.0	36.1	35.1
97	43.6	42.7	41.7	40.8	39.8	38.9	37.9	37.0	36.1	35.1
98	43.6	42.7	41.7	40.8	39.8	38.9	37.9	37.0	36.0	35.1
99	43.6	42.7	41.7	40.8	39.8	38.9	37.9	37.0	36.0	35.1

Table II: Joint Life and Last Survivor Expectancy (continued)									
AGES	40	41	42	43	44	45	46	47	48	49
100	43.6	42.7	41.7	40.8	39.8	38.9	37.9	37.0	36.0	35.1
101	43.6	42.7	41.7	40.8	39.8	38.9	37.9	37.0	36.0	35.1
102	43.6	42.7	41.7	40.8	39.8	38.9	37.9	37.0	36.0	35.1
103	43.6	42.7	41.7	40.8	39.8	38.9	37.9	37.0	36.0	35.1
104	43.6	42.7	41.7	40.8	39.8	38.8	37.9	37.0	36.0	35.1
105	43.6	42.7	41.7	40.8	39.8	38.8	37.9	37.0	36.0	35.1
106	43.6	42.7	41.7	40.8	39.8	38.8	37.9	37.0	36.0	35.1
107	43.6	42.7	41.7	40.8	39.8	38.8	37.9	37.0	36.0	35.1
108	43.6	42.7	41.7	40.8	39.8	38.8	37.9	37.0	36.0	35.1
109	43.6	42.7	41.7	40.7	39.8	38.8	37.9	37.0	36.0	35.1
110	43.6	42.7	41.7	40.7	39.8	38.8	37.9	37.0	36.0	35.1
111	43.6	42.7	41.7	40.7	39.8	38.8	37.9	37.0	36.0	35.1
112	43.6	42.7	41.7	40.7	39.8	38.8	37.9	37.0	36.0	35.1
113	43.6	42.7	41.7	40.7	39.8	38.8	37.9	37.0	36.0	35.1
114	43.6	42.7	41.7	40.7	39.8	38.8	37.9	37.0	36.0	35.1
115+	43.6	42.7	41.7	40.7	39.8	38.8	37.9	37.0	36.0	35.1

Table II: Joint Life and Last Survivor Expectancy (continued)

AGES	50	51	52	53	54	55	56	57	58	59
50	40.4	40.0	39.5	39.1	38.7	38.3	38.0	37.6	37.3	37.1
51	40.0	39.5	39.0	38.5	38.1	37.7	37.4	37.0	36.7	36.4
52	39.5	39.0	38.5	38.0	37.6	37.2	36.8	36.4	36.0	35.7
53	39.1	38.5	38.0	37.5	37.1	36.6	36.2	35.8	35.4	35.1
54	38.7	38.1	37.6	37.1	36.6	36.1	35.7	35.2	34.8	34.5
55	38.3	37.7	37.2	36.6	36.1	35.6	35.1	34.7	34.3	33.9
56	38.0	37.4	36.8	36.2	35.7	35.1	34.7	34.2	33.7	33.3
57	37.6	37.0	36.4	35.8	35.2	34.7	34.2	33.7	33.2	32.8
58	37.3	36.7	36.0	35.4	34.8	34.3	33.7	33.2	32.8	32.3
59	37.1	36.4	35.7	35.1	34.5	33.9	33.3	32.8	32.3	31.8
60	36.8	36.1	35.4	34.8	34.1	33.5	32.9	32.4	31.9	31.3
61	36.6	35.8	35.1	34.5	33.8	33.2	32.6	32.0	31.4	30.9
62	36.3	35.6	34.9	34.2	33.5	32.9	32.2	31.6	31.1	30.5
63	36.1	35.4	34.6	33.9	33.2	32.6	31.9	31.3	30.7	30.1
64	35.9	35.2	34.4	33.7	33.0	32.3	31.6	31.0	30.4	29.8
65	35.8	35.0	34.2	33.5	32.7	32.0	31.4	30.7	30.0	29.4
66	35.6	34.8	34.0	33.3	32.5	31.8	31.1	30.4	29.8	29.1
67	35.5	34.7	33.9	33.1	32.3	31.6	30.9	30.2	29.5	28.8
68	35.3	34.5	33.7	32.9	32.1	31.4	30.7	29.9	29.2	28.6
69	35.2	34.4	33.6	32.8	32.0	31.2	30.5	29.7	29.0	28.3
70	35.1	34.3	33.4	32.6	31.8	31.1	30.3	29.5	28.8	28.1
71	35.0	34.2	33.3	32.5	31.7	30.9	30.1	29.4	28.6	27.9
72	34.9	34.1	33.2	32.4	31.6	30.8	30.0	29.2	28.4	27.7
73	34.8	34.0	33.1	32.3	31.5	30.6	29.8	29.1	28.3	27.5
74	34.8	33.9	33.0	32.2	31.4	30.5	29.7	28.9	28.1	27.4
75	34.7	33.8	33.0	32.1	31.3	30.4	29.6	28.8	28.0	27.2
76	34.6	33.8	32.9	32.0	31.2	30.3	29.5	28.7	27.9	27.1
77	34.6	33.7	32.8	32.0	31.1	30.3	29.4	28.6	27.8	27.0
78	34.5	33.6	32.8	31.9	31.0	30.2	29.3	28.5	27.7	26.9
79	34.5	33.6	32.7	31.8	31.0	30.1	29.3	28.4	27.6	26.8

AGES	50	51	52	53	54	55	56	57	58	59

Table II: Joint Life and Last Survivor Expectancy (continued)

AGES	50	51	52	53	54	55	56	57	58	59
80	34.5	33.6	32.7	31.8	30.9	30.1	29.2	28.4	27.5	26.7
81	34.4	33.5	32.6	31.8	30.9	30.0	29.2	28.3	27.5	26.6
82	34.4	33.5	32.6	31.7	30.8	30.0	29.1	28.3	27.4	26.6
83	34.4	33.5	32.6	31.7	30.8	29.9	29.1	28.2	27.4	26.5
84	34.3	33.4	32.5	31.7	30.8	29.9	29.0	28.2	27.3	26.5
85	34.3	33.4	32.5	31.6	30.7	29.9	29.0	28.1	27.3	26.4
86	34.3	33.4	32.5	31.6	30.7	29.8	29.0	28.1	27.2	26.4
87	34.3	33.4	32.5	31.6	30.7	29.8	28.9	28.1	27.2	26.4
88	34.3	33.4	32.5	31.6	30.7	29.8	28.9	28.0	27.2	26.3
89	34.3	33.3	32.4	31.5	30.7	29.8	28.9	28.0	27.2	26.3
90	34.2	33.3	32.4	31.5	30.6	29.8	28.9	28.0	27.1	26.3
91	34.2	33.3	32.4	31.5	30.6	29.7	28.9	28.0	27.1	26.3
92	34.2	33.3	32.4	31.5	30.6	29.7	28.8	28.0	27.1	26.2
93	34.2	33.3	32.4	31.5	30.6	29.7	28.8	28.0	27.1	26.2
94	34.2	33.3	32.4	31.5	30.6	29.7	28.8	27.9	27.1	26.2
95	34.2	33.3	32.4	31.5	30.6	29.7	28.8	27.9	27.1	26.2
96	34.2	33.3	32.4	31.5	30.6	29.7	28.8	27.9	27.0	26.2
97	34.2	33.3	32.4	31.5	30.6	29.7	28.8	27.9	27.0	26.2
98	34.2	33.3	32.4	31.5	30.6	29.7	28.8	27.9	27.0	26.2
99	34.2	33.3	32.4	31.5	30.6	29.7	28.8	27.9	27.0	26.2
100	34.2	33.3	32.4	31.5	30.6	29.7	28.8	27.9	27.0	26.1
101	34.2	33.3	32.4	31.5	30.6	29.7	28.8	27.9	27.0	26.1
102	34.2	33.3	32.4	31.4	30.5	29.7	28.8	27.9	27.0	26.1
103	34.2	33.3	32.4	31.4	30.5	29.7	28.8	27.9	27.0	26.1
104	34.2	33.3	32.4	31.4	30.5	29.6	28.8	27.9	27.0	26.1
105	34.2	33.3	32.3	31.4	30.5	29.6	28.8	27.9	27.0	26.1
106	34.2	33.3	32.3	31.4	30.5	29.6	28.8	27.9	27.0	26.1
107	34.2	33.3	32.3	31.4	30.5	29.6	28.8	27.9	27.0	26.1
108	34.2	33.3	32.3	31.4	30.5	29.6	28.8	27.9	27.0	26.1
109	34.2	33.3	32.3	31.4	30.5	29.6	28.7	27.9	27.0	26.1

Table II: Joint Life and Last Survivor Expectancy (continued)									
AGES	**50**	**51**	**52**	**53**	**54**	**55**	**56**	**57**	**58**	**59**
110	34.2	33.3	32.3	31.4	30.5	29.6	28.7	27.9	27.0	26.1
111	34.2	33.3	32.3	31.4	30.5	29.6	28.7	27.9	27.0	26.1
112	34.2	33.3	32.3	31.4	30.5	29.6	28.7	27.9	27.0	26.1
113	34.2	33.3	32.3	31.4	30.5	29.6	28.7	27.9	27.0	26.1
114	34.2	33.3	32.3	31.4	30.5	29.6	28.7	27.9	27.0	26.1
115+	34.2	33.3	32.3	31.4	30.5	29.6	28.7	27.9	27.0	26.1

Table II: Joint Life and Last Survivor Expectancy (continued)

AGES	60	61	62	63	64	65	66	67	68	69
60	30.9	30.4	30.0	29.6	29.2	28.8	28.5	28.2	27.9	27.6
61	30.4	29.9	29.5	29.0	28.6	28.3	27.9	27.6	27.3	27.0
62	30.0	29.5	29.0	28.5	28.1	27.7	27.3	27.0	26.7	26.4
63	29.6	29.0	28.5	28.1	27.6	27.2	26.8	26.4	26.1	25.7
64	29.2	28.6	28.1	27.6	27.1	26.7	26.3	25.9	25.5	25.2
65	28.8	28.3	27.7	27.2	26.7	26.2	25.8	25.4	25.0	24.6
66	28.5	27.9	27.3	26.8	26.3	25.8	25.3	24.9	24.5	24.1
67	28.2	27.6	27.0	26.4	25.9	25.4	24.9	24.4	24.0	23.6
68	27.9	27.3	26.7	26.1	25.5	25.0	24.5	24.0	23.5	23.1
69	27.6	27.0	26.4	25.7	25.2	24.6	24.1	23.6	23.1	22.6
70	27.4	26.7	26.1	25.4	24.8	24.3	23.7	23.2	22.7	22.2
71	27.2	26.5	25.8	25.2	24.5	23.9	23.4	22.8	22.3	21.8
72	27.0	26.3	25.6	24.9	24.3	23.7	23.1	22.5	22.0	21.4
73	26.8	26.1	25.4	24.7	24.0	23.4	22.8	22.2	21.6	21.1
74	26.6	25.9	25.2	24.5	23.8	23.1	22.5	21.9	21.3	20.8
75	26.5	25.7	25.0	24.3	23.6	22.9	22.3	21.6	21.0	20.5
76	26.3	25.6	24.8	24.1	23.4	22.7	22.0	21.4	20.8	20.2
77	26.2	25.4	24.7	23.9	23.2	22.5	21.8	21.2	20.6	19.9
78	26.1	25.3	24.6	23.8	23.1	22.4	21.7	21.0	20.3	19.7
79	26.0	25.2	24.4	23.7	22.9	22.2	21.5	20.8	20.1	19.5
80	25.9	25.1	24.3	23.6	22.8	22.1	21.3	20.6	20.0	19.3
81	25.8	25.0	24.2	23.4	22.7	21.9	21.2	20.5	19.8	19.1
82	25.8	24.9	24.1	23.4	22.6	21.8	21.1	20.4	19.7	19.0
83	25.7	24.9	24.1	23.3	22.5	21.7	21.0	20.2	19.5	18.8
84	25.6	24.8	24.0	23.2	22.4	21.6	20.9	20.1	19.4	18.7
85	25.6	24.8	23.9	23.1	22.3	21.6	20.8	20.1	19.3	18.6
86	25.5	24.7	23.9	23.1	22.3	21.5	20.7	20.0	19.2	18.5
87	25.5	24.7	23.8	23.0	22.2	21.4	20.7	19.9	19.2	18.4
88	25.5	24.6	23.8	23.0	22.2	21.4	20.6	19.8	19.1	18.3
89	25.4	24.6	23.8	22.9	22.1	21.3	20.5	19.8	19.0	18.3

Table II: Joint Life and Last Survivor Expectancy (continued)

AGES	60	61	62	63	64	65	66	67	68	69
90	25.4	24.6	23.7	22.9	22.1	21.3	20.5	19.7	19.0	18.2
91	25.4	24.5	23.7	22.9	22.1	21.3	20.5	19.7	18.9	18.2
92	25.4	24.5	23.7	22.9	22.0	21.2	20.4	19.6	18.9	18.1
93	25.4	24.5	23.7	22.8	22.0	21.2	20.4	19.6	18.8	18.1
94	25.3	24.5	23.6	22.8	22.0	21.2	20.4	19.6	18.8	18.0
95	25.3	24.5	23.6	22.8	22.0	21.1	20.3	19.6	18.8	18.0
96	25.3	24.5	23.6	22.8	21.9	21.1	20.3	19.5	18.8	18.0
97	25.3	24.5	23.6	22.8	21.9	21.1	20.3	19.5	18.7	18.0
98	25.3	24.4	23.6	22.8	21.9	21.1	20.3	19.5	18.7	17.9
99	25.3	24.4	23.6	22.7	21.9	21.1	20.3	19.5	18.7	17.9
100	25.3	24.4	23.6	22.7	21.9	21.1	20.3	19.5	18.7	17.9
101	25.3	24.4	23.6	22.7	21.9	21.1	20.2	19.4	18.7	17.9
102	25.3	24.4	23.6	22.7	21.9	21.1	20.2	19.4	18.6	17.9
103	25.3	24.4	23.6	22.7	21.9	21.0	20.2	19.4	18.6	17.9
104	25.3	24.4	23.5	22.7	21.9	21.0	20.2	19.4	18.6	17.8
105	25.3	24.4	23.5	22.7	21.9	21.0	20.2	19.4	18.6	17.8
106	25.3	24.4	23.5	22.7	21.9	21.0	20.2	19.4	18.6	17.8
107	25.2	24.4	23.5	22.7	21.8	21.0	20.2	19.4	18.6	17.8
108	25.2	24.4	23.5	22.7	21.8	21.0	20.2	19.4	18.6	17.8
109	25.2	24.4	23.5	22.7	21.8	21.0	20.2	19.4	18.6	17.8
110	25.2	24.4	23.5	22.7	21.8	21.0	20.2	19.4	18.6	17.8
111	25.2	24.4	23.5	22.7	21.8	21.0	20.2	19.4	18.6	17.8
112	25.2	24.4	23.5	22.7	21.8	21.0	20.2	19.4	18.6	17.8
113	25.2	24.4	23.5	22.7	21.8	21.0	20.2	19.4	18.6	17.8
114	25.2	24.4	23.5	22.7	21.8	21.0	20.2	19.4	18.6	17.8
115+	25.2	24.4	23.5	22.7	21.8	21.0	20.2	19.4	18.6	17.8

AGES	70	71	72	73	74	75	76	77	78	79
\multicolumn{11}{c}{**Table II: Joint Life and Last Survivor Expectancy (continued)**}
70	21.8	21.3	20.9	20.6	20.2	19.9	19.6	19.4	19.1	18.9
71	21.3	20.9	20.5	20.1	19.7	19.4	19.1	18.8	18.5	18.3
72	20.9	20.5	20.0	19.6	19.3	18.9	18.6	18.3	18.0	17.7
73	20.6	20.1	19.6	19.2	18.8	18.4	18.1	17.8	17.5	17.2
74	20.2	19.7	19.3	18.8	18.4	18.0	17.6	17.3	17.0	16.7
75	19.9	19.4	18.9	18.4	18.0	17.6	17.2	16.8	16.5	16.2
76	19.6	19.1	18.6	18.1	17.6	17.2	16.8	16.4	16.0	15.7
77	19.4	18.8	18.3	17.8	17.3	16.8	16.4	16.0	15.6	15.3
78	19.1	18.5	18.0	17.5	17.0	16.5	16.0	15.6	15.2	14.9
79	18.9	18.3	17.7	17.2	16.7	16.2	15.7	15.3	14.9	14.5
80	18.7	18.1	17.5	16.9	16.4	15.9	15.4	15.0	14.5	14.1
81	18.5	17.9	17.3	16.7	16.2	15.6	15.1	14.7	14.2	13.8
82	18.3	17.7	17.1	16.5	15.9	15.4	14.9	14.4	13.9	13.5
83	18.2	17.5	16.9	16.3	15.7	15.2	14.7	14.2	13.7	13.2
84	18.0	17.4	16.7	16.1	15.5	15.0	14.4	13.9	13.4	13.0
85	17.9	17.3	16.6	16.0	15.4	14.8	14.3	13.7	13.2	12.8
86	17.8	17.1	16.5	15.8	15.2	14.6	14.1	13.5	13.0	12.5
87	17.7	17.0	16.4	15.7	15.1	14.5	13.9	13.4	12.9	12.4
88	17.6	16.9	16.3	15.6	15.0	14.4	13.8	13.2	12.7	12.2
89	17.6	16.9	16.2	15.5	14.9	14.3	13.7	13.1	12.6	12.0
90	17.5	16.8	16.1	15.4	14.8	14.2	13.6	13.0	12.4	11.9
91	17.4	16.7	16.0	15.4	14.7	14.1	13.5	12.9	12.3	11.8
92	17.4	16.7	16.0	15.3	14.6	14.0	13.4	12.8	12.2	11.7
93	17.3	16.6	15.9	15.2	14.6	13.9	13.3	12.7	12.1	11.6
94	17.3	16.6	15.9	15.2	14.5	13.9	13.2	12.6	12.0	11.5
95	17.3	16.5	15.8	15.1	14.5	13.8	13.2	12.6	12.0	11.4
96	17.2	16.5	15.8	15.1	14.4	13.8	13.1	12.5	11.9	11.3
97	17.2	16.5	15.8	15.1	14.4	13.7	13.1	12.5	11.9	11.3
98	17.2	16.4	15.7	15.0	14.3	13.7	13.0	12.4	11.8	11.2
99	17.2	16.4	15.7	15.0	14.3	13.6	13.0	12.4	11.8	11.2

Table II: Joint Life and Last Survivor Expectancy (continued)

AGES	70	71	72	73	74	75	76	77	78	79
100	17.1	16.4	15.7	15.0	14.3	13.6	12.9	12.3	11.7	11.1
101	17.1	16.4	15.6	14.9	14.2	13.6	12.9	12.3	11.7	11.1
102	17.1	16.4	15.6	14.9	14.2	13.5	12.9	12.2	11.6	11.0
103	17.1	16.3	15.6	14.9	14.2	13.5	12.9	12.2	11.6	11.0
104	17.1	16.3	15.6	14.9	14.2	13.5	12.8	12.2	11.6	11.0
105	17.1	16.3	15.6	14.9	14.2	13.5	12.8	12.2	11.5	10.9
106	17.1	16.3	15.6	14.8	14.1	13.5	12.8	12.2	11.5	10.9
107	17.0	16.3	15.6	14.8	14.1	13.4	12.8	12.1	11.5	10.9
108	17.0	16.3	15.5	14.8	14.1	13.4	12.8	12.1	11.5	10.9
109	17.0	16.3	15.5	14.8	14.1	13.4	12.8	12.1	11.5	10.9
110	17.0	16.3	15.5	14.8	14.1	13.4	12.7	12.1	11.5	10.9
111	17.0	16.3	15.5	14.8	14.1	13.4	12.7	12.1	11.5	10.8
112	17.0	16.3	15.5	14.8	14.1	13.4	12.7	12.1	11.5	10.8
113	17.0	16.3	15.5	14.8	14.1	13.4	12.7	12.1	11.4	10.8
114	17.0	16.3	15.5	14.8	14.1	13.4	12.7	12.1	11.4	10.8
115+	17.0	16.3	15.5	14.8	14.1	13.4	12.7	12.1	11.4	10.8

Table II: Joint Life and Last Survivor Expectancy (continued)

AGES	80	81	82	83	84	85	86	87	88	89
80	13.8	13.4	13.1	12.8	12.6	12.3	12.1	11.9	11.7	11.5
81	13.4	13.1	12.7	12.4	12.2	11.9	11.7	11.4	11.3	11.1
82	13.1	12.7	12.4	12.1	11.8	11.5	11.3	11.0	10.8	10.6
83	12.8	12.4	12.1	11.7	11.4	11.1	10.9	10.6	10.4	10.2
84	12.6	12.2	11.8	11.4	11.1	10.8	10.5	10.3	10.1	9.9
85	12.3	11.9	11.5	11.1	10.8	10.5	10.2	9.9	9.7	9.5
86	12.1	11.7	11.3	10.9	10.5	10.2	9.9	9.6	9.4	9.2
87	11.9	11.4	11.0	10.6	10.3	9.9	9.6	9.4	9.1	8.9
88	11.7	11.3	10.8	10.4	10.1	9.7	9.4	9.1	8.8	8.6
89	11.5	11.1	10.6	10.2	9.9	9.5	9.2	8.9	8.6	8.3
90	11.4	10.9	10.5	10.1	9.7	9.3	9.0	8.6	8.3	8.1
91	11.3	10.8	10.3	9.9	9.5	9.1	8.8	8.4	8.1	7.9
92	11.2	10.7	10.2	9.8	9.3	9.0	8.6	8.3	8.0	7.7
93	11.1	10.6	10.1	9.6	9.2	8.8	8.5	8.1	7.8	7.5
94	11.0	10.5	10.0	9.5	9.1	8.7	8.3	8.0	7.6	7.3
95	10.9	10.4	9.9	9.4	9.0	8.6	8.2	7.8	7.5	7.2
96	10.8	10.3	9.8	9.3	8.9	8.5	8.1	7.7	7.4	7.1
97	10.7	10.2	9.7	9.2	8.8	8.4	8.0	7.6	7.3	6.9
98	10.7	10.1	9.6	9.2	8.7	8.3	7.9	7.5	7.1	6.8
99	10.6	10.1	9.6	9.1	8.6	8.2	7.8	7.4	7.0	6.7
100	10.6	10.0	9.5	9.0	8.5	8.1	7.7	7.3	6.9	6.6
101	10.5	10.0	9.4	9.0	8.5	8.0	7.6	7.2	6.9	6.5
102	10.5	9.9	9.4	8.9	8.4	8.0	7.5	7.1	6.8	6.4
103	10.4	9.9	9.4	8.8	8.4	7.9	7.5	7.1	6.7	6.3
104	10.4	9.8	9.3	8.8	8.3	7.9	7.4	7.0	6.6	6.3
105	10.4	9.8	9.3	8.8	8.3	7.8	7.4	7.0	6.6	6.2
106	10.3	9.8	9.2	8.7	8.2	7.8	7.3	6.9	6.5	6.2
107	10.3	9.8	9.2	8.7	8.2	7.7	7.3	6.9	6.5	6.1
108	10.3	9.7	9.2	8.7	8.2	7.7	7.3	6.8	6.4	6.1
109	10.3	9.7	9.2	8.7	8.2	7.7	7.2	6.8	6.4	6.0

AGES	80	81	82	83	84	85	86	87	88	89
Table II: Joint Life and Last Survivor Expectancy (continued)										
110	10.3	9.7	9.2	8.6	8.1	7.7	7.2	6.8	6.4	6.0
111	10.3	9.7	9.1	8.6	8.1	7.6	7.2	6.8	6.3	6.0
112	10.2	9.7	9.1	8.6	8.1	7.6	7.2	6.7	6.3	5.9
113	10.2	9.7	9.1	8.6	8.1	7.6	7.2	6.7	6.3	5.9
114	10.2	9.7	9.1	8.6	8.1	7.6	7.1	6.7	6.3	5.9
115+	10.2	9.7	9.1	8.6	8.1	7.6	7.1	6.7	6.3	5.9

Table II: Joint Life and Last Survivor Expectancy (continued)

AGES	90	91	92	93	94	95	96	97	98	99
90	7.8	7.6	7.4	7.2	7.1	6.9	6.8	6.6	6.5	6.4
91	7.6	7.4	7.2	7.0	6.8	6.7	6.5	6.4	6.3	6.1
92	7.4	7.2	7.0	6.8	6.6	6.4	6.3	6.1	6.0	5.9
93	7.2	7.0	6.8	6.6	6.4	6.2	6.1	5.9	5.8	5.6
94	7.1	6.8	6.6	6.4	6.2	6.0	5.9	5.7	5.6	5.4
95	6.9	6.7	6.4	6.2	6.0	5.8	5.7	5.5	5.4	5.2
96	6.8	6.5	6.3	6.1	5.9	5.7	5.5	5.3	5.2	5.0
97	6.6	6.4	6.1	5.9	5.7	5.5	5.3	5.2	5.0	4.9
98	6.5	6.3	6.0	5.8	5.6	5.4	5.2	5.0	4.8	4.7
99	6.4	6.1	5.9	5.6	5.4	5.2	5.0	4.9	4.7	4.5
100	6.3	6.0	5.8	5.5	5.3	5.1	4.9	4.7	4.5	4.4
101	6.2	5.9	5.6	5.4	5.2	5.0	4.8	4.6	4.4	4.2
102	6.1	5.8	5.5	5.3	5.1	4.8	4.6	4.4	4.3	4.1
103	6.0	5.7	5.4	5.2	5.0	4.7	4.5	4.3	4.1	4.0
104	5.9	5.6	5.4	5.1	4.9	4.6	4.4	4.2	4.0	3.8
105	5.9	5.6	5.3	5.0	4.8	4.5	4.3	4.1	3.9	3.7
106	5.8	5.5	5.2	4.9	4.7	4.5	4.2	4.0	3.8	3.6
107	5.8	5.4	5.1	4.9	4.6	4.4	4.2	3.9	3.7	3.5
108	5.7	5.4	5.1	4.8	4.6	4.3	4.1	3.9	3.7	3.5
109	5.7	5.3	5.0	4.8	4.5	4.3	4.0	3.8	3.6	3.4
110	5.6	5.3	5.0	4.7	4.5	4.2	4.0	3.8	3.5	3.3
111	5.6	5.3	5.0	4.7	4.4	4.2	3.9	3.7	3.5	3.3
112	5.6	5.3	4.9	4.7	4.4	4.1	3.9	3.7	3.5	3.2
113	5.6	5.2	4.9	4.6	4.4	4.1	3.9	3.6	3.4	3.2
114	5.6	5.2	4.9	4.6	4.3	4.1	3.9	3.6	3.4	3.2
115+	5.5	5.2	4.9	4.6	4.3	4.1	3.8	3.6	3.4	3.1

Table II: Joint Life and Last Survivor Expectancy (continued)									
AGES	**100**	**101**	**102**	**103**	**104**	**105**	**106**	**107**	**108**	**109**
100	4.2	4.1	3.9	3.8	3.7	3.5	3.4	3.3	3.3	3.2
101	4.1	3.9	3.7	3.6	3.5	3.4	3.2	3.1	3.1	3.0
102	3.9	3.7	3.6	3.4	3.3	3.2	3.1	3.0	2.9	2.8
103	3.8	3.6	3.4	3.3	3.2	3.0	2.9	2.8	2.7	2.6
104	3.7	3.5	3.3	3.2	3.0	2.9	2.7	2.6	2.5	2.4
105	3.5	3.4	3.2	3.0	2.9	2.7	2.6	2.5	2.4	2.3
106	3.4	3.2	3.1	2.9	2.7	2.6	2.4	2.3	2.2	2.1
107	3.3	3.1	3.0	2.8	2.6	2.5	2.3	2.2	2.1	2.0
108	3.3	3.1	2.9	2.7	2.5	2.4	2.2	2.1	1.9	1.8
109	3.2	3.0	2.8	2.6	2.4	2.3	2.1	2.0	1.8	1.7
110	3.1	2.9	2.7	2.5	2.3	2.2	2.0	1.9	1.7	1.6
111	3.1	2.9	2.7	2.5	2.3	2.1	1.9	1.8	1.6	1.5
112	3.0	2.8	2.6	2.4	2.2	2.0	1.9	1.7	1.5	1.4
113	3.0	2.8	2.6	2.4	2.2	2.0	1.8	1.6	1.5	1.3
114	3.0	2.7	2.5	2.3	2.1	1.9	1.8	1.6	1.4	1.3
115+	2.9	2.7	2.5	2.3	2.1	1.9	1.7	1.5	1.4	1.2

Table II: Joint Life and Last Survivor Expectancy (continued)						
AGES	110	111	112	113	114	115+
110	1.5	1.4	1.3	1.2	1.1	1.1
111	1.4	1.2	1.1	1.1	1.0	1.0
112	1.3	1.1	1.0	1.0	1.0	1.0
113	1.2	1.1	1.0	1.0	1.0	1.0
114	1.1	1.0	1.0	1.0	1.0	1.0
115+	1.1	1.0	1.0	1.0	1.0	1.0

Table III: Uniform Lifetime Table					
Age	Applicable Divisor	Age	Applicable Divisor	Age	Applicable Divisor
70	27.4	86	14.1	101	5.9
71	26.5	87	13.4	102	5.5
72	25.6	88	12.7	103	5.2
73	24.7	89	12.0	104	4.9
74	23.8	90	11.4	105	4.5
75	22.9	91	10.8	106	4.2
76	22.0	92	10.2	107	3.9
77	21.2	93	9.6	108	3.7
78	20.3	94	9.1	109	3.4
79	19.5	95	8.6	110	3.1
80	18.7	96	8.1	111	2.9
81	17.9	97	7.6	112	2.6
82	17.1	98	7.1	113	2.4
83	16.3	99	6.7	114	2.1
84	15.5	100	6.3	115+	1.9
85	14.8				

Table IV: Survivor Benefit Limits

Excess of Employee's Age Over Beneficiary's Age	Applicable Percentage	Excess of Employee's Age Over Beneficiary's Age	Applicable Percentage
10 years or less	100%	28	62%
11	96%	29	61%
12	93%	30	60%
13	90%	31	59%
14	87%	32	59%
15	84%	33	58%
16	82%	34	57%
17	79%	35	56%
18	77%	36	56%
19	75%	37	55%
20	73%	38	55%
21	72%	39	54%
22	70%	40	54%
23	68%	41	53%
24	67%	42	53%
25	66%	43	53%
26	64%	44 and greater	52%
27	63%		

Index

A

Account balance
  for required distribution calculations,
    86–91, 104–105
  and substantially equal periodic
    payments, 95
  See also Applicable distribution period
Active participant. *See* Participant
Actuaries, consulting with, 10, 11, 90
Adjusted gross income (AGI)
  calculating, 194
  and converting an IRA to a Roth IRA,
    202–203
  and early distribution tax, 66–67
  overview, 5, 63, 195
  and Roth IRA contributions, 15, 42
  and traditional IRA contribution
    deductions, 12
ADP. *See* Applicable distribution period
Advantages and disadvantages
  of conversion to a Roth IRA at retirement,
    34–35
  of direct rollovers at retirement, 32
  of fixed amortization method, 89–90
  of fixed annuitization method, 92
  of multiple beneficiaries, 127–128
  of naming your estate as beneficiary,
    164–165
  of paying ordinary income tax on
    distributions, 31, 41

  of required minimum distribution
    method, 87
  of rollover or conversion to a Roth IRA,
    200–204
  of Roth IRAs, 196
  of 10-year averaging, 37–38
  of trusts, 188–189
  See also Pitfalls
After-death exception, 64, 148, 178
After-tax contributions
  and charitable donations, 53
  claiming losses on, 29, 53, 95, 133
  conversion to Roth IRA, 204, 206, 207
  distribution of, 196–197, 206
  early distributions, 206, 217
  and income tax computations, 31, 36
  overview, 5, 22, 63, 195, 213
  pro rata distribution of earnings and,
    213–215
  and required distributions, 123–124
  and rollovers, 55
  and tax calculations, 68–69
  in traditional IRAs, 27–29, 31, 53, 196,
    201–202, 207
  withholding exemption, 46
  See also Roth 401(k)s; Roth IRAs
After-tax dollars, 22, 195
Aggregation rule for IRAs and TDAs,
  108–109, 124
AGI. *See* Adjusted gross income

Almost-qualified retirement plans, 15. *See also* Qualified annuities; Tax-deferred annuities

Alternate payees, 44–45, 131–134, 166–167, 190–191

Amortization, 22, 83, 87–90, 95–96

Amortization calculator, online, 88–89

Ancestor, definition of, 63

Annuities
  beneficiaries of, 129–131, 165
  definition of, 83, 140, 172
  distribution rules, 165, 190
  income taxes before retirement, 35–38, 40–41
  individual retirement annuities, 12
  irrevocable annuities, 165
  overview, 116, 117, 129
  required distribution rules, 128–131
  term certain, 117, 128, 129, 130
  See also Income taxes on qualified plans and qualified annuities at retirement; Qualified annuities; Tax-deferred annuities

Annuitization method for required distributions, 90–92, 95–96

Annuity factor, 90, 91

Annuity factor calculator, online, 91

Anti-alienation rule, 43

Applicable distribution period (ADP)
  for alternate payee with separate account, 132, 166
  determining, 121–123
  overview, 117
  for required distributions during your lifetime, 120
  and spouse as sole beneficiary of a trust, 126–127

for spouse beneficiaries, 145, 186–187

for spouse beneficiary's beneficiaries, 150–154, 178–179

B

Bankruptcy Abuse Prevention and Consumer Protection Act (2005), 17

Bankruptcy protection for retirement plans, 17

Basis
  exceeding fair market value of IRAs, 29
  of inherited retirement plans, 30, 40
  and net unrealized appreciation, 22, 38–40, 68
  overview, 22, 26–28
  of Roth 401(k)s or Roth IRAs, 29

Beneficiaries
  of alternate payees, 132
  of annuities, 129–131
  default beneficiaries, 126
  designating, 125–128
  distribution rules if not named, 102, 104
  and 5-year holding period for Roth accounts, 197, 215
  nonspouse beneficiary's beneficiaries, 153–154
  overview, 5, 101, 172, 195, 213
  primary, 117, 127, 140, 164, 172, 189
  spouse beneficiary's beneficiaries, 148–150, 178–179
  See also Designated beneficiaries; Multiple beneficiaries; Nonspouse beneficiaries; Spouse beneficiaries; *entries beginning with* "distributions to beneficiaries"

Borrowing rules for loans from qualified retirement plans, 49–51

Brokerage firm. *See* Custodians and trustees
Bypass trusts and estate planning, 162, 163–164, 188–189

C

Calculators, online, 88–89, 91
Capital gains treatment
    alternate payees not eligible, 45, 52
    for distributions at retirement, 38, 39–40
    IRAs ineligible for, 53, 55
    tax-deferred compounding versus, 21, 23–25
    TDAs ineligible for, 16, 52
Charitable contributions from IRAs, 53
Child support payments, 76
Chronic error penalty, 107
Church plans, 118
Contingent beneficiaries
    overview, 117, 127–128, 140
    primary beneficiary disclaiming interest in favor of, 141, 173
    trust as, 164, 189
Contributions. *See* After-tax contributions; Pretax contributions
Contributory IRAs. *See* Traditional contributory IRAs
Conversion to a Roth IRA
    inherited retirement plans, 42–43, 103, 182
    nonspouse beneficiaries, 153, 182
    overview, 26, 30, 34–35, 200, 201–204
    paying income tax with converted amounts, 206
    spouse beneficiaries, 148, 178
    tax on distributions from, 201–204
    withdrawing converted amounts too soon, 206, 207

See also Rollovers
Corporations, qualified plan rules for, 11
Creditor protection for retirement plans, 17
Custodians and trustees
    and aggregation rules, 109
    and charitable contributions from IRAs, 53
    IRS revenue procedure for death of IRA participant, 159, 171
    and multiple beneficiaries, 155, 157–158, 185–186
    overview, 22
    record keeping requirements, 105
    RMD notice and calculations by, 106, 124–125, 167
    tax forms from, 69–70, 75, 92–94, 173
    and trusts, 126–127, 161
Custodian-to-custodian transfers
    avoiding distribution with, 151, 158, 181, 186
    avoiding withholding with, 46, 109
    for conversion to a Roth IRA, 153, 182
    direct rollovers, 32–34, 41, 46, 47, 49
    at divorce or separation, 55–56, 76
    of overpayments into a Roth IRA, 204
    for recharacterizing Roth IRA contributions, 204–205
    rollovers versus, 54
    splitting accounts for multiple beneficiaries, 158, 186
    for TDAs, 105

D

Death
    after-death exception, 64, 148, 178
    after RBD, 103–104, 173–178, 180–181, 210

before RBD, 102–103, 157–160, 209

ending substantially equal periodic payments, 95

of nonspouse beneficiary, 153–154, 181

and Roth 401(k)s, 218

and Roth IRAs, 209–210

of spouse beneficiary, 148–150, 178–179

See also Beneficiaries; Post-death distributions

Deductible contribution, 5

Default beneficiaries, 126

Deferral period, definition of, 101, 140, 172, 195

Defined benefit plans, 10

Defined contribution plans, 100

Designated beneficiaries

deadline for determining, 140–141

determining, 139–141, 184

disclaimer in favor of contingent beneficiaries, 141

overview, 125–128, 160–161

timely distribution to charity beneficiaries, 141

See also No designated beneficiary

Direct rollovers, 32–34, 41, 46, 47, 49

Disability, effect on distributions, 64–65, 95, 198

Disabled, definition of, 65

Disadvantages. *See* Advantages and disadvantages; Pitfalls

Disclaimer, 140, 141, 164, 173, 188–189

Distribution

choosing an option, 159–160, 186

definition of, 5, 22, 172, 195

overview, 63, 83, 101

See also Distributions; *Pro rata* distribution

Distribution rules

on fair market value of property, 28–30

immediate taxation, 26

on losses within your plan, 29, 53, 95, 133

overview, 6

for qualified plans, 6

See also Beneficiaries; Five-year rule; Tax rules

Distributions

and ADP, 121–123

hardship distributions, 51–52

for health insurance premiums, 76–77

for higher education expenses, 77–78

and RBD, 118–120

to spouse beneficiary before RMDs were started, 144–148

See also Early distributions; Required distributions; Substantially equal periodic payments

Distributions to your beneficiaries after your RBD, 169–191

administrative details, 171–173

annuities, 190

applicable distribution period, 178–179, 186–187

beneficiary's beneficiaries, 178–179, 181

custodian-to-custodian transfers, 181, 182, 186

deferral period, 172

and multiple beneficiaries, 185–186

nonspouse alternative payees of a QDRO payment, 190–191

nonspouse beneficiary, 181

overview, 103–104, 171, 172, 173–178, 180–181, 210

from Roth 401(k)s, 218

from Roth IRAs, 210

spouse beneficiary, 174–175, 178–179

trust as contingent beneficiary, 189

Distributions to your beneficiaries before your RBD, 137–168

alternate payee under terms of a QDRO, 166–167

annuities, 165

applicable distribution period, 145, 150–154, 166

custodian-to-custodian transfers, 151, 153, 158

determining designated beneficiaries, 139–141

distribution methods, 141–144

estate as beneficiary, 164–165

multiple beneficiaries, 155–160, 163, 167

and multiple beneficiaries, 155, 157–158

nonspouse beneficiary, 153–154

overview, 102–103, 139, 140

from Roth 401(k)s, 218

from Roth IRAs, 209

spouse beneficiary, 148–150

trust as contingent beneficiary, 164

See also Five-year rule

Dividends from ESOPs, 66

Divorce

and alternate payee under terms of a QDRO, 131–134, 166–167, 190–191

anti-alienation rule, 43

and distribution rules with QDRO, 131–134

and IRAs, 55–56, 76

and tax rules, 30

See also Qualified Domestic Relations Order

E

Early distributions from Roth IRAs, 202, 204, 205–207

Early distribution tax/penalty, 61–79

calculating the tax, 68–69

for early withdrawals from retirement plans, 33, 47

exceptions to, 62–68

inherited plan exemption, 41

on IRA distributions, 56, 75–79

overview, 57, 62, 63

private letter rulings, 64

on QDRO distribution, 45

reporting the tax, 69–75

on SIMPLE IRAs, 79

Earned income, 5, 195

Education, hardship withdrawals for paying, 51–52

Eligibility

for conversion to a Roth IRA at retirement, 34, 202–204

for direct rollovers at retirement, 32, 41, 46

paying ordinary income tax on distributions, 31, 40, 41, 52

for 10-year averaging, 35–36, 41

Eligible employee, definition of, 5

Emergency fund, Roth IRA as, 197

Employee Retirement Income Security Act (ERISA—1974), 17

Employees

eligible employee, definition of, 5

leaving a job after age 55 and early distribution tax, 66, 75

Employee stock ownership plans (ESOPs), 10, 66

Employer plans, 55, 66, 212–213

Employers
  and income tax withholding, 26, 33, 46–49, 56, 83
  and profit-sharing plans versus money purchase pensions, 9
  retirement plans as incentives, 6, 16
  security distribution rules at retirement, 38–40, 48–49
  and SEPs, 13
ERISA (Employee Retirement Income Security Act of 1974), 17
Errors
  chronic errors, 107
  excess contributions, 78–79, 108, 110
  innocent blunder penalty, 106–107, 112–113
  liability for uncorrected errors, 106–107, 108
  See also Penalties
ESOPs (employee stock ownership plans), 10, 66
Estate, 140, 172, 209
Estate as beneficiary, 164–165
Estate planning and bypass trusts, 162, 188–189
Eviction, hardship withdrawals for paying rent prior to, 51–52
Exception code for substantially equal periodic payments, 94
Exceptions to no-modification rule, 95–96
Excess contributions, 78–79, 108, 110
Exclusion amount, 162

F

Fair market value (FMV), 22
Federal midterm interest rate, 88, 91
Federal tax levy as early distribution, 68

First home purchase with an early distribution from an IRA, 78
Five-year holding period for Roth accounts, 197–198, 207–209, 214, 215–216
Five-year rule
  and alternate payee's beneficiary, 166–167
  for avoiding penalties, 112
  and beneficiary's beneficiary, 149, 154
  multiple beneficiaries on a single account, 156–157
  no designated beneficiary, death before RBD, 154–155, 156, 160–161
  nonspouse beneficiary, death before RBD, 152, 154
  overview, 142–143
  as plan-specific option or requirement, 102, 141, 143–144, 150–151, 157, 166
  for plans without a beneficiary, 102–103
  for Roth 401(k)s, 218
  for Roth IRAs, 209
  and spouse beneficiary's beneficiary, 149
Fixed amortization method for required distributions, 87–90, 95–96
Fixed annuitization method for required distributions, 90–92, 95–96
Fixed payment implications, 90
Fixed payment modifications, 90, 94–97
FMV (fair market value), 22
Foreclosure, hardship withdrawals for paying mortgage prior to, 51–52
401(k) plans, 8, 13, 213. *See also* Roth 401(k) plans
403(a) plans, 100
403(b) plans. *See* Tax-deferred annuities
457 plans (government plans), 100, 116, 139, 200, 201

G

Gainful activity, 65
Government plans (457 plans), 100, 116, 139, 200, 201
Government's reasons for retirement plans, 4, 6, 40, 209
Grandfather provisions, 101, 104–105

H

Hardship distributions, 51–52, 56
Health insurance premiums, paying from an IRA, 76–77
Higher education expenses, paying from an IRA, 77
Home purchase with an early distribution from an IRA, 78

I

Income taxes
    early distribution tax rules for non-Roth IRAs, 75–79
    on inherited plans, 41–43
    on IRAs, 53–56
    overview, 26–30
    on QDRO distributions, 133–134
    for tax-deferred annuities, 52
    See also Distribution rules; U.S. Tax Code
Income taxes on qualified plans and qualified annuities at retirement, 30–40
    compute with 10-year averaging, 35–38
    compute with capital gain rates, 38
    conversion to a Roth IRA, 34–35
    employer stock rules, 38–40
    ordinary income tax, 31, 40, 41, 52
    overview, 30–31
    roll over your distribution, 32–34
Income taxes on qualified plans and qualified annuities before retirement, 35–38, 40–41
Income tax withholding
    exemptions, 56, 83
    as plan administrator requirement, 26, 33, 46–49
Individual retirement annuities, 12
    See IRAs; Traditional contributory IRAs
Ineligible rollover penalty, 107–109
Inflation and fixed payment modifications, 90
Inherited retirement plans
    aggregation ineligibility, 108–109, 124
    basis of, 30, 40
    conversion to a Roth IRA, 42–43, 103
    early distribution tax/penalty exemptions, 41
    name on the account, 158–159, 171, 186
    rollovers, 41–42, 103, 107–109
    and tax rules, 30, 41–43
    10-year averaging for distributions, 43
Innocent blunder penalty, 106–107, 112–113
Interest rate for substantially equal periodic payment computations, 84, 88, 90–91
Investment returns, 31, 197–200, 199
IRAs (individual retirement accounts)
    aggregation rule for required distributions, 108–109, 124
    charitable contributions from, 53
    early distribution tax rules for non-Roth IRAs, 75–79
    excess contribution penalty, 110
    income tax rules, 53–56
    ineligible for conversion to Roth IRA, 148, 178
    overview, 12–15

required distributions and ex-spouse, 134

rollover IRAs, 13, 75–79, 146–148

SEPs, 13, 58, 75–79, 200, 201–204

SIMPLE IRAs, 14–15, 58, 79, 200, 201–204

transfers versus rollovers, 54

trust as beneficiary, 163

See also Roth IRAs; Traditional contributory IRAs

Irrevocable annuities, 165

Irrevocable trusts, 117, 126, 140

IRS (Internal Revenue Service)

plan guidelines and leeway

private letter rulings, 64

revenue procedure on custodian reporting requirements, 159, 171

See also Private letter rulings; U.S. Tax Code

IRS Form 1040, *U.S. Individual Income Tax Return,* 69, 71–72

IRS Form 1099R, *Distributions From Pensions, Annuities, Retirement or Profit-Sharing Plans, IRAs, Insurance, Contracts, etc.,* 69, 70

IRS Form 4972, *Tax on Lump-Sum Distributions,* 220–223

IRS Form 5329, *Additional Taxes on Qualified Plans and Other Tax-Favored Accounts,* 73–74, 75, 93–94, 110–111, 225–232

IRS Form 5330, *Return of Excise Taxes Related to Employee Benefit Plans,* 233–251

IRS Form 5498, *IRA Contribution Information,* 159, 252

IRS Form 8606, *Nondeductible IRAs,* 253–263

IRS Revenue Ruling 2002-62, 82, 90, 264–269

Itemized deductions, 63

J

Joint and survivor annuity, 130–131

Joint and survivor annuity with term certain, 131

Joint Life and Last Survivor Table (Table II)

for ADP determination, 121–123

for MRD calculation, 85–86, 125, 133

overview, 102, 273–290

for rollovers by spouse beneficiaries, 176–177

and term certain payments, 128, 130

with young spouse beneficiaries, 102, 121, 122, 123, 174–175

Joint life expectancy, 83

K

Keoghs for self-employed people, 11

L

Life annuities, 128, 129, 131

Life annuities with term certain, 129

Life expectancy assumptions for substantially equal periodic payment computations, 84

Life expectancy factor, 85

Life expectancy rule

five-year-rule versus, 141–142

multiple beneficiaries on a single account, 156–157

for nonspouse beneficiaries, death before RBD, 150–151

for spouse beneficiaries, 144–146

Life expectancy tables

Survivor Benefit Limits Table, 130–131, 292

See also Joint Life and Last Survivor
Table; Single Life Expectancy Table;
Uniform Lifetime Table
Loans from IRAs, 54, 56
Loans from qualified retirement plans,
49–52
Losses within your plan, 29, 53, 95, 133

M
Marginal tax bracket, 22
Married couples filing separately, 203
MDA (minimum distribution allowance),
36–37
Medical expenses, 51–52, 66–67
Minimum distribution allowance (MDA),
36–37
Minimum distributions. *See* Required
minimum distributions
Modifications to fixed payments, 90, 94–97
Modified adjusted gross income (modified
AGI), 194, 202–203, 204–205
Money purchase pension plans, 9, 10–11
Mortality table, 90
Mortality tables, 90, 92
Mortgage payments, borrowing from
qualified plans for, 50–51
Multiple beneficiaries
beneficiaries and alternate payees as, 167
and custodians or trustees, 155, 157–158,
185–186
disadvantages of naming, 127–128
one account, 155–160, 183–187
of one trust, 163, 188
separate accounts, 132–133, 155, 166–167
splitting accounts, 133, 157–160, 185–187
spouse as one of, 103, 160, 186–187

Multiple distributions and 10-year averaging,
38
Multiple retirement plans, 27–28, 36, 84,
214–215
Municipal bonds, 199

N
Net unrealized appreciation, 22, 38–40, 68
No designated beneficiary
acceleration of distributions due to, 139,
142
deadline for determining designated
beneficiary, 140–141
death after RBD, 183
death before RBD, 154–155, 156
default beneficiary versus, 125–126
multiple designated beneficiaries with
one nonqualifying, 127, 156, 172–173
overview, 125, 160–161
No-modification rule, 94–97
Nondeductible contributions, 22, 195. *See
also* After-tax contributions
Nondiscrimination rules, 5, 6, 16
Nonqualified distributions
from Roth 401(k)s, 215
from Roth IRAs, 199–200, 205–207
Nonqualified retirement plans, 6, 16
Nonspouse alternative payees of a QDRO
payment, 44–45, 131–134, 166–167,
190–191
Nonspouse beneficiaries
of annuities, 130–131, 165
distributions after your RBD, 103–104,
180–182
distributions before your RBD, 102–103,
150–154
overview, 125–126

and rollover or conversion options, 41–43
transferring retirement plan assets into an inherited IRA, 103
of trusts, 161, 187
Nonspouse beneficiary's beneficiaries, 153–154, 181

O

One-rollover-per-year rule, 54, 201, 204
Online calculators, 88–89, 91
Ordering of Roth IRAs distributions, 207–209

P

Participant, 5
Participation rules, 5, 13
Penalties
    avoiding with direct rollovers, 49
    for breaking no-modification rule, 96–97
    chronic errors, 107
    for excess contributions, 108, 110
    ineligible rollovers, 107–109
    for innocent blunders, 106–107, 112–113
    liability for uncorrected errors, 106–107, 108
    for not taking required distributions, 57, 100, 106–110, 121
    overview, 57
    on QDRO distributions, 133–134
    reporting to IRS, 110–111
    See also Early distribution tax
Period certain, 140, 172. *See also* Term certain annuities
Pitfalls
    of conversion to a Roth IRA at retirement, 35

of direct rollovers at retirement, 32–34
of standard rollovers for distributions, 46–49
of 10-year averaging, 38
See also Advantages and disadvantages
Post-death distributions
    continuity requirement after RBD, 174, 176, 177
    and designated beneficiary, 173
    overview, 64
    plan's instructions on, 150–151
    spouse's election to not take distributions, 146, 147, 176, 177
    tax reporting, 69–75
    to trust beneficiaries, 161
    See also Distributions to your beneficiaries after your RBD; Distributions to your beneficiaries before your RBD
Pretax contributions
    and charitable donations, 53
    and conversion to Roth IRA, 26, 34, 148, 153, 178, 182
    for employer stock, 39
    and required distributions, 123–124
Pretax dollars, 22
Pretax earnings, 212, 213, 214–215, 217
Primary beneficiaries
    definition of, 172
    naming spouse as, 164, 189
    overview, 117, 127, 140
Principal residence, 63
Private letter rulings
    on after-death exception, 178
    for creative minimum distribution calculations, 85
    on estate as beneficiary, 164–165

for inflation-related modifications to fixed payments, 90

for interest rates higher than guidelines, 88

overview, 64

on trust-as-beneficiary rollovers by spouse, 164, 189

for variable payments under the annuity factor method, 91

Profit-sharing plans, 7–9, 51–52

Pro rata distribution

of after-tax dollar contributions to traditional IRAs, 196

of earnings and after-tax contributions, 213–215

overview, 22

as reasonable method for splitting retirement plan proceeds, 133

of Roth 401(k)s, 217

tax on distribution of Roth IRA or Roth 401(k)s, 27

Purchasing a principal residence, hardship withdrawals for paying, 51–52

Q

Qualified annuities

ineligible rollover penalty, 107–108

overview, 16

permissible rollovers, 58

See also Income taxes on qualified plans and qualified annuities at retirement; Qualified Domestic Relations Order

Qualified distributions

from Roth 401(k)s, 217

from Roth IRAs, 197–199, 205, 207

and 10-year averaging, 43

Qualified Domestic Relations Order (QDRO)

alternate payees under terms of, 44–45, 131–134, 166–167, 190–191

and early distribution tax, 68, 75–76

IRAs not addressed by, 55–56

overview, 43–45

and required distributions, 131–134

and rollovers, 134

and TDAs, 52

Qualified retirement plans

administrator's reluctance to maintain separate accounts, 155

converting to a Roth IRA, 200, 201–204

ESOPs, 10, 66

excess contribution penalty, 110

ineligible rollover penalty, 107–108

overview, 9–12

permissible rollovers, 58

profit-sharing plans, 7–9, 51–52

rollover to a Roth IRA, 201

See also Income taxes on qualified plans and qualified annuities at retirement; Qualified Domestic Relations Order

Qualified trusts, 125, 126–127

R

RBD (required beginning date), 101, 117–120, 129–131, 142

Recalculated life expectancy, 83

Record keeping, 92, 105

Refund of excess allowable contribution, 68

Required beginning date (RBD), 101, 117–120, 129–131, 142

Required distributions

annuity rules, 128–131

computing the amount, 120–125, 145–146, 184

death after beginning date, 103–104

death prior to beginning date, 102–103
determining the APD, 121–123
during your lifetime, 101–102, 116–117
funds ineligible for rollovers, 33, 107–109
grace period for first time withdrawal, 111
ineligible for rollover or conversion, 203
overview, 100–101
penalty for not taking, 57, 100, 106–110, 121
from Roth 401(k)s, 217–218
Roth IRAs exempt from, 105–106, 209–210, 218
spouse's failure to take, 146, 147, 176, 177
for tax-deferred annuities, 104–105
timing of, 156
waiver for 2009 distributions, 100, 116, 139
waiver of penalty, 111–113
See also Required minimum distributions; Rollovers
Required minimum distributions (RMDs)
advantages and disadvantages, 87
charitable contributions as part of, 53
computation of, 85–89
switching from another method to, 95–96
See also Required distributions; Substantially equal periodic payments; 10-year averaging
Retirement plans
conversion to Roth IRA, 148, 178, 202
converting assets to Roth IRA, 201–204
multiple plans, 27–28, 36, 84, 214–215
nonqualified, 6, 16
overview, 4–6
profit-sharing plans, 7–9, 51–52

QDRO and separate versus no separate account, 132–133, 166–167
Retirement plans, almost-qualified, 15. *See also* Qualified annuities; Tax-deferred annuities
Retirement plans, plan-specific rules
avoiding a penalty with, 112
distributions after death before RBD, 102–103
versus IRS rules, 34, 42, 63, 143–144
Retirement plans, qualified
defined benefit plans, 10
employee stock ownership plans, 10
Keoghs for self-employed people, 11
money purchase pension plans, 9
profit-sharing plans, 7–9
stock bonus plans, 9
target benefit plans, 10–11
See also IRAs
Revenue procedure for custodians, 159, 171
Revocable trusts, 117, 140
RMDs. *See* Required minimum distributions
Rollover IRAs, 13, 75–79, 146–148
Rollovers
avoiding penalties, 49
direct, 32–34, 41, 46, 47, 49
direct rollovers, 32–34, 41, 46, 47, 49
of distributions received before retirement, 40–41
distribution versus, 26
of employer stock into a traditional IRA, 39–40
hardship distributions ineligible for, 52
ineligible funds, 33, 107–109
of inherited retirement plans, 41–42
for nonspouse beneficiaries, 151, 153, 159, 181–182

one-rollover-per-year rule, 54
overview, 58, 133–134
penalties for ineligible rollovers, 107–109
permanent nature of, 33
pitfalls of direct rollovers at retirement, 32–34
post-death of a spouse, 64
from Roth 401(k) to Roth 401(k), 215–216
from Roth 401(k) to Roth IRA, 216
from Roth IRA to Roth IRA, 200–201
for spouse beneficiaries, 143, 146–148, 176–178
for spouse or former spouse alternate payee of a QDRO, 45, 134
spouse's inherited IRA, 103
standard rollovers, 46–49
substantially equal periodic payments ineligible for, 83
of TDA distributions, 52
for transferring an IRA to an ex-spouse, 76
trust beneficiaries ineligible for, 163–164
See also Conversion to a Roth IRA
Roth 401(k)s, 211–218
basis of, 26–28
early distribution tax, 216–217
multiple plans, 214–215
nonqualified distributions, 215
overview, 8–9, 212, 213
permissible rollovers, 58
required distributions, 217–218
rollovers into, 33, 212–213, 214–215
Roth IRAs versus, 196, 212–213, 214–215, 217–218
taxation of distributions, 212–216
Roth accounts, five-year holding period for, 197–198, 207–209, 214, 215–216

Roth IRAs, 193–210
basis of, 26–28
considering multiple Roth IRAs as a single Roth IRA, 208
ordering of distributions, 207–209
overview, 15, 194, 195
permissible rollovers, 58
required distributions, 105–106, 209–210
rollovers into, 33, 40, 216
Roth 401(k)s versus, 196, 212–213, 214–215, 217–218
traditional IRAs compared to, 194–196, 205, 209
See also Conversion to a Roth IRA
Roth IRAs, tax on distributions from conversions and rollovers, 200–204, 206–207
conversion to Roth IRA, 201–204
correcting errors by recharacterizing, 204–205
early distributions, 205–207
investment return distributions, 197–200
nondeductible contributions, 196–197, 206
nonqualified distributions, 199–200, 205–207
overview, 196
qualified distributions, 197–199, 205, 207
rollover from Roth IRA, 200–201

S

Self-employed individuals, 11, 13, 17, 77, 79, 118
Separate accounts for multiple beneficiaries, 132–133, 155, 166–167
Separation, marital, 55–56, 76, 131–134. See also Qualified Domestic Relations Order
Separation from service, definition of, 63

SEPs. *See* Simplified employee pensions

SIMPLE IRAs
    converting to a Roth IRA, 200, 201–204
    overview, 14–15
    permissible rollovers, 58
    rollover to a Roth IRA, 201
    specific early distribution rule for, 79

Simplified employee pensions (SEPs)
    converting to a Roth IRA, 200, 201–204
    overview, 13, 75–79
    permissible rollovers, 58
    rollover to a Roth IRA, 201

Simplified Incentive Match Plan for
  Employees. *See* SIMPLE IRAs

Single Life Expectancy Table (Table I)
    for ADP determination, 174–175
    computing required distribution for
      alternate payee with separate account,
      132
    for minimum distribution calculations,
      85–86, 88, 89
    and multiple beneficiaries, 128
    for multiple beneficiaries, 156–157, 160
    for nonspouse beneficiaries, 151, 154
    overview, 272
    for spouse beneficiaries, 145–146,
      148–149, 163
    with trust as beneficiary, 126–127

60-day rule, 33, 54, 55

Splitting accounts for multiple beneficiaries,
  133, 157–160, 185–187

Spouse as alternate payees, 166

Spouse beneficiaries
    after-death exception, 64, 148, 178
    after RMDs were started, 173–179
    of annuities, 165
    applicable distribution period, 145,
      186–187
    before RMDs were started, 144–149
    death of, 148–150
    life expectancy rule option, 144–146
    more than 10 years younger, 122, 123
    as one of multiple beneficiaries, 160,
      186–187
    options for distributions from inherited
      retirement plan, 103, 104
    overview, 144
    rollovers, 143, 146–148, 176–178
    as sole beneficiary, 160, 173–179, 187
    of tax rules, 187–188
    timeline for rollover of deceased spouse's
      IRA, 147–149, 176, 177–178
    of trusts, 161, 163
    See also Young spouse beneficiaries

Spouse beneficiary's beneficiaries, 148–150,
  178–179

Spouse or former spouse as alternate payee
  under a QDRO, 44–45, 131–134, 166–167,
  190–191

Standard deduction, 63

Standard rollovers, 46–49

Step-up basis rules, 30, 40

Stock bonus plans, 9

Substantially equal periodic payments
    for avoiding early distribution penalty,
      81–97
    computing payment amount, 84–92
    fixed amortization method, 87–90, 95–96
    fixed annuitization method, 90–92, 95–96
    overview, 65–66, 82–84
    See also Required minimum distributions;
      10-year averaging

Survivor Benefit Limits Table, 130–131, 292

T

Table I. *See* Single Life Expectancy Table

Table II. *See* Joint Life and Last Survivor Table

Table III. *See* Uniform Lifetime Table

Table IV – Survivor Benefit Limits Table, 130–131, 292

Target benefit plans, 10–11

Tax basis. *See* Basis

Tax bracket, 22, 25. *See also* Capital gains treatment

Tax code. *See* U.S. Tax Code

Tax-deductible expenses, 5

Tax deferral, 5

Tax-deferred annuities (TDAs)
  aggregation rule for required distributions, 108–109, 124
  converting to a Roth IRA, 200, 201–204
  income tax rules for, 52
  overview, 16, 101
  permissible rollovers, 58
  required distribution rules, 104–105
  rollover to a Roth IRA, 201
  See also Qualified Domestic Relations Order

Tax-deferred compounding, 21, 23–25

Tax-free investments, 199

Tax rates and MRDs, 119

Tax Rate Schedule (1986), 224

Tax reporting
  distributions from retirement plans, 124–125, 167, 173
  early distribution tax, 69–75
  post-death distributions, 69–75
  Roth IRA overpayments, 204–205
  substantially equal periodic payments, 92–94

Tax rules
  conversion to a Roth IRA, 26, 30, 34–35, 42–43
  divorce or inheritance and, 30
  income tax withholding, 26, 33, 46–49, 56, 83
  and loans from qualified retirement plans, 49–51
  net unrealized appreciation, 22, 38–40
  nondeductible contributions, 22, 195
  overview, 21–26
  pretax contributions, 26, 34, 39, 53
  See also After-tax contributions; Basis; Capital gains treatment; Penalties; Roth IRAs, tax on distributions from; *entries beginning with* "income taxes"

TDAs. *See* Tax-deferred annuities

10-year averaging
  eligibility for, 35–36, 41
  and employer stock at retirement, 39
  income taxes on qualified plans and qualified annuities at retirement, 35–38
  for inherited retirement plan distributions, 43
  IRAs ineligible for, 55
  for QDRO plan participants, 44–45
  TDA ineligible for, 52

Term certain, 140, 172

Term certain annuities, 117, 128, 129, 130

Titling an inherited IRA, 171

Traditional contributory IRAs
  after-tax contributions in, 27–29, 31, 53, 196, 201–202, 207
  converting assets to Roth IRA, 201–204
  overview, 12–13, 195
  permissible rollovers, 58
  rollover of employer stock into, 39–40

Roth IRAs compared to, 194–196, 205, 209

tax rules, 196

Transferring Roth 401(k)s, 212

Transfers versus rollovers, 54. *See also* Custodian-to-custodian transfers

Trust beneficiaries, 161–164, 187–189

Trustees. *See* Custodians and trustees

Trusts

as beneficiary of retirement plan, 158

bypass trusts, 162, 163–164, 188–189

irrevocable, 117, 126, 140

qualified trusts, 125, 126–127

revocable, 117, 140

U

Uniform Lifetime Table (Table III)

for ADP determination, 121–123

computing required distributions, 132, 133

and designated beneficiary, 125

for minimum distribution calculations, 85–88

for multiple beneficiaries, 128

overview, 102, 291

and term certain payments, 128, 130

U.S. Tax Code, 4, 6, 16, 112

U.S. Tax Code key sections

on early distributions, 79, 210

on required distributions, 113, 135, 167, 191

rollovers, QDROs, withholding rules, prohibited transactions, 58

Roth 401(k)s, 218

on Roth IRAs, 210

on substantially equal periodic payments, 97

types of retirement plans, 17

V

Vested benefit, 5

Vested interests and loans, 50

Vesting rules, 13

W

Waiting periods for Roth IRAs, 205

Waiver

for 60-day rule, 55

correcting mistake in order to receive, 106

definition of, 101

for failure to take required distributions, 111–113

of required distributions for 2009, 100, 116

Withdrawals. *See* Distributions

Withholding. *See* Income tax withholding

Y

Young nonspouse beneficiaries

of annuities, 130–131

and required distributions, 180

Young spouse beneficiaries

and required distributions, 102, 121, 122, 123, 174–175

and rollover of deceased's retirement plan, 147–148, 177–178

NOLO Keep Up to Date

 1 Go to **Nolo.com/newsletter** to sign up for free newsletters and discounts on Nolo products.

- **Nolo Briefs.** Our monthly email newsletter with great deals and free information.

- **Nolo's Special Offer.** A monthly newsletter with the biggest Nolo discounts around.

- **BizBriefs.** Tips and discounts on Nolo products for business owners and managers.

- **Landlord's Quarterly.** Deals and free tips just for landlords and property managers, too.

2 And don't forget to check **Nolo.com/updates** to find free legal updates to this book.

Let Us Hear From You

 3 Comments on this book? We want to hear 'em. Email us at feedback@nolo.com.

RET9

NOLO Catalog

BUSINESS	PRICE	CODE
Business Buyout Agreements (Book w/CD-ROM)	$49.99	BSAG
The California Nonprofit Corporation Kit (Binder w/CD-ROM)	$69.99	CNP
California Workers' Comp	$34.99	WORK
The Complete Guide to Buying a Business (Book w/CD-ROM)	$24.99	BUYBU
The Complete Guide to Selling a Business (Book w/CD-ROM)	$34.99	SELBU
Consultant & Independent Contractor Agreements (Book w/CD-ROM)	$34.99	CICA
The Corporate Records Handbook (Book w/CD-ROM)	$69.99	CORMI
Create Your Own Employee Handbook (Book w/CD-ROM)	$49.99	EMHA
Dealing With Problem Employees	$44.99	PROBM
Deduct It! Lower Your Small Business Taxes	$34.99	DEDU
The eBay Business Start-Up Kit (Book w/CD-ROM)	$24.99	EBIZ
Effective Fundraising for Nonprofits	$24.99	EFFN
The Employer's Legal Handbook	$49.99	EMPL
The Essential Guide to Family & Medical Leave (Book w/CD-ROM)	$49.99	FMLA
The Essential Guide to Federal Employment Laws	$44.99	FEMP
The Essential Guide to Workplace Investigations (Book w/CD-ROM)	$39.99	NVST
Every Nonprofit's Guide to Publishing	$29.99	EPNO
Form a Partnership(Book w/CD-ROM)	$39.99	PART
Hiring Your First Employee: A Step-by-Step Guide	$24.99	HEMP
Form Your Own Limited Liability Company (Book w/CD-ROM)	$44.99	LIAB
Home Business Tax Deductions: Keep What You Earn	$34.99	DEHB
How to Form a Nonprofit Corporation (Book w/CD-ROM)—National Edition	$49.99	NNP
How to Form a Nonprofit Corporation in California (Book w/CD-ROM)	$49.99	NON
How to Form Your Own California Corporation (Binder w/CD-ROM)	$59.99	CACI
How to Form Your Own California Corporation (Book w/CD-ROM)	$39.99	CCOR
How to Run a Thriving Business: Strategies for Success & Satisfaction	$19.99	THRV
How to Write a Business Plan (Book w/CD-ROM)	$34.99	SBS
Incorporate Your Business (Book w/CD-ROM)—National Edition	$49.99	NIBS
Investors in Your Backyard (Book w/CD-ROM)	$24.99	FINBUS
The Job Description Handbook (Book w/CD-ROM)	$29.99	JOB
Legal Guide for Starting & Running a Small Business	$34.99	RUNS
Legal Forms for Starting & Running a Small Business (Book w/CD-ROM)	$29.99	RUNSF
LLC or Corporation?	$24.99	CHENT
The Manager's Legal Handbook	$39.99	ELBA
Marketing Without Advertising	$20.00	MWAD
Music Law: How to Run Your Band's Business (Book w/CD-ROM)	$39.99	ML
Negotiate the Best Lease for Your Business	$24.99	LESP

Nolo's Crash Course in Small Business Basics (Audiobook on 5 CDs) .... $34.99 ABBIZ
Nolo's Quick LLC .... $29.99 LLCQ
Nonprofit Meetings, Minutes & Records (Book w/CD-ROM) .... $39.99 NORM
The Performance Appraisal Handbook (Book w/CD-ROM) .... $29.99 PERF
The Progressive Discipline Handbook (Book w/CD-ROM) .... $34.99 SDHB
Retire—And Start Your Own Business (Book w/CD-ROM) .... $34.99 BOSS
Small Business in Paradise: Working for Yourself in a Place You Love .... $19.99 SPAR
The Small Business Start-Up Kit (Book w/CD-ROM)—National Edition .... $29.99 SMBU
The Small Business Start-Up Kit for California (Book w/CD-ROM) .... $29.99 OPEN
Smart Policies for Workplace Technologies: Email, Blogs,
   Cell Phones & More (Book w/CD-ROM) .... $29.99 TECH
Starting & Building a Nonprofit: A Practical Guide (Book w/CD-ROM) .... $29.99 SNON
Starting & Running a Successful Newsletter or Magazine.. $29.99 MAG
Tax Deductions for Professionals .... $34.99 DEPO
Tax Savvy for Small Business .... $36.99 SAVVY
The Work From Home Handbook .... $19.99 USHOM
Wow! I'm in Business .... $21.99 WHOO
Working for Yourself: Law & Taxes for Independent Contractors,
   Freelancers & Consultants.. $39.99 WAGE
Working With Independent Contractors (Book w/CD-ROM).. $34.99 HICI
Your Limited Liability Company (Book w/CD-ROM).. $49.99 LOP
Your Rights in the Workplace... $29.99 YRW

CONSUMER
How to Win Your Personal Injury Claim... $34.99 PICL
Nolo's Encyclopedia of Everyday Law.. $29.99 EVL
Nolo's Guide to California Law .... $34.99 CLAW
Your Little Legal Companion (Hardcover) .... $9.95 ANNIS

ESTATE PLANNING & PROBATE
8 Ways to Avoid Probate .... $21.99 PRAV
The Busy Family's Guide to Estate Planning (Book w/CD) .... $24.99 FAM
Estate Planning Basics .... $21.99 ESPN
Estate Planning for Blended Families: Providing for Your Spouse & Children in a
   Second Marriage... $34.99 SMAR
The Executor's Guide: Settling a Loved One's Estate or Trust.. $39.99 EXEC
Get It Together: Organize Your Records (Book w/CD-ROM) .... $21.99 GET
How to Probate an Estate in California .... $49.99 PAE
Make Your Own Living Trust (Book w/CD-ROM).. $39.99 LITR
Nolo's Simple Will Book (Book w/CD-ROM) .... $36.99 SWIL
Plan Your Estate .... $44.99 NEST
Quick & Legal Will Book (Book w/CD-ROM) .... $21.99 QUIC
Special Needs Trusts: Protect Your Child's Financial Future (Book w/CD-ROM)............. $34.99 SPNT

FAMILY MATTERS

Always Dad: Being a Great Father During & After a Divorce .... $16.99 DIFA
Building a Parenting Agreement That Works .... $24.99 CUST
The Complete IEP Guide: How to Advocate for Your Special Ed Child .... $34.99 IEP
Divorce & Money: How to Make the Best Financial Decisions During Divorce .... $34.99 DIMO
Divorce Without Court: A Guide to Mediation & Collaborative Divorce .... $34.99 DWCT
Do Your Own California Adoption (Book w/CD-ROM) .... $34.99 ADOP
Every Dog's Legal Guide: A Must-Have for Your Owner .... $19.99 DOG
The Guardianship Book for California .... $34.99 GB
A Judge's Guide to Divorce (Book w/CD-ROM) .... $24.99 JDIV
A Legal Guide for Lesbian & Gay Couples (Book w/CD-ROM) .... $34.99 LG
Living Together: A Legal Guide for Unmarried Couples (Book w/CD-ROM) .... $34.99 LTK
Nolo's Essential Guide to Divorce .... $24.99 NODV
Nolo's IEP Guide: Learning Disabilities .... $29.99 IELD
Parent Savvy .... $19.99 PRNT
Prenuptial Agreements (Book w/CD-ROM) .... $34.99 PNUP

GOING TO COURT

Becoming a Mediator .... $29.99 BECM
Beat Your Ticket: Go to Court & Win—National Edition .... $21.99 BEYT
The Criminal Law Handbook: Know Your Rights, Survive the System .... $39.99 KYR
Everybody's Guide to Small Claims Court—National Edition .... $29.99 NSCC
Everybody's Guide to Small Claims Court in California .... $29.99 CSCC
Fight Your Ticket & Win in California .... $29.99 FYT
How to Change Your Name in California (Book w/CD-ROM) .... $34.99 NAME
Legal Research: How to Find & Understand the Law .... $39.99 LRES
Nolo's Deposition Handbook .... $34.99 DEP
Nolo's Plain-English Law Dictionary .... $29.99 DICT
Represent Yourself in Court: How to Prepare & Try a Winning Case .... $39.99 RYC
Win Your Lawsuit: A Judge's Guide to Representing Yourself in
    California Superior Court .... $39.99 SLWY

HOMEOWNERS, LANDLORDS & TENANTS

Buying a Second Home (Book w/CD-ROM) .... $24.99 SCND
The California Landlord's Law Book: Evictions (Book w/CD-ROM) .... $44.99 LBEV
The California Landlord's Law Book: Rights & Responsibilities (Book w/CD-ROM) ...... $44.99 LBRT
California Tenants' Rights .... $29.99 CTEN
Deeds for California Real Estate .... $27.99 DEED
The Essential Guide for First-Time Homeowners .... $19.99 USOWN
Every Landlord's Guide to Finding Great Tenants (Book w/CD-ROM) .... $24.99 FIND
Every Landlord's Legal Guide (Book w/CD-ROM) .... $44.99 ELLI
Every Landlord's Property Protection Guide (Book w/CD-ROM) .... $29.99 RISK
Every Landlord's Tax Deduction Guide .... $34.99 DELL
Every Tenant's Legal Guide .... $34.99 EVTEN

First-Time Landlord: Your Guide to Renting Out a Single-Family Home.......................... $19.99 USFTL
For Sale by Owner in California (Book w/CD-ROM).. $29.99 FSBO
How to Buy a House in California .... $34.99 BHCA
Leases & Rental Agreements (Book w/CD-ROM) .... $29.99 LEAR
Neighbor Law: Fences, Trees, Boundaries & Noise.. $29.99 NEI
Nolo's Essential Guide to Buying Your First Home (Book w/CD-ROM) .... $24.99 HTBH
Renters' Rights: The Basics .... $24.99 RENT
Saving the Family Cottage: A Guide to Succession Planning for Your
   Cottage, Cabin, Camp or Vacation Home.. $29.99 COTT
Selling Your House in a Tough Market: 10 Strategies That Work.................................... $24.99 DOWN

IMMIGRATION

Becoming a U.S. Citizen: A Guide to the Law, Exam & Interview .... $24.99 USCIT
Fiancé & Marriage Visas.. $34.99 IMAR
How to Get a Green Card .... $29.99 GRN
Student & Tourist Visas... $29.99 ISTU
U.S. Immigration Made Easy .... $39.99 IMEZ

MONEY MATTERS

101 Law Forms for Personal Use (Book w/CD-ROM) .... $29.99 SPOT
The Busy Family's Guide to Money .... $19.99 USMONY
Chapter 13 Bankruptcy: Keep Your Property & Repay Debts Over Time........................ $39.99 CHB
Credit Repair (Book w/CD-ROM) .... $24.99 CREP
Easy Ways to Lower Your Taxes .... $19.99 USLOT
The Foreclosure Survival Guide .... $21.99 FIFO
How to File for Chapter 7 Bankruptcy.. $29.99 HFB
The New Bankruptcy: Will It Work for You?... $24.99 FIBA
Nolo's Guide to Social Security Disability (Book w/CD-ROM) .... $29.99 QSS
The Sharing Solution: How to Prosper by Sharing Resources, Simplifying Your Life &
   Building Community .... $24.99 SHAR
Solve Your Money Troubles: Debt, Credit & Bankruptcy .... $24.99 MT
Stand Up to the IRS... $29.99 SIRS
Stopping Identity Theft: 10 Easy Steps to Security .... $19.99 USID
Surviving an IRS Tax Audit .... $24.95 SAUD

RETIREMENT & SENIORS

Get a Life: You Don't Need a Million to Retire Well.. $24.99 LIFE
IRAs, 401(k)s & Other Retirement Plans: Taking Your Money Out............................... $34.99 RET
Long-Term Care: How to Plan & Pay for It .... $24.99 ELD
Nolo's Essential Retirement Tax Guide .... $24.99 RTAX
Retire Happy: What You Can Do Now to Guarantee a Great Retirement .... $19.99 USRICH
Social Security, Medicare & Government Pensions... $29.99 SOA
Work Less, Live More: The Way to Semi-Retirement .... $17.99 RECL
The Work Less, Live More Workbook (Book w/CD)... $19.99 RECW

PATENTS AND COPYRIGHTS

All I Need Is Money: How to Finance Your Invention .... $19.99 FINA

The Copyright Handbook: What Every Writer Needs to Know (Book w/CD-ROM) ...... $39.99 COHA

Getting Permission: How to License & Clear Copyrighted
  Material Online & Off (Book w/CD-ROM) .... $34.99 RIPER

How to Make Patent Drawings .... $29.99 DRAW

The Inventor's Notebook .... $24.99 INOT

Legal Guide to Web & Software Development (Book w/CD-ROM) .... $44.99 SFT

Nolo's Patents for Beginners .... $29.99 QPAT

Patent, Copyright & Trademark: An Intellectual Property Desk Reference .... $39.99 PCTM

Patent It Yourself .... $49.99 PAT

Patent Pending in 24 Hours .... $34.99 PEND

Patent Savvy for Managers: Spot & Protect Valuable Innovations in Your Company .... $29.99 PATM

Patent Searching Made Easy .... $39.99 PATSE

Patenting Art & Entertainment .... $39.99 PATAE

Profit From Your Idea (Book w/CD-ROM) .... $34.99 LICE

The Public Domain .... $34.99 PUBL

Trademark: Legal Care for Your Business & Product Name .... $39.99 TRD

What Every Inventor Needs to Know About Business & Taxes (Book w/CD-ROM) .... $21.99 ILAX

SOFTWARE

Call or check our website at www.nolo.com for special discounts on Software!

LLC Maker—Windows $89.99 LLP1

PatentEase Deluxe 6.0—Windows .... $349.00 PEAS

Quicken Legal Business Pro 2009—Windows $109.99 SBQB9

Quicken WillMaker Plus 2009—Windows $89.99 WQP9

Special Upgrade Offer

Save 35% on the latest edition of your Nolo book

Because laws and legal procedures change often, we update our books regularly. To help keep you up-to-date, we are extending this special upgrade offer. Cut out and mail the title portion of the cover of your old Nolo book and we'll give you 35% off the retail price of the New Edition of that book when you purchase directly from Nolo. This offer is to individuals only. Prices and offer subject to change without notice.

Order Form

Name

Address

City

State, Zip

Daytime Phone

E-mail

Our "No-Hassle" Guarantee

Return anything you buy directly from Nolo for any reason and we'll cheerfully refund your purchase price. No ifs, ands or buts.

☐ Check here if you do not wish to receive mailings from other companies

Item Code	Quantity	Item	Unit Price	Total Price

Method of payment

☐ Check   ☐ VISA

☐ American Express

☐ MasterCard

☐ Discover Card

Subtotal	
Add your local sales tax (California only)	
Shipping: RUSH $12, Basic $6 (See below)	
"I bought 2, ship it to me FREE!" (Ground shipping only)	
TOTAL	

Account Number

Expiration Date

Signature

Shipping and Handling

Rush Delivery—Only $12

We'll ship any order to any street address in the U.S. by UPS 2nd Day Air* for only $12!

* Order by 9:30 AM Pacific Time and get your order in 2 business days. Orders placed after 9:30 AM Pacific Time will arrive in 3 business days. P.O. boxes and S.F. Bay Area use basic shipping. Alaska and Hawaii use 2nd Day Air or Priority Mail.

Basic Shipping—$6

Use for P.O. Boxes, Northern California and Ground Service.

Allow 1-2 weeks for delivery.

U.S. addresses only.

For faster service, use your credit card and our toll-free numbers

Call our customer service group Monday thru Friday 7am to 6pm PST

 Phone
1-800-728-3555

 Fax
1-800-645-0895

 Mail
Nolo
950 Parker St.
Berkeley, CA 94710

Order 24 hours a day @ www.nolo.com